D1736407

cSUR-UT Series: Library for Sustainable Urban Regeneration
Volume 10

Series Editor: Shinichiro Ohgaki, Tokyo, Japan

cSUR-UT Series: Library for Sustainable Urban Regeneration

By the process of urban development in the 20th century, characterized by suburban expansion and urban redevelopment, many huge and sophisticated complexes of urban structures have been erected in developed countries. However, with conventional technologies focused on the construction of structures, it has become difficult to keep urban spaces adaptable to environmental constraints and economic, social and cultural changes. In other words, it has become difficult for conventional technologies to meet social demands for the upgrading of social capital in a sustainable manner and for the regeneration of attractive urban space that is not only safe and highly efficient but also conscious of historical, cultural and local identities to guarantee a high quality of life for all. Therefore, what is needed now is the creation of a new discipline that is able to reorganize the existing social capital and the technologies to implement it.

For this purpose, there is a need to go beyond the boundaries of conventional technologies of construction and structural design and to integrate the following technologies:

(1) Technology concerned with environmental and risk management
(2) Technology of conservation and regeneration with due consideration to the local characteristics of existing structures including historical and cultural resources
(3) Technologies of communication, consensus building, plan making and space management to coordinate and integrate the individual activities initiated by various actors of society

Up to now, architecture, civil engineering, and urban engineering in their respective fields have, while dealing with different time-space scales and structures, accumulated cutting-edge knowledge and contributed to the formation of favorable urban spaces. In the past, when emphasis was put on developing new residential areas and constructing new structures, development and advancement of such specialized disciplines were found to be the most effective.

However, current problems confronting urban development can be highlighted by the fact that a set of optimum solutions drawn from the best practices of each discipline is not necessarily the best solution. This is especially true where there are relationships of trade-offs among such issues as human risk and environmental load. In this way, the integration of the above three disciplines is strongly called for.

In order to create new integrated knowledge for sustainable urban regeneration, the Center for Sustainable Urban Regeneration (cSUR), The University of Tokyo, was established in 2003 as a core organization of one of the 21st Century Centers of Excellence Programs funded by the Ministry of Education and Science, Japan, and cSUR has coordinated international research alliances and collaboratively engages with common issues of sustainable urban regeneration.

The cSUR series are edited and published to present the achievements of our collaborative research and new integrated approaches toward sustainable urban regeneration.

A. Sorensen, J. Okata (Eds.)

Megacities

Urban Form, Governance, and Sustainability

André Sorensen
Associate Professor
University of Toronto Scarborough
Cities Centre
455 Spadina Avenue, Suite 400
Toronto
Ontario, M5S 2G8
Canada
sorensen@utsc.utoronto.ca

Junichiro Okata
Professor
Department of Urban Engineering
School of Engineering
The University of Tokyo
7-3-1 Hongo, Bunkyo-ku
Tokyo 113-8656
Japan
okata@up.t.u-tokyo.ac.jp

ISSN 1865-8504 e-ISSN 1865-8512
ISBN 978-4-431-99266-0 e-ISBN 978-4-431-99267-7
DOI: 10.1007/978-4-431-99267-7
Springer Tokyo Dordrecht Heidelberg London New York

Library of Congress Control Number: 2010931386

Cover photograph by André Sorensen
Cover graphic: Urban form of Istanbul; © Neyran Turan

Printed on acid-free paper

Springer is part of Springer Science+Business Media (www.springer.com)

Preface

This book builds on a research project that was undertaken from 2003 to 2010 by the Mega-City Research Group at the Center for Sustainable Urban Regeneration, at The University of Tokyo, and the international workshop on world megacities held 7–8 March 2008 by the Center for Sustainable Urban Regeneration (cSUR) at The University of Tokyo.

Obviously, the sustainability issues of megacities including Tokyo, which is the largest megacity in the world, has been one of the major topics studied by cSUR since it was established in 2003.In September of 2004, cSUR held an international conference on sustainable urban regeneration, and we invited research on varied sustainability issues of Asian megacities including Seoul, Beijing, Manila, Bangkok, and Tokyo.With the basic knowledge derived from the conference and the preliminary study of the sustainability challenges of Tokyo, we held a presentation titled "Toward a Comparative Study on Spatial Planning Issues and Approaches in Diverse Megacities" at the 2006 World Planning School Congress, 11–16 July 2006 in Mexico City, at which we invited core research members engaged in comparative studies of the sustainability problems of world megacities from the point of view of urban form and spatial planning. Thus, the core editorial team of this book, consisting of André Sorensen, Alfonso Valenzuela, Haryo Winarso, Akito Murayama, and myself, was established in early 2007. This team planned the workshop, invited candidate authors, and held the workshop in March 2008 in Tokyo.

In the workshop, 20 papers on 20 megacities were presented. It was an intensive, exciting and fruitful workshop. At the closing session, all participants decided to publish those papers and discussions as a book for researchers, experts, students, and all those who are interested in the challenges of sustainability of world megacities. It is my great happiness to see this book, which is the fruit of the labor of all authors and editorial staff.

I would particularly like to thank André Sorensen for taking on the editing duties, Philippa Campsie for her careful copy-editing work, and the editorial staff members at Springer Japan for their work in shepherding the book into print. cSUR is grateful for the generous funding (as a 21st Century COE Program 2003–2008 and a Global COE program after 2008) from the Japanese Ministry of Education, Culture, Sports and Technology that allowed us to hold the workshop and produce this volume. Finally, on behalf of cSUR, I would like to thank everyone who participated in the Sustainable Urban Regeneration (COE) program and the megacity research project. We will continue to pursue the theme, and we welcome your comments and responses to the following pages.

Junichiro Okata
Co-Director, Center for Sustainable Urban Regeneration
Professor, Department of Urban Engineering,
The University of Tokyo

Contents

List of Contributors

Sang-Chuel Choe
Professor
Graduate School of Environmental Studies
Seoul National University
Republic of Korea
choesc@snu.ac.kr

Dana Cuff
Director, cityLAB
and
Professor
UCLA Department of Architecture and Urban Design
USA
dana.cuff@aud.ucla.edu

José Salazar Ferro
Professor
Universidad Nacional de Colombia
Colombia
jasalazarf@unal.edu.co
and
Universidad de los Andes
Colombia
salazarf@cable.net.co

Jyoti Hosagrahar
Director
Sustainable Urbanism International
Graduate School of Architecture, Planning, and Preservation
Columbia University
USA
and
India
jh2443@columbia.edu

Kwang-Joong Kim
Associate Professor
Graduate School of Environmental Studies
Seoul National University
Republic of Korea
kjkim@snu.ac.kr

Ali Madanipour
Professor of Urban Design
School of Architecture
Planning and Landscape
Newcastle University
UK
ali.madani@ncl.ac.uk

Akito Murayama
Department of Environmental Engineering and Architecture
Graduate School of Environmental Studies
Nagoya University
Japan
murayama@corot.nuac.nagoya-u.ac.jp

Junichiro Okata
Professor
Department of Urban Engineering
School of Engineering
The University of Tokyo
Japan
okata@up.t.u-tokyo.ac.jp

Eduardo Reese
Instituto del Conurbano
Universidad Nacional de General Sarmiento
Argentina
ereese@ciudad.com.ar

The English version of this text was prepared by Hayley Henderson

Philipp Rode
Executive Director
Urban Age Programme
London School of Economics and Political Science
UK
P.Rode@lse.ac.uk

Ananya Roy
Professor
Department of City and Regional Planning
University of California Berkeley
ananya@berkeley.edu

Paulo Sandroni
Professor
Department of Economics
Getulio Vargas Foundation
São Paulo, Brazil
paulo.sandroni@fgv.br

Sidh Sintusingha
Assistant Professor
Faculty of Architecture Building and Planning,
The University of Melbourne
Australia
ssint@unimelb.edu.au

André Sorensen
Associate Professor
Department of Geography and Programme in Planning
University of Toronto
Canada
sorensen@utsc.utoronto.ca

Neyran Turan
Assistant Professor
Rice University School of Architecture
USA
fnt1@rice.edu

Alfonso Valenzuela-Aguilera
Professor
Universidad Autónoma del Estado de Morelos
Mexico
aval@uaem.mx

Haryo Winarso
Head of Urban Planning
and Design Research Division
School of Architecture
Planning and Policy Development
Institute of Technology Bandung
Indonesia
haryowinarso@yahoo.com

1. Introduction: Megacities, Urban Form, and Sustainability

André Sorensen and Junichiro Okata

Of the many changes to our world wrought during the twentieth century, one of the most profound was the transformation of human settlement systems. A century ago the vast majority of the world's population was rural, embedded in social and economic systems tied to agricultural production and living in dispersed, small-scale settlements. Now, for the first time in human history, more than half the world's population is urban, after a century of massive migrations from rural hinterlands to burgeoning cities. In this urban transformation of the globe, one of the most dramatic and momentous developments has been the emergence of giant cities, often referred to as "megacities."

In 1950 there were two cities in the world with a population of more than ten million people: New York and Tokyo. By 1975 there were three, with the addition of Mexico City. By 2007 there were 19 cities with populations of more than ten million, of which four were in developed countries and 15 were in developing countries. It is projected that by 2025 that number will increase to 27, of which 22 will be in developing countries (UNDESA 2008: 10). In 2007 megacities accounted for about 9% of the world urban population, but although they represent only a minority of global population, megacities loom disproportionately large in economic flows, political processes, social stresses, and environmental risks. It is therefore no exaggeration to suggest that megacities will play a central role the future of human civilization, and that meeting the challenges they present is a key to global environmental and social sustainability.

A basic premise of this book is that the urbanization patterns achieved during the next four decades will be critical to the long-run sustainability and livability of the globe, and that megacities are a central part of that challenge. Over that period it is projected that the world's urban population

A. Sorensen and J. Okata (eds.), *Megacities: Urban Form, Governance, and Sustainability*,

will grow by just over three billion from the current 3.29 billion in 2007 to 6.4 billion in 2050, and 95% of that increase will be in developing countries (UNDESA 2008: 3). Just as important is the fact that if current trends hold, by 2050 the urban transition will be largely completed – 70% of the global population will live in cities and the period of greatest urban growth and development will be over.

The next 40 years therefore present either a crucial opportunity to create more sustainable urban areas, or alternatively to dig ourselves ever further into the wasteful, unsustainable, unjust, and unhealthy patterns of urban development that have dominated in recent decades. This next period is critical, as the urban form patterns established during the transition from rural to urban are enduring. Basic patterns of urban form, once established, become increasingly difficult and more costly to alter.

Through 15 in-depth case studies by researchers around the world, this book examines many of the major challenges facing megacities today. The contributors, all prominent researchers on their respective cities, were invited to an International Workshop on Megacities in March 2008 by the Centre for Sustainable Urban Regeneration of the University of Tokyo to discuss, debate, and share ideas about contemporary megacity challenges. Participants were asked to examine contemporary issues at the intersection of urban sustainability, urban form, and governance in their megacity. Regrettably, one participant from China was unable to attend the workshop, and another was unable to contribute a chapter to this book.

This introductory chapter briefly outlines our understanding and working definitions of sustainability and megacities, identifies the distinctions between megacities in the developed and developing countries, and frames the major questions addressed by the contributors. Detailed case studies of 15 megacities form the main body of the book, organized in three major groups of cities: Asia, Europe and North America, and Latin America. The main findings are brought together in the conclusions chapter, which draws out the major sustainability issues of urban form, land development, infrastructure provision, and governance, and the linkages between these examined in the individual case studies.

1.1 A World of Giant Cities

Despite a flurry of research on megacities during the late 1980s and 1990s (Dogan and Kasarda 1988; Fuchs et al. 1995; McGee and Robinson 1995; Gilbert 1996), there has been relatively little such work recently, apart from several excellent monographs on individual cities. It is clear that we need a much better understanding not just of how current megacities are changing, but also of how to make effective interventions in those changes. Production of the built environment is ultimately a social and political as well as an economic process, in the sense that it is the outcome of many millions of decisions and priorities. Learning better ways to make decisions together about the direction of urban change, in ways that foster greater livability for all inhabitants – not just the tiny minority who can buy their own protected enclaves – is one of the greatest sustainability challenges facing the globe.

In particular, rapid urbanization in poor countries has meant that key elements of infrastructure, such as water supply, waste removal, flood prevention, and rapid transit, which make giant cities more livable in developed countries, are often lacking for the majority of the population in these countries, leading to poverty, sickness, and preventable death on a scale scarcely imaginable (Davis 2006; Pieterse 2008; Brugmann 2009). Vast populations lack reliable and affordable access to clean drinking and washing water and live in informal settlements where basic public facilities such as water supply, sewers, and schools are non-existent. Although often economically vibrant and providing affordable footholds in the city (Benjamin 2004), these areas – often located on floodplains, on steep mountain slopes, or near garbage dumps – marginalize the poor and inflict on them heavy health burdens and exceptional environmental risks. The dilemma is to achieve better environments without destroying the flexibility, affordability, and dynamism of such poor areas of cities.

The failure of contemporary patterns of urbanization is not restricted to poor countries. Even in developed countries, economic restructuring, the weakening of social welfare systems, the abandonment of social housing programs, the downloading of responsibilities to municipal governments, and increased competition for inward investment have led to social polarization, poverty, and social pathologies such as homelessness. In some developed countries, planning has contributed to the production of sterile, monofunctional city areas that require long-distance commuting and prevent the creative adaptive re-use of older urban areas. The increased global mobility of capital and a shift from investment in productive capacity to investment in a securitized real estate industry has seen the emergence of an increasingly international development industry that has contributed greatly to the destabilization of urban livability and reduced access to housing for the poor and middle classes, as well as being a primary cause of the global economic and financial collapse since 2008.

Further, the failure to adequately manage urban fringe land development has led to wasteful urban sprawl, political fragmentation, and the rapid decline of many central cities, especially in the United States. Sprawl causes increased air pollution, long-distance commuting, heavy energy use, and wasted land. Worse, in poor countries the informalization of peri-urban land development is not just a matter of planning or governance failure, but as Roy (2005) argues, implicates the state in creating spaces of exception that facilitate social segregation and land development profits.

In both developed and developing countries, rapid urban growth during the last 30 years without adequate governance and planning regimes has facilitated an accelerating process of socio-spatial polarization, in which the wealthy are increasingly self-segregating in gated communities and fortified enclaves, and in many cities have successfully withdrawn from contributing their share of resources to provide public goods. In many megacities, elites are able to ensure that municipal investment in infrastructure and facilities benefits themselves disproportionately, producing a self-reinforcing process of segregated high-amenity communities for the wealthy, isolated from the environmental and social problems of poorer areas.

Although this contemporary urban crisis is far graver and on a vaster scale than that of the mid-nineteenth century that prompted the great urban reform movements of the end of that century, it is still largely ignored by those who are not directly affected. The magnitude of the problems, and the fact that trends in most relevant indicators are moving in the wrong direction render contemporary patterns of urbanization discouraging for those concerned about sustainability, social equity, and ecological integrity at the local and global scales. In this context, linking the concepts of "sustainability" and "megacities" may appear absurd, but we argue that the role of megacities in this urban crisis does, in fact, present significant insights about the meanings of sustainability and unsustainability.

1.2 Sustainable Megacities?

A review of the enormous literature on sustainable cities is neither possible nor necessary here (see Owens 1986; Stren et al. 1992; Haughton and Hunter 1994; Campbell 1996; Sorensen et al. 2004). The concept of sustainability has been so influential, however, and used in such a wide range of contexts that its meaning has become somewhat diffuse, so it is necessary to make explicit our approach. The seminal Brundtland Report (World Congress on Environment and Development 1987: 43), defined sustainability as "development that meets the needs of the present without compromising the ability of future generations to meet their own needs." The key insight of that work was that both the overexploitation of global natural resources by the North, and the failure to meet basic needs in the South are generators of unsustainable outcomes. Intergenerational equity and transfrontier equity have since become central concepts of sustainable development.

Campbell (1996: 298) developed this perspective concisely in his "planners' triangle" diagram, in which the three corners of the triangle represent the three fundamental priorities of economic development, environmental protection, and social equity, with the three sides of the triangle representing the "resource conflict" between economy and environment, the "property conflict" between economic growth and social justice, and the "development conflict" between social justice and environmental protection, with sustainable development located in the middle. Campbell argues convincingly that the idea of sustainable development will be particularly effective if "it acts as a lightning rod to focus conflicting economic, environmental, and social interests. The more it stirs up conflict and sharpens the debate, the more effective the idea of sustainability will be in the long run" (1996: 297). Therefore, pretending that there is some singular solution to these conflicts is not helpful. Instead it is necessary to continue to negotiate strategies to manage these enduring conflicts between the usually divergent priorities of environment, economy, and social equity, at all different scales.

So, the point is not to imagine a perfectly sustainable megacity. In a profound sense, megacities are inherently unsustainable, with their vast consumption of resources drawn from distant elsewheres, and equally vast production of wastes that are routinely exported elsewhere. The challenge is instead to keep looking for ways of reducing the ecological impacts of cities, achieving greater social equity, and strengthening economic functions to accomplish the first two priorities. The goal, in other words, is not sustainable cities per se, but cities that contribute to sustainable development (Satterthwaite 1997).

Urban growth has always involved overcoming existing limits and thresholds of risk and dysfunction, either through market processes, education, planning, technology, infrastructure provision, or a combination of those. A new understanding introduced by the sustainability debate, especially with the recognition of global climate change as a pressing environmental issue, is that limits are a permanent reality, not to be overcome, but to be embraced as a way of accelerating technological and governance change that reduces megacities' environmental footprints. The development and elaboration of an imaginary of unsustainability, risk, and disaster is part of the process of framing different future pathways and priorities of planning and governance in each megacity.

Each megacity has a legacy of built form, patterns and understandings of property rights, and planning and governance cultures that structure the ways in which issues of sustainability are framed, the kinds of solutions that can be imagined and proposed, and the policy approaches that are actually implemented. Different actors understand and prioritize sustainability issues in diverse ways, from the intimate and hyperlocal to the regional and ecosystemic. Developing a political and planning framework that addresses megacity sustainability in meaningful ways must engage a range of different actors at different scales and in different sectors. The structure, capacity, and nature of that engagement have a profound influence on the equity, environmental, and economic impacts of those processes.

In all of the cities examined here, concepts of sustainable development and fears of unsustainable development have been influential and in some cases have produced innovative and even transformative changes. The goal is not to cherry-pick success stories, but to examine how issues of megacity development, urban form, sustainability, and unsustainability are conceived and reconceived, how governance processes are influenced by these ideas and either block or facilitate their implementation, and how these processes in turn influence outcomes on the ground.

1.2.1 Defining Megacities

Definitions of "megacity" vary, from a population threshold as low as four million (Dogan and Kasarda 1988), to eight million (Richardson 1993; Gilbert 1996) or ten million (Ward 1990; UNDESA 2008). But as Gilbert (1996) notes, this threshold is arbitrary, and there is no theoretical basis for believing that the issues facing a city of eight million are qualitatively different from those of a city of ten million. There are also great difficulties in deciding where to draw the line when counting megacity populations, as population data is usually collected for specific political jurisdictions, and megacities are continually growing beyond those political lines. So the precise threshold is not as important as the fact that cities of eight or ten million face significantly different challenges from those of cities of a hundred thousand or one million, and that the number of such giant cities is rapidly increasing.

As yet there is little systematic research or reliable comparable data on the precise ways in which urban issues vary with city size, and the goal here is not to attempt a contribution to the long and inconclusive optimal city size debate (see Richardson 1973; Begovic 1991). Most variables do not vary consistently with city size (Richardson 1973; Gilbert 1996: 4), and as the studies collected here show, the most pressing issues can be quite different in two cities even of similar size. Nor is there a singular urban problematic or agenda common to all megacities. Several major issues do seem characteristic of megacities, however, and come up repeatedly in the studies here. These include air pollution, water supply, waste management, transportation, housing, growth management, and governance, although these manifest themselves variously in different places. Our suggestion is not, therefore, that these cities face identical problems, but simply that they share a number of issues and that a close examination of the challenges and responses to these issues in different contexts will be valuable.

1.2.2 Giant Cities in Developed and Developing Countries

We argue in the conclusions that it is increasingly necessary to move beyond a simple divide between megacities in developed and developing countries, but first it is important to acknowledge profound differences between cities in developed and developing countries. As White and Whitney (1992: 16) showed, cities in rich and poor countries differ not only in the kinds of sustainability issues that are most critical, but also in their capacity to manage them. They argued that in developing countries, job opportunities, water supply, transportation, and air pollution are likely to be much bigger problems in large cities than in small and medium-sized cities, while in developed countries, pollution, crime, and housing tend to pose greater problems in large cities than in smaller ones.

More recent research suggests that the fundamental difference is not just wealth, although that is important, but the speed and timing of growth. As has often been noted, the pace of urbanization has accelerated during the last two centuries. While a city like London took over a century to grow from one to seven million people, Tokyo took half that time, and cities like Delhi are making the same transition in a few decades. Cities in developing countries are also growing faster than early industrializing cities in Europe, which had the "pressure release" of massive exports of population to colonies in the new world; such emigration is proportionately much less today. Most of the huge migrations of poor people from rural hinterlands are towards cities like Delhi, Istanbul, and Sao Paulo, rather than to other countries.

The increasing speed of urbanization has had major consequences: building infrastructure takes time as well as money, and rapid growth often means that there is not enough of either to keep up with needs. Perhaps more fundamentally, political processes and governance institutions take time to evolve and generate the effective frameworks to manage the complex systems that make giant cities more livable – such as public utilities commissions to finance, build, and maintain infrastructure, inter-municipal councils and agreements to share responsibilities, or coroners' juries to determine liability and propose remedies for institutional failure, among hundreds of others.

An important analysis of how the speed and timing of urbanization create different experiences in different countries is the "urban environmental transition" hypothesis, which suggests that cities go through a sequence of environmental challenges as they get wealthier (see McGranahan et al. 1999; Marcotullio 2007). In the first stage, they must deal primarily with "brown" environmental issues – clean water supply and waste management. As they increase in wealth and industrial development, "grey" issues of air and water pollution become increasingly important. In the third stage, the "green" environmental agenda of sustainable ecosystems and life-support systems comes to the fore.

There are also important temporal and scale components of this analysis, in that as cities develop, neighborhood-scale brown issues that have immediate health impacts are overcome, and the focus shifts to larger city-region-scale issues of industrial air and water pollution. Wealthier cities struggle with ecosystemic challenges that are regional or global in scale, such as acid rain, ozone depletion, and global warming.

Intrinsic to this analysis is the suggestion that environmental burdens are increasingly displaced to ever-greater scales. Brown issues affect primarily those creating the waste and others nearby, but grey issues tend to be dispersed – for example by tall smokestacks – over much wider areas. Finally, the wealthiest cites are able to export the "green" environmental burdens of their consumption throughout the globe not only by shipping toxic waste to unregulated dumps and materials recyclers in distant locations, but also by consuming natural resources and manufactured products whose primary environmental impacts are in other (usually poorer) places. And of course, the consumption of carbon-based fuels is much higher per capita in rich cities and countries, yet the wastes that contribute to global warming are dumped into a global waste-sink.

To this analysis Marcotullio (2007) adds an important further insight: this series of environmental challenges has been radically "telescoped" into an ever-shorter period, so that whereas cities in early industrializing countries had centuries to deal with brown issues and then grey and green issues sequentially, building gradually to their governance capacity and norms, developing countries today are dealing with all three simultaneously. As he concisely puts it, "environmental challenges in developing cities are occurring *sooner* (at lower levels of income), rising *faster* (over time for similar ranges of income), and emerging *more simultaneously* (as sets of problems) than previously experienced by developed cities" (Marcotullio 2007: 46, italics in original). The challenges of livability are thus much greater, and in many ways qualitatively different for cities in developing countries today than they were in cities at a similar stage of development in developed countries decades ago.

Another major difference between megacities has to do with the timing of major urban growth relative to prevailing ideologies of development and governance. The shifts in political and economic ideology that have occurred during the last 30 years have had profound impacts on planning and governance institutions. During the 1950s and 1960s the dominant economic model for developing countries was import-substitution, the promotion of national industrial champions, and the creation of the bureaucratic, infrastructural, and technological support structure to enable their growth. Since the 1970s, however, the hegemonic idea of best practices for development has shifted towards neo-liberal formulas of open markets, reduced government, and lower taxes. At the same time, accelerating globalization means that cities are more thoroughly integrated into global financial, technological, and production systems than before, with cities in the global South systemically at a disadvantage, gaining primarily low-value-added production functions and heavy environmental burdens, while (some) cities in the developed countries gain an increasing share of high-value-added command and control functions (Sassen 1991; Dicken 1998).

One profound consequence of this shift has been a transformation of the way urban infrastructure is understood, built, and managed. The institutional frameworks of urban infrastructure provision – for example for water supply or public transit – established during the former period are in almost all cases very different from those established during the latter period. As Graham and Marvin (2001) and a growing literature on "splintering urbanism" show, in the earlier era a "modern infrastructural ideal" assumed that the right way to build infrastructure was as public monopolies delivering integrated and standardized networks throughout urban areas. Now it is more likely that service delivery is fragmented, delivered by both public- and private-sector actors, with huge and growing disparities in provision between well-served and un-served areas.

These new patterns are in part a product of new technologies that allow efficiency in much smaller networks, and a shift in which new kinds of networks are being provided (cellphones vs. sewerage). But it is also fundamentally a shift in ideology, towards a withdrawal of the state, increased urban competition, and a neoliberal emphasis on privatization, full-cost pricing, and the elimination of cross-subsidies. There is also heavy pressure from international organizations such as the World Bank and International Monetary Fund, for example, which promote the privatization of water supply systems. Furthermore, the "unbundling" of infrastructure allows increasing segmentation of urban space into highly networked areas for those who can afford to pay, and unserviced areas for the less powerful and less able to pay, thereby promoting enclave developments for the rich (Graham and Marvin 2001: 383).

Graham and Marvin (2001) describe this as a process of "splintering cities." They argue that the decline of the "modern infrastructure ideal" in the second half of the twentieth century has led in many cities to the abandonment of the goal of public provision of municipal services throughout the urbanized area. This shift is producing an increased differentiation between high-value locations served by modern infrastructure and deprived locations that are bypassed by it. This trend is having profound impacts on cities in developing countries that did not have infrastructure networks in place before the onset of the current period and the decline of the modern infrastructure ideal. At the same time, these impacts are seen in many more developed cities where processes of social polarization are often exacerbated by highly uneven service provision.

As discussed in the conclusions chapter, the challenges of sustainability, urban form, infrastructure provision, and governance are closely linked. Although megacities in developing countries experience these challenges in acute forms, cities in more developed countries face many of these fundamental issues too. This book does not attempt to highlight solutions achieved in rich cities for transfer to poorer cities, since learning and innovation is taking place in all the cities examined here. Without minimizing the challenges faced by rapidly growing megacities in developing countries, we are also seeing shared challenges, dilemmas, and policy approaches among the megacities in all countries.

The detailed case studies of 15 megacities around the world are organized around a shared set of concerns and questions about issues of sustainability, land development, urban governance, and urban form. The main questions that framed our investigations are: What are the most pressing issues of sustainability and urban form in each megacity? How are major issues of sustainability understood and framed by policymakers? Is urban form considered a significant component of sustainability issues in public debates and public policy? Who are the key actors in framing urban sustainability challenges and in shaping urban change? How is unsustainability, risk, or disaster imagined?

References

Begovic B (1991) The economic approach to optimal city size. Progr Plann 36:93–161
Benjamin S (2004) Urban land transformation for pro-poor economies. Geoforum 35(2):177–187
Brugmann J (2009) Welcome to the urban revolution: how cities are changing the world. Viking, Canada, Toronto
Campbell S (1996) Green Cities, growing cities, just cities? Urban planning and the contradictions of sustainable development. J Am Plann Assoc 62(3):296–312
Davis M (2006) Planet of slums. Verso, London
Dicken P (1998) Global shift: transforming the world economy. Guilford Press, New York
Dogan, M, Kasarda, JD (eds) (1988) The metropolis era, vol 1. A world of giant cities. Sage, Newbury Park, CA
Fuchs RJ, Brennan E, Chamie J, Uitto J, Lo F-C (eds) (1995) Mega-city growth and the future. United Nations University Press, Tokyo
Gilbert A (ed) (1996) The mega-city in Latin America. United Nations University Press, Tokyo
Graham S, Marvin S (2001) Splintering urbanism: networked infrastructures, technological mobilities and the urban condition. Routledge, London
Haughton G, Hunter C (1994) Sustainable cities. Jessica Kingsley, London
Marcotullio PJ (2007) Variations of urban environmental transitions: the experiences of rapidly developing Asia-Pacific cities. In: Marcotullio PJ, McGranahan G (eds) Scaling urban environmental challenges: from local to global and back. Earthscan, London, pp 45–68
McGee TG, Robinson IM (eds) (1995) The mega-urban regions of Southeast Asia. University of British Columbia Press, Vancouver
McGranahan G, Songsore J, Kjellen M (1999) Sustainability, poverty and urban environmental transitions. In: Satterthwaite D (ed) Sustainable cities. Earthscan, London, pp 107–130
Owens SE (1986) Energy, planning and urban form. Pion, London
Pieterse, EA (2008) City futures: confronting the crisis of urban development. Zed Books, London, New York; UCT Press, Capetown, South Africa
Richardson HW (1973) The economics of urban size. Saxon House, Lexington
Richardson HW (1993) Efficiency and welfare in LDC mega-cities. In: Kasarda JD, Parnell AM (eds) Third world cities: problems, policies and prospects. Sage, Newbury Park, CA, pp 32–57
Roy A (2005) Urban informality: toward an epistemology of planning. J Am Plann Assoc 71(2):147–158
Sassen S (1991) The global city: New York, London, Tokyo. Princeton University Press, Princeton, NJ
Satterthwaite D (1997) Sustainable cities or cities that contribute to sustainable development? Urban Stud 34(10):1667–1691

Sorensen A, Marcotullio PJ, Grant J (eds) (2004) Towards sustainable cities: East Asian, North American and European perspectives. Ashgate, Aldershot, England
Stren RE, White R, Whitney JB (eds) (1992) Sustainable cities: urbanization and the environment in international perspective. Westview Press, Boulder, CO
UNDESA (2008) World urbanization prospects: the 2007 revision. United Nations Department of Economic and Social Affairs, New York
Ward PM (1990) Mexico City: the production and reproduction of an urban environment. Belhaven Press, London
White R, Whitney JB (1992) Cities and the environment: an overview. In: Stren RE, White R, Whitney JB (eds) Sustainable cities: urbanization and the environment in international perspective. Westview Press, Boulder, CO, pp 8–51
World Congress on Environment and Development (1987) Our common future. Oxford University Press, Oxford

Part I
Asia

2. Tokyo's Urban Growth, Urban Form and Sustainability

Junichiro Okata and Akito Murayama

2.1 Introduction

Tokyo, the largest mega-region in the world so far with 35 million inhabitants in 2007, has experienced a rapid growth in the twentieth century with various issues associated with urban form and urban environment. Some issues were solved and others remain to be solved. If Tokyo is evaluated as one of the most efficient, productive and sustainable mega-regions in the world, it is the result of rapid urban growth and development in the twentieth century. After that, Tokyo has been facing new challenges as it left the phase of rapid growth and entered the phase of no- or low-growth, depopulating and aging society. In this respect, Tokyo is a leading or an instructive mega-region in the world. At the same time, Tokyo must take part in the global effort to achieve sustainability. This chapter focuses on the history of Tokyo's urban growth, the diversity of urban form issues in Tokyo, some previous successes in solving urban environmental problems and some new challenges facing efforts to enhance urban sustainability.

In this chapter, the term "Tokyo" refers to Tokyo region comprised of Tokyo Metropolitan Government (TMG) jurisdiction and the surrounding three prefectures of Kanagawa, Chiba and Saitama, covering 13,551 km^2 and accommodating 35 million inhabitants. As of January 2008, there were 23 wards, 26 cities, five towns and eight villages in TMG jurisdiction, and there were total of four designated cities, 91 cities, 59 towns and five villages in the three prefectures. "Central Tokyo" in this chapter roughly refers to central three wards of Chuo, Chiyoda and Minato, and inner five wards of Shibuya, Shinjuku, Toshima, Bunkyo and Taito. The 23-ward area is the former city of Tokyo before it was abolished in 1943, that now comprises the central city area of the current Tokyo metropolitan region, with a population of about 8.7 million.

A. Sorensen and J. Okata (eds.), *Megacities: Urban Form, Governance, and Sustainability*,

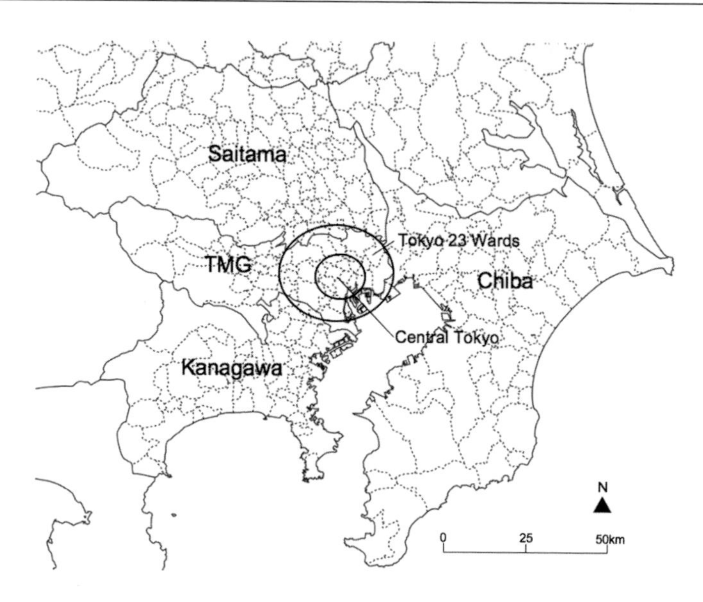

Fig. 2-1. Tokyo Metropolitan Government (TMG) jurisdiction, prefectural and municipal boundaries in Tokyo

Although there are governmental organizations for TMG, the three prefectures as well as wards, cities, towns and villages, there is no governmental organization or planning body for the whole Tokyo (region) (Fig. 2-1).

2.2 History of Tokyo's Urban Growth

During the twentieth century Tokyo experienced a significant urban expansion due to rapid population growth. Figure 2-2 shows the expansion of densely inhabited district with population of 40 persons/ha or more. The population of Tokyo grew from 7.5 million in 1920 to nearly 35 million in 2007. The major planning issue for twentieth century Tokyo was to expand and intensify the urban area in order to accommodate this rapid growth.

Tokyo began as the national capital city called 'Edo' which was constructed by the Shogun Tokugawa Ieyasu after 1600, and it grew to be one of the largest metropolises in the world by the early 1700s. After the imperial restoration in 1860s, when reformers overthrew the feudal system in a bid to modernize Japanese society and economy, Edo was renamed to Tokyo (East-Capital-City), and was remodeled into a modern city by introduction of railway, tram and trunk road network, modern water supply and modern parks until 1910s.

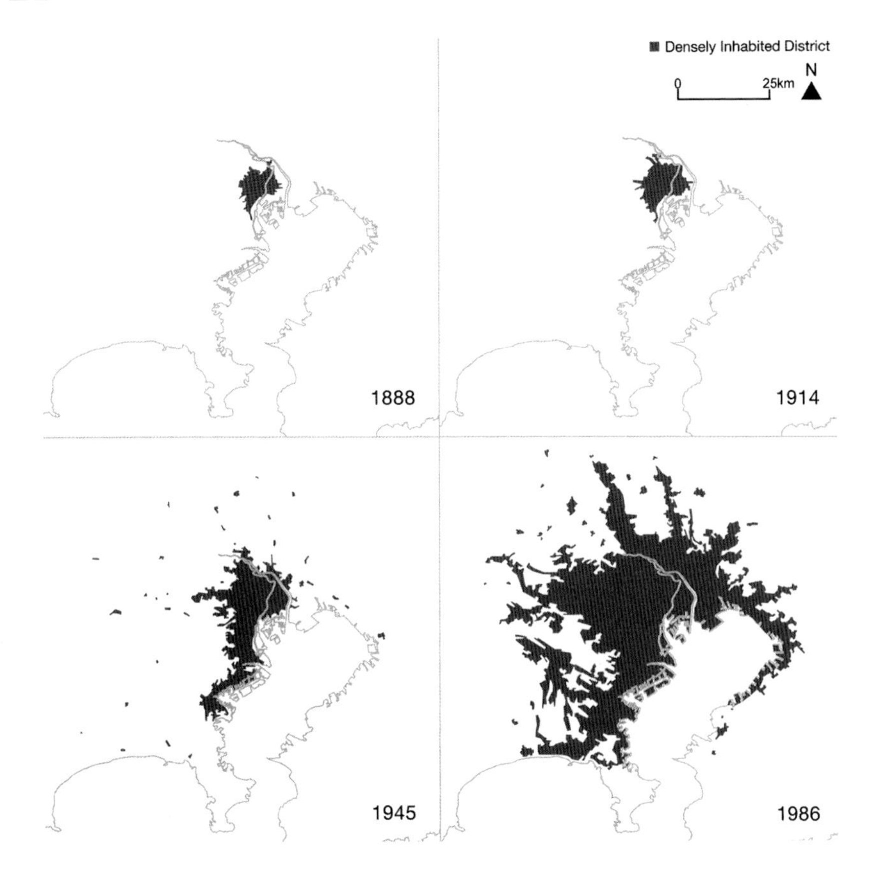

Fig. 2-2. Expansion of densely inhabited district (Okata et al. 2005)

In the middle of 1920s, Tokyo's urban area started to grow past the fringe of the former city of Edo's urban area, heavy industrial factories located in peripheral area of Tokyo, which caused severe conflict with local residents. The local government of Tokyo and the National Government needed to introduce a kind of subdivision control system or development control system to prevent un-planned and un-controlled suburban development, and use-zoning system for managing pollution/nuisance problems. A new City Planning Law was enacted in 1919, the main elements of which were a simple zoning system similar to New York City's and the designated building line system similar to the German district development plan system (Bebau-ungs Plan).

However, the designated building line system introduced in the 1919 Law did not work well in order to inhibit un-planned small scale sub-division or plot-by-plot development with insufficient infrastructure, because unlike the German system, all roads wider than 2.7 m (4 m after revision in 1938), were automatically designated as building lines, enabling development on the lot attached to the road. Subsequently, small-scale development or plot-by-plot development spread over sub-urban area where very primitive road network existed for farming and rural life. But, the typical suburban development in Tokyo until 1950s was low dense single family housing for emerging middle class citizens, those sub-urban development generally provided decent or minimal living environment even if it had only self-supplied well water and no flush toilet. So, as many sub-urban railways were developed in the 1920s, rapid sub-urbanization started under very weak planning system introduced in 1919, and the big earthquake in 1923 accelerated the suburban development of Tokyo.

Since 1930s, ideas and plans for greenbelt that controls suburban expansion were developed until the late 1950s, but greenbelt was never implemented. Firstly, in late 1930s, the Tokyo Regional Greenbelt Plan was established and the land was purchased by local governments, but the major part of the land was sold to local farmers as the farming land reform initiative after the war. Secondly, 'Green Belt Zoning' that regulate coverage ratio under 10% was designated around existing urban area of Tokyo as a part of the post war restoration plan of Tokyo, but local building authorities failed to enforce such a strict regulation in the context of 'postwar liberalism' and rapid population growth. Thirdly, in the first National Capital Region's Development Plan established in 1958, a 'greenbelt and new towns' scheme similar to the Greater London Plan 1944 was introduced, but as the plan was only advisory, there was no effective action to implement the green belt. Thus, Tokyo's urban expansion was largely led by railway constructions and developments along railway lines without being controlled by a strong urban land use plan nor a greenbelt policy until the end of 1960s.

Before 1960, Japan was still a 'rural' country where over the half of households live in rural areas. In the 1960s, the post war baby boomers immigrated for job and higher education from rural area and provincial small towns into metropolitan regions including Tokyo, Osaka and Nagoya. They were accommodated in dormitories or lodgings at first, then moved to small wooden apartment houses, public or social housings, or small suburban single family housing if they were lucky enough. Also, condominium apartment houses became popular in Tokyo since 1970s. As the planning system and sub-division control system in 1960s was still very weak, the level of infrastructure of those housing was very poor. However minimum level of urban services such as water supply and elementary education were mandatory responsibilities of local governments (the idea of 'Civil Minimum' was very popular in late 1960s in Japan), Tokyo was able to successfully accommodate the flood of immigrant population in not-informal settlement with no-less-than minimum level of living environment. It seems possible that if the planning power in Japan or Tokyo had been stricter before the 1960s, then more illegal or informal settlements lacking minimum levels of infrastructure and social services would have developed, and Tokyo might have experienced much more serious problems in the 1960s and would not have grown into the world's largest megacity. Finally, in 1968, City Planning Law was significantly revised and a kind of growth boundary system that controls expansion of urban area, more precise zoning system that may protect good residential environment, and the development permission system that ensures a certain level of infrastructure of development were introduced (Fig. 2-3).

Railway construction was one of the national modernization policies, and the national railway network connecting central Tokyo and other cities in Japan was established by the end of the nineteenth century. Beginning in the 1920s, private railway companies purchased huge areas of land in the suburbs of Tokyo and developed housing estates or garden suburbs. Private railway companies were able to pay for the railway constructions by the profits they made from selling or leasing the developed housing estates and

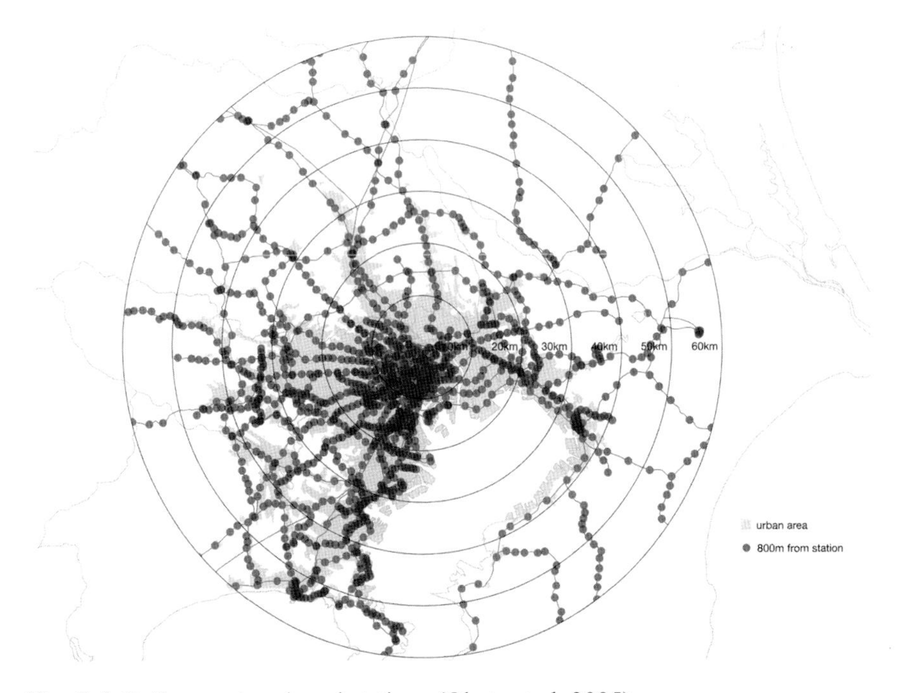

Fig. 2-3. Railway network and stations (Okata et al. 2005)

commercial areas around the stations. Public corporations also developed large-scale housing estates along railway lines in the suburbs starting in the 1960s such as Tama New Town and Chiba New Town. These new towns were developed as garden suburbs or "bed towns" of Tokyo. On the other hand in central Tokyo, the subway network has been developed continuously since 1927. As a result, nearly 73% of morning commuters to Tokyo 23 Wards used railway lines while only 9% of them used private automobiles in 1998 (Nakamura et al. 2004). Others used bus, bicycle or foot. Not only the railway system is well equipped, but also the season ticket discount for commuter was introduced since before the war, employers usually pay commuting cost to employees, major companies often inhibit employees to commute by a private car because of limitation of parking place and reparations risk for car accidents caused by employees, and traffic congestion in commuting time in Tokyo is so terrible that makes commuting to central Tokyo from suburb impossible in fact. Thus, Tokyo is clearly one of the world's most public transportation oriented megacities (Cervero 1998).

With the high concentration of office and commercial functions in central Tokyo and the development of housing estates along railway lines in the suburbs, Tokyo has grown to a transit-oriented, mono-centric region at least from a macroscopic point of view. The daytime and nighttime population density by distance from Tokyo station clearly show this pattern. In the future, with the decrease of working population, it may become more difficult to maintain today's sophisticated railway system and a mono-centric spatial structure. In addition, suburbs without sufficient public transit services have already become automobile-oriented.

Regarding the current land use planning of Tokyo, Urban Area, Agricultural Area, Forestry Area, Natural Park Area and Natural Reserve Area are designated based on National Land Use Planning Act and the five land use related laws: City Planning Law, Law Concerning the Improvement of Agricultural Promotion Areas, Forest Law, Natural Park Law and Nature Conservation Law. Land use in these areas is controlled by the regulations of their respective laws. In fact, this land use plan is not really a plan with particular visions or strategies but merely a map showing where each law is effective. Some areas overlap. The land use related laws are administered by different sections of the national government, and at the local level do not provide an effective land management system (Sorensen 2002) (Fig. 2-4).

Land use in Urban Area (and only in Urban Area) is controlled by the regulations of the City Planning Law. Urban Area is divided by a kind of urban growth boundary line into Urbanization Promotion Area (UPA) and Urbanization Control Area (UCA) in principle. Besides those 'divided' Urban Areas, Undivided Urban Areas exist as small provincial towns

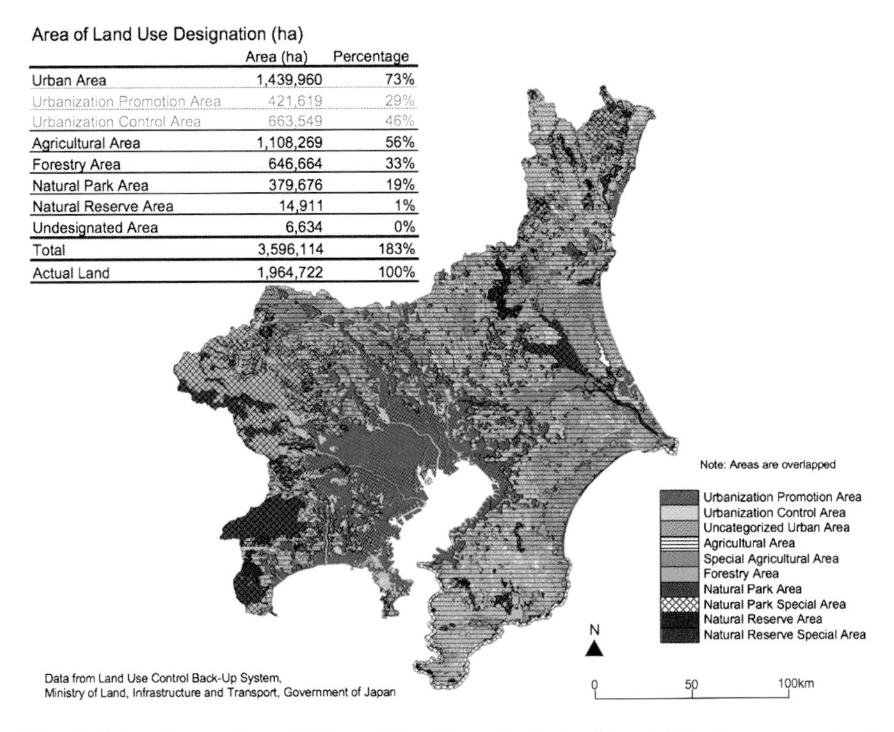

Area of Land Use Designation (ha)

	Area (ha)	Percentage
Urban Area	1,439,960	73%
Urbanization Promotion Area	421,619	29%
Urbanization Control Area	663,549	46%
Agricultural Area	1,108,269	56%
Forestry Area	646,664	33%
Natural Park Area	379,676	19%
Natural Reserve Area	14,911	1%
Undesignated Area	6,634	0%
Total	3,596,114	183%
Actual Land	1,964,722	100%

Fig. 2-4. Land use plan of Tokyo (The figure includes Ibaraki Prefecture north of Chiba Prefecture) (Ministry of Land, Infrastructure and Transport, Government of Japan)

peripheral or outside of metropolitan regions. Twelve category 'basic' zoning zone must be designated in UPA, regulating use, building coverage ratio, floor area ratio, building height, etc. in conjunction with the Building Standard Law. Agricultural, Forestry, Natural Park and Natural Reserve Areas have "special areas" within themselves to further strengthen land use restrictions. Roughly, natural resources and farmlands are protected in the "special areas". On the other hand, developments that meet certain conditions are permitted in areas outside "special areas", often causing the destruction of natural resources or farmlands.

Although Tokyo left the phase of rapid growth, transportation infrastructures, both roads and railways, are continuously developed. The completion of the three express ring roads (Central Circular Route, Tokyo 'Gaikan – Outer Circular' Expressway and Metropolitan Inter-city Expressway) first planned around 40 years ago are long-awaited for to mitigate traffic congestions in central Tokyo and to connect suburban cities. Other arterial roads are also proposed. Railway projects include constructing new lines and elevating existing railway lines to reduce level road crossings that became increasingly congested as trains became more frequent.

From 2000 to 2005, population growth was observed in selected areas of Tokyo. Growing areas include waterfront areas (Minato, Chuo and Koto Wards), residential areas within Tokyo 23 Wards (Nerima, Setagaya, etc.) and suburban residential areas (Machida City and Aoba-Ku, Yokohama City). Condominiums ("mansion" or apartment for sale, not for rent) are built in larger scale in these areas: the share of condominiums with more than 100 units/building increased from 14% in 1995 to 58% in 2005, and the share of apartments with more than 200 units/buildings is as high as 38% in 2005. On the other hand, population decline was observed in the outer suburbs. People are coming back to the selected areas of Tokyo including central Tokyo. (Ministry of Land, Infrastructure and Transport, Government of Japan 2007).

2.3 Diversity of Urban Form Issues in Tokyo

As a result of rapid urban growth and a relatively weak planning system, Tokyo is a patchwork of various types of urban space with diverse urban form issues. Some of the major issues are as follows.

2.3.1 Several Kinds of Urban Sprawl

Most of Urban Areas in the mega-regions in Japan are divided into Urbanization Promotion Area (UPA) where development is promoted and Urbanization Control Area (UCA) where urban development is not permitted in principle. Some Urban Areas called Undivided Urban Areas (UUA) are not divided into UPA and UCA. There are several kinds of urban sprawls in Urban Area, somewhat different from urban sprawl in North America where it is generally considered as the expansion of urban area with insufficient urban infrastructure such as streets, parks and utilities.

Firstly, in UPA, not only large-scale planned developments but also small-scale or 'single lot' developments are permitted as long as each building lot is attached to a street which width is 4 m or wider in principle, causing urban sprawl by incremental accumulation of small scale 'mini-developments' and 'plot-by-plot' developments. Secondly, in UCA, certain developments such as housing for farmers' sons, retail facilities for the locals or public facilities are permitted, contributing to urbanization. Thirdly, in UUA where land use regulation is generally loose, various kinds

Fig. 2-5. Mini-development

of developments including large-scale commercial developments were possible. Thus, urban sprawl can be observed both in UPA, UCA and UUA. Urbanization in UCA and UUA has been controlled mainly by Agricultural Land designation in Agricultural Area where agricultural land is protected to promote productive agriculture (Figs. 2-5 and 2-6).

As a response to continuing urban sprawl and downtown decline, City Planning Law was recently amended to permit large-scale commercial developments exclusively in commercial, neighborhood commercial and quasi-industrial zoning zones, that are to be designated by a local government with consent of its higher government which is responsible for regional location management of major commercial centers. This response might have been too late since many large-scale commercial developments have already occurred in urban fringe areas since the early 1990s.

2.3.2 Transit-Oriented Development (TOD)

As explained in the previous section, Tokyo is transit-oriented in terms of a regional structure. Urban areas around railway stations are generally high density and pedestrian-oriented. Major transit terminals such as Tokyo,

Fig. 2-6. Development in UCA

Ueno, Ikebukuro, Shinjuku, Shibuya, Shinagawa, Kawasaki, Yokohama, Omiya and Chiba stations are surrounded by high-density mixed-use area of retail, commercial and office uses, and suburban stations often have supermarkets and shopping streets around them (Fig. 2-7).

However, road infrastructure around many of the suburban stations is not well provided, resulting in narrow sidewalks unfriendly to baby strollers and wheelchairs, and small rotaries difficult to access by buses, taxis and private automobiles. In addition, lack of reasonable bicycle parking facilities often leads to illegal bicycle parking on narrow sidewalks (Fig. 2-8).

Recently, there are controversies regarding TOD visions, for example, in Shibuya and Shimokitazawa station areas. While the governments try to promote functional TOD with large-scale redevelopment and modern infrastructure, many people including local people and urban professionals emphasize the importance of vernacular urban form and pedestrian-oriented environment.

2.3.3 Intensification of Urban Centers

The population of central Tokyo had increased continuously since the end of World War II until 1986, but decreased from 1987 to 1996 due to

Fig. 2-7. Major transit terminal area

Fig. 2-8. Suburban station area

skyrocketing land value by the bubble economy and its aftereffect. Since 1997, population of central Tokyo has been recovering, activating various housing developments.

Significant among those are super-high-rise residential towers and small-size three-story single-family housing. Super-high-rise residential towers are often developed on former industrial sites in the Tokyo Bay waterfront, or on large lots (sometimes assembled from several smaller lots) in existing urban areas. In some cases, the former is accompanied with the issues of insufficient infrastructure and public services particularly public schools, and the latter by neighborhood conflicts provoked by the destruction of valued landscapes and by buildings that block sunlight (Fujii et al. 2007). Also very common is the redevelopment large single-family dwellings into small-size three-story single-family housing is often developed after a large property was divided into smaller pieces, leading to fragmentation and the loss of large single-family housing properties in central Tokyo (Figs. 2-9 and 2-10).

Constructions of one-room (studio) apartments, both high-rise and low-rise, are active in central Tokyo, in response to the increasing number of single person households. Residential apartments for families are being

Fig. 2-9. Super-high-rise residential tower

Fig. 2-10. Small-size three-story housing

constructed in suburban centers around railway stations for people who put high priority on the convenience of commuting (Fig. 2-11).

Many mixed-use (mix of office and commercial with or without residential uses) redevelopment projects mostly planned during the bubble economy in the 1980s have been completed in recent years such as Roppongi Hills, Shiodome Sio-Site and Tokyo Midtown (Fig. 2-12).

2.3.4 Redevelopment of Brownfields

In the Tokyo region, industrial areas of various sizes are dispersed throughout the region, but the largest concentration is in Tokyo Bay Waterfront Area that holds Keihin Industrial Area (4,400 ha) and Keiyo Industrial Area (4,700 ha). These industrial areas were the engines of Japan's economic growth in the twentieth century, but they are now experiencing a gradual change as they entered the globalizing twenty-first century (Fig. 2-13).

Recently, there has been a drastic movement among companies in these industrial areas such as the mergers of oil and steel companies or relocation of plants to foreign countries, which result in the generation of potential

Fig. 2-11. One-room apartment tower

sites for redevelopment. On the other hand, research and development institutions have been located, introducing new land uses to the industrial areas. Thus, these areas call for the integrated methodology of brownfield regeneration and planning, including remediation of contaminated soil, as they gradually evolve from the heavy industrial base to a new urban area that potentially accommodates research and development institutions, light industry, business and commercial facilities, housing and other uses.

Fig. 2-12. Mixed-use redevelopment

Fig. 2-13. Keihin Industrial Area

2.3.5 Conservation of Historic Areas

Based on the Law for the Protection of Cultural Properties, preservation districts for groups of historic buildings can be designated by local municipalities to provide technical and financial support from government. There are only two preservation districts in Tokyo region: Sawara in Chiba Prefecture (7.1 ha) and Kawagoe in Saitama Prefecture (7.8 ha), both developed as merchant towns in the pre-modern period (Denkenkyo; Hiramoto 2005).

While these districts are well conserved, there are many other areas in Tokyo that are not eligible to be designated as preservation districts but have certain levels of historic or vernacular environment. These areas often confront with high pressure of redevelopment since land use and building regulations in Japan are generally loose, and neighborhood conflicts never stop. Such examples are Yanaka and Kagurazaka in central Tokyo. In these areas, attempts are being made to create future visions based on local consensus and implementation measures including regulations or incentives by City Planning Law, the recently enacted Landscape Law or local ordinances as necessary.

2.3.6 Improvement of Vernacular or Popular Settlements

Population growth and urban expansion of Tokyo in the twentieth century was so rapid and sub-division control system (or detailed district development planning system) was so weak that most of the inner urban areas are not provided with sufficient infrastructure such as well-planned streets and parks, and still occupied by mainly low-rise high-density obsolete wooden housings. The improvement of such vernacular unplanned settlements continues to be a great challenge, particularly as although they provide convenient and affordable housing for both young and aged people they are highly vulnerable to earthquake and fire disasters.

Tokyo Metropolitan Government has designated 11 major improvement areas totaling around 2,400 ha where improvement projects are promoted to mitigate potential earthquake disasters in low-rise high-density wooden housing areas. In Higashi Ikebukuro, one of the designated major (Department of Urban Development, Tokyo Metropolitan Government 2003) improvement areas, the collaborative work of residents, consultants and government officials since the mid-1980s has been able to complete ten plaza projects with fire extinguishers and hydrants, several fire-proof cooperative housings and one 6 m-wide disaster-proof street as an emergency escape route in case of disaster (Fig. 2-14).

Dealing with continued building of "mini-development" urban areas presents another set of issues. For ongoing "mini-developments" in

Fig. 2-14. Designated improvement area

residential–agricultural mixed-use areas such as Tagara in Nerima Ward, Tokyo, a district plan that designates future streets, wall setbacks, minimum lot sizes, building design and fence structure seems to be the most effective approach. On the other hand, it is very difficult and expensive to improve an established or already built-up "mini-development" urban area such as Takashina in Kawagoe City, Saitama Prefecture, because of the severe lack of public space and facilities (Fig. 2-15).

Recently, illegal "Blue Tent" settlements can be observed in large parks and riverbanks in central Tokyo. They started as homeless concentrations but now are becoming increasingly permanent, and form a new type of informal settlement. So far, no effective measure has been found for this kind of settlement.

2.3.7 Maintenance and Improvement of the Suburbs

As Tokyo entered the phase of no- or low-growth, depopulating and aging society, with people moving back to central Tokyo after the collapse of the bubble economy, maintenance and improvement of the suburbs has become a new issue. Many suburban housing estates, both multi-family and single family, were developed in the 1960s and the 1970s, the age of

Fig. 2-15. Built-up mini-development area

rapid growth. Baby-boomers who purchased housing in those estates are now retiring and most of their children have already left home. Decline of schools and shops, and growing demand for social services mean that it is questionable if these suburbs will be socially and economically sustainable in the future. Measures to maintain the suburbs might include provision of various community services to support the lives of the aged population, regeneration of multi-family housing estates to attract diverse population and local management of vacant properties (Fig. 2-16).

Parts of Tokyo suburbs not well served by public transit have automobile-oriented urban structure and landscape. Improvement of landscape in commercial strips along arterial roads, for example, might be an issue particularly from the aesthetic point of view (Fig. 2-17).

2.4 Previous Successes in Solving Urban Environmental Problems

Tokyo has experienced various urban environmental problems due to the rapid growth and concentration of population and industries. The problems include environmental pollution such as air pollution, water pollution and ground subsidence, delays in providing sewage systems and the limitation of waste disposal sites. Tokyo Metropolitan Government (TMG) has successfully

Fig. 2-16. Suburban housing estate

Fig. 2-17. Commercial strip along arterial road

solved many of these problems, taking creative measures ahead of the national government and leading other prefectures in the region. It is useful to examine some examples.

2.4.1 Fighting Against Environmental Pollution in the 1970s

In the late 1950s, with the growing concentration of population and industries in TMG jurisdiction, environmental pollution increasingly became a serious problem. The air pollution caused by sulfur dioxide (SO_2) generated by burning heavy oil that had become the main energy source replacing coal.

Responding to the problem, the national government enacted the Air Pollution Control Law and started to take various measures. The measures were, however, emissions regulations based on "Diffusion Theory" where higher stacks would diffuse the pollutants more widely with less impact at ground. These regulations are effective for pollutions in large industrial areas. However, in areas like Tokyo where urban environmental pollution is caused by numerous concentrated sources such as small and medium-sized factories and building heating systems, such regulations were not effective and higher stacks would simply spread the pollution to surrounding residential areas.

To solve this air pollution problem in Tokyo, TMG introduced its original regulations on fuel use to reduce the emissions of sulfur dioxide instead of merely diffusing it. It was estimated that burning heavy oil caused about 150,000 tons of sulfur content per year in 1970. The "Program to Protect Residents of Tokyo from Environmental Pollution" had a target to reduce the emissions to 80,000 tons per year, or 1964 level, that generally satisfied the Environmental Quality Standard.

Besides these regulations on fuels based on the Pollution Prevention Ordinance of 1969, TMG implemented measures such as the promotion of fuel shift to electricity and gas, and the introduction of district heating and cooling systems. As a result, sulfur dioxide concentrations in Tokyo started to decrease. The Environmental Quality Standards were achieved at all general air pollution monitoring stations in 1983 and also at all roadside air pollution monitoring stations in 1985 and thereafter (source of data?).

In addition to regulations on fixed generation sources such as factories, TMG established measures for air pollution caused by the rapid increase of automobiles. TMG established the system of giving instructions and advice on the installation of exhaust gas reduction devices (catalyst re-combustion devices) for in-use vehicles. The goal was to reduce carbon monoxide that was highly concentrated at intersections.

Thus, TMG in the 1970s developed various measures leading Japan's environmental administration for both fixed and mobile sources.

2.4.2 Reducing and Recycling Waste in the 1990s

The issue of waste became increasingly serious in the 1970s with the spread of lifestyles based on mass production, mass consumption and mass disposal. After the World War II, constructing waste incineration plants and securing landfill sites had always been big issues. The delay in the development of facilities was often seen as a restricting factor of urban sustainability.

The amount of waste in Tokyo 23 wards was reduced due to the two oil shocks in 1974 and 1979, and was stable until the middle of the 1980s. However, the output of waste per capita began to increase again in the bubble economy of the late 1980s. The amount of waste increased by more than a million tons from 3.79 million tons in 1984 to 4.90 million tons in 1989.

On the other hand, the final landfill disposal site for Tokyo 23 Wards was filled close to its total capacity. Under such critical circumstances, TMG decided to transform the concept of measures from the prompt disposing of generated waste to reducing and recycling waste.

In 1989, TMG clarified the critical situation of waste disposal and started the "Tokyo Slim" campaign. The campaign asked residents of Tokyo to take actions on their own to reduce waste. With the increasing interest in the issue of waste through "Tokyo Slim" campaign, TMG introduced a variety of measures and programs to reduce and recycle waste. In the "Tokyo Waste Conference" in 1991, action plan to reduce waste was drawn up and the "My Bag Campaign" was developed to reduce packaging waste. In the same year, on-site instructions were started in order for owners of a building within Tokyo 23 wards with a total floor area of 3,000 m^2 or more to select a person responsible for waste management and submitting a waste reuse plan. In 1995, TMG set up a "Discussion Group Considering 'Tokyo Rules' for Waste Reduction" to establish its original rules. Tokyo rules included the proposal to collect PET bottles at retail outlets, measures for collecting and recycling used paper, bottles and cans included in household waste and measures to charge all commercial waste.

Since the start of the "Tokyo Slim" campaign in 1989, the series of measures taken for over 10 years have resulted in the increase of the annual amount of recycling in Tokyo 23 wards from 300,000 tons to about one million tons. These efforts by TMG were again ahead of the national government and other large cities in policy-making.

2.4.3 "No Diesel Strategy" Campaign Since 1999

Although TMG significantly reduced sulfur dioxide and carbon monoxide pollutions, the concentration of nitrogen dioxide and suspended particle matter generated mainly by automobiles still failed to meet the Environmental Quality Standards. Particularly, particulate matter (PM) generated from diesel engines had been pointed out to have an adverse impact on health.

As a response, in the summer of 1999, TMG started the "No Diesel Strategy" campaign asking residents and businesses in Tokyo to intensively discuss the possible measures to be taken. The campaign initially proposed the following five measures:

1. No diesel vehicles to be driven, sold, or bought in TMG jurisdiction
2. Obligation to replace commercial diesel vehicles with an alternative gasoline vehicle
3. Development of an exhaust gas purifying device and obligation to install it on diesel vehicles
4. Correction of the preferable tax rate on diesel fuel
5. Early development of vehicles meeting the new long-term regulations

In December 2000, these draft measures were incorporated into the "Tokyo Metropolitan Environmental Security Ordinance", an overall revision of the Tokyo Metropolitan Pollution Prevention Ordinance of 1969. The new ordinance was enforced in 2003. Three prefectures neighboring to TMG jurisdiction, namely, Saitama, Chiba, and Kanagawa prefectures, established similar ordinances, and the regulations on the operation of diesel vehicles were implemented comprehensively in Tokyo.

In TMG jurisdiction alone, there were 202,000 diesel vehicles subject to the regulations to be enforced in October 2003. However, neither the installation of particulate matter reduction devices or the replacement of unqualified diesel vehicles had made much progress as of a year before the enforcement of the regulations. So, TMG began the "Illegal Diesel Vehicle Elimination" campaign to smoothly implement the regulations.

Before starting the "No Diesel Strategy" campaign, the Environmental Quality Standards for suspended particulate matter was not achieved in any of the roadside air pollution monitoring stations. However, after the implementation of the measures, significant achievements were realized so that the Environmental Quality Standards were achieved in all stations except one.

Starting in January 2005, all gasoline and diesel fuel was made sulfur-free by the decisive step taken by the Petroleum Association of Japan.

2.5 New Challenges to Enhance Urban Sustainability

2.5.1 Energy-Saving and a Shift to Renewable Energy

Energy is the most fundamental element needed to support urban activities. The limitation of energy resource and global/urban warming caused by excessive use of energy are considered as the most important issues in enhancing urban sustainability. TMG started to take comprehensive measures on global warming issue ("Stop Global Warming, Tokyo Strategy") after developing the current Tokyo Metropolitan Environmental Master Plan in 2002. To realize an energy-saving city and a shift to renewable energy, TMG started the following measures (Bureau of Environment, Tokyo Metropolitan Government 2006).

The first measure was taken to reduce greenhouse gas emissions from existing facilities. TMG introduced the Tokyo CO_2 Emission Reduction Program where large-scale factories, offices, commercial facilities and public facilities were obligated to develop a 5-year plan for greenhouse gas reduction. These facilities were responsible for about 40% of CO_2 emissions in industrial and business sectors in Tokyo. Their activities were then evaluated and announced to the public. This program was implemented in April 2005 and more than 1,000 facilities submitted their plans.

It is also important to improve the energy-saving performance of newly constructed buildings. Since those buildings constructed in the era of rapid growth in the 1970s are now being demolished and reconstructed, there are opportunities to construct energy-saving buildings. TMG started to implement the Tokyo Green Building Program in 2002 to obligate large-scale building owners to develop and submit their plans for improving environmental performance when reconstructing or expanding. Since condominiums account for more than 50% of newly built large-scale buildings, the Tokyo Metropolitan Condominium Environmental Performance Indication Program was also started in 2005.

CO_2 emissions in the domestic sector account for a quarter of the total, and 70% of CO_2 emissions in the domestic sector are by the use of electricity. TMG has introduced the Energy Efficiency Labeling System for Home Appliances to promote the purchase of energy-saving home appliances. The display of energy efficiency labels in shops started in 2002 as a voluntary measure, with the cooperation of large home appliance retailers. It was institutionalized in 2005 based on a new Ordinance. The display of energy efficiency labels in shops initiated by TMG has already spread to 22 prefectures.

CO_2 emissions from vehicles account for about 20% of the total. Tokyo Environmental Distribution Project, including traffic demand reduction through the joint delivery of goods for department stores, is being promoted. In 2006, the Revision of Vehicle Emission Reduction Program was introduced, which promotes well-planned actions for reducing CO_2 emissions by businesses that use vehicles. Other new measures will also be developed, including the promotion of using public transportation instead of private automobiles and the enhancement of environmentally conscious driving technology.

The Tokyo Green Energy Program, a program started in Japan targeting electric power suppliers, started in 2005, obligating them to take measures to reduce the CO_2 emissions and to develop a plan to introduce renewable energy. In order to clarify the strategy to expand renewable energy use to a full-scale, TMG developed the Tokyo Renewable Energy Strategy and proposed a target to increase the ratio of renewable energy to the total energy consumed in TMG jurisdiction to about 20% by 2020.

2.5.2 Tokyo After 10 Years Plan

Tokyo After 10 Years Plan, published in the end of 2006 by Tokyo Metropolitan Government, set a near future vision of Tokyo growing to a higher level in the fields of urban infrastructure, environment, security, culture, tourism and industry. The plan presented the following eight goals to be accomplished in the next 10 years. (Headquarters of the Governor of Tokyo, Tokyo Metropolitan Government 2006)

1. Recover Beautiful Tokyo Embraced by Water and Green Corridors
2. Tokyo will be Reborn by the Three Ring Roads
3. Realize the City with Least Environmental Load in the World
4. Reinforce Reliance on Tokyo by Creating Disaster-Proof City
5. Create the World-Leading Urban Model for Hyper Aged Society
6. Establish the Presence of Tokyo by the City's Attractiveness and Industry
7. Create a Society that Any High-Motivated People can Challenge
8. Provide a Dream for Children of the Next Generation through Sports

In order to implement the plan speedy and surely, interdepartmental "Joint Strategic Meeting for Environmental City Building" was established within TMG. Under the meeting, two headquarters were established, namely "Carbon Minus City Building Promotion Headquarters" and "Green City Building Promotion Headquarters". The two headquarters launched their 10 years projects (Tokyo Metropolitan Government 2007).

Carbon Minus Tokyo 10 Years Project is an effort to realize a city with least environmental load in the world. It will establish a new urban model in the twenty-first century and spread it to Asia and rest of the world. The project consists of the following five parts: The development of Tokyo-Originated Energy Strategy Using World-Class Energy Saving Technologies, Realization of a City with the Most Renewable Energy Use, Realization of Sustainable Transportation Network, Development of New Environmental Technologies and Creation of Environmental Businesses and Carbon Minus Movement.

On the other hand, Green Tokyo 10 years project is an effort to recover beautiful Tokyo embraced by water and green corridors. It will promote the networking of existing greenery and the provision of new greenery. The project consists of the following five parts: Shaping Green Road Network, Creation of Greenery in the Gaps of Urban Space, Creating Green Center in Neighborhood, Conservation of Existing Greenery and Creation of High Quality Greenery and Green Movement that Involves Local Governments and Businesses.

2.6 Conclusion

The major planning issue of the twentieth century Tokyo was to expand and intensify the urban area in order to accommodate rapid growth. Until the 1960s urban expansion was controlled neither by a strict planning system nor by a greenbelt but by developments around railway stations. Though experiencing very rapid urban growth and with a relatively weak planning system, Tokyo had barely accommodated the flood of immigrant population and had provided not less than minimum level of living environment and social services. From the viewpoint of urban form, Tokyo is a patchwork of various types of urban space with diverse urban issues. As Japan entered the phase of no- or low-growth, depopulating and aging society, it is not possible or not necessary to change the current spatial structure of Tokyo so drastically. It is more realistic to improve or conserve existing urban spaces incrementally to enhance quality of life in a sustainable manner. As there is a diversity of urban issues, diverse and creative approaches are needed. The major problem of Tokyo's planning is that so many areas have no clear future vision of urban space. Mixed use and vibrant looking vernacular urban places, often praised by European and American planners and urban designers, are merely the incidental results of market economy and loose land use/building regulations, and are actually vulnerable in many ways. In order to shape attractive urban space through the regeneration of existing urban space, it is important in each area to establish a future vision and to implement measures for realization. The high-density mixed-use "urban village" concept now becoming popular worldwide, might give hints to many areas in Tokyo.

Tokyo has experienced various urban environmental problems since the 1970s due to the rapid growth and concentration of population and industries. Tokyo Metropolitan Government (TMG) has successfully solved many of these problems, taking creative measures ahead of the national government and leading other prefectures in Tokyo Region. With the recognition of the limitation of energy resource and global/urban warming caused by excessive use of energy being the most important urban sustainability issues, TMG has started to work on some new measures related to the efficient use of energy. "Carbon Minus Tokyo 10 Years Project" and "Green Tokyo 10 Years Project" are new official initiatives to pursue a sustainable city. It should be noted that this chapter focused on the efforts of Tokyo Metropolitan Government and did not look in to the efforts of other prefectures and local governments.

In Tokyo, urban growth and urban form issues have not been considered explicitly in relation to environmental issues or sustainability issues. Rather, environmental issues were tackled with mainly technological improvements and promotion of eco-life-style. Also, greenery issues were tackled with enhancing and improving existing greenery structure. There is no explicit policy to reorganize or redesign the existing urban form or land use pattern in order to enhance the sustainability of Tokyo.

Since the level to be accomplish is not so high, it might be easy to accomplish current 'improving and enhancing' approach. However, If we must reach higher goal in respect with environmental issues and 'hyper aged society' issues, we cannot help but adopt more ambitious and difficult approach that reorganize spatial form and infrastructures including innovative public transportation system, comfortable and easy-to-access public spaces and pedestrian environment, and effective and efficient social service system especially for aged people and working mothers.

References

Based on the GIS data in (2005) from the Ministry of Land, Infrastructure and Transport, Government of Japan, Data from land use control back-up system (Tochiriyou Chousei Sougou Shien Network System)

Bureau of Environment, Tokyo Metropolitan Government (2006) Tokyo Metropolitan Government Environmental White Paper 2006

Cervero R (1998) The transit metropolis: a global inquiry. Island Press, Washington, DC

Department of Urban Development, Tokyo Metropolitan Government (2003) Disaster-proof urban improvement promotion plan (Bousai Toshizukuri Suishin Keikaku)

Denkenkyo, Introduction to Japan's preservation districts. http://www.denken.gr.jp/. Accessed 30 April 2008

Fujii S, Okata J et al (2007) Inner-city redevelopment in Tokyo: conflicts over urban place, planning governance, and neighborhoods. In: Sorensen A, Funck C (eds) Living cities in Japan: citizens' movements, machizukuri and local environments. Routledge, London, pp 247–266

Headquarters of the Governor of Tokyo, Tokyo Metropolitan Government (2006) Tokyo 10 years after. http://www.chijihon.metro.tokyo.jp/10years_after/index.htm. Accessed 30 April 2008

Hiramoto K (ed) (2005) Tokyo project. Nikkei BP

Ministry of Land, Infrastructure and Transport, Government of Japan (2007) 2006 Annual report of capital region development (Heisei 18 Nendo Shutoken Seibi nikansuru Nenji Houkoku)

Nakamura H, Ieda H et al (2004) Infrastructure of Tokyo (Tokyo No Infurasutorakuchaa), 2nd edn. Gihoudou

Okata J, Murayama A et al (2005) 21 Profiles of Tokyo. In: SUR (Sustainable Urban Regeneration), vol 2. Center for Sustainable Urban Regeneration, The University of Tokyo, pp 10–31

Sorensen A (2002) The making of urban Japan: cities and planning from Edo to the 21st century. Routledge, London

Tokyo Metropolitan Government (2007) Materials for joint strategic meeting for environmental city building (Kankyo Toshizukuri Senryaku Goudou Kaigi). http://www2.kankyo.metro.tokyo.jp/kikaku/strategy-meeting/index_1.htm. Accessed 30 April 2008

3. In Search of Sustainable Urban Form for Seoul

Kwang-Joong Kim and Sang-Chuel Choe

3.1 Introduction

The global urban population is currently increasing by about 65 million a year, a number roughly equivalent to the total population of France. The growth of megacities and of megacity regions poses a great challenge to sustainable development and the environmental, economic, and social stability of nations and the world.

Although urban processes in major regions of the world are superficially similar, sustainable urban development approaches must take into account differences in the level of urbanization and in urban patterns, which are highly culture-bounded. In this regard, many theoretical and cross-cultural approaches to sustainable urban form have been suggested and debated since the 1990s (Breheny 1992; Jenks 1996, 2000, 2005; Jenks and Burgess 2000; Sorensen et al. 2004; Williams et al. 2000). Cautious conclusions have been drawn that there is no universal paradigm for sustainable urban form.

Korea's experience in shaping its capital region's metropolitan form provides some lessons, as this metropolitan area has tested three major policies germane to the discussion of sustainable urban form worldwide: a greenbelt, inner-city renewal, and planned outward development. These three policies have transformed Seoul's metropolitan form, channeling countless individual developments into the current shape, pattern, and structure of the Seoul metropolitan area (SMR) (Fig. 3-1).

This chapter reviews how these policies came about and how they have influenced the SMR's urban form. Particular attention is given to sustainability issues related to these policies, the resulting urban form, and lessons from Seoul's unique experience.

A. Sorensen and J. Okata (eds.), *Megacities: Urban Form, Governance, and Sustainability*,

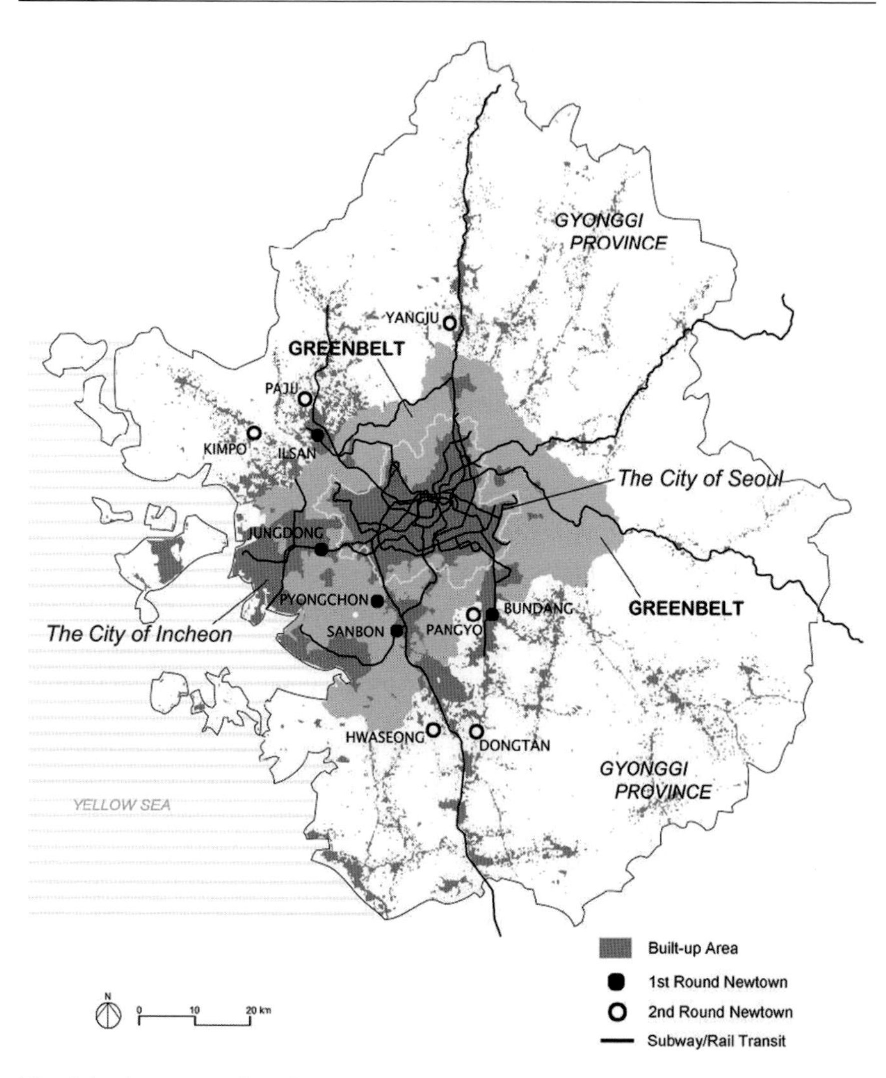

Fig. 3-1. The metropolitan form of SMR – the built-up area, greenbelt and new towns

3.2 Evolution of the Metropolitan Urban Form of Seoul

The Seoul Metropolitan Region (SMR) includes the cities of Seoul and Incheon and the province of Gyonggi. Seoul is the capital of South Korea and the central city of SMR. Incheon is an independent city to the west of Seoul with a population of more than two million people. Gyonggi Province surrounds Seoul and Incheon with its own cities, towns, and rural jurisdictions.

The SMR has gone through a period of rapid growth over the past 50 years, experiencing a population increase from 3.2 million in 1960 to 11.9 million in 1980 and 23.8 million in 2005, or 48.3% of the national population. The city of Seoul alone has grown from 2.4 million in 1960 to 10.3 million in 2005, and is one of the 25 world megacities of more than ten million inhabitants. The explosive growth of SMR has coincided with equally rapid economic growth and urbanization at the national level.

Seoul's suburbanization is a late twentieth-century phenomenon. In the 1960s and 1970s, the city government of Seoul laid out massive subdivisions around the traditional city center. Middle-class people left the ill-planned city center to move to this suburban area, including Gangnam south of the Han River, which offered modern houses and infrastructure and a homogeneous social milieu (Lee 2003). This grid-patterned, plot-division-led expansion took place within the city limits of 605 km^2. Since then, however, Seoul has undergone a unique metropolitanization process to become one of the world's largest urban agglomerations (Fig. 3-2).

Along with the first suburban wave, the city adopted a greenbelt policy in 1971 based on the greenbelts in the UK. Encircling Seoul's boundary at a distance of 15 km from the city core, the greenbelt has had a profound impact on the subsequent metropolitan growth of Seoul (Choe 2004a, b). It was intended to prevent urban sprawl, to protect the agricultural land around the city, and to preserve the natural environment.

During the 1970s, much of Seoul's growth was contained inside the greenbelt, although the city's population rose from five million in 1971 to eight million in 1980. The 1980s saw a second wave of suburbanization beyond the greenbelt, which was due to the enlarged network of roadways and to increasing automobile ownership. As vacant land in Seoul was used up during the 1980s, development pressure jumped over the greenbelt and urban growth continued throughout the SMR as a whole.

Outlying areas within commuting distance from Seoul began to exhibit a high rate of growth, as population and economic activities moved out from the saturated central city (Kim and Jung 2001). This time, suburban development extended as far as 25 km from the city core. It was at this same time, however, that residential renewal began to surge inside the greenbelt.

Although the dual process of inner renewal and outer expansion was largely a market-led process, two public policies deserves much credit in shaping market forces into a particular metropolitan form. Inside the greenbelt (that is, within the inner city of Seoul), the renewal policy of the City of Seoul governed changes in density, development patterns, and the formal character of a ten-million-person megacity. Outside the

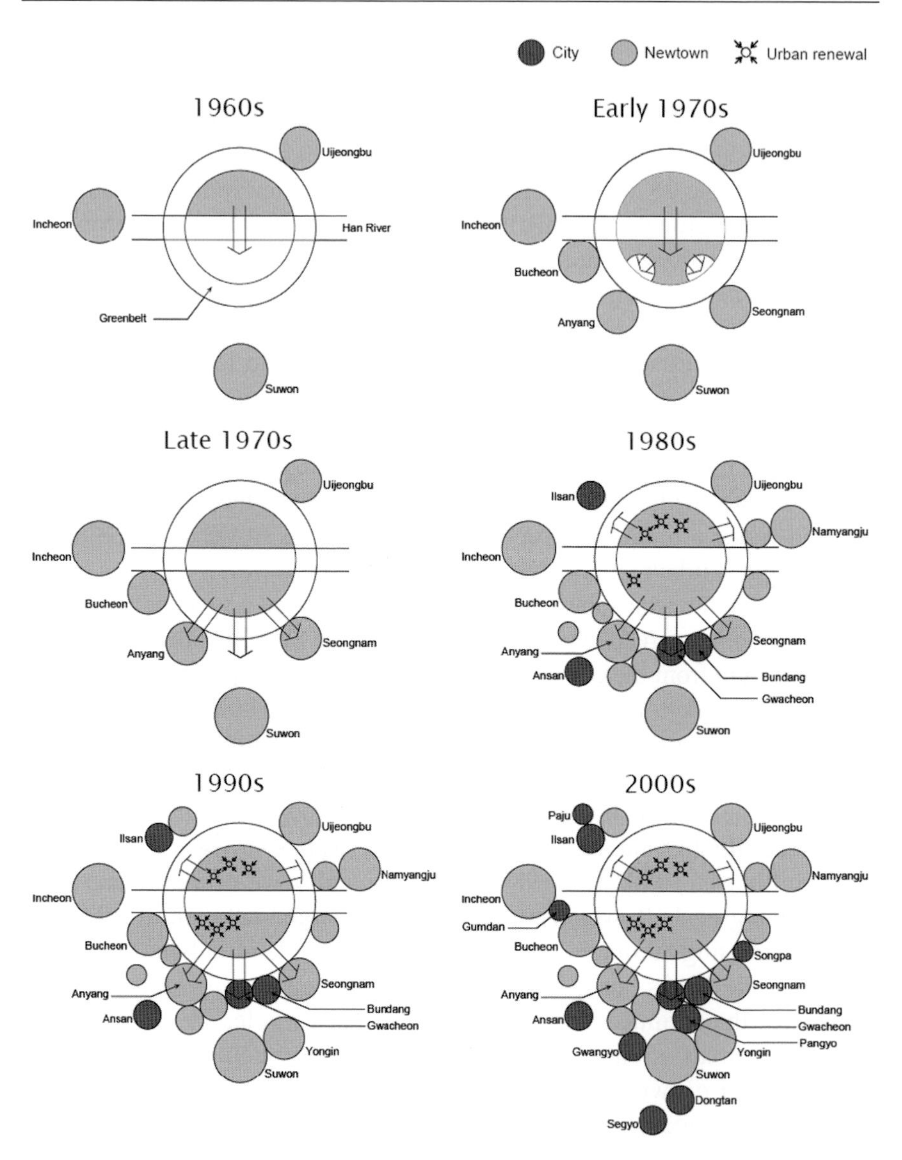

Fig. 3-2. Diagrammatic illustration of inner compaction and outer expansion of Seoul metropolitan region: 1960s–2000s

greenbelt, the new town policy of the central government accelerated new waves of the metropolitanization of Seoul.

By 2000, Seoul's metropolitan form had been much extended, while population growth in the center city of Seoul had leveled off. The Seoul

Development Institute estimated that the built-up area of Seoul metropolitan area grew 1.5 times, from 778 km^2 in 1985 to 1,173 km^2 in 1998, consuming an equivalent amount of green and open spaces (Kim and Jung 2001). The force propelling densification of the inner city and suburbanization outside the city was housing construction. During the 20-year period of the 1980s and 1990s, a total of 2.9 million housing units were built. Of those units, 1.5 million were government projects. What follows is a detailed discussion of three major policies that created the current urban form of SMR.

3.2.1 The Greenbelt

The greenbelt was a central government policy in that it represented a national defense initiative. It was created not only to contain urban expansion but also to protect the city from North Korean artillery attack. Yet, in urban planning terms, the main objectives in introducing the greenbelt were to prevent urban sprawl, to protect agricultural land, and to preserve the natural environment. Searching for a planning tool to meet all three objectives, the Korean government examined the UK's greenbelt policy in 1971. A greenbelt policy had been tried in Japan in the late 1960s, but had failed because of strong opposition from residents and landowners. Given Korea's dictatorial regime, however, the government was able to impose this policy and a greenbelt ranging from 10 to 20 km wide was hastily designated around Seoul, known as the Seoul Metropolitan Greenbelt.

However, Korea's greenbelt policy has not very successful in containing urban sprawl around Seoul, and has resulted in distortions of urban growth patterns. As Tankel (1963) has observed, the greenbelt was about as useful in containing urban sprawl as a leather belt is useful in curbing obesity. The preservation of open space can influence urban form, but not the density of development. This is exactly what has happened in Korea.

In designating the greenbelt around Seoul, the government felt that urban sprawl would be contained as long as vacant land remained in Seoul for urban uses. However, the greenbelt resulted in the densification of the inner city and unplanned development beyond the greenbelt. Over time, the density differential inside and outside the greenbelt has equalized (Choe 2004a, b). Some areas outside the greenbelt have been developed at even higher densities than parts of the inner city. Some of the densest areas in the region are those adjacent to the greenbelt, as people take advantage of the free amenity the greenbelt offers.

In spite of the failure of the greenbelt to contain urban sprawl, Korea's greenbelt policy has had two positive outcomes. First, it has ensured the intensification of the inner city and promoted the creation of compact satellite towns within commuting distance of the city. Satellite towns tend to cluster as close as possible to the greenbelt to offer greater accessibility to the central city. The greenbelt has thus contributed to more compact development of the metropolitan area as a whole.

Second, the key goal of the greenbelt policy has changed from "belt" to "green." Along with an increasing awareness of environmental problems and the limits of conventional planning tools to bring about sustainable urban development, planners since the 1980s have worked to redefine the objectives and uses of greenbelts. During a debate at the Royal Town Planning Institute in 1993, several prominent UK planners criticized the indiscriminate use of greenbelts in containing urban sprawl. They suggested that greenbelt policies could also, by creating more contained forms of development, promote more sustained patterns of urban growth.

In 1995, the revision of Planning Policy Guidance Note 2 in the UK suggested that greenbelts had a positive role in fulfilling the following objectives (Steeley and Gibson 1998):

1. To provide opportunities for access to the open countryside for the urban population
2. To provide opportunities for outdoor sport and outdoor recreation near urban areas
3. To retain attractive landscapes, and enhance landscapes, near to where people live
4. To improve damaged and derelict land around towns
5. To secure nature conservation interests
6. To retain land in agricultural, forestry, and related uses

Given the changing objectives of the British greenbelt policies and the evolving urban growth management practices, including New Urbanism, in the US, planners are redefining the objectives and practical applications of greenbelts. After a half-century's indulgence in unbounded low-density sprawl, urban growth boundaries have been introduced in several states and local jurisdictions in the US.

The consequences of Korea's 30-year experiment with British greenbelt policy are still unclear. While Korea's metropolitan greenbelt has not curbed urban expansion, the introduction of the greenbelt was the most important determinant in shaping the current urban form of the SMR, resulting in the densification of the inner city and the concentrated nuclear development of new towns beyond the greenbelt. It has at least checked

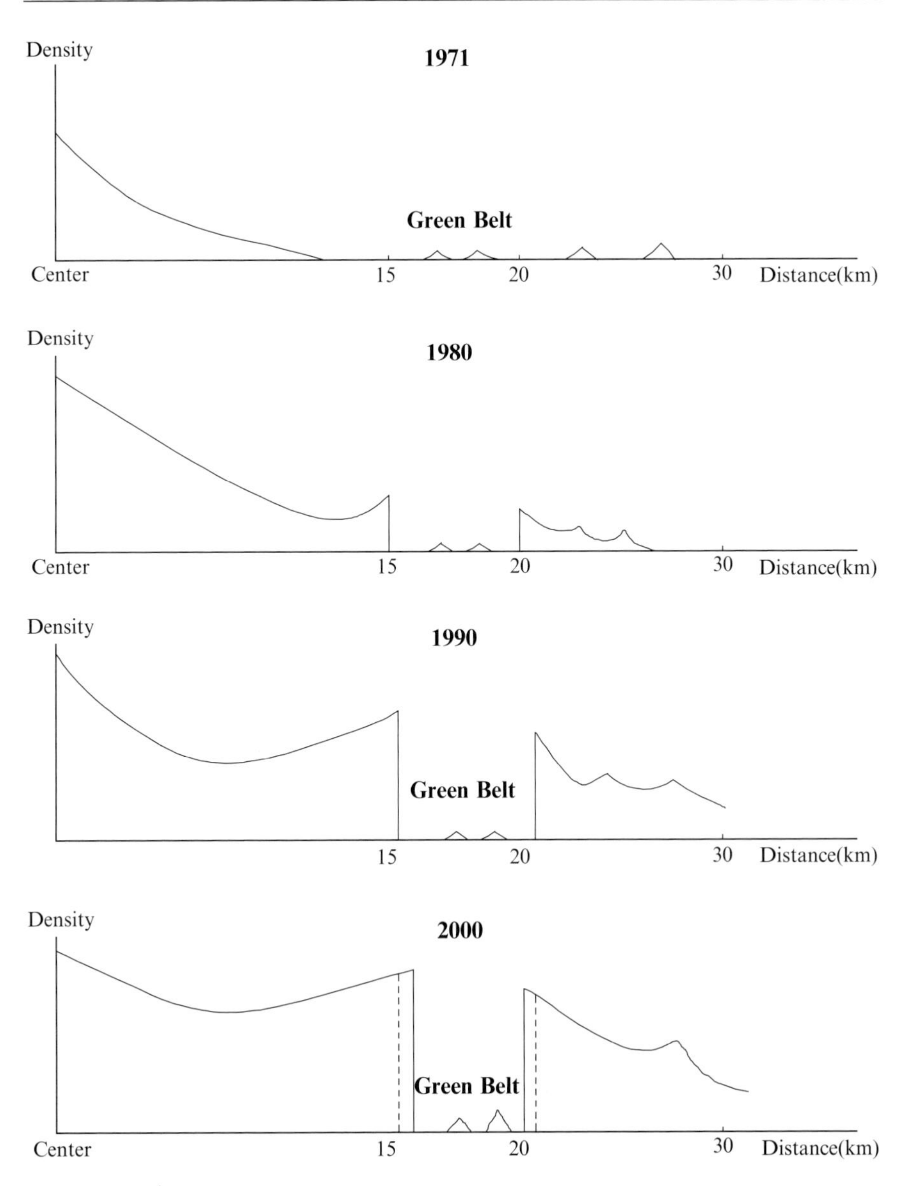

Fig. 3-3. Changing density gradients in Seoul metropolitan region (Source: Choe 2004a)

unbounded low-density urban sprawl and has secured green and open spaces accessible to the urban population, acting as an "urban lung" to mitigate air pollution and providing a reserve of land for future urban growth (Fig. 3-3).

3.2.2 Inner City Renewal

While urbanization beyond the greenbelt extended Seoul's built-up area to 30 km from the city center, extensive redevelopment took place inside the greenbelt through the late 1980s to the 1990s. Both private- and public-sector residential renewal projects raised density in the center city, making Seoul a forest of apartment buildings (Kim 2004b). The process replaced Seoul's old form, which had developed in the 1960s and 1970s, mainly through two public residential renewal policies known as Jae-Gae-Bal (JGB: replacing deteriorated houses with high-rise apartments) and Jae-Gun-Chuk (JGC: replacing low-rise apartments with high-rise apartments) (Fig. 3-4).

JGB was originally conceived as squatter clearance program in the 1960s and evolved into a general approach to renewing substandard housing. It galvanized redevelopment in the middle of the 1980s because of its profit-making development formula. The City permitted high density, landowners provided the sites, and construction companies carried out the renewal process, from demolition to apartment construction. In return, landowners were rewarded by the creation of new apartment units and construction companies profited from selling the extra units in the market. High-density development benefited both landowners and construction companies during a time of chronic housing shortages.

Fig. 3-4. Example of inner city renewal: residential redevelopment sites are shown with the existing low-rise area

JGC employed the same development method as JGB. These residential renewal programs were applied to 415 districts, where about 180,000 housing units were constructed during the 1990s. They accounted for almost half of Seoul's new housing supply in that period, absorbing enormous housing demand from the rapidly growing middle class. Seoul grew from five million people in 1970 to ten million in 1990, while Korea managed one of the fastest-growing economies.

Even more aggressive renewal policies were implemented in the late 1990s. The steep increase in housing prices in the affluent Gangnam area south of the Han River caused a sense of relative deprivation among lower-income residents, mainly in the Gangbuk area north of the Han River. While the central government relaunched its new town program to respond to this problem, the Seoul city government carried out a radical renewal of the Gangbuk area. The renewal area was very large and included multiple residential sites. In undertaking active clearance and infrastructure provision, the city hoped that the Gangbuk area would be renewed and that property values would increase.

The City of Seoul named these large-scale urban renewal schemes within the existing city the "New Town Policy." The name could be confused with the outer new town policy of the central government, so here it will be referred to as "new town in town" (NIT). Between 2002 and 2005, there were three rounds of NIT designation. In 2002, three demonstration NIT districts were designated. Even before these demonstration projects were launched, 12 NITs were designated in 2003, followed by 11 more in 2005. Policy-makers and property owners alike supported this bold move in the belief that complete renewal of their neighborhood would ensure a balance between Gangbuk and Gangnam and increase property values. In the planning community, some argued that this inner-city intensification was superior to the outer new town policy of the central government because it promoted a compact city, environmental sustainability, and smart growth.

NIT is a redevelopment scheme. Two-thirds of the designated areas was to be cleared and redeveloped. The existing JGB and JGC methods have been applied, in that individual building activities are prohibited for the sake of collective joint renewal. It is noteworthy, however, that NIT plans on average do not increase the population of an area, and therefore do not bring about an increase in population density. NIT is primarily intended to improve the physical condition of the area. Moreover, NIT areas are low-income neighborhoods in which most residents are tenants who occupy small, closely spaced rental units, yielding high population or household densities with relatively low floor-area density. Since NIT plans accommodate the equivalent number of people and households, they lead to a significant increase in floor-area density, i.e. larger housing units.

Table 3-1. Aggregated changes in ten selected NIT (new town in town) projects in Seoul

	Existing	Planned	Change
Area (ha) – A	646	646	No change
Population – B	273,070	271,850	−1,220
Household	109,630	106,950	−2,680
Population density (B/A)	422	420	−2
Residential land (ha)	414	371	−43
Commercial land (ha)	44	63	19
Business land (ha)	139	167	28
Ratio of road (%)	15.7	13.9	−1.8
Ratio of park (%)	2.0	6.6	4.4
Ratio of school site (%)	0.9	7.3	6.4

Source: Assembled from Seoul Metropolitan Government website information

As seen in Table 3-1, NITs accommodate approximately the same number of people and households while providing more open space, public facilities, and commercial uses by reducing the footprint of residential land uses and reducing the space used for roads. Without exception, two-to-five-story buildings are replaced by apartment buildings of 20 or more stories with outdoor open spaces. The existing fine street networks are replaced by wider superblock roads. The significant increase of commercial and business land use implies that NITs seek a mixed land use, although the existing residential land uses are already highly mixed. The plans for each NIT employs such sustainable elements as pedestrian amenities, bikeways, green corridors, and eco-friendly materials, among others. Although the total population remains virtually the same, the population density in some areas is as high as 400 persons per hectare.

Features such as high population densities, inner-city revitalization, mixed land uses, walkable communities, and environment-friendly design align with current theories of the compact city and sustainable planning and design. At the same time, however, NITs represent a form of gentrification. Among the existing households, more than 60% are tenants. After renewal is complete, public rental housing units will be available to only 35% of them, as the current law requires. Further, the realization of these projects relies on market mechanisms.

NIT policy depended on a national law that promoted urban clearance through the relaxation of development controls and the provision of financial subsidies. In the Special Promotion Law for Urban Renewal, the national law enacted in 2005 to support NIT policy, deregulation was more highlighted than public resource commitment.

3.2.3 Suburban New Town Development

Government-initiated new towns are not new in the history of Seoul. Seoul itself was a new town built in the fourteenth century, and in the 1980s the inner area of Seoul grew through the development of further new towns. Gaepo (936 ha), Goduck (335 ha), Mokdong (430 ha), and Sanggye (330 ha) were planned new towns inside the greenbelt, each accommodating 80,000–170,000 people. These huge apartment towns were previously outlying agricultural fields or forests between 10 and 16 km from the city center. Housing supply was the main impetus behind this planned urban expansion within the city boundary. They were called "new city areas," meaning newly built-up areas, rather than "new towns."

The *bona fide* new towns, in name as well as suburban location, came in the late 1980s. In 1987, the housing supply ratio (the ratio of housing units to households) in Seoul was 50.6–100 and the number of households was growing faster than the population, causing severe housing shortages. At the same time, private money accumulated by a growing economy generated uncontrollable speculative home buying. In a hurried response, the central government, while encouraging aggressive inner-city renewal in central Seoul, also constructed the first five new towns, intending to boost the housing supply quickly and reinvigorate the slumping domestic economy (Ahn and Ohn 2001). Thus the impetus of the new town policy was both economic and political.

These new towns were master-planned. Each one ranged from 160,000 to almost 400,000 inhabitants. Most housing was in the form of high-rise apartments. As Table 3-2 shows, the gross population density of new towns ranged from 19,700 to 39,600 persons per square kilometer, higher than the density of the City of Seoul (16,364 person per square kilometers). New town building in Seoul's outlying area occurred at a distance of 20–25 km from the city core of Seoul. New towns are either beyond or inside the greenbelt (Fig. 3-1). Often linked by transit lines to the center of Seoul, car dependency is lower than 40%, although the commuting time is about 1 h.

These five new towns provided 293,000 new housing units for 1.2 million residents in less than 7 years, or as much as 20% of Seoul's total housing stock. This massive housing supply stabilized housing prices: the 32% annual increase in 1990 fell to 0.7% in 1995. Despite this dramatic effect, the new towns faced heavy criticism soon after their construction. The most common complaint was the lack of self-sufficiency. As most people commuted to central Seoul, traffic congestion became a serious problem. Furthermore, new town brought haphazard developments caused by land speculation around them.

Table 3-2. Selected suburban new towns in the Seoul metropolitan region

	Distance from centre (km)	Area (ha)	Pop. (000s)	Density (pop/ha)	Residential FAR (%)	Rail transit	Work in Seoul (%)	Car use (%)
First round new towns								
Bundang	20	1,964	390	197	184	Linked	53.1	36.3
Ilsan	20	1,574	276	174	169	Linked	41.2	38.6
Pyongchon	20	511	168	327	204	Linked	46.6	NA
Sanbon	25	420	168	396	205	Linked	52.2	NA
Jungdong	25	545	166	301	225	Linked	23.9	NA
Second round new towns (under construction or planned)								
Pangyo	20	931	80	86	161	Linked	NA	NA
Hwaseong	35	904	121	134	173	No	NA	NA
Kimpo	30	1,185	154	130	170	No	NA	NA
Paju	25	941	125	133	174	No	NA	NA
Yangju	30	611	79	130	165	No	NA	NA
Dongtan	40	904	121	134	80–220	No	NA	NA

Source: Adapted from Kim (2007)

Fig. 3-5. Example of suburban sprawl in Yongin area: individual apartment construction encroaching green spaces

Given these problems in the early stage of new town development, the government suspended its new town policy and allowed small-scale housing estate development and individual development (Fig. 3-5). However, the problems of new towns have only been aggravated, as new development has proliferated without adequate infrastructure. In 1997, the government turned to a "mini-new-town" policy whereby smaller new towns were developed in outlying areas beyond the greenbelt. In the Seoul metropolitan area, 2,580 a were devoted to mini-new-town development after 1998. The chief purpose of this policy was to supply housing sites. However, the mini-new-town policy was not considered a viable alternative to larger new towns: the towns were too small to support transit lines or to be economically self-sufficient.

These problems led to the introduction of a new urban-rural unitary planning system through the enactment of the National Land Use and Planning Law, which involves a new land use control system based on the catchphrase of "no plan, no development" (Choe 2004a, b).

On the other hand, over time, the five new towns have shown an increasing degree of self-sufficiency as their commercial, business, and educational facilities are developed (Fig. 3-6). The general consensus is that self-sufficiency does not come overnight and the new towns were far better

Fig. 3-6. Planned new town Bundang: neighborhood commercial establishments in front of a subway station

than unplanned or sporadic development. Their contribution to the stabilization of housing price was also acknowledged. As housing prices skyrocketed again in the late 1990s, the central government turned again to a large-scale new town policy, while the city of Seoul adopted its NIT policy.

In 2001, the second round of new town construction was announced: six more large-scale new towns were to be built within 5 or 6 years (Table 3-2). These new towns are farther outside the greenbelt, between 30 and 40 km from Seoul city center. These extended locations have benefited from the newly built Capital Region Second Ring Highway. Reflecting an increased personal income level of over $10,000 and increased homeownership (82% in the SMR), these new towns offer lower densities and more open spaces than the first round of new towns.

The second round of new towns was subject to Planning and Design Standards for New Towns, drafted by the central government. This new town development standard was devised in 2004 in an effort to improve the proposed new towns compared to those in the first round. Interestingly, the standard calls for the environmental, social, and economic sustainability of the new towns. It applies to sites of larger than 330 ha and its criteria includes social mix, self-sufficiency, optimal density, transit use, energy saving, ecological awareness, traffic calming, urban forestry, barrier-free environments, and compact development, among others. Using these guidelines and requirements, the second-round new towns employed various sustainable concepts such as extensive bikeways, public transit, storm water reuse, eco-friendly sewage treatment, minimum 20% green space, and commercial and business centers for self-sufficiency. While supporting the compact city model, however, the guidelines state that the site should not exceed medium density, that is, no more than 150 people per hectare. The second-round new towns fit these criteria with an average of 130 people per hectare, while first-round new towns have 175–400 people per hectare.

Despite the inclusion of elements of sustainability in their plans, the assessment has yet to come, as these new towns are still under construction. Their location, 40 km away from the Seoul's city center, was based on the research finding that commuting to Seoul sharply decreased at this distance, and thus, if the new towns offered sufficient business opportunities, they would be self-sufficient. However, since these new towns rely on the outer ring highway of the SMR, their commuting and traffic patterns remain to be seen.

Some of the new towns are already visible. Closely clustered 30-to-40-story apartment buildings rise in the middle of rice fields with a backdrop of distant mountain ranges. The interim assessment of the Korean Planners Association is that they represent a high-quality living environment and sustainable design (Kim 2007). Yet these new towns are deemed unduly concentrated along the corridor of the Kyungbu Express Highway, which is likely to cause traffic congestion. Also, the landowners received high levels of compensation from the government for land for these massive new towns. Unbridled, small-scale individual developments proliferating around new towns may be a further unintended negative effect (Fig. 3-5). Finally, many people believe that the development of outlying new towns causes the decline of the inner city. Considerable debate still swirls around the new towns.

These three policies – the greenbelt, inner-city renewal, and outer new town development – explain to some extent how and why Seoul's metropolitan region has taken the form it has and provide grounds for debate on sustainable metropolitan areas. Seoul's urban form, of course, is not shaped by these three policies alone. Other land use controls, topographical constraints, land availability, and the government system have also played roles in the evolution of the SMR. The outcome of these forces is a metropolitan region that is dense, discontinuous, heterogeneous, and amorphous, and presents some issues of sustainable urban form.

3.3 Seoul's Metropolitan Form and Sustainability Issues

From a satellite image, the impact of the greenbelt and topography is evident in Seoul's overall metropolitan form. The encircling greenbelt separates the dense center city of Seoul from outer new towns and other urbanized areas. Urban expansion follows a linear pattern along the topographically constrained corridors to the north, east, and south. To the west, the region is open to the Yellow Sea and allows a coalescence of the cities of Incheon and Seoul along the Kyung-In corridor.

To the naked eye, the SMR defies the classic notion of a density gradient, which assumes declining density with distance from the city center. Dense developments and tall buildings are found throughout the entire metropolitan region, both inside and outside the greenbelt.

The greenbelt, inner-city renewal, and outer new town development have been the main public policies that have shaped the SMR. Whether the resulting form is sustainable is hard to say, either because there is little consensus on how to gauge the sustainability of a particular urban form or because no comprehensive and reliable data is available for the assessment. Some exploratory and comparative discussion may serve as a useful examination for the time being.

3.3.1 Compactness: Population Density Vs. Building Density

Compactness has multiple dimensions. It relates to the degree of population density, morphological agglomeration, and building accumulation. It can be examined at the scale of the metropolitan region, the city, the district, or the block.

In terms of population density, Seoul is one of the most compact center cities as well as most compact metropolitan areas in the world. Based on available 1999 and 2000 data, Kim et al. (2002) compare the population density of selected world megacities: Seoul at 16,364 persons per square kilometers is more dense than Tokyo's 23 urban districts (13,092 persons per kilometer), New York's five boroughs (9,721), or London's 32 boroughs (4,671). When it comes to built-up area density (or net density), Seoul is distinct from other cities, because 40% of the land within the city boundary is not built up, therefore the net density is approximately 27,000 person per square kilometers.

At the metropolitan level, the gross density (metropolitan population relative to metropolitan area) requires careful interpretation, as each urban region has unique boundaries. Hence the population density of the built-up area (net population density) provides useful information on the compactness of the metropolitan area. An estimate based on satellite images of the built-up area shows Seoul's net metropolitan population density is 21,500 persons per square kilometer (Kim et al. 2002). Using the same approach, Tokyo's net metropolitan density yields 31,152 persons per square kilometers, Beijing 16,345, and Paris 5,925. At the metropolitan level, Tokyo seems to offer the densest form of metropolitan living. Nonetheless, it is clear that Seoul is one of the densest megacities of the world.

Seoul provides a unique example of a compact city. While the Western notion of compact city largely means an increase in population density, Seoul has followed policies that increase physical compactness, as evidenced in inner-city renewal projects. Indeed, at the block level, Seoul's building density in the central business district is no higher than that of many Western megacities. For example, downtown Seoul averages about 3.0 FAR, while New York's Manhattan exceeds 10.0 FAR and Paris has 5.0 FAR (Kim 2004a). Seoul's recent downtown renewal projects are intended to achieve 10.0 FAR. At the same time, Seoul has residential densities of 1.5 FAR on average and allows new apartment development as high as 2.5 FAR – a much higher level of residential density than that found in Western cities.

These different density dimensions have complicated compact city discussions in Korea's planning community, since neither advocates nor opponents have made this crucial distinction. Given the initial low-density development of the inner-city area, Seoul needed to develop a more compact physical form. However, it is debatable whether Seoul should be more compact in terms of population density.

While dense living provides a number of benefits associated with theories of sustainable development, negative impacts are also in evidence, such as overcrowding, traffic congestion, bad air quality, noise, and soaring housing prices. As Richardson et al. (2000) point out, these problems might not be entirely a direct consequences of high density. It is undeniable, however, that density makes a difference to the quality of space. Indeed, some economists have argued that the greenbelt contributed to oversaturation of the inner city, causing unduly high land prices and housing costs (Kim 1998). And as in Hong Kong, excessive high-rise and high-density development is viewed as a cause of environmental degradation (Zhang 2000).

3.3.2 Morphological Dimensions

Another dimension of sustainable urban form is the shape of the city. The same population or building floor space can be accommodated in many different shapes. All kinds of city shapes have appeared in urban history such as rectangular, circular, linear, or star (Duany et al. 2003). Each shape is associated with different performance dimensions in energy consumption, social interaction, and land use efficiency. Morphological dimensions can thus be crucial in achieving sustainable form.

As seen in Fig. 3-1, Seoul's metropolitan form takes the shape of a jellyfish: the densely patterned and agglomerated inner city is attached to several linear corridors along narrow valleys radiating out from the city, linked by either radial or circular highways. Seoul's mountainous topography presents constraints on urban expansion. Indeed, most of greenbelt area comprises mountain slopes not suitable for urban expansion.

Size and connection are also important aspects of sustainable urban form. With a relative short history of urban growth and suburbanization, Seoul's metropolitan built form is smaller than that of, for example, Tokyo or Paris. One estimate (Kim et al. 2002) shows that the built-up area of Seoul metropolitan area is 990 km^2, smaller than Tokyo's 1,076 and Paris's 1,848. In addition, the SMR's 990-km^2 built-up area is less contiguous than that of other world megacities with a longer metropolitan history such as Tokyo, New York, London, or Paris.

As Fig. 3-1 shows, Seoul's metropolitan form is agglomerated within 10-km-radius where the center cities of Seoul, Incheon, Bucheon, Seongnam, and Anyang are concentrated. Outside the center, built-up areas are scattered along transportation corridors. The greenbelt leaves room for additional conglomeration. In fact, parts of the greenbelt have been used for public interests such as affordable housing. The issue is politically sensitive, however, as the greenbelt is linked to the issues of environmental conservation and over-concentration of the SMR.

The sustainability issue, then, is how to link the region in a sustainable manner. Seoul's bus lines are extensive, but it has a limited network of rail lines that could carry larger numbers of people with lower levels of pollution. Nine subway lines serve the center of Seoul: only four lines connect with outer areas. Only the first-round new towns have direct linkage to Seoul by subway. Of the six second-round new towns that are under construction, only one will be served by rail transit: the remaining five, located 30–40 km from the center of Seoul, will have to rely on automobiles and buses. Unlike megacities in Western countries or Japan, the SMR lacks regional commuter rail lines and light rail transit.

3.3.3 Concentration Vs. Decentralized Concentration

The City of Seoul's NIT policy and the central government's new town policy represent the concurrent processes of concentration and decentralized concentration. These local and central government policies have often come into conflict over jurisdictional interests. Originally, both policies were devised to address specific problems such as the physical improvement of the inner city or housing shortages. Yet as the two levels of government insist on the superiority of one policy over the other, the debate entails issues of sustainability.

Seoul's NIT policy matches Western theories on inner-city regeneration, the reuse of existing infrastructure, transit-oriented development, and mixed-use development, among others. Indeed, NIT documents are filled with these ideas and promise to provide healthy, sustainable communities. Though smaller in extent, the areas redeveloped under the NIT policy have denser populations (more than 300 persons per hectare) than the new towns. Energy conservation and the preservation of rural open space are also benefits of the NIT policy compared with new towns. Yet this property-led renewal involves a massive displacement of low-income tenants and small shopkeepers (Hong 2003). It also often involves a thoughtless clearance of usable buildings, and causes a further deterioration of the area by renewal designation that prohibits individual reconstruction for the sake of later collective redevelopment (Kim and Yoon 2003).

The central government's new towns have been much criticized as bedroom communities lacking the workplaces that would make them self-sustaining. The government's instant city-making has been also under attack for not offering a sense of place. Nonetheless, the new towns have been well accepted by middle-class people who moved there in search of good housing, a good environment, and investment value (Kwon and Lee 1995; Lim et al. 2002; Cheon 2004). Given the size of the new towns and the consumer base of middle-class households, the new town business centers have now filled up with offices, institutions, and a wide range of commercial uses, providing goods and services to the residents. The governmental development guidelines also ensured adequate provision of schools, parks, and other public facilities and infrastructure. The new towns are also dense enough to support transit service: new towns are often well linked by mass transportation networks. New town plans normally adopt the concept of transit-oriented development. Thus, this planned mode of decentralized concentration has some similarities to western suburban development models of New Urbanism.

Indeed, although they are still not entirely self-sufficient (Jung 2006), the first-round new towns show increasing degrees of self-sufficiency and transit use. As Table 3-2 shows, in four of the first-round new towns, about 40% of the residents travel to work in Seoul. In Jungdong, a new town close to the city of Incheon and the Kyung-in industrial corridor, only 23.9% of commuters work in Seoul. The auto dependency of commuters is less than

40% in the two largest new towns of Bundang and Ilsan, thanks to a network of transit and bus lines (Table 3-1).

In the SMR as a whole, the number of commuters has increased substantially. From 1990 to 2000, about 250,000 commuters lived within 20-km radius of the center and about 130,000 within 20–40 km. Thus outer expansion has increased commuting distances. By one estimate, SMR consumes about 172 million Bbl a year, of which 60% is consumed by the transportation sector (Hwang 2001). Since a significant portion of total transportation energy consumption is accounted for by private automobiles, more housing is needed in inner-city job centers and more jobs are needed in outer areas (Lee 2007).

3.4 Conclusion

As a capital region in a rapidly growing economy, Seoul Metropolitan Area has absorbed a population increase of 20 million since 1960. Under this enormous development pressure, it has experimented with a greenbelt, inner city densification, and decentralized concentration. These policies were devised to meet specific and limited goals, not as part of a comprehensive view of sustainable urban form. Nonetheless, Seoul offers some lessons to other megacities, as these concepts has been widely discussed as viable options for sustainable planning and design worldwide.

Seoul's greenbelt experience shows that this means of growth management should be carefully scrutinized as to its possible impact on metropolitan form. As intended, this containment policy indeed contributed to the intensification of inner area. However, despite its substantial width (10–20 km), the greenbelt could neither curb nor contain urban growth, because of the rapid pace of growth in the region. Rather, it changed the growth pattern: the intensification of the inner city has coincided with dense developments in suburban areas outside the greenbelt. The result is that the greenbelt now serves as a vital green open space in the middle of a dense metropolitan area. With extensive hiking trails, it is a popular leisure destination for millions of residents. The excessive densification and the restricted land supply might be shortcomings, but these outcomes fit with the principles of sustainable urban form.

Inside the greenbelt, urban renewal has led to the further intensification of the inner city of Seoul, where land prices have increased steeply. Seoul is now one of the densest cities in the world. As Western sustainability theories advocate, Seoul's dense living provides social benefits such as heavy transit use, reduced energy use, a balance of housing and jobs, the conservation of rural land, and urban vitality. However, as Zhang (2000) notes about the Hong Kong case, excessive intensification can cause environmental degradation. It is necessary to monitor the impact of high-rise and high-density development on urban sustainability, as many Asian cities exhibit this form of urban change. Seoul's experience also shows that market-driven inner-city intensification involves widespread gentrification, loss of usable buildings, and the excessive use of building materials.

The outer new town development also has pros and cons. The new towns were created to provide large amounts of housing quickly and thus lacked the sophistication of good city making. Yet, master-planned under the government development standards, outer new towns have physical amenities and good infrastructure. The initial lack of self-sufficiency has been much eased as new towns have matured. Like Western suburbanization processes, commercial activity and jobs have followed residential development. The size and density of the new towns support elements of sustainable planning and design such as mass transit, town centers, business facilities, and public parks that would otherwise not be possible. Not all new towns were originally supported by mass transit, but later transit provision is likely as transportation corridors develop over the coming years. All these features have contributed to limiting the new town residents' auto-dependency for commuting to 40%. Further efforts should be devoted to improve outer new towns with more social mix, increased self-sufficiency and better transit linkages, while making them more walkable, diverse, and affordable. Finally, given the development pressure within the SMR, it is undeniable that planned new towns have prevented or limited much worse sprawl.

The urban form of the SMR as a whole presents a number of positive elements arising from dense agglomeration. High levels of mass transit use, extensive mixed-used development, and intensive use of brownfields are all positive signs of a sustainable future. However, Seoul poses the issue of long-term sustainability. Development has taken place within a short period of time in both the inner city and the outer suburbs. And most new developments have entailed joint landownership of apartment complexes. The aging of buildings occurs simultaneously and the unit of change is getting increasingly large due to joint ownership. This will lead simultaneous blight of buildings and, to renew them, will require a responsive agreement from the multiple landowners. While Seoul has seen some concerted collective decision-making, it has never been easy. Little attention has been paid to how to ensure continued population turnover and renewal. Seoul's metropolitan form will test its flexibility and adaptability to urban change in the future.

References

Ahn K-H, Ohn Y-T (2001) Metropolitan growth management policies in Seoul: a critical review. In: Kwon W-Y, Kim K-J (eds) Urban management in Seoul: policy issues and responses. Seoul Development Institute, Seoul

Breheny MZ (1992) Sustainable development and urban form. Pion, London

Cheon H-S (2004) Motivation and types of migration of newtown residents in Seoul metropolitan region. Kyongginondan, Spring (in Korean)

Choe S-C (2004a) Reform of planning controls for an urban–rural continuum in Korea. In: Sorensen A et al (eds) Towards sustainable cities: East Asian, North American and European perspectives on managing urban regions. Ashgate, Aldershot, UK

Choe S-C (2004b) The thirty-year's experiment with British greenbelt policy in Korea: a convergent path to sustainable development. In: Richardson H, Bae CC (eds) Urban sprawl in Western Europe and the US. Ashgate, Aldershot, UK

Duany A, Plater-Zyberk E, Alminana R (2003) The new civic art: elements of town planning. Rizzoli, New York

Hong I-O (2003) Study on residents in urban renewal district in Seoul: impact of clearance renewal on local residents, research report. Seoul Development Institute and Korea Center for City and Environment Research (in Korean)

Hwang K-H (2001) Land use strategies for shaping the capital region transportation fuel-efficient growth pattern. Kyonggi Research Institute, research report 2001–11 (in Korean)

Jenks M, Burton E, Williams K (eds) (1996) The compact city: a sustainable urban form? E & FN Spon, London

Jenks M (2000) The appropriateness of compact cities to developing countries. In: Jenks M, Burgess R (eds) Compact cities: sustainable urban forms for developing countries. Spon Press, London

Jenks M, Dempsey N (eds) (2005) Future forms and design for sustainable cities. Architectural Press, Oxford, UK

Jenks M, Burgess R (eds) (2000) Compact cities: sustainable urban forms for developing countries. Spon Press, London

Jung H-Y (2006) Comparative study on characteristics between urban rehabilitation in built-up area and new town development. Research Report (SDI 06-R-03), Seoul Development Institute (in Korean)

Kim K-H (1998) An evaluation of green belt policy and major issues for reform. Hous Stud 6(2):127–148 (in Korean)

Kim K-J (ed) (2004a) International urban form study. Seoul Development Institute, Seoul

Kim K-J (2004b) Residential rebuilding boom and planning response. In: Sorensen A et al (eds) Towards sustainable cities: European, American and Asian perspectives. Ashgate, Aldershot, UK

Kim M-H, Jung H-Y (2001) Spatial patterns and policy issues of the Seoul metropolitan region. In: Kwon W-Y, Kim K-J (eds) Urban management in Seoul: policy issues and responses. Seoul Development Institute, Seoul

Kim K-J, Jung H-Y, Kim Y-R, Yun H-R (eds) (2002) Seoul and world cities: comparative reference on urban context and infrastructure. Seoul Development Institute, Seoul
Kim K-J, Yoon I-S (2003) Urban renewal and change of the 20th century Seoul. In: Kim K-J (ed) Seoul, 20th century: growth and change of the last 100 years. Seoul Development Institute, Seoul
Kim K-J et al (2002) Comparative reference on urban context and infrastructure. Seoul Development Institute, Seoul (in Korean)
Kwon Y-W, Lee J-W (1995) Spatial pattern of migration in Seoul metropolitan region. J Korea Plann Assoc 30(4):21–39 (in Korean)
Lee K-S (2003) Seoul's urban growth in the 20th century: from a pre-modern city to a global metropolis. In: Kim K-J (ed) Seoul 20th century: growth and change of the last 100 years. Seoul Development Institute, Seoul
Lee J-I (2007) The effect of change of the spatial structure and transportation modal split on the transportation energy consumption. Seoul Development Institute, research report 2007-R-01 (in Korean)
Lim C-H, Lee C-M, Sohn J-R (2002) Analysis of migration pattern of Seoul suburban area. J Korea Plann Assoc 3(4):95–108 (in Korean)
Richardson HW et al (2000) Compact cities in developing countries: assessment and implications. In: Jenks M, Burgess R (eds) Compact cities: sustainable urban forms for developing countries. Spon Press, London
Sorensen A et al (eds) (2004) Towards sustainable cities: East Asian, North American and European perspectives on managing urban regions. Ashgate, Aldershot, UK
Steeley G, Gibson M (1998) UK greenbelt policy: a review. Paper presented at the international seminar on management of greenbelt areas, Korea Research Institute for Human Settlements, Seoul, Korea, December 11
Tankel SB (1963) The importance of open space in urban patterns. In: Wingo L (ed) City and space. Johns Hopkins University Press, Baltimore
Williams K, Burton E, Jenks M (eds) (2000) Achieving sustainable urban form. E & FN Spon, London
Zhang XQ (2000) High-rise and high-density compact urban form: the development of Hong Kong. In: Jenks M, Burgess R (eds) Compact cities: sustainable urban forms for developing countries. Spon Press, London

4. Sustainable Development, Urban Form, and Megacity Governance and Planning in Tehran

Ali Madanipour

As a city of 7.8 million people in a province of 13.4 million, Tehran faces major challenges in sustainable development. This paper presents a brief history of Tehran's development, followed by a discussion of its urban form, governance and planning processes, and some of the major challenges that face the city today, primarily environmental pollution, traffic congestion, and management of urban growth, as well as social divide and environmental risks.

4.1 Emergence of a Metropolis

The first time Tehran is mentioned in history is in an eleventh-century chronicle, where it is noted as a small village north of the ancient city of Ray, Tehran's predecessor and now a southern suburb of the metropolis. A Spanish visitor in 1404 described it as very large with no walls, well supplied with everything, and delightful. Its significance grew when a bazaar and square-shaped town walls with four gates were built in 1553. Over time, it became a garrison town, a trading center, a regional capital, a temporary court, and eventually the capital of the Persian empire in 1786. Its population grew from 15,000 in 1796 to 50,000 in little more than a decade.

By the mid-nineteenth century, four residential neighborhoods surrounded the walled citadel, the roofed bazaar, and the city's two focal points – Citadel Square and the Herbs Market Square. Tehran exerted a limited control as the administrative center of an empire formed of a collection of loosely connected provinces with relatively self-sufficient, closed agrarian economies and multi-ethnic communities (Madanipour 1998, 2008) (Fig. 4-1).

During the nineteenth century, the empire lost some territory to the advancing Russian and British empires, and export crops replaced subsistence crops.

A. Sorensen and J. Okata (eds.), *Megacities: Urban Form, Governance, and Sustainability*,

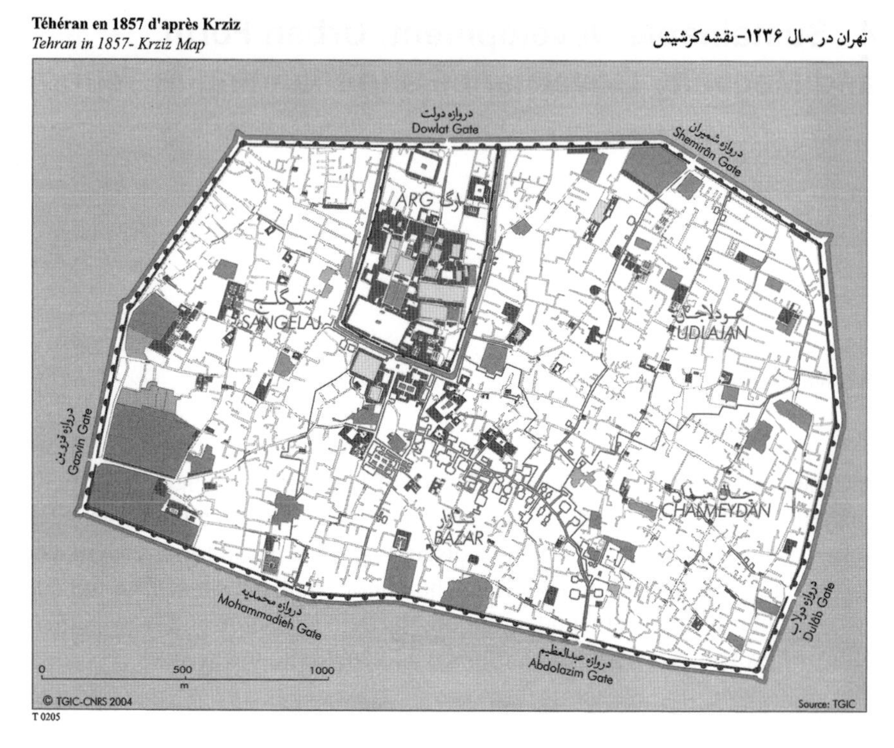

Fig. 4-1. Map of Tehran in 1857: a walled, traditional Middle Eastern city (Source Tehran Municipality)

Iran entered the new world system of capitalist economies as a peripheral partner, exporting raw materials and importing manufactured goods. From 1868 on, a major program of modernization transformed the capital. The urban area grew by 4.5 times, and new walls and gates were built, as well as new institutions, buildings, streets, and neighborhoods. The new urban structure introduced a north–south divide, separating the rich from poor and the modern from the traditional, establishing a character for the city that has been maintained ever since.

With a population of 300,000 at the end of the century, Tehran was a hotbed of tensions, which would unfold in a century of social unrest and revolutionary struggle. In 1906, Tehran and other large cities were the main sites of a revolution that resulted in the establishment of a constitution and a parliament. Economic decline and the First World War, however, limited the effectiveness of the revolution and its new institutions.

Following a coup d'état in 1921, Reza Shah started a new dynasty, Pahlavi (1925–1979). His immediate tasks were the centralization of government and the consolidation of his power by the creation of a new army, a reorganized government bureaucracy, and a new system of court patronage. To integrate the fragmented provinces into a unified national space, transport networks were developed across the country. The past was associated with administrative inefficiency, tribal anarchy, clerical authority, and social heterogeneity. This was to be replaced by a future marked by cultural uniformity, political conformity, and ethnic homogeneity (Abrahamian 1982).

In the 1930s, Tehran underwent a radical transformation to symbolize this change. New royal palaces were built and the old royal compound was replaced by a new government quarter. The city walls and gates were pulled down and a network of wide streets cut through the urban fabric, creating an open matrix for the easy movement of goods and vehicles across a unified urban space. This created a new basis for the growth of the city in all directions and defined a new character for the city (Fig. 4-2).

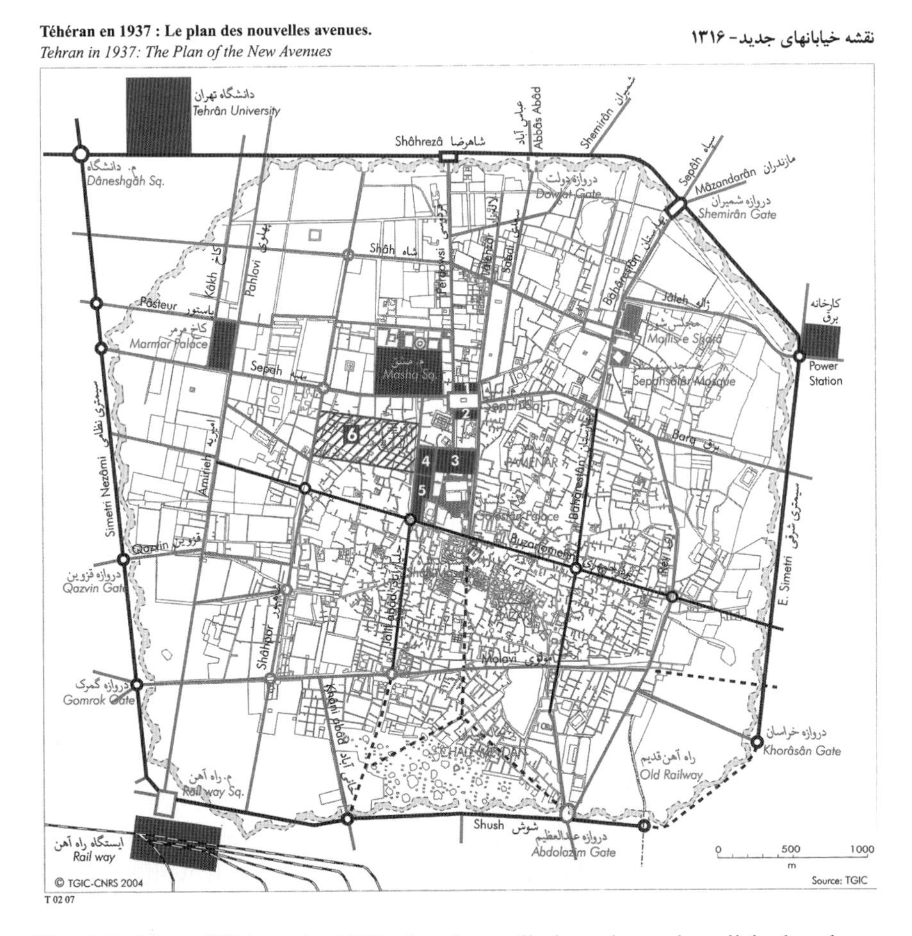

Fig. 4-2. Map of Tehran in 1937: the city walls have been demolished and new streets have structured the growing city (Source Tehran Municipality)

The postwar period witnessed rapid and unregulated growth of the city through speculative development. During the Second World War, Reza Shah's sympathy for Germany led to the Allied occupation of the country in 1941 and his abdication in favor of his son Muhammad Reza Shah. By the end of the decade, Tehran's population had passed the one million mark. The nationalization of the oil industry by the prime minister and the international economic blockade that followed led to the overthrow of the government by a U.S.-supported coup d'état in 1953 in favor of the shah. An industrialization drive encouraged private investment for import-substituting industries, most of which were established in the area around Tehran. By 1956, the population had reached 1.56 million.

Land reform in the early 1960s redistributed agricultural land from large feudal landowners to sharecropping farmers and nationalized forests and pastures. At that same time, women were given new rights, including voting. A large-scale revolt against the reform program headed by the clergy and the bazaar merchants was a rehearsal for the revolution 15 years later. Oil revenues rose substantially, especially after 1973, to reach 87% of foreign exchange earnings in 1977. The oil boom, industrialization, modernization, and new construction increased the population to 4.59 million in 1976. The city continued to grow and change, with new motorways, high-rise buildings, and large satellite towns. This was a prosperous period in Tehran's history, but also one in which social divide and political oppression intensified.

An economic downturn, international pressure, and internal disapproval of the shah's model of development and government prepared the ground for social unrest. After 2 years of mass demonstrations which united most shades of political opinion, the monarchy was toppled in 1979 and replaced by an Islamic Republic, a system that uneasily combined the rule of clergy with parliamentary republicanism. The revolution was followed by 8 years of war with Iraq, and a period of continuous international tensions, which often resulted in the neglect and decline of the capital city. Only after the normalization of the 1990s did the city start to recover with further expansion, and construction of parks, motorway networks, and high-rise buildings (Fig. 4-3).

4.2 Patterns of Urban Form

The key patterns of urban form in Tehran include a north–south duality, an axial urban structure, the decline of the center coupled with suburban sprawl, and the transformation of the street system, land use, and building form. The distinctive topography of the region has also had a major

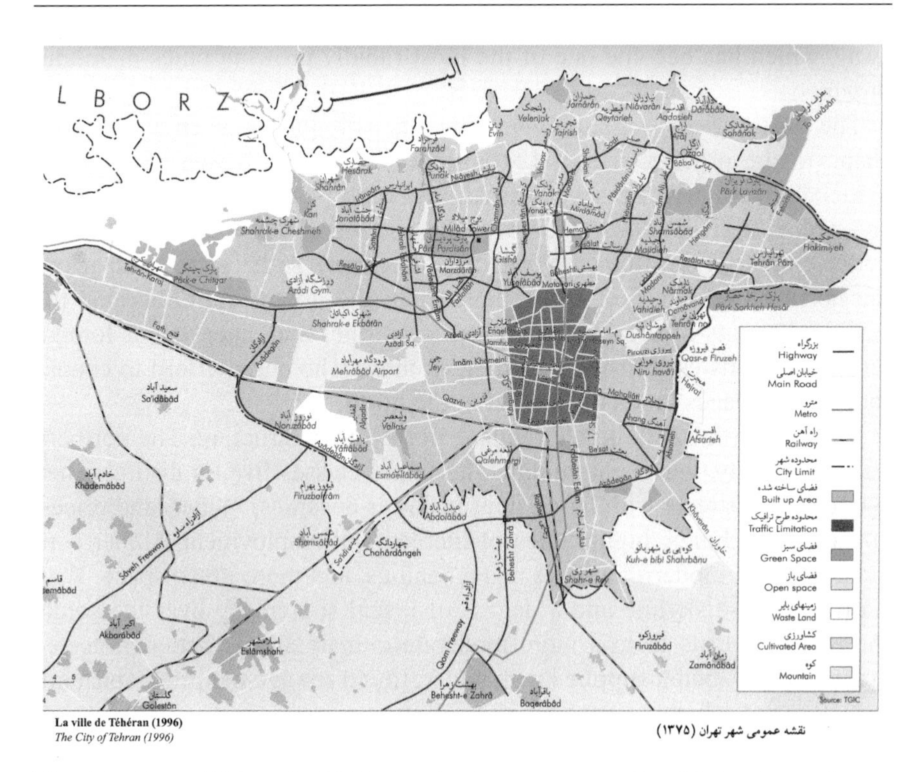

Fig. 4-3. Map of Tehran in 1996: the city has grown considerably in size and area, becoming a major metropolis (Source Tehran Municipality)

influence on the qualities of urban space. The city of Tehran is located on the southern slopes of the Alborz chain of mountains, not far from the Damavand ridge – the summit can be seen from the city on bright days. Twenty kilometers immediately to the north lies the To-Chal ridge, 3,933 m high, which dominates the city (Lockhart 1960). To the south, Tehran stretches to Kavir, the central desert of Iran. The center of the city is on the longitude of 51 degrees 26 minutes east and the latitude of 35 degrees 41 minutes north (Kariman 1976:8). The northernmost limit of the city, as established by the municipality, is the contour of 1,800 m above sea level, 640 m higher than the city's southeastern border, which is 1,160 m high. The desert on the southern outskirts of the city, 30 km away from the northern heights, is even lower. This dramatic difference in height has had significant impacts on the characteristics of urban space in Tehran.

The wall of mountains has limited the growth of the city to the north and, to a lesser extent, to the east. To the south, the desert is a barrier to expansion, although a less definitive one than the mountains. It is on its western side that the city has gradually stretched towards the city of Karaj, 40 km away, which has become one of the most rapidly growing cities in Tehran province.

The north–south slope on which the city is built has given a particular shape to the process of social stratification. The north was traditionally associated with privileges, such as a better supply of water, a higher defensive value, a visual dominance over the south and the countryside, and a better climate. From the early nineteenth century, some of the villages to the north of Tehran, now incorporated into the urban fabric, became the summer retreats of royal and aristocratic families and, later, major foreign embassies. This established a pattern, as those who could afford to choose their living places gradually moved to the north.

A clear north–south divide remains in the urban structure. The northern half of the city, where the middle and upper classes live, is distinguished by tree-lined streets with larger houses, lower densities, higher land prices, smaller households, higher rates of literacy and employment, higher concentrations of modern facilities and amenities, and more green space. With a more diverse skyline and a degree of visual supremacy over the south, the north benefits from a more moderate climate and is better protected against floods, better supplied with underground sewage facilities, and, until recently, less subject to atmospheric pollution.

The south lies at the opposite end of the spectrum in relation to these characteristics. Despite attempts by the revolutionary government, the north–south divide remains a key feature of the city's spatial structure and social conditions. Although there have been some successes in improving the conditions of the south, the strong social divide is still clearly visible in Tehran, with serious manifestations, such as homelessness, informal settlements, and crime (Tabrizi and Madanipour 2006).

There is also a recognizable difference between the core and periphery of the city. The central areas, comprising the old city and its northward expansion between 1868 and the Second World War, are where most of the business activities and services are concentrated. Some of the historic parts of the city suffer from neglect and decline, while the city has grown outwards into the surrounding areas. The rural settlements around Tehran, which have been engulfed by its expanding fabric, are the main nuclei of many new suburbs, which have developed through the gradual addition of new built-up areas. Developed by the private sector on a speculative basis, most of the post-Second World War suburban developments focused on housing.

The pace of urban development was so fast that the provision of services and infrastructure could not keep up with the needs of the new areas. The old city, with its limited facilities, had to provide infrastructure and services for an ever-increasing population. The planning system, with its policy of containment of growth within municipal boundaries, also contributed to further concentration of facilities in the center. Nevertheless, after the initial stages of concentration in the central areas, there has been a growing decentralization and suburbanization of services, encouraged by both public and private agencies.

Another characteristic of Tehran's urban structure has been its axial form: there is a central axis linking the south-centre to the northernmost areas, along which many facilities and amenities are located. This primary axis is formed of several north–south streets, among which one street, Vali Asr, predominates. A secondary, east–west axis intersects the main axis at right angles and centers on a single street, Enghelab. The major squares along these two main axes of the urban structure are the city's focal points and have the highest land prices.

The change in the street system from traditional to modern is another characteristic of Tehran's urban form. The traditional system, designed for walking, was a hierarchical distribution of narrow, twisting, partly-roofed streets leading to buildings grouped around cul-de-sacs. The spine of this pattern was a local high street – a bazaar. With the introduction of the motor car and the rise in its ownership, the urban form has been transformed. An orthogonal network of roads was imposed on the traditional pattern, gradually eliminating the cul-de-sacs. The new network was an open matrix designed to ease the flow of automobiles and people.

In the traditional city, land uses were clearly separated from one another, whereas the new city has a more mixed-use structure. In its initial stages, the government encouraged commercial uses to spread out from the central bazaar to support the newly laid out street network. This change was mainly due to the state's desire to dismantle the monopoly of the bazaar merchants over the economic space and activities, but it was also due to the bazaar's limited capacity to accommodate new businesses.

The city expanded rapidly without any consensus on the way it should develop or any effective planning system. Even when planning and zoning were established, the limited powers of municipalities to enforce planning control resulted in the development of mixed-use areas.

Alongside other changes in urban form, there has been a change in building form: from one- or two-story, inward-looking, courtyard buildings to higher, more open buildings, although still enclosed within walled courtyards. At the same time, there has been a change from living in single family houses to apartment living. The change in building form has been largely associated with the changes in the street system and in the way development pressure and population growth have transformed the habits and demands of a large urban society (Fig. 4-4).

Fig. 4-4. The morphology of the city has changed, with high rise buildings replacing garden suburbs, with inevitable impact on the quality of urban environment

The urban form, therefore, consists of a large population increasingly living in apartments in taller buildings, connected by a car-based infrastructure, in an ever-expanding metropolis. This fragmented pattern of development goes through cycles of building booms and densification, and gradually matures through mixed use and infill development, but also declines through obsolescence and neglect.

4.3 Urban Governance

The city of Tehran is run by a municipal organization in conjunction with a city council (Tehran Municipality 2008). The task of the 15 elected members of the city council is to select and monitor the activities of a mayor, who acts as executive manager of the city. The central municipality oversees 22 district municipalities, each run by a district mayor who is supported by advisors and deputies. Overlaps and ambiguities create obstacles to the effective operation of this hierarchical organization.

The relationship between the city council and the mayor is one of the most crucial elements of the institutional arrangements, which is marked at times by visible tensions. The tensions between the mayor and the council are part of the teething problems of the city council's re-emergence after a long period of inactivity. The institutional structure of a city council and a mayor was introduced after the 1906 Constitutional Revolution. Since then, however, the council has been operating intermittently, and has often been subject to the control of central government. Twenty years after the revolution of the 1970s, the city council was re-introduced in 1999. But from the beginning, its relationship with different mayors was tense, partly because of the developmental nature of the council's establishment and operation. Pressure for more democratization also led to the development of elected neighborhood advisory councils in 2006, the impacts of which are yet to be fully assessed.

Another important relationship is between the mayor and the central government. Rather than an independent organization responsive to citizens, the municipality is seen as a branch of the central government in charge of delivering certain services. The history of modern municipalities in Iran, exemplified in Tehran, is a constant struggle between democratic aspirations for local autonomy and the central government's assertion of its powers. In the absence of the city council, mayors were appointed by the Ministry of the Interior. The relationship between the mayor and the city council on the one hand, and with the Ministry of the Interior on the other, can generate a tense power relationship.

The post of mayor in Tehran is a very prominent political position. During the 1990s, the mayor of Tehran was invited to participate in cabinet meetings of the central government. However, in an unsettled political scene, in which different factions and groups compete for power, the position is subject to constant controversy and power struggles. It is a post that could pave the way to a presidential position, as it did for the last mayor of Tehran, Mahmoud Ahmadinejad. Therefore, much sensitivity is associated with the office of mayor in the capital city.

The distribution of power and responsibilities between the municipality and government ministries is another source of tension. The administration of Iran is based on sectoral management. Local branches of different ministries engage in development, deliver services, and deal with major urban and national problems according to their own capacities. A local organization such as a municipality finds it very difficult to cross the divide between these different public agencies. This vertical intervention in urban development and management is often in contrast to the municipal responsibility of managing the city at a horizontal level. The overlap of issues and interests between local public agencies and the municipality often leads to a confusion of responsibilities, undermining the municipality's role (Tehran Municipality 1996).

Tehran is also the seat of the national government. The country's spiritual leader, its president, parliament, and ministries are based in Tehran. Before them, the shah, the court, the foreign dignitaries, and all the state apparatus were based in Tehran. This has traditionally created a massive concentration of the country's elite in Tehran, powerful figures who have an interest and considerable influence in the affairs of the city.

The national government and their local agencies intervene in the governance of the city through both official and informal channels. Given the presence of the national government, almost half of those working in Tehran are employed in the public sector. The concentration of public-sector employees in the city makes its social and economic life closely tied to nuances of public-sector management and finances.

Tehran municipality's activities fall into three categories: administrative services, urban services, and urban development. Administrative services deal with revenue, renewal tax, and organizational issues. Urban services deal with keeping the city clean, environmental maintenance and improvement, fire fighting and security, traffic, urban transport, social services, and the distribution of drinking water. The urban development functions include development planning, development and improvement of infrastructure for water, sewage and transportation systems, as well as sports, entertainment, cultural, and tourist facilities. Some municipal functions have been transferred to other organizations, including health control and combating contagious diseases, price control, supervision of weights and other standards, and the preparation of trade regulations.

Each municipal district is further divided into neighborhoods, of which there are 112 in total. In addition to municipal districts and neighborhoods, Tehran is subdivided in different ways by service organizations, including water and wastewater, regional electricity, gas, post, telecommunication, tax, civil registration, land registration, property registration, social security, police, employment and social affairs administration. Each has its own organization and subdivision of the city (Habibi and Hourcade 2005:48). These subdivisions, however, do not coincide with one another, causing overlaps and ambiguities in urban management.

The relationship between the central municipality and its district municipalities is also a source of tension and ineffectiveness. Within a hierarchical bureaucratic organization, district mayors historically avoided making independent decisions. The 1990s drive for effectiveness led to some devolution of power to districts, followed by huge controversies about the misuse of resources. The privatization of some services further complicated the city's governance arrangements, creating further overlaps and ambiguities.

Some courts do not acknowledge the legal status of municipal planning documents. When the municipality attempts to limit landowners' right to develop their property, some courts have ignored the planning documents and regulations and supported landowners. They take the position that Islamic laws sanction private property rights and the municipality is not in a position to undermine those rights. Another hindrance to the authority of the Tehran municipality is its limited spatial domain of activities. Most of the recent growth of the metropolis has taken place beyond the official boundaries of the city, outside the municipality's jurisdiction. This limitation means that suburban developments, some of which have a major impact on the metropolis, remain outside an effective, overall management structure.

The city's management, therefore, suffers from a multiplicity of agencies and the absence of an authority in charge of managing the city with an overall perspective and responsibility. This institutional crisis has resulted from the passage to a more democratic and accountable governance coupled with a degree of privatization and devolution of responsibilities.

4.4 Planning the Megacity

Several phases of planning have enabled the growth of the city: from the building of walls in the sixteenth century to the nineteenth-century enlargement of the city and the early twentieth-century imposition of a new street network on the old city, which laid the foundation for a massive urban explosion in the second half of the twentieth century (Madanipour 2006). In this process, the changing patterns of land use, street layout, and building form have transformed the city from a traditional Middle Eastern city to a modern metropolis.

Speculative development in the mid-twentieth century, especially after the Second World War, created a fragmented urban pattern. In Tehran, as a deputy mayor of the city noted in 1962, "the buildings and settlements have been developed by whoever has wanted in whatever way and wherever they have wanted," resulting in a city that was "in fact a number of towns connected to each other in an inappropriate way" (Nafisi 1964:426). By the 1960s, the desire for a degree of control over this growth had become overwhelming. As a result, a consortium of the Iranian consultants Aziz Farmanfarmaian Associates and the American firm of Victor Gruen Associates was commissioned to produce a comprehensive plan, which was approved in 1968.

According to these consultants, the city's problems were high density, especially in its central areas, the expansion of commercial activities along the main roads, pollution, inefficient infrastructure, widespread unemployment in poorer areas, and the continuous migration of low-income groups to Tehran. Their solution was to transform the city's physical, social, and economic fabric (Farmanfarmaian and Gruen 1968).

Echoing fashionable planning ideas of the time (Abercrombie 1945; Mumford 1954; Gruen 1964), the plan recommended reducing the density and congestion of the city center and growing westward in a linear, polycentric form. The city would be formed of ten large urban districts, separated from each other by greenbelts, each with about 500,000 inhabitants, a commercial and an industrial center, and high-rise buildings. Each district would be subdivided into a number of areas and neighborhoods. An area, with a population of about 15,000–30,000, would have a high school and a commercial center and other necessary facilities. A neighborhood, with about 5,000 inhabitants, would have a primary school and a local commercial center. The districts and areas would be linked by a transportation network, which would include motorways, rapid transit routes, and bus routes. The stops on each rapid transit route would be developed as nodes for concentration of activities with a high residential density. A number of redevelopment and improvement schemes in the existing urban areas would involve relocating 600,000 people from the central areas to other parts of the city (Farmanfarmaian and Gruen 1968).

Within a decade, the plan's implementation was thwarted by the revolution and the war, and its 25-year lifespan came to an end in the early 1990s. Its impact on the reorganization of neighborhoods and districts was negligible, but it continued to be the basis for infrastructure development. Much of the road network construction since the 1990s has been based on the 1968 plan provisions, even though the public transit system has been slow to develop, compared to the network of highways across the city.

A new plan was prepared in the 1990s, followed by a municipal policy document that set the city's priorities. The impacts of these documents were, however, limited. A strategic plan for the metropolitan region in 2002 recommended the establishment of a metropolitan authority, but this recommendation was not implemented. A new comprehensive plan for Tehran was prepared in 2006. It is a strategic plan that links up the 22 plans for municipal districts. Twenty-two consultants were commissioned to prepare plans for all the municipal districts, while a consortium of consultants, led by Boum Sazegan, was given the task of preparing a comprehensive strategic plan. Despite much controversy among the professional elite, this plan has gone through the necessary legal stages and is now ready for implementation.

According to the new comprehensive plan, the city suffers from a lack of effective planning, exacerbated by the impacts of selling density rights to support the municipal budget and paying no attention to the city's strategic roles at national and international levels. Other problems include under-regulated development beyond the city's boundaries, as well as environmental pollution, traffic congestion, poor protection against earthquake risk, a shortage of public spaces and facilities, lack of land use regulation, and a haphazard townscape. The city has reached its limits of growth and has no more capacity to grow any further. The plan's proposals include setting and maintaining clear boundaries for the city, consolidating its population at maximum 8.6 million, improving physical infrastructure and environmental conditions, providing new employment opportunities, controlling densities and land uses, improving transportation infrastructure and managing demand, and promoting the development of a polycentric urban area (Boum Sazegan 2006).

Given Tehran's institutional and substantive complexities, it is not yet clear whether this new document, and the planning process more broadly, can meet the challenges of moving towards a more livable and sustainable megacity. Several disjunctions in the planning process undermine its chances of success.

The municipality is in charge of implementing the plan, which has been prepared by private consultants and approved by the Ministry of Housing and Urban Development. The in-house capacity of the central and local municipalities for development and feedback is limited. There are plans to introduce a municipal department as a permanent home for the city's comprehensive plan, which could be in charge of monitoring its implementation and revision.

4.5 Challenges of Sustainable Development

Environmental sustainability is an urgent concern in Tehran, both for the population suffering from severe atmospheric pollution, and for the policy makers whose credibility and legitimacy are under threat. As early as 1971, a Department of the Environment was established for environmental protection. The revolutionary government recognized the significance of environmental concerns. The article 50 of the new Constitution considers it "a public duty to protect the environment where the present and future generations are to have a thriving social life. Thus, any form of activities, whether economic or otherwise, that causes pollution of or irreparable damage to the environment is prohibited." (Iran DoE 2009).

Since the 1990s, following the period of normalization that followed the revolution and the war, the discourses of environmental sustainability have been growing in Iran, as evidenced in the appointment of a high-profile deputy-president for the environment and the increasing number of green NGOs and activists. Tehran City Council has also established a committee devoted to the environment, and in 2003 the municipality set up an Environment and Sustainable Development Task Force, headed by a Mayor's special adviser. The Task Force has six working groups: water and sewage, energy, solid waste, air pollution, information, and environmental education. In 2007 it produced a 682-page report, titled *Green Workbook*, which lists the municipality's policies and activities to promote environmental sustainability (Tehran Municipality 2007). This publication indicates the growing awareness of the need for sustainable development in the city, even if it is not well integrated into all areas of activity.

Here we touch on the most pressing environmental problem in Tehran, which is closely related to its urban form and planning – namely air pollution, primarily caused by automobiles, as well as household fuels and industrial activities. The city is engulfed in an arc of high mountains, and local winds are not strong enough to clear the city air. The result has been mounting environmental pollution, reaching such dangerous levels that on some days schools are closed and vulnerable people are advised to stay at home.

According to research, 70% of Tehran's pollution is produced by automobiles. Many of the city's cars are more than 20 years old and newer cars are produced at low environmental standards. During a typical morning rush hour, 216 tonnes of carbon monoxide, 29 tonnes of hydrocarbons, and 6 tonnes of nitrogen oxides are released into the atmosphere (Tehran Municipality 2004a:143).

Automobiles are responsible for more than just air pollution. Traffic conditions in Tehran are extremely bad, and Iran suffers from one the highest rates of road accidents in the world. In 2001, the growing number of deaths on Tehran roads reached about 30% of all deaths (Tehran Municipality 2004a:36). Traffic jams are part of everyday life, caused by the large number of cars on the roads (estimated to be up to 2.1 million in Tehran), erratic behavior by motorists in driving and parking, disregard of traffic regulations by pedestrians, and a host of other problems (Tehran Municipality 2004a) (Fig. 4-5).

There are 132 km^2 of roads in the city, accounting for almost one-fifth of the total urban area. According to Tehran Municipality's traffic research center (Tehran Municipality 2004a:6), every day the city's residents make 11.5 million trips, with the following mode splits: private cars (29%), bus and metro (24%), taxis (20%), minibuses (11%), motorcycles (9%),

Fig. 4-5. The intersection of the two main urban axes, showing Vali Asr, the primary street of the city, which runs north south across Tehran

coaches (4%), and vans (3%).[1] Minibuses are part of the public transport system, working along fixed routes but with no fixed schedules or stops, while shared taxis carry passengers along the main roads. In addition to regulated taxis, many private cars operate as informal taxis along the main roads. Traffic jams are often caused by the way these different vehicles stop for passengers at any point along the road.

A number of solutions have been proposed for managing traffic and reducing air pollution. In the aftermath of the revolution, a radical scheme was introduced which limited vehicular access to central areas. An area of 22 sq km was designated which private cars could not enter during weekdays. This scheme had an initial impact on traffic jams, but has also led to the decentralization of some activities.

[1]According to Tehran Metro's managing director (Hashemi 2006:44), the number of daily trips in 2004 was more than 12 million, with the following mode splits: private car (23%), bus (23%), taxi (20%), minibus (13%), metro (7%), and other (14%), which includes shared taxis, jitney cars (cars or vans that operate as demand warrants on mostly fixed routes without fixed schedules or stops), and motorcycles. The discrepancy between the two data sets may be attributable to the different areas of coverage and different years of data.

The metro system, which has been in the making since the 1970s, is 90 km long with 42 stations, accounting for 10% of all journeys in 2005. The target of the Tehran Metro company, which is owned by the municipality, is to grow to a 170-km long network and account for 40% of all journeys in the city by 2020 (Hashemi 2006).

Other initiatives, such as managed traffic lights, a central traffic management center, dedicated bus routes, traffic-calming measures, public education, and stricter enforcement of traffic regulations (for example, in wearing seatbelts), have also been introduced. Enforcement of alternate days for odd and even number plates to enter the central areas, and a recent rationing of subsidized petrol have had some impact on traffic volumes in Tehran. Conversion from petrol to natural gas for buses and taxis, and the introduction of incentives for replacing old cars with newer ones are among the environmental measures to reduce atmospheric pollution.

Since the 1990s, the city has implemented a scheme to improve the quality of urban environment, balance the distribution of green spaces across the city, and combat air pollution by developing pocket parks on vacant land and planting large areas of new urban trees, particularly in the less privileged southern parts of the city. The scheme was recognized by the UN Habitat as good practice. Other environmental problems, such as contaminated underground water tables, are caused by the lack of a citywide sewage infrastructure, a problem the city has yet to address.

4.6 Environmental Risks

Environmental risks are risks to the natural and built environment caused by attitudes and patterns of development by Tehranis. Three of the most important are earthquake risks, flood risks, and threats to historic environments.

Tehran sits at the foot of Alborz mountains, on a number of major fault lines. The old city was not located on any fault line, but many of its new areas are. In the event of a serious earthquake, which has been experienced in other parts of Iran, the number of casualties would be enormous. In selecting sites for housing development, earthquakes have not been a consideration, so many affluent areas may be just as exposed to a disaster as poor areas. In coping with a disaster and its aftermath, the better-off would have more resources, but the poor will have stronger community support. Civil defense arrangements are also in place. Local mobilization was strong after the revolution, and so there is some capacity to act. Iran has a long history of earthquakes and it can mobilize its resources fairly quickly.

The government commissioned a Japanese organization to prepare a study on the risks of earthquake in Tehran and what to do to avoid dangerous consequences. At different times, there has even been talk of relocating the capital, but this would leave most of the people in place and would not address the problems caused by such a disaster.

The city has building codes to ensure that buildings are safe in the case of earthquakes, but much of the physical fabric was built before enforcement of these codes, particularly the smaller domestic buildings. Also, enforcement is not always effective. The low quality of construction exposes many buildings to an earthquake risk.

Coping with this risk demands stronger planning awareness and intervention in site selection, better enforcement of building regulations, and community training for disaster management. Unfortunately, there is a sense of fatalism in Iran, which prevents people from engaging with the issue and demanding action from the authorities.

Flooding is another environmental risk, as Tehran is also vulnerable to flows of the excess water from heavy rains. Canals and seasonal rivers, called *maseel*, have traditionally channeled this excess water away from built-up areas. Since the *maseels* have been used to safeguard the city from flood, they are not usually found in the older areas near the city center and the south. In the built-up areas around the suburban villages and along the main arteries, the *maseel* originally played an important role as the physical boundaries of growth, creating gaps in the urban fabric. However, in some areas they have been filled and built upon by speculators, leading to major disasters. These disasters, with few exceptions, such as the major flood of the summer of 1987 in the north city, have always affected the poor neighborhoods of the south. These southern neighborhoods have also suffered from poor sewage disposal and water distribution, because the slope of the city favors the north.

Finally, the city's built heritage is at risk. Praise of the new and disregard for the old have dominated twentieth-century attitudes towards the built environment. Old buildings are easily pulled down as land prices go up and the gap between exchange value and use value widens. During the revolution several ancient monuments around the country were demolished, either because of hostility towards the past monarchies or for what were considered utilitarian reasons. This utilitarianism, which in its extreme forms touches on vandalism, appears in sharp contrast with the values of a revolution whose stated aims were to revive tradition and to contradict the disenchantments of modernism. Yet these sensitivities, which were manifest in the area of cultural and religious norms and behavior, were hardly extended to dealing with the built environment (Madanipour 2003). This can also be observed in dealing with political institutions. After all, the revolution uprooted a very traditional institution, the monarchy, and replaced it with a very modern one, the republic. As such, the government has continued the modernist tradition of the recent history, despite its traditionalist appearances (Fig. 4-6).

Tehran's old core continues to be neglected, as it is seen to be outdated and dilapidated. By the mid 1990s, only 38 buildings in the city were listed and a further 12 were in the process of being protected. The Bazaar and Oudlajan districts have at least 5,000 buildings of historical and architectural merit, although no specific action is being taken to protect them (Tehran Municipality 1996:242). Tehran's conservationists argue that the conservation of the old core would give the city a degree of historic continuity and could be used to promote cultural activities (Safamanesh 1993). However, rather than protecting the city center, the municipality's policy of decentralizing activities can be a further blow to the old core by depriving it of some of its economic base (Tehran Municipality 1996).

Elsewhere in the city, especially in the northern areas, historic gardens and buildings are under threat from development pressure. A new policy of urban renewal has designated large parts of the old core and poorer neighborhoods as "worn out," and huge funds are being raised to redcvelop them

Fig. 4-6. Historic buildings are under pressure from development: a new metro station is replacing some old buildings

radically. It is partly this absence of continuity in the built environment that has given rise to frequent complaints about the loss of identity in Tehran.

4.7 Managing Urban Growth

The tools of managing urban growth in Tehran have included municipal service boundaries, density limits, and new town development. The overall density of population in Tehran is 110 persons per hectare (the city population was 7.8 million in 2006, in an urban area of 707 sq km, up from a population of 6.7 million in 1996). Densities in some southern and eastern districts are 365 persons per hectare, while the newly added western districts have densities as low as 11 persons per hectare (Tehran Municipality 2004b:23).

Controlling the growth of the city's population has been an urgent item on the municipal agenda for a long time, but efforts to do so have generally met with little success. Over the years, therefore, city authorities have expanded municipal boundaries to allow for urban growth and manage densities. In 1956, with a population of 1.56 million in an area of 110 sq km, the city's density was 140 persons per hectare; in 1966, the population had risen dramatically to 2.86 million in an area of 243 sq km, but its density was 115 persons per hectare. By 1970, the population had grown to 3.7 million in an area of 305 sq km and a density of 122 persons per hectare (Doxiadis Associates International 1972).

These figures show that Tehran's density today is less than it was 50 years ago; even though its population has grown more than fivefold, its municipal area has been enlarged almost sevenfold. The experience of living in the city, however, does not reflect these figures. Congested streets, a skyline of tall buildings, and a large urban region that lies beyond municipal boundaries, all contribute to a sense of higher densities, overcrowding, and a faster pace of life.

Population growth in Iran dramatically slowed down during the last decade, reaching 1.6% per annum year between 1996 and 2006; but migration remains a major cause of urban growth and the decline of regions. Although population growth in the city of Tehran has slowed, it has accelerated in the suburbs, particularly in speculative and informal settlements. Between 1996 and 2006, the city of Tehran grew by 15% as compared to 30% growth in Tehran Province for the same period. The rate of population growth in Tehran Province, which includes these marginal cities and towns, was 2.6% per annum between 1996 and 2006, one of the fastest in the country. This province attracted more than 600,000 immigrants from other parts of the country during this decade.

While suburban growth eased some pressure on Tehran City Council, the problems of the urban region grew. The natural limits of mountains and desert have shaped the growth of Tehran. The 1968 plan had envisaged 5-year cycles in which municipal boundaries would grow to accommodate population growth. The enforcement of the first cycle of 5-year boundaries, which had major impacts on land prices, was hugely controversial, as it set limits on the supply of land for development. The second cycle, however, was not implemented, as the country entered a period of instability. After the revolution, municipal boundaries were expanded to the maximum 25-year boundary which had been envisaged by the plan.

The 1968 plan had proposed a reduction in the density of central areas, by relocating up to 600,000 population from the center to new development areas, which would have reduced the city's density to about 85 persons per hectare by the end of the plan's period in 1992 (envisaging a maximum population of 5.5 million in an area of 650 sq km). It set density limits in housing development, so that some more affluent areas in the north could have a maximum 150 persons per hectare, while allowing some areas in the south to have up to 500 persons per hectare. But the population explosion inside the city and in the surrounding areas continued. In the 1980s, some studies were conducted to investigate the relocation of the capital to another site, but the enormous cost of such an undertaking put an end to the idea. Instead, a policy of rapid urban improvement was adopted.

To pay for the rapid improvement policy, and to make the municipality financially independent, the plan's density limits were relaxed and the municipality entered a new relationship with developers. Through negotiation and payment of fees to the municipality, developers could obtain permission to change land use and density limits on their land. Development pressure in Tehran, in response to the continued population growth and high land prices, was met through facilitating new development.

After the end of the 8-year war, the feeling was that people expected some improvement in their living standards, and a program of regeneration and renewal was inevitable. Tehran had been neglected during the war, and had been undermined by revolutionaries who thought it had been unduly favored by the previous regime, at the expense of small towns and rural areas. After a decade of nationalization and state control, this was a time in which privatization of services and organizations was beginning, fostering a more intensive use of private-sector resources in postwar reconstruction.

The bonus zoning policy became known as "density selling." It transformed the urban landscape very quickly and became very controversial. Northern Tehran, which had been a place of large two-storey villas, turned into clusters of luxury towers. Southern Tehran was also transformed by the replacement of single-family houses by apartment blocks of up to five or six stories. As a result, Tehran has become more and more a city of apartment dwellers. In this process, the municipality became financially autonomous, undertaking vast infrastructure programs. A program of highway construction expanded the network of fast roads, as planned by the 1968 comprehensive plan. Large and small parks, cultural centers, youth centers, municipal shopping centers, and a range of other services were introduced. The policy of capturing the value of land for development of urban infrastructure changed the conditions of municipal services as dramatically as it did the face of the city. At its peak, according to unofficial reports, value capture accounted for 80% of the city's revenue.

A major urban renewal initiative, the Navab Project, transformed a high-density part of southern Tehran. The project was financed by issuing government bonds, which were quickly sold in the market. Old low-rise buildings were replaced with high-rise buildings with a highway running down the middle. This project was hailed by the administration as the model for the renewal of entire southern Tehran. At the same time, there was a reorganization of municipal management towards a more devolved distribution of powers, to enable district municipalities to take a stronger role in decision-making about their areas.

The policy of value capture continues to this day in one form or another, and has been adopted by other cities. It was not introduced as a tax, but a flexible negotiated settlement, which has, nevertheless, become more systematized and institutionalized, and the city is constantly under pressure to reduce it in size and proportion. Today it is based on a standard density of 1.2 floor area ratio (FAR) for the city as a whole, to which additional costs are added for additional density, often in the form of additional floors. It is calculated on the basis of a complicated formula, published by the Municipality, in which location in the city, width of the adjacent road, building height, land value, size of development, construction materials, and type of land use are taken into account. By a rough estimate, it amounts to 5 or 6% of the price of a new apartment.

To help with the regeneration of run-down areas, some bonuses in designated areas are provided to help with the assembly of adjacent sites and developing multi-story buildings. The provision of parking is also subject to these calculations: all new developments are expected to include adequate off-road parking spaces, but if adequate parking is not provided, it can be compensated for by additional charges.

As density selling rides on the cycles of building boom, it is not a sustainable source of income for the municipality. With the fluctuations in oil revenue that followed the international financial crisis in 2008 and the closely associated fluctuations in the development industry, Tehran municipality is facing financial problems. Furthermore, in granting development permission, the city did not pay enough attention to planning considerations such as the availability of support services, or impacts on neighbors or on urban infrastructure. Tall buildings were built in narrow roads, with no regard for the impact that their development might have on neighboring areas.

Densification and a preference for tall buildings date from before the revolution. But it was in the 1990s that these policies were expanded to large parts of the city. Value capture also generated large amounts of money, which brought accusations of embezzlement. The mayor of Tehran was put on a controversial trial and jailed, even though he was later pardoned. The mayor's downfall was interpreted not as the result of his wrongdoing, but of political clashes between reformists and conservatives at all levels of the state.

Discontent with tall building development led to a ban on tall buildings and a limit of five stories was imposed on new development in Tehran. This measure led to a flight of capital to other urban areas, resulting in a slowdown in the development industry in Tehran and a building boom in other parts of the country. Regional capitals, envious of the tall buildings in Tehran wanted their own share of the building boom, and some introduced their own density-selling schemes. This created considerable tensions, especially in historic cities such as Isfahan, where a battle between conservation and development has played out for several years. Development capital also moved to the coastal regions of the Caspian Sea, where in a short period of time, within an under-regulated planning environment, much of the agricultural area of this green region was paved over for holiday villas for the Tehrani middle class. Investment also went to neighboring countries in the Persian Gulf; in particular, Iranian capital has played a considerable role in the development of new housing in Dubai.

The new comprehensive plan expresses caution about further densification, because it attracts more people to the city, rather than providing appropriate services to the existing population. As the aim of the plan is to limit the growth of the city's population, it includes stricter density controls. The plan proposes to stabilize the urban density to about 120 persons per hectare (8.6 million people within the current boundaries is envisaged to be the maximum carrying capacity of the city), and a FAR of 1.2 in residential areas across the city to keep density under control (Boum Sazegan 2006). Some have argued, however, that compared to cities such as Paris, Tehran's density is still not high enough, and it should be allowed to increase further (Habibi and Hourcade 2005).

The notion of controlling the city's population through setting density limits within a strict administrative boundary goes back to Tehran's first comprehensive plan, and it had little success at the time. The failure was partly due to the revolutionary period's disruption, but also, more fundamentally, to the limitation of the plan's tools and the local government's ability to enforce it. This is also the case for the new plan. As the demand for land has intensified in a city sandwiched between deserts and mountains, the building form has changed in response, accommodating more people in the same amount of space. Furthermore, the city's main growth has taken place beyond these boundaries, where Tehran municipality cannot reach, and where smaller municipalities positively encourage expansion and development. As a result, the urban region as a whole continues to grow, and setting population limits may only be a target for municipal service delivery, rather than a reflection of reality. The policy could well be ineffective, as well as exclusionary.

Meanwhile the cost of housing is so high that living in the city is becoming unaffordable for many young residents. Luxury apartments at up to $18,000 U.S. per square meter have been reported in the city. The government's policy for affordable housing is the promotion of mass production and new towns. New towns were part of the growth management strategy for Tehran and other large cities in the country. Five new towns were introduced in the 1990s, which have been partly developed by now. But their distance from the city is such that they have not been found attractive by potential residents. The prospect of long-distance commuting to the city has meant that new towns have not met their population targets, and therefore they have had a limited impact on the growth of population and density in the city.

4.8 Conclusion

The historic pattern of development in Tehran has created a fragmented urban fabric, spreading in all possible directions, resulting in a congested, polluted, socially polarized, and resource-consuming metropolis. Several factors, such as the mixed pattern of land use, investment in rapid transit and subsidies for buses, and the drive for higher densities may lead to improvements. But at present, with inadequate public transport and continued growth beyond municipal boundaries, Tehran's governance and planning processes are not well equipped to address the environmental risks that face the city. Addressing the problems of sustainable development, such as air pollution, earthquake risks, growth management, building quality control, and social inequality, all require a more strategic governance arrangement in the metropolitan region, and a stronger and more democratically accountable municipality. Some city officials and other stakeholders readily admit some of these shortcomings, such as the limits to city boundaries and the absence of a regional approach to governance, the lack of sufficient attention to the demands of sustainable development, or the needs for further democratization of the city's governance. With the new master plan for the city, many debates for the future of the city have started, which may help further articulate these concerns.

References

Abercrombie P (1945) Greater London Plan 1944. HMSO, London

Abrahamian E (1982) Iran between two revolutions. Princeton University Press, Princeton, NJ

Boum Sazegan Consultants (2006) Tarhe Jame Tehran 1385 (Tehran comprehensive plan 2006). Tehran Municipality, Tehran

Doxiadis Associates International (1972) Iran: Teheran action program. Doxiadis Archives, Athens

Farmanfarmaian A, Gruen V (1968) Tarh-e Jame-e Tehran. Sazman-e Barnameh va Budgeh, Tehran

Gruen V (1964) The heart of our cities. Thames and Hudson, London

Habibi SM, Hourcade B (2005) Atlas of Tehran metropolis. Tehran Geographic Information Centre, Tehran

Hashemi M (2006) Keeping costs low and traffic moving with the Tehran metro extension. Publ Transport Int 4:44–49

Iran DoE (2009) Iran Department of Environment. http://www.irandoe.org/en/. Accessed 13 January 2009

Kariman H (1976) Tehran dar Gozashteh va Hal. Iran's National University Press, Tehran

Lockhart L (1960) Persian cities. Luzac, London

Madanipour A (1998) Tehran: the making of a metropolis. Wiley, Chichester

Madanipour A (2003) Modernization and everyday life: urban and rural change in Iran. In: Mohammadi A (ed) Iran encountering globalization: problems and prospects. RoutledgeCurzon, London, pp 137–148

Madanipour A (2006) Urban planning and development in Tehran. Cities 23(6): 433–438

Madanipour A (2008) Tehrān. In: Encyclopædia Britannica, Encyclopædia Britannica Online. http://www.britannica.com/EBchecked/topic/585619/Tehran. Accessed 28 August 2008

Mumford L (1954) The neighborhood unit. Town Plann Rev 24:256–270

Nafisi A (1964) Shahrdari-e Tehran. In: Masael-e Ejtemai-e Shahr-e Tehran. A colloquium by Institute of Social Research and Study, University of Tehran. Tehran University Press, Tehran, pp 424–434

Safamanesh K (1993) Baft-e tarikhi-e Tehran va nahveh-ye barkhord ba an. Abadi 8(1372):6–17

Tabrizi LR, Madanipour A (2006) Crime and the city: domestic burglary and the built environment in Tehran. Habitat Int 30(4):932–944

Tehran Municipality (1996) Barnameh-ye Avval-e Shahrdari-e Tehran, 'Tehran 80', 1375–1380, Ketab-e Barnameh. Markaz-e Motale'at va Barnamehrizi, Shahrdari-e Tehran, Tehran

Tehran Municipality (2004a) Motaleate Hamlo Naghl va Traffic. Tehran Municipality, Tehran

Tehran Municipality (2004b) Karabarye Arazi. Tehran Municipality, Tehran

Tehran Municipality (2007) Karnameh Sabz (Green Workbook). Environment and Sustainable Development Task Force, Tehran. http://www.tehran.ir/portals/0/other/green_workbook/index.html. Accessed 13 January 2009

Tehran Municipality (2008) Tehran Municipality website. www.tehran.ir/. Accessed 15 April 2008

Nafisi A (1964) Shahedari-e Tehran. In: Masael-e Ejtemai-e Shahr-e Tehran. A colloquium by Institute of Social Research and Study, University of Tehran. Tehran University Press, Tehran, pp 124–184

[illegible]

5. Re-Forming the Megacity: Calcutta and the Rural–Urban Interface*

Ananya Roy

5.1 Introduction

The city of Calcutta (renamed Kolkata in 2001) is a stark manifestation of the stereotype of the Third World megacity. Imagined as a "black hole" of poverty, deprivation, disease, and suffering, Calcutta is seen as the quintessential urban problem, in need of reform and intervention. Such a stereotype rests on two key assumptions. First, it is assumed that the "crisis" of the megacity is synonymous with the crisis of poverty and its concentration in slums, squatter settlements, and other types of urban informality – for example Mike Davis's (2006) apocalyptic narrative of a "planet of slums." Second, such megacities are assumed to be disconnected from systems of global capitalism and thus understood to be "off the map" – this occurs, for example, in the global cities/world cities framework of Sassen (1991) and others (for an important critique of the global cities framework, see Robinson 2002).

In this essay, I call into question such assumptions and thereby seek to "re-form" the idea of the megacity. I argue that far from being "off the map," cities such as Calcutta are integrated into systems of global capitalism, particularly through processes of "reform" (read: liberalization) that have been at work for well over a decade now. The discourses and practices of reform are both indigenous and imposed; together they spin intricate connections between Calcutta and the global economy – from the attempt to

*While the name Calcutta was changed to Kolkata in 2001, I continue to use the Anglicized term in my work. I do so since the city, despite the nativist renaming, is itself a colonial construction, an urban artifact whose founding act is inextricably linked to the founding of the British empire in South Asia.

A. Sorensen and J. Okata (eds.), *Megacities: Urban Form, Governance, and Sustainability*,

model the city as a world-class metropolis to efforts to attract transnational investment. In the case of Calcutta, I also argue that its urban crisis is not so much about the concentration of poverty, although this is in fact a horrific reality, but rather that such a crisis is produced and managed by the very logic of planning and governance in the city. In this sense, Calcutta "re-forms" commonsense readings of Third World megacities. It also "re-forms" common sense understandings of urban sustainability.

The limits of Calcutta's urban growth lie not in its dense slums, which are surprisingly resource-efficient, but rather in the enclave developments at its rural edges. Most significant, these limits are increasingly marked by dissent and struggle, as emergent social movements and political alliances call into question the instruments of planning and governance through which territorial expansion is produced and legitimated. This crisis of legitimacy indicates the ways in which the Third World Megacity is a lively terrain of urban politics where neither outcomes of neoliberalism nor those of social justice are guaranteed. With this framework in mind, I argue that cities such as Calcutta cannot be understood through delineations of its land use; rather they must be understood through the urban politics that shapes the logic of planning.

5.2 Millennial Calcutta

The Calcutta metropolitan area comprises the city of Calcutta, which falls under the jurisdiction of the Kolkata Municipal Corporation (KMC), and several towns and villages under the jurisdiction of various municipalities and local governments. The Kolkata Municipal Corporation, established in 1876, is organized into administrative wards, each with an elected councilor, and governed by a Mayor-in-Council system. The KMC is responsible for the city's infrastructure and urban services. The statutory and development planning of the larger metropolitan region, however, resides in the Calcutta Metropolitan Development Authority (KMDA), which was established in 1970 and granted extensive planning powers by the *West Bengal Town and Country (Planning & Development) Act*, 1979. While the KMC is an elected body and thus shaped by the politics of democratic representation, and while the KMDA is an appointed body and thus somewhat immune from local accountability, they together constitute a rather coherent regime of planning.

In this essay I will focus on this regime of planning, with particular attention to the growth taking place in the peri-urban fringes of the metropolis. To this end, I am more concerned with the regulatory role of the KMDA and less with the KMC's infrastructure provision and management roles. The latter are clearly important, especially in a city that cannot cope with its infrastructure needs; however, it is the former that gives shape and contour to the metropolis and that triggers the question of the possible limits to metropolitan expansion in Calcutta. The analysis that follows focuses on two instances of metropolitan planning: the first is a series of "sweeps" meant to clear the city of informal vendors; the second is a set of planned townships and enclave developments that have dramatically urbanized formerly rural tracts at the edges of the city.

In December 1996, the city of Calcutta witnessed an unusual event. Almost overnight, thousands of informal vendors, known as hawkers, who had long occupied the city's sidewalks were evicted and their stalls demolished. The Left Front regime, the world's longest-serving democratically elected communist government, had lent its support to these hawkers for many years. But suddenly, in a sweep euphemistically nicknamed "Operation Sunshine," Left Front–affiliated government functionaries were eager to eradicate hawking. The move was hailed internationally: *Newsweek* magazine (March 1997) trumpeted that the "world's worst city" was cleaning up its act.

The KMC played a central role in Operation Sunshine. In many ways, this "sweep" was the municipality's first high-profile effort to render informal, even criminal, the very structures of vending and hawking that had long been established features of the city's commercial landscape. But the sweep was also an attempt to recuperate a city of air and light, governed by values of hygiene, order, and beauty. Both official and popular discourses cast the event as a return to *bhadralok* Calcutta. The world *bhadralok* is appropriately polyvalent, meaning not only a distinctive elite with colonial roots but also "gentlemanly." Operation Sunshine was meant to re-establish the "gentleman's city" (Roy 2004).

This attempt to symbolically as well as physically remake the city is not surprising. In the late 1990s, the city was in the first stages of its "reform" period, and Operation Sunshine provided the first glimpse of a New Communism that was eager to prepare the city as a greenfield site for transnational investment, especially that by "non-resident Indians." The effort to territorialize the values of hygiene, order, and beauty revived an older mission of the KMC itself. The corporation, established in colonial times, derived its power from the idea of local self-government that animated colonial governance in British India. The emblem of the corporation, complete with a crown, embodied the sheer fact of colonial rule and the strange paradox of local self-government under conditions of imperial power.

Fig. 5-1. The symbol of the Kolkata Municipal Corporation

In 1961, the corporation adopted a new emblem (Fig. 5-1) with traditional icons of Bengali and Indian identity – from the eight-spoked wheel symbolizing industry and progress, to the Mayurpankshi boat, symbolizing naval trade in ancient Bengal, to the lotus symbolizing beauty and culture. At the top of the emblem are the words "Purosree Bibardhan" in old Bengali script, a phrase that can be translated as the enhancement of the city's well-being. At the center is a hand shooting fire. It is worth noting how the KMC itself describes this particular icon: "A Hand of Fire typifying Purity and High Ideals in the hands of the body politic. It also stands for removal of diseases, filth and tardiness" (http://www.kolkatamycity.com/about_kmc_emblem.asp). The KMC's self-conscious discussion of its own emblem is an interesting glimpse into the symbolic and discursive order of Calcutta's regime of planning.

But Operation Sunshine may have been only a rehearsal for the drama of urban expansion that was to quickly unfold in "millennial" Calcutta. In the last decade, the predominantly rural, eastern perimeter of the metropolis has been rapidly urbanized, mainly through three types of development.

The first are planned townships initiated by state entities such as the West Bengal Housing Board and KMDA. These include Rajarhat, also called New Town, and the East Kolkata and Baishnabghata-Patuli townships.

The older township of Salt Lake City (renamed Bidhan Nagar) serves as a precedent for this type of development.

The second are enclave developments that function as mini-townships and that are either underwritten by private investments or are public–private partnership projects. The latter include the City Centre commercial complex in Salt Lake and the Hiland Park and Udayan condominium housing complexes further south, each of which involved a partnership between the KMDA and a private corporation such as Bengal Ambuja or United Credit Belani Group. Other enclave developments are being wholly financed by private capital, such as the plans by Shriram Properties, partnering with Walton Street Capital and Starwood Capital Group, to build a $1.25-billion township on the site of the former Hindustan Motors plant in Uttarpara. The master plan for this project will be created by the international architectural firm HOK. Such private townships have been facilitated by the central government's granting of permission, in 2002, for 100% foreign direct investment in the development of integrated townships (Sengupta and Tipple 2007: 2013).

The third type of development are housing subdivisions driven by private developers that transform the landscape of wetlands and paddy cultivation into one of dispersed suburbanization. These developments often take place stealthily and involve transactions between sharecroppers with de facto rights to agricultural land, real estate developers, and middle-class urbanites seeking suburban plots of land.

What are the planning instruments and processes that facilitate, shape, and manage such processes of urban expansion? The role of the KMDA is obviously crucial. Indeed, the KMDA presents itself as "the agency of city planning," claiming that "it sculpts new areas and townships, develops physical infrastructure as well as provides basic services like water, drainage, and waste management" (http://www.cmdaonline.com/profile.html). The instruments used to "sculpt" the metropolitan landscape are those of land-use planning such as Land Use Development Control Plans that delineate development control zones. The KMDA also prepares "perspective plans", the most recent one titled "VISION-2025." This plan starts with the premise that "Kolkata's long history as a colonial city, and its unplanned growth over the centuries, had resulted in the KMDA inheriting a chaotic civic entity with deteriorating urban environment" (http://www.cmdaonline.com/profile.html). VISION-2025 presents a set of development strategies to manage and reform the metropolis. In addition, the KMDA is the main vehicle for all national and state-level urban policies, such as the Jawaharlal Nehru National Urban Renewal Mission (JNNURM), which will channel infrastructure and services projects worth millions of dollars over the next

5 years to Calcutta. The KMDA also implements and manages various internationally funded development projects, such as the Kolkata Slum Improvement Programme, funded by the Urban Poverty Office of DFID, and the Kolkata Urban Development Programme, funded by the World Bank.

But the "plan" as an instrument of metropolitan change is only one piece of the story. It is thus important to make the case for an analysis of planning that transcends land-use concerns as well as the formal plan. For example, Krueckeberg (1995) has argued that while land use is a central concept in planning, the issue of property deserves equal attention. He notes that by focusing on the utilitarian question of where things belong, planners forget to ask *to whom* things belong. In the case of Calcutta, it is necessary to therefore turn to the political logic of its planning regime, which can be designated as "informality."

Informality is commonly understood as a sphere of unregulated activities that exists outside the formal order of urbanization. While most scholars acknowledge that informal work and housing are governed by norms and rules, they designate such frameworks of governance as "extra-legal," emerging as a response to the bureaucratic restrictions of the planned processes of state regulation (see, for example, de Soto 1989, 66). I argue that such a contrast between planned formality and unplanned informality, between a legal, formal order and an extra-legal order, does not hold in a city such as Calcutta. Instead I interpret informality as a mode of urbanization and planning involving a system of both land acquisition and regulation. Building on the arguments laid out in Roy (2003) and Roy and AlSayyad (2004), I emphasize that informality does not exist in a bounded sector that lies outside the formal and the legal; rather it exists at the very heart of sovereignty and is a key instrument of state power.

Such a conceptualization leads to the argument that instead of drawing a distinction between what is formal and what is informal, it may be more useful to see the formal as itself marked by illegality, ambiguity, and exceptionality. The formal plan then is nothing more than a shadow cast on a screen; it is real, but its reality is more fluid and illusory than we tend to believe. In the case of Calcutta, the question to then ask is how such forms of informality establish both the premise and limits of urban growth and expansion, especially at the peri-urban fringes of the metropolitan region. Here is a glimpse of this process.

From Operation Sunshine to the planned townships at the edges of the city, millennial Calcutta presents itself as the antithesis to chaotic, informal urbanization. The "reform" of Calcutta through liberalization is meant to establish a "gentleman's city" as an explicit counterpoint to the popular and vernacular city. And yet such urban development is itself facilitated through a volatility and violence that reveals the manner in which the formal city is in fact deeply informalized, its rules and norms arbitrary and fickle. There are, of course, official instruments of planning at work, for example "vesting" – the means by which the state can appropriate private land either in the public interest or in keeping with various land ceiling regulations, including the *Urban Land Ceiling Act*. This act, which is being repealed in many Indian states, imposed a ceiling on vacant parcels over a certain size in India's large cities and empowered the state to acquire land in excess of the ceiling. Such instruments of vesting take on peculiar potency in a metropolitan region that, in earlier work, I have characterized as "unmapped" (Roy 2003). By this I mean a context of planning marked by the absence of centralized, agreed-upon, and knowable land records, an absence that makes it impossible to fix land ownership and thus land appropriation and transfer.

While "unmapping" may seem to indicate a failure of planning, a profound lack of rationality, it is better understood as a productive force, one that produces a distinctive sort of planning and state power. It is "unmapping" that gives the state territorialized flexibility to implement populist or developmentalist projects. Thus, in the 1970s and 1980s, the Left Front settled the agricultural land of the eastern fringes of Calcutta with sharecroppers, squatters, and resettled slum-dwellers. This settlement took place through land invasions, or "extra-judicial" processes of vesting – the informal appropriation and deployment of the formal instrument of the state. In the late 1990s, with a new imperative afoot, the Left Front embarked on a process of displacement, evicting these occupants to make way for townships, condominium complexes, and suburban homes. The earlier round of "vesting" was declared illegal (even though it had been undertaken by the same political apparatus) and a new round of "vesting" was launched in the name of public purpose – this time, suburban development.

Such a transition cannot be understood as a shift from informal urbanization to formal urban development. Rather the settling of the eastern edges of Calcutta through the distribution of de facto land rights is a central component of the sovereign power of the Left Front government; this "extra-judicial" history is indeed the history of the state in the Calcutta metropolitan region. In a similar vein, rendering these de facto rights informal and illegal in the late 1990s marks a new political moment in which the Left Front has sought to establish alliances with the urban middle class, that "gentlemanly" elite which longs for a city of hygiene and order. And the new urban developments on the eastern fringes can themselves be considered informal subdivisions, with many of them violating planning bans on the conversion of agricultural land into urban uses.

Here then is a space of exception created by the sovereign power of the state, a territorialized flexibility that allows the state to create value. Theorists have long talked about how the state deploys power through the technologies of mapping, zoning, and planning. But in Calcutta, the territorialized flexibility of the estate is made possible through the unique regulatory regime of "unmapping," whereby the ownership and status of land in the peri-urban fringes are maintained in a state of constant uncertainty and negotiability. This is an important issue, because it means that we cannot think about these urban processes as ones in which an informal sector is regulated and managed by the state; rather, the state *itself* is deeply informalized. The major axis of differentiation then lies not between what is formal and informal, but rather within informality: how some forms of informality are legalized and utilized by the state while others are criminalized and disciplined.

The major story about Indian peri-urbanization is how and why informal elite subdivisions are celebrated as a new global India, while slums and squatter settlements are vilified. This, of course, is the politics of class. But it is also the functioning of informality as a mode of the production of space. Informality produces an uneven geography of spatial value, thereby facilitating urban development. In Indian cities, with the consolidation of neoliberalism, there has also been a "privatization of informality." While informality was once primarily associated with public land and practiced in public space, it is today a crucial mechanism in wholly privatized and marketized urban formations. It is this territorialized flexibility, rather than the statutory powers of the KMDA, that has made possible the expansion of the Calcutta metropolitan region and the consolidation of a New Communism.

The story is not unique to Calcutta. In many other Indian cities, including Delhi and Bangalore, the peri-urban edge is the most active frontier of urban development, a space where squatter settlements, paddy cultivation, and new gated enclaves abut one another. In the last decade, the urbanization of these rural fringes has proceeded with brazen speed. Farmland has been rapidly converted into residential subdivisions, shopping malls, and entertainment complexes to ensure the production of the bourgeois city. At the same time, Indian cities have deployed aggressive strategies of slum demolition, criminalizing the poor and evicting squatters. The result is not unlike what Graham and Marvin (2001) designate as "splintering urbanism" or what Benjamin (2000), in his work on Bangalore, designates as the division between "local" and "corporate" economies – a dense terrain of slum economies contrasted with the private enclaves of global industry, with highly differentiated access to urban infrastructure and resources.

This enclave urbanism has a near-exclusive focus on middle-class and high-end urban development, much of it catering to "non-resident Indians."

Calcutta's insertion into the global economy of the late twentieth century took place not through industrial, financial, or technological capital, but through property capital, and a distinctively transnational type of property capital at that – what Bose (2008) calls "diasporic capital." Despite the emergence of an information technology sector in Calcutta, the growth of the metropolis is driven by real-estate developments and speculations. This is a raw and often brutal manifestation of a Lefebvrian (1974) "production of space," in which space is both a commodity and a means of production. In order to reverse the region's history of deindustrialization and capital flight, the Left Front's New Economic Policy has placed its bets on urban real estate. Planning priorities have also been reworked to fit this agenda, with a jump in metropolitan expenditures on housing and new area developments and cuts to expenditures on slum redevelopment (Chakravorty and Gupta 1996; Shaw 2005). But will this approach be enough to build a solid economic base for the region? And whose city will this be?

It is obvious that in such urban calculations the city's poor remain marginalized and neglected. The influx of property capital has yielded only the most informalized and casualized jobs for the city's poor, such as construction work and domestic service. And in millennial Calcutta, the flurry of housing developments has bypassed the city's low-income and poor households. While the public–private partnerships involve cross-subsidy schemes meant to provide housing to LIG and MIG (Low-Income and Middle-Income) social groups, Sengupta (2006) and Sengupta and Tipple (2007) conclude that low-income households, while making up 80% of the city's population, are rarely served in the various township developments that have emerged. Indeed, Sengupta (2006) is right to characterize the situation as one of liberalizing reform where there is a "privatization" of public housing in Calcutta. The "mass housing" of the fringes has turned out to be a "bourgeois landscape of aestheticized gentrification" (Roy 2003, 156).

But once again, this situation cannot be read as a failure of planning or lack of planning. There is in fact a well-articulated logic of planning at work here. The Left Front has not simply sponsored development that excludes the poor. In an even bolder move, it has strategically capitalized on the context of "unmapping" to render informal and illegal the claims of squatters to EWS and LIG (Economically Weak Section and Low-Income Group) housing, as in the case of the Patuli housing colony. Here, in 1996, the Left displaced poor squatters – who met the social criteria for this housing – and waged a vigorous struggle to make this highly subsidized housing available to middle-class families, who did not necessarily need the subsidies and who clearly did not fit the criteria of either EWS or LIG beneficiaries. Since then Patuli has become a suburban extension of the "gentleman's city," one enabled by a series of state strategies.

5.3 The Politics of the Mega-City

The terrain of metropolitan expansion is a contested one. I am particularly interested in how the moment of "reform" (read: liberalization) in Indian cities is marked by fierce dissent. Indeed, it can be argued that the question of democracy in India is now entangled with the urban question, and that it is vitally important to examine the possibilities and impossibilities of citizenship and belonging in Indian cities – even though the majority of Indians still live in the countryside and are dependent on agriculture.

The story of Calcutta, for example, is inevitably a story of the rural–urban interface where the rural poor migrate from the region's villages and make a difficult living in the city as domestic servants and day laborers, squatting in peripheral spaces. In the 1990s, such rural–urban movements took on a more intense form with the daily commuting of poor women from villages to the city on crowded local trains, a daily commute against hunger and rural deprivation. Dubbed the "automatic washing machines," these women are the laboring bodies that reproduce the everyday routines of the city. These moving and migrating bodies are part of a larger socio-economic structure that can be understood as the "feminization of livelihood" (Roy 2003).

In a context of deindustrialization and economic restructuring, with growing male unemployment and underemployment, women have become the primary earners in poor households. At the same time, these sectors of employment, such as domestic service, have become increasingly casualized and informalized. As Breman (2003: 4354), notes, these migrants and commuters "have left the village but whether they have arrived at the city is a debatable issue … they are kept in a footloose condition on the outskirts of the metropolis." This "footloose condition" – between city and countryside and in the city – marks the territorialized vulnerability of the rural–urban poor. These trends are not unique to Calcutta. Scholars, particularly in the Latin American context, have charted the formation of a "new urban marginality," a "hyper-shantytown" characterized by deproletarianization and labor informalization (Auyero 2000; Perlman 2003; Wacquant 2007).

In the face of such marginality, it is worth asking: should not such a city be exploding in a politics of resistance? Urban politics, of course, is not simply the politics of the poor. One of the most striking features of Indian urbanism is the emergence of the forms and structures of middle-class politics. Framed as "good governance," these self-organized initiatives seek to reform government, improve service delivery, and assert the rights and needs of middle-class neighborhoods. Many of them are "protection of place" associations that initiate and mobilize evictions and the demolition of slums and squatter settlements. Amita Baviskar, in the context of

Delhi, has rightly labeled these forms of urban democracy a "bourgeois environmentalism," one that asserts the rights of "consumer-citizens" to "leisure, safety, aesthetics, and health" and thereby devalorizes the citizenship of those who are poor and propertyless.

But the politics of the poor is also a complex configuration of patronage and clientelism. In the case of Calcutta, urban politics has usually taken the form of populism, whereby squatters and slum-dwellers are able to establish tenuous access to land, livelihood, and shelter. However, they are rarely able to convert this tenuous access into a secure and permanent right to the city. A key feature of urban populism is the manner in which the informalized poor are constantly sorted and resorted into groups of beneficiaries and non-beneficiaries, a political logic that is uncertain and arbitrary in the way that it manufactures loyalty and consent. In Calcutta, such forms of urban populism are mediated through structures of "marginalized masculinity" – poor men who reinscribe their powerlessness and power as clients of patronage (Roy 2003). In this way, through home and community, political consent is reproduced on an everyday basis in the geography of Calcutta's informal settlements.

In recent years, a new politics seems to be emerging in Indian cities, a radical rather than populist mobilization of the poor. Thus, there is now considerable optimism about urban politics in India and what may be seen as "insurgent citizenship," to borrow a phrase from Holston's (2007) work on Brazil. Inspired by the self-organizing logic of slum-dwellers and organizations of poor women, Appadurai (2002) argues that the politics of informality is "deep democracy," the remaking of the rules and norms of citizenship from below. Similarly, Chatterjee (2004) makes a distinction between "civil" and "political" societies. Civil society is bourgeois society and in the Indian context, an arena of institutions and practices inhabited by a relatively small group of people able to make claims as fully enfranchised citizens. By contrast, political society is the constellation of claims made by those who are only tenuously and ambiguously right-bearing citizens. The "paralegal" practices and negotiations of this political society are for Chatterjee the politics of many people in most of the world.

> The paralegal then, despite its ambiguous and supplementary status in relation to the legal, is not some pathological condition of retarded modernity, but rather part of the very process of the historical constitution of modernity in most of the world.

In other words, the very forces that have converged to set the stage for a harsh moment in Indian urbanism (the criminalization of the urban poor; the imagining of Indian cities as global cities; the bourgeois claim to clean, green, and beautiful spaces) have also unleashed social movements and protest. For example, in the winter of 2004–2005, Mumbai city authorities put into motion "Vision Mumbai," the bold report of the global consulting firm, McKinsey and Company, promoted by an elite NGO, Bombay First. Seeking to remake Mumbai as the next Shanghai, the state violently demolished long-standing slums, instantly rendering 300,000 people homeless. The demolitions came to be known as the "Indian tsunami" and were condemned as a human rights disaster by international authorities (Roy 2009). While NGOs such as SPARC (Society for the Promotion of Resource Centres) had once made the case for "demolitions to dialogue," they were now confronted with an unprecedented scale and intensity of erasure and violence.

But the demolitions sparked a different politics. The National Alliance of People's Movements (NAPM), led by Medha Patkar and other Narmada Dam activists, organized evicted slum-dwellers around the idea of "struggle." Diagnosing Vision Mumbai as yet another expression of "imperialist globalisation based on neoliberalism," the movement sought to counter the persistent forms of displacement through which frontiers of accumulation are forged. NAPM framed the "Shanghaification of Mumbai" as primarily an issue of rights, in particular, whether the urban–rural poor have a "right over urban space" (Patkar and Athialy 2005): "In Mumbai, 60% live in the slums. Shouldn't they have a right over 60% of the land in Mumbai?"

Perhaps the most prominent struggle has been at the far edges of Calcutta's metropolitan orbit. At two sites, Singur and Nandigram, peasants, sharecroppers, and squatters have refused to make way for the Left Front's development projects. The Left Front has deployed violent means to enact a Special Economic Zone in the village of Nandigram, to house a chemical industry complex supported by Indonesian investors. The plight of the peasant rebellion has captured national and international attention. In Calcutta, a cultural elite shocked at the left's use of violence against the rural poor, has turned suspicious of New Communism, and taken to marching in the streets against the Left Front, returning medals and awards, and holding public hearings.

The Nandigram struggle has become a symbol of a much broader struggle against the spatial instruments of neoliberal development: eminent domain, special economic zones, land acquisition, displacement. It represents a rejection of "Chinese-style development" and a repudiation of India's efforts to benchmark its progress in relation to other Asian "miracle" economies. In particular, it has become a cause of struggle against the state, for such "public-purpose" projects require more of the state than simply the acquisition of land. In the case of Special Economic Zones, the state creates zones of exception (Ong 2006), suspending laws and creating exceptional benefits for corporate investors. The exceptional nature of such exceptions have suddenly become starkly visible.

The violence of the state in Nandigram is neither new nor unique. Its precedents lie in the eastern fringes of Calcutta, and in the frontier of development that has been carved out here for the last decade. The peasant rebellion in Nandigram and the formation of the Bhoomi Uchchhed Pratirodh Committee (Committee to Resist Displacement) is supported by the opposition party, the Trinamul Congress, led by Mamata Banerjee. In elections held in May 2008, the Left Front suffered defeat in the state districts most affected by the politics of land acquisition and displacement for development projects. This, too, is not new. In 1996, as the Left Front set out to displace squatters and sharecroppers from the eastern fringes of the city, the Trinamul Congress established its political legitimacy by mobilizing the rural–urban poor. This frontier politics shaped the rise of the Trinamul Congress as a national political force; Nandigram is simply the maturation of such struggles, although it seems to be remaking the political map of West Bengal in unprecedented fashion.

Commenting on the recent victories in the districts of East Midnapore and South 24-Parganas, opposition leader Mamata Banerjee argued that the results were a "mandate against state-sponsored terrorism" and that the people had voiced their protests against the move to "grab farmland from the poor in the name of industrialization" (*Telegraph*, May 22, 2008). Can we read this statement as the politics of resistance, that which seeks to reform the reformed Third World megacity? The story is, in fact, more complex and returns us to the practices of informality.

A recent article published in the Calcutta newspaper, the *Telegraph* (Siddiqui 2008), notes that while the Trinamul Congress has been resisting the displacement of peasants in Nandigram, it has also been grabbing land in Calcutta. At issue is a plot of land owned by a transnational Indian. The land borders a Trinamul-run neighborhood "club," and Trinamul party bosses insist that they require use of the land for various party activities. Such neighborhood clubs are important nodes in the political infrastructure of West Bengal, where political parties establish their credentials as patrons and mark the territory of their influence. There are three elements to the competing claims of the landowner and the Trinamul Congress. First, the current owner's father had bought the property a few months after India's independence. In 1976, through the act of "vesting," the state government acquired two-thirds of this land under the *Urban Land Ceiling Act*. In 1996, with the death of her father, the current owner applied for and received the mutation certification (recording the change in the ownership and title of the land) from the KMC for the remaining piece of land. Second, for all of this time the property was unoccupied, allowing the Trinamul Congress to make a moral claim in favor of occupying vacant land; in other words, an argument about adverse possession. The current owner was warned that any efforts to reclaim the land would lead to a "Nandigram." Finally, a senior Trinamul Congress leader and MLA interviewed about the matter argued the following: "It's right that the local people have occupied her vacant land, but she is not our voter and we don't want to antagonise so many refugees for her sake. This is not a public interest matter."

I provide the details of this particular land dispute because it makes visible the political logic of urbanization in Calcutta. It is a logic of patronage and one that crafts a complex cartography of zones of exception. It is impossible to fix what is formal and what is informal, for the law itself is rendered ambiguous, fluid, and open to multiple interpretations. While the struggles to resist displacement are significant, they do not necessarily alter this logic. Indeed, they may even strengthen it.

5.4 Re-Forming the Megacity

The "urbanization of neoliberalism" (Brenner and Theodore 2002) is an important feature of *fin-de-millenaire* development. The metropolis is an important site for the consolidation of various circuits of capital, from finance capital to property capital. At the same time, cities in different world-regions are indelibly shaped by neoliberal agendas of entrepreneurial planning, gentrification, public–private development projects, and the privatization of infrastructure. In keeping with broader discourses of liberalization, these neoliberal transformations have commonly been billed as "reform," as is the case with Indian cities. Such "reform" is made possible by the aggressive role of the state in sponsoring and subsidizing urban development, and by transnational investors and "diasporic capital." It is also extended through the material and discursive role of international development institutions that seek to reform, upgrade, and improve megacities.

For example, in the case of Calcutta, various development institutions ranging from the World Bank to DFID (UK Department for International Development) to the Asian Development Bank have funded environmental improvement, capacity-building, and governance initiatives. This essay has argued that the implementation of "reform" in Calcutta has to be understood in light of the political logic of urbanization. This logic pervades the informalized rationality of the state as well as the dissent and protests unleashed by state action. It is productive in that it produces development, albeit through displacement and violence; but it is also paralyzing in that it locks urban futures into an endgame of land grabs and renders land-use calculations irrelevant and irrational.

Cities such as Calcutta thus re-form the very concept of the Third World megacity. The challenge of this megacity lies not in its population density or its shortage of resources or its planning bureaucracy or its infrastructure shortfalls. A better plan will not address the key issues at stake in Calcutta. Calcutta's challenge lies in the very logic that drives its growth and gives shape to its metropolitan form. It is a logic that allows the poor to survive through access to a meager and diminished structure of substantive citizenship – informalized and casualized wage-earning labor at the margins of the global economy and fragile and tenuous shelter at the margins of the metropolis. (For the poor, this fate may be better than the one they would face by remaining in India's countryside, where the agrarian crisis looms large. And it is possibly a better fate than that of the poor in so-called global cities that have successfully criminalized the informal practices of the poor, such as the criminalization of the homeless in North American cities.)

It is also a planning logic that produces a dis-integrated city. The irony is that both the public and private new townships of Calcutta boldly proclaim that they are world-class "integrated" townships. But this particular planning vocabulary refers to the integration of uses and services within each township, not across the metropolitan region. While these townships are created in the name of the public interest, and often through processes of displacement and land acquisition that invoke this public purpose, their spatial logic is that of secessionary enclaves rather than that of integrated infrastructure.

It is worth asking whether cities were ever defined by integration or whether they have always been splintered and fractured spaces. Clearly Calcutta's colonial history, with its sharp division of White Town and Black Town, gives the lie to any nostalgic referencing of a unified public infrastructure undertaken in the name of a singular public interest. But the current geography of enclave urbanism is significant because it calls into question the anxieties that are often expressed about Third World megacities. Calcutta's planning challenge does not lie in its landscape of slums, which seemingly remains outside the formal, legal order and defies state regulation. Rather, it lies in planning itself, in a ruling regime that unmaps the city and renders ambiguous legal systems of property and territory. Calcutta's frontier of urban development is driven by an informalized state that can undermine or sidestep its own edicts. In other words, the state, as sovereign power and keeper of the law, can declare an exception to the law.

Dasgupta (2007: 324–325) notes that in the eastern fringes of Calcutta, the state government has rarely followed its own proclaimed policies (notably the *Town and Country Planning Act* of 1979) of protecting agricultural land and wetlands. Similarly, in Delhi, Baviskar (2003: 92) shows how, in the 1980s, with economic liberalization, the Delhi Development Authority facilitated the development of Delhi's fringes, often transferring land to cooperatives of urban professionals. Equally important is the issue that the citizens on whose behalf such measures are being taken are often non-resident Indians. As Bose (2007) has argued, with liberalization, the Indian nation-state has been paying particular attention to the "Global Indian." The luxury enclaves on the fringes of Indian cities such as Calcutta are part of global property markets where both the developers and buyers are transnational elites. What then are governance and politics in such a city?

In such a city it is possible to negotiate – work, housing, services, political power, but is it possible to be secure? In such a city it is possible to gain access to resources, but is it possible not to lose access to resources? In such a city the law can be challenged, but can the law protect? In such a city it is possible to survive, but is it possible to thrive?

References

Appadurai A (2002) Deep democracy: urban governmentality and the horizon of politics. Publ Cult 14(1):21–47

Auyero J (2000) The hyper-shantytown: neoliberal violence(s) in the Argentine slum. Ethnography 1:93–116

Baviskar A (2003) Between violence and desire: space, power, and identity in the making of metropolitan Delhi. Int Soc Sci J 55(175):89–98

Benjamin S (2000) Governance, economic settings, and poverty in Bangalore. Environ Urban 12(1):35–56

Bose P (2007) Dreaming of diasporas: urban developments and transnational identities in contemporary Kolkata. Topia 17:111–130

Bose P (2008) Home and away: diasporas, developments, and displacements in a globalizing world. J Intercult Stud 29(1):111–131

Breman J (2003) At the bottom of the urban economy. Econ Polit Wkly 38(39): 4151–4158

Brenner N, Theodore N (2002) Cities and the geographies of 'actually existing neoliberalism. Antipode 34(3):349–379

Chakravorty S, Gupta G (1996) Let a hundred projects bloom: structural reform and urban development in Calcutta. Third World Plann Rev 18:415–431

Chatterjee P (2004) The politics of the governed: reflections on popular politics in most of the world. Columbia University Press, New York

Dasgupta K (2007) A city divided? Planning and urban sprawl in the eastern fringes of Calcutta. In: Shaw A (ed) Indian cities in transition. Orient Longman, New Delhi

Davis M (2006) Planet of slums. Verso, New York
De Soto H (1989) The other path: the invisible revolution in the Third World. I.B. Taurus, London
Graham S, Marvin S (2001) Splintering urbanism: networked infrastructures, technological mobilities, and the urban condition. Routledge, London
Holston J (2007) Insurgent citizenship: disjunctions of democracy and modernity in Brazil. Princeton University Press, Princeton
Krueckeberg D (1995) The difficult character of property. J Am Plann Assoc 61(3): 301–309
Lefebvre H (1991) The production of space. Basil Blackwell, New York
Ong A (2006) Neoliberalism as exception: mutations in citizenship and sovereignty. Duke University Press, Durham
Patkar M, Athialy J (2005) The Shanghaification of Mumbai. Countercurrents.org. http://www.countercurrents.org/hr-athialy110805.htm. Accessed January 15, 2008
Perlman J (2003) Marginality: from myth to reality in the favelas of Rio de Janeiro. In: Roy A, AlSayyad N (eds) Urban informality: transnational perspectives from the Middle East, Latin America, and South Asia. Lexington Books, Lanham
Robinson J (2002) Global and world cities: a view from off the map. Int J Urban Reg Res 26(3):531–554
Roy A (2003) City requiem, Calcutta: gender and the politics of poverty. University of Minnesota Press, Minneapolis
Roy A (2004) The gentleman's city. In: Roy A, AlSayyad N (eds) Urban informality: transnational perspectives from the Middle East, Latin America, and South Asia. Lexington Books, Lanham
Roy A (2009) Civic governmentality: the politics of inclusion in Mumbai and Beirut. Antipode 41(1):159–179
Roy A, AlSayyad N (eds) (2004) Urban informality: transnational perspectives from the Middle East, Latin America, and South Asia. Lexington Books, Lanham
Sassen S (1991) The global city: New York, London, Tokyo. Princeton University Press, Princeton
Sengupta U (2006) Liberalization and the privatization of public rental housing in Kolkata. Cities 23(4):269–278. doi:10.1016/j.cities.2006.01.003
Sengupta U, Tipple AG (2007) The performance of public-sector housing in Kolkata, India, in the post-reform milieu. Urban Stud 44(10):2009–2027
Shaw A (2005) Peri-urban interface of Indian cities: growth, governance and local initiatives. Econ Polit Wkly 40:129–136
Siddiqui IA (2008) Land grab in Nandigram's name, law be damned. The Telegraph, April 2
The Telegraph (2008) Bargain Chips for Mamata. http://www.telegraphindia.com/1080522/jsp/siliguri/story_9304657.jsp
Wacquant L (2007) Urban outcasts: a comparative sociology of advanced marginality. Polity, Cambridge

6. Landscapes of Water in Delhi: Negotiating Global Norms and Local Cultures

Jyoti Hosagrahar

6.1 Introduction

Today more than half of the world's population lives in cities. With anticipated increases in urbanization in Asia and Africa, addressing the growing needs of water and sanitation in cities has become one of the most urgent and pressing issues in urban sustainability. As the megacities of the world are home to such a large proportion of the urban population, the issue of water is particularly acute. Given the magnitude and complexity of the water question, this chapter focuses on water as one significant aspect of urban sustainability in megacities.

International organizations and development specialists have identified the main issue as the widening gap between the demand for and the supply of water and sanitation services (UN/WWAP 2003). Experts have identified overexploitation of water sources especially groundwater, pollution, and health outcomes as some of the most significant concerns (UN/WWAP 2003). Furthermore, recognition of the relationship between poverty, slums, water, and sanitation has led to international targets integrated into the UN Millennium Development Goals. The objective, as stated, is to reduce by half, by 2015, the proportion of people without sustainable access to safe drinking water.[1]

Recent scholarship on and interventions into the management of urban water have addressed everything from technologies of purification and delivery to the technologies of saving and storing water; from the economics of penalizing industrial polluters to the pricing of water. From slums

[1]One of the targets in the Millennium Development Goals states: "Halve, by 2015, the proportion of the population without sustainable access to safe drinking water and basic sanitation."

A. Sorensen and J. Okata (eds.), *Megacities: Urban Form, Governance, and Sustainability*,

to sanitation, water is problematized as a commodity to be manufactured, distributed, and used. These different threads are useful and necessary to discussions of urban sustainability. However, I seek to contribute to discussions of water and urban sustainability by investigating the historical antecedents of the contemporary "water problem." In this chapter, I offer a reading of the cultural landscape of one megacity with a view to examining the underlying biases in the discourse on water. My premise is that a particular view of modernity has framed contemporary approaches and interventions.

Delhi, located on the banks of the River Yamuna, was established more than 2,000 years ago. According to Hindu mythology, Yamuna was a river that fell from heaven to earth. Today, Delhi is India's second-largest metropolis after Mumbai. It has a population of more than 16 million, and has increased by 52% in just a decade.[2] Delhi is one of the oldest cities in the world that has been continuously inhabited. Capital of several empires from ancient to modern times, the site of numerous historical monuments and archaeological sites, Delhi contains both a historic walled city and the seat of government in New Delhi. Today, the National Capital Region of Delhi, the second largest commercial center in South Asia after Mumbai, extends across three states, and includes several major satellite towns and 165 villages.

Delhi also faces an acute water crisis today. The demand for water in 2005–2006 was estimated to have been 963 million gallons per day (mgd) while the water supply managed by the Delhi Jal Board provided for only 650 mgd. Scientists, economists, and policy analysts have been engaged for some time in analyzing and suggesting interventions to solve the urban water crisis in Delhi. The prescriptions have ranged from the World Bank's proposals to privatize water supply with a view to improving the efficiency of the governance of water to microbial analysis to improve the quality of the water treatment (Bosch 2005). The Center for Science and Environment has proposed various methods of water harvesting for individuals and communities to adopt. Yet questions of demand, supply, governance, and water quality have obscured a historical perspective on the transformations in the city's social and spatial relationships to water.

A close look at the city's development from the early eighteenth century to the present reveals enormous changes in the relationships between people, the state, and water in its many dimensions. Like many pre-modern societies, Delhi had local practices of building and settlement planning that were historically rooted and deeply embedded in the culture. But modernity and

[2]The Census of India, 2001, estimated the population at 13.8 million. It was expected to be over 15 million by the end of 2002. The urban population increased by 52% between 1991 and 2001.

colonization dismantled these local knowledges of geography, terrain, and settlement planning through neglect, destruction, and erasure and replaced them with utilitarian interpretations of natural resources and technologically driven approaches for their use. The dilemmas between universal modern globality and unique traditional locality are evident in the transformations in the cultural landscapes of water. Rapid urbanization in the postcolonial period and the most recent phase of globalization has further exacerbated the commodification of natural resources with sprawling swaths of squatter settlements on the one hand and equally vast areas of new "technology parks" for a global communications industry on the other.

The first section of the paper looks at the development of the historic walled city in the seventeenth century, when the pre-modern hydrological landscape included a system of underground canals, surface canals, stepped wells, ponds, tanks, and household wells. The second section examines the transformations under British colonial rule in the nineteenth century with the introduction of piped water supply, water closets, and sanitary engineering. In addition to the engineering skills and funds required to put the new systems in place, these new technologies required a rationalized and efficient legal and administrative apparatus to deliver them. Not only was the knowledge not local, but the institutions and administrative mechanisms they required were also imposed as an import.

The third and fourth sections look at two different post-colonial (post 1947) landscapes of Delhi. The third section focuses on the rapid proliferation of slums and squatter settlements in the city and conflicted efforts by the state and community development agencies to improve water and sanitation provisions for these settlements. The fourth section looks at the recent mushrooming of private townships devoted to global corporate offices and housing for a new generation of global corporate elites. Large-scale development projects such as DLF City or Gurgaon in metropolitan New Delhi, were established on agricultural land and depend heavily on groundwater that is now at a perilous low in the entire urban area of Delhi.

Through a historical perspective on Delhi's development, I identify five key transformations in the cultural landscape of water: (1) the geographies of access, (2) the technologies of extraction and distribution, (3) the socio-economic organization of water, (4) institutional structures and governance mechanisms, and (5) water's symbolic significance. The cultural upheavals of rapid urbanization, modernity, and colonialism in the nineteenth and twentieth centuries brought about displacements in the cultural landscapes of water. Taking a historical approach relocates questions of sustainability from singular and modernist definitions to multiple interpretations that suggest ways of redressing these displacements as a necessary step towards sustainability.

6.2 The Historic Walled City of Shahjahanabad

Delhi has been the site of many cities in its 2,000-year history. The present capital of New Delhi is the eighth city of Delhi. Shahjahanabad, the walled, historic city known today as Old Delhi, was established as a sovereign city of the Mughals in 1638. In the earliest known capital city, and each of the subsequent cities, the rulers made provisions for water supply for the city. In addition to the River Yamuna, some of the elements that characterized the system included canals, *dighi*, *nahar*, *qanat*, ponds, wells, *baoli*, and the layout of the city itself.

Since the twelfth century, *baoli* were significant elements in the cultural landscape of Delhi that supplied ground water to the city. *Baoli* were tanks with steps on four sides leading down to the water. They were secular structures constructed as a way to access groundwater as well as to harvest and store rain water. *Baoli*, which were designed to minimize evaporation, served the dual purpose of offering surface water for drinking as well as recharging underground aquifers. Some had pulley systems in place for drawing water and anyone could access them. Some elaborate *baoli* also had chambers below ground, which served as places to escape from the searing heat of the summer. One of the earliest surviving *baoli* in Delhi is Angtal Baoli near Qutub Minar. Iltutmush is credited with building numerous *baoli* in the thirteenth century, including the Gandhak-ki-Baoli and the Hauz-i-Shamsi. Maulvi Zafar Hasan described the Gandhak-ki-Baoli as being in five tiers. Feroz Shah Tughlaq in particular is credited with constructing many *baoli* and laying out many gardens.

In the fourteenth century, the Tughlaq kings built canals to divert water from the river Yamuna. In moving his capital to Delhi, the Mughal King Shahjahan developed an elaborate system of canals and tanks called *dighi* to bring water to the city from the river. Shahjahan ordered Ali Mardan Khan, an important minister in his court from Persia, to bring the waters of the River Yamuna to the city and his palace. Ali Mardan Khan built a canal that not only brought water from the Yamuna to the palace, but also linked to another canal bringing water from the Sirmaur hills located near present-day Najafghar.[3] Water from the basin of another smaller river, the Sahibi, was also brought to the canal.

The river in Shahjahan's Delhi, as in many pre-modern societies, had aesthetic, social, symbolic, and functional significance. The river served as a defense mechanism (as a moat for the royal fort), a transportation route for goods and travel, a source of fertile alluvial soil from annual flooding,

[3]See www.rainwaterharvesting.org.

a source of fish for the local population, and, most significantly, a source of water for the urban households. *Dhobi* or washermen would go to the river to wash clothes for the urban dwellers. Steps going down to the water formed *ghats* where people could wash, pray, and bathe. Women and men would go to the river at different times for bathing and recreation. Kings and the nobility displayed their benevolence by constructing such places of public convenience. The *baoli*, as well as the *ghats* along the river, served as important community centers where people could gather, socialize, and escape the heat. The river was also a place of spiritual connection and religious deification. The Nigambodh Ghat along the Yamuna remains even today the most significant cremation ground in Delhi and a place for the performance of last rites for many Hindus.

Water from the main canals was channeled into underground *qanat* throughout the city that in turn fed some *nahar* or small channels that were both functional and aesthetic elements of urban design.[4] The royal planners of Delhi laid the main street in an east-west direction to protect it against the hot summer winds from the south. In the seventeenth and eighteenth centuries, the Faiz *nahar* (channel) ran through the two main streets. Lined with stone, it ran all the way from Lahore Gate at the western end of the city through the royal palace on the east, opening up to square or octagonal pools at intervals. To the south, a *nahar* ran down the center of Faiz Bazaar. Water from the Tughlaq canals supplied the Faiz *nahar*, as well as the palaces, mosques and gardens of the city. Water from the *nahar* and the *qanat* pooled into ponds in squares and the private gardens and courtyards. Outside the city wall were green areas used for leisure activities. In addition to gardens within the city, a number of orchards with gardens in their midst ringed the city. Agricultural estates lay between and beyond them (Hosagrahar 2005).

Dighi were square, rectangular, or stepped wells. These were used as reservoirs and people were not allowed to wash or bathe at these, unlike the *ghats* (steps) along the river. Sluice gates were often included as they fed orchards, gardens, or agricultural land. The well-to-do often had their own smaller *dighi* and a large number of houses had wells. *Kahar* or *bhishti* (water carriers) were usually hired to draw water from the public *dighi* and

[4]Samuel Noe has suggested that the canals represented a considerable engineering achievement and that their pattern is central to understanding the form and structure of Shahjahan's Delhi. He also suggests that the entire city was originally designed as a paradise garden in the tradition of Islamic design in medieval Persia. Although one may question his assertion that geometry was the primary determinant of Delhi's form, his analysis is valuable in pointing out the significance of engineering in the layout of Shahjahanadad (Noe 1989).

deliver them to the households. Within the royal palaces and in the mansions of the elite, small pools of water cooled the courtyards and flowed into the baths. Water in the courtyards was an aesthetic as well as cooling element. Sometimes the water trickled from small fountains so that the sound of falling water adding to the aesthetic experience of the courtyards and gardens. The pools of water cooled the spaces around them by evaporation in the hot, dry climate. In the courtyards, the flowing water was also used for washing and ablutions.

During the seventeenth and eighteenth centuries, the houses of the well-to-do consisted of a complex of single- or double-storied structures, open pavilions, and large gardens within a walled compound. The streets formed a web of narrow winding lanes, but the interior of residences contained courtyards, with rooms and pavilions arranged around them. Shady trees and shrubs in the courtyard provided fruit and flowers, and medicinal herbs grew around the water fountain or pond. Humbler dwellings also included small open spaces, and were often arranged around a larger communal open space that might include a well. Temples, neighborhoods, and many individual houses, even the smaller ones, had wells attached to them. The well water was used for drinking and cooking. Neighborhood wells also served as gathering places, especially for women. Hauz Khazi, the second-largest square in the walled city of Delhi (after Chandni Chowk), also had a well which was the principal source of water for the area around.

In 1843, Shahjahanabad had 607 wells. During the summer months when the canals and *dighi* ran dry, the wells were the main source of water. Ponds, *dighi*, and wells also served for rainwater harvesting and storage as well as a means of recharging groundwater. During the latter part of the nineteenth century, officials declared the well water polluted and instituted piped water supply in its place. Today 80% of the wells are closed because the water is contaminated by the sewer system and water in the remaining wells has turned brackish.

6.3 Colonialism and Urban Growth[5]

The British conquered Delhi in 1803 and established imperial rule from 1857 until 1947, when India became an independent republic. This was also the period in which the city expanded and grew vastly beyond the walls.

[5]For a discussion of the integral relationship between modernity and colonialism in Delhi, see Hosagrahar (2005).

Several things happened during the nineteenth and early twentieth centuries to alter dramatically the pre-modern cultural landscape of water in Delhi.

By about the middle of the eighteenth century, it appeared that the desert to the southwest of Delhi was starting to impinge on the city. The water pressure in the Yamuna River dropped and the course of the river also changed somewhat (Prashad 2001). Although the reasons for the drop in the level of water in the Yamuna are not clear, warfare, deforestation, and overcropping, along with extensive felling of hardwoods by the British East India Company, had all brought environmental changes to the region in the eighteenth and early nineteenth centuries (Hill 2008). Political uncertainty and chaos in Delhi during the eighteenth century and loss of the region around Delhi to British rule in the early part of the nineteenth century had together resulted in the neglect of the Shahjahani drains and canals. Without regular maintenance and cleaning, and without the water pressure to flush them out, Shahjahan's elaborate system of canals had started to dry up and the Shahjahani drains had started to resemble cesspools (Prashad 2001).

Despite their decline, the existing hydrological system could have been repaired and made effective once again. When W.H. Greathed, Deputy Superintendent of Delhi Canals in the colonial government, studied the engineering systems existing in the city in 1852, he praised the Shahjahani systems and made a series of recommendations to improve the existing networks of water supply and drainage (Greathed 1852). However, for the British, modernity and progress were intimately related to science. Standing in opposition to religion, myth, superstition, and metaphysics, the British saw science, technology, and medicine as important aspects of their imperial mission to "civilize" other cultures.[6]

The needs of the city were no doubt growing and the available sources diminishing, yet the overwhelming preference for the symbolic value of science influenced the cultural landscape of water in Delhi in several ways. First, existing practices with regard to water were systematically rejected and replaced by new ones. In valorizing the achievements of Western science and technology in shaping the urban landscape, official colonial discourse discounted Indian scientific traditions. European interpretations of modernity demanded a complete rejection of inherited traditions. Furthermore, British colonial rule in northern India during the latter half of the nineteenth century was preoccupied with establishing the superiority of the British Empire over the Mughal. As a consequence, officials chose

[6]Gyan Prakash's and David Arnold's excellent studies on the cultural authority of science and its relationship to colonialism are illuminating on this point. See Prakash (1999) and Arnold (2000).

to replace in entirety the hydrological system in Delhi rather than update existing systems and supplement them with new technologies. Equating modernity with technological achievement drove the British to demonstrate their superiority by opting for the most advanced engineering solutions for the provision of water supply and sanitation, including piped water supply to individual houses and underground sewage systems.

The absence of an integrated approach to water management meant that efforts were focused singularly on finding specific solutions to problems viewed narrowly. Officials favoured scientific calculations and medical rationales, and the documents of the time contain endless specifications about the size of ferules and pipes and so on, but the basis of these specifications are not clear. In addition, water was not available in the expected quantities and systems were not placed evenly across the city. Outside the city, colonial technologies such as weirs, dams, and barrages, oriented towards delivering perennial irrigation for settled agriculture, were, in most instances, not merely incompatible with traditional systems, but aimed at eliminating them (D'Souza 2006). As in the provision of other infrastructure such as roads and sewage, in the supply of water the emphasis was on efficiency of movement and distribution and water's functional use.

Second, the emphasis on utilitarian ideals meant that the multiple and complex cultural relationship of people to water was reduced to a functional commodity to be consumed by individuals. The discourse on water shifted to engineering the efficient delivery of water for use by individuals in their households. Since the colonial government was making a capital investment in the technologies, a profit motive dominated both the provision and the pricing of infrastructure.[7] The preoccupation with quantities, distances, and mechanisms of distribution of water meant the meanings of water and relationships of people over water that constituted the cultural landscape were ignored and altered, resulting in dislocations.

[7]Vast amount of funds spent on the military expeditions of the Indian Army under the British Empire left little money for state projects during the late nineteenth century. Local authorities were largely required to raise their own funds for improvement projects. The Delhi Municipal Committee had very little money. As my review of municipal records and proceedings over several years in the late nineteenth century shows, large, capital-intensive projects were not only expected to pay for themselves, but to bring in some profits as well. Kumar and Habib (1982) have noted that works of "Internal Improvement" were explicitly a commercial proposition. Such works were to be "essentially based on the idea of their being profitable in a pecuniary point of view.… If it cannot reasonably be predicted that such work will be profitable in this sense, it should not be undertaken" (Report of a Committee 1858).

Yet the imagined ideal of technological solutions had to negotiate on the ground with the realities of funding and the availability of water. For instance, during the early 1920s, municipal officials estimated that the requirement for running water-carriage latrines was 8–10 gallons per capita per day. Not being able to fund or secure adequate amounts of water, officials in Delhi were forced to continue the traditional system of relying on the human labor of *mehtar* (sweepers) and *bishti* (water carriers) to solve the city's sanitation problems while attempting to put in place the most technologically advanced water treatment and sewage treatment plants. *Mehtar* serviced the pit latrines of houses, carrying refuse to designated spots outside the city walls where they developed and sold manure.[8] The *mehtar* also swept neighborhood streets on local contract. While most houses had wells for water supply, *bishti* were water carriers whose primary occupation was to collect and sell water from the community tanks and *baoli* in leather containers slung over their shoulders. From selling drinking water in the bazaars to supplying daily water to homes without wells, the *bishti* formed a human water supply system in the city. Eventually the municipality was forced to recognize the power of the *mehtar*, otherwise socially outcast and invisible, and contract them officially to clean and sweep the city (Hosagrahar 2005).

In another instance, the Municipal Committee proposed a new water supply scheme as the first and most important scheme of its establishment.[9] Water was to be collected from the River Yamuna and purified before distribution so that filtered water would be supplied throughout the city in pipes that traveled underground. Officials assumed that "well-to-do gentlemen" would be willing to pay extra rates to have pipes laid to bring water into their homes and "save their women from parading themselves in public."[10] In fact, the families that could afford maids and domestic help had them collect the water necessary for the household. Well-to-do families were reluctant to pay the extra money to obtain piped water. Furthermore, from the perspective of most residents, the *baoli* and community wells also served as

[8]"Sweeper" is a term that colonial officials used to refer to those who collected refuse and cleaned toilets and streets. Such people were considered untouchable according to traditional caste divisions.

[9]Letter from Major C.A.M. Mahon, Deputy Commissioner, Delhi, dated 1882, to Lieutenant W.M. Wiley, Commissioner and Superintendent, Delhi Division. Commissioner's Office, Delhi Division, File #206, Carton Box #11, 1869–1882.

[10]Letter from Major C. A. M. Mahon, Deputy Commissioner, Delhi, dated 1882, to Lieutenant W. M. Wiley, Commissioner and Superintendent, Delhi Division, Commissioner's Office, Delhi Division, File #206, Carton Box #11, 1869–1882.

important community centers for interaction. Receiving piped water supply into the individual homes would have removed this social function of the wells and *baoli*.

Third, interventions and debates on water were increasingly dominated by a discourse on sanitation and health. From the mid nineteenth century, public health was a growing concern in the cities of Western Europe and the new "sanitary science" was significant in shaping actions and policies in urban areas. Previous experiences with the plague and cholera in Europe and in India and newly evolving ideas about hygiene and infectious diseases emphasized the need for the provision of clean, potable water and the appropriate disposal of waste. Rhetoric about sanitation masked the slow and minimal success of many of projects and the stark and growing inequalities in the city's population.

In 1869 the Municipal Committee proposed installing an advanced network of wells, canals, and pipes to supply piped drinking water to households. After funds had been arranged and the final design approved, construction work on the waterworks project began in 1882.[11]

Despite the seemingly egalitarian goals of public health, the interventions reinforced and deepened inequities in the city. The concern over the health of the troops and the perception of mysterious illnesses and death in the tropics were instrumental in shaping an unequal structure of sanitation in Delhi – a legacy that has continued until this day. For instance, the British cleaned, cleared, and reopened the Ali Mardan Canal during the 1820s, providing a source of fresh water. However they drew substantially more water per capita for the Civil Lines (where the civilian European population of Delhi resided) and the Cantonment (where the colonial military personnel resided) than for the rest of the city (Gupta 1981). As a result of the uneven development of the sanitation system from the 1840s, the inhabitants began to make ad hoc arrangements of their own, such as using the city ditch or the glacis around the fort wall as a sewage receptacle (Prashad 2001). They also complained in numerous written petitions and newspaper articles about the growing unsanitary conditions within the city, such as clogged drains that formed cesspools. By 1894 a mere 146 private houses had water connections, most of them in the Civil Lines and Lothian Road areas inhabited by Europeans.

The creation of New Delhi as the new imperial capital exacerbated the new geographies of inequality. The new city was located on land that was more than five times the size of Shahjahan's walled Delhi and away from the River Yamuna rather than along its banks. The layout of New Delhi was

[11]Narayani Gupta has discussed the politics and burdens of taxation in detail. Gupta (1981).

premised on the use of modern engineering technology to bring purified and piped water to individual homes. New waterworks were set up further north of the old city. While New Delhi was flush with funds for such projects, the colonial government was unwilling or unable to support the advanced engineering solutions for the walled city, which required a substantial capital investment. This further aggravated the inequalities.

Finally, colonial policies towards the governance and management of water had the dual effect of making water a commodity for purchase while wresting responsibility from the community in caring for and managing water sources and placing them with the municipality. Municipalization of Delhi in 1968 dramatically altered the system of governance in the city. Where benevolent royalty and nobility historically established *dighi*, *baoli*, wells, and *ghats*, and where communities once followed unwritten codes on their maintenance and use (such as never bathing on the steps of a *baoli* or *dighi* for instance), the responsibility of providing and maintaining water supply and sanitary services now fell squarely on the municipality.

The new technologies of water provision also required a complex legal and administrative apparatus to deliver them, in addition to the engineering skills and funds necessary to install them. Not only was the knowledge not local, the administrative mechanisms they required were also non-local. For instance, water supply provisions were based on scientific calculation of household demand, giving the residents and their institutions no role in maintaining or managing the piped water supply. Scientific calculations for the provision of services assumed that the space of the city was a socially undifferentiated territory needing rationally provided facilities and that the residents were undifferentiated beings. Clearly, not everyone in the city had equal or plentiful access to water in the traditional systems of water provision. Wells were territorial for religious sects and communities, hence conflicts were commonplace over their use, especially during the dry summer months. Yet the systems and practices embodied in generations of accumulated knowledge and experience of dealing with the local patterns of rain, drought, floods, and soil involved the engagement of everyday users. The egalitarian ideals of municipal governance replacing the decentralized traditional practices was intended to serve all citizens and areas of the city equally, but in fact it did not.

During the late nineteenth and early twentieth centuries, Delhi's population increased exponentially. Transformations in land ownership and cropping patterns under colonialism had the dual effect of changing the water needs of irrigation in the countryside and bringing large numbers of people to the city (Raychaudhuri and Habib 1981). Finally, by the 1930s and 1940s, the idea of relieving congestion in the walled city by creating model living environments outside the walled area took root. So began the first phase of planned, low-density, residential developments through state acquisition of orchards, gardens, and agricultural land (Hosagrahar 2005). Not only were these new model neighborhoods (products of the Delhi Improvement Trust) premised on rationalized and efficient provision of piped water and sewage disposal, but they also built on land that had formed gardens and orchards that had once nourished the city and provided valuable open space. The design of the neighborhoods with detached houses, wider orthogonal streets, walled rooms, and internal courtyards made them less responsive to the local climate and required electrical devices to cool them down.

Thus British colonial rule in Delhi saw the decline, elimination, and sometimes appropriation of a number of "traditional" technologies (D'Souza 2006). This is not to romanticize nostalgically about local knowledge or traditional systems of water management or to argue against attempting anything new. The point is that modernity saw it necessary to reject in totality the inherited practices and structures rather than remedy their deficiencies or supplement them.

6.4 The Water Crisis in Postcolonial Delhi

The commodification of water as well as the rejection of traditional technologies, practices, and institutions for the management of water that began with nineteenth-century modernity and colonialism became well-established norms in postcolonial Delhi. The partition of the Indian Empire into the independent nations of India and Pakistan brought a deluge of refugees to Delhi. As the population grew rapidly, the imperial city grew into an enormous metropolis. Providing modern infrastructure to all citizens became an urgent concern of the government in the new republic.

Today the metropolitan area of Delhi has spread to an area of 1,500 km^2, stretching across three states and including several smaller towns and urban villages, a vast, urban agglomeration of over 16 million people with a population that has grown by 41% in the last 15 years. The value of buildable land is so much higher than that of agricultural land that landowners on the edge of the ever-expanding metropolis see their property as a gold mine, the value of which can be realized only as real estate.[12] Technological capabilities and the objectives of rationalized development dictate a mode of urban development that can conquer rocky terrain, fill in flood-prone

[12]Based on conversations with property owners, municipal officials, and real estate agents during the author's field work in Delhi, 2002–2004.

areas, eliminate orchards, and control the internal climate of buildings using technology. Bungalows in gardens and villas at the edge of the city have been replaced by dense apartment blocks. The edge continues to move ever further out as more agricultural land is devoured.

The demand for water continues to grow. The Bhakra Nangal Dam, the River Yamuna, and the River Ganga at some distance are Delhi's three main sources of water. The Tehri Dam and other large projects bring the waters of the Yamuna and the Ganga to the metropolis. Groundwater from private and public tube wells or raised by hand pumps made up the shortfall. However, with increasing urbanization and rising population, the large-scale extraction of groundwater has resulted in the fall of the water table to dangerous levels. Furthermore, the quality of the water too, is severely compromised, since a substantial portion of Delhi's sewage flows untreated into the River Yamuna and sewage seeps into underground aquifers. The water crisis in Delhi today has multiple dimensions, from its quantity and quality to its governance.

First are concerns about the amount of water available and ways to address water scarcity. Clearly, the city's population and its water needs are growing rapidly without a corresponding increase in the sources or amount of water. The demand is expected to grow to 1,600 million gallons a day (mgd) versus a proposed treatment capacity of 990 mgd. The shortfall in supply has resulted in excessive extraction of groundwater.

The Center for Science and Environment, an advocacy and public-interest NGO in New Delhi, reports that the groundwater table in Delhi has dropped sharply. Compared to a level of 10–13 m below the surface at the time of India becoming independent in 1947, the water table is now as low as 100 m or more in certain places. On average, the groundwater is currently falling at the rate of 3.3 m/year. This water has not been replenished at the same rate: Delhi receives a total average rainfall of around 600 mm/year, of which 80% is received in 3 months from July to September. In areas such as Mehrauli, which has seen dramatic expansion of residential and commercial development, groundwater levels have dropped about 20 m just in the last 60 years.[13] Yet these areas have remained as areas of significant growth and expansion.

The unreliability of supply is another issue. According to one study, on average households in Delhi were getting 13 h of supply a day; 13% of households did not receive water at all and only about 40% had water around the clock (Zérah 2000). These shortages have led to changes in living and working patterns, as people adapt to the limited supply by installing storage devices and plan their activities according to the timing of the water supply.

[13]www.cseindia.org.

Second, of the water that is available for use, quality and potability vary. Pollution from industrial effluents, upstream fertilizer run-off, and the city's wastewater affects the quality of water sources. Groundwater quality is further affected by leakage from sewage pipes and inadequately serviced sanitary pits. The Energy Resources Institute calls the Yamuna a dead river, because the National Capital region is a mere 1% of the river's total catchment area but generates more than 50% of its pollutants. Yamuna water enters Delhi at Wazirabad and leaves it 22 km farther downstream at Okhla. Delhi receives relatively clean water at Wazirabad but converts it into deadly source of disease for people living downstream. Only about 55% of the population of Delhi is served by the sewage system and about 15% by on-site sanitation systems, while the remaining have no access to sanitation facilities at all. Even at the treatment plants, only a part of the sewage generated in the city is treated (Delhi Development Authority 2005). The quality of groundwater is also deteriorating and in several places it has been found to be unfit for human consumption.[14]

Third, new geographies of inequity are created by water. Delhi ranks highest among the Indian metropolitan centers for availability of water per person, about 280–300 l per capita per day (lpcd).[15] According to the Bureau of Indian Standards, the average water requirement of a Delhi citizen is 160 l per capita daily. Even these estimates mark the reality of the wide variation in water supply received across the different neighborhoods in Delhi. A recent report reveals that people in Mehrauli receive only 29 lpcd and those in Narela receive 31 lpcd, while those in the Cantonment get 509 lpcd, those in Lutyen's Delhi 462 lpcd, and those in Karol Bagh 337 lpcd.[16] The Center for Science and Environment also predicts that unless the depleted water table in Mehrauli is maintained or replenished, Mehrauli will experience desertification within the next 10 years.[17] An inadequate sewer system, leaking pipes, and blocked drains compound the problem.

The figures on supply and demand and the foregoing discussion masks the grim daily struggles for water by 78% of Delhi's citizens, who live in substandard settlements. Almost 46% of the population still does not have access to piped water supply and has to collect or buy 30–90 lpcd. In just four decades the squatter population in Delhi has increased 40-fold from 12,749 families in 1951 to about 485,000 in 1991 (Sharma and Gupta no date) and in 2001 the Census of India 2001 estimated the slum population of Delhi at 2,029,755. The figure

[14]www.cseindia.org.

[15]www.cseindia.org.

[16]www.cseindia.org.

[17]www.cseindia.org.

will be several times greater today. The ever-escalating value of real estate has resulted in the floodplains of the River Yamuna being built up by squatters. According to the Energy Resources Institute, about 750,000 people live in slums along the 22-km stretch of the river in Delhi (Energy Resources Institute (no date)). Squatting on public land devoid of basic infrastructure creates problems at the very outset with flooding and poor sanitary conditions. Furthermore, the nature of materials used for building houses as well as the storage of inflammable recycled material have made these settlements extremely vulnerable to fire (Véronique and Ramanathan 2007).

In contrast to the unplanned developments facing water scarcity are the poorly planned townships and neighborhoods mushrooming on what was once farmland around the ever-expanding edges of the city. In the last decade, Gurgaon, a corporate park and home to DLF City, one of Asia's largest private townships, has emerged as a significant center of global business. A world of glittering malls, glossy corporate offices, and vast gated enclosures containing multistory blocks of luxury apartments, Gurgaon epitomizes, for many observers, modernity in India. The spaces are largely designed, supported, and inhabited by those identifying with the forms of modernity adopted and promoted by corporate powers in Europe and North America. Gurgaon's apartment complexes, office parks, shopping malls, schools, hospitals, and golf courses are all fed largely by privatized infrastructure (Hosagrahar 2007). Urban villages with entirely different land use and ownership patterns are hemmed in by new developments that have taken over their agricultural lands (Delhi Development Authority 2005). Extensive construction activity and groundwater extraction has disturbed the hydrological balance, leading to decline in the productivity of wells, increasing pumping costs, and rising demands for energy.[18] The water table has dropped by 7 m between 2003 and 2007.[19] The rate of depletion is considerably higher than what it was for

[18]www.cseindia.org.

[19]The journal *Down to Earth*, published by the Center for Science and Environment in New Delhi, notes that during the 1980s, private developers in Gurgaon had hundreds of private borewells and were drawing water free of cost. The water table today is 40 m below ground level while Gurgaon, home to multinational companies and apartment complexes of the well-heeled employees in the IT sector, depends heavily on groundwater for its needs. According to the Central Ground Water Board (2004), 70% of its present need is met through groundwater. Yet, no figures are available on how many borewells are operating or how much groundwater is being extracted.

[20]Central Ground Water Board, 2004. The Central Ground Water Board is a government agency. The rate of depletion, which is about 4.5 m/year over four years, can be compared to the earlier figure of 22.5 m in the 27 years between 1980 and 2007 (http://cgwb.nic.in/).

27 years before that.[20] A study by the Central Ground Water Commission has already cautioned that there will be no groundwater left in 10 years' time in Gurgaon if the water level continues to fall at the current rate, even as new luxury apartments continue to be built.

The ridge to the southwest of Delhi was a rocky hill that was densely forested at one time. Its terrain had historically formed a natural barrier to the growth of the city. Further, according to the Central Ground Water Authority, this area is a special water recharge area for the underlying aquifers, as the fractured and weathered rocks allow rainwater to percolate underground and replenish the groundwater.[21] A massive *baoli* is still in evidence on the Ridge near the historic Flagstaff Tower. Built at the time of Feroz Shah Tughlaq, the *baoli* is believed to have been encircled by a series of chambers similar to other *baoli* of the time. This area stands threatened by the ever-expanding circle of investor and commercial interests that hope to reap profits from building mega-malls on the ridge.

A final dimension of the water crisis in Delhi has to do with the governance mechanisms and the institutional structures for managing water. At the moment, several government agencies are involved with monitoring and distribution of water supply and sanitation, of which the most important are the Delhi Jal Board, the Municipal Corporation of Delhi, the New Delhi Municipal Corporation, the Central Pollution Control Board, Yamuna Action Plan, and the Central Ground Water Commission. However, each agency seems to function independently with little coordination among them. For instance, a government audit last year indicted the Jal Board for having spent $200 million, yielding "very little value." Similarly, the construction of more sewage treatment plants has done little to ease the flow, in part because sewage lines are badly clogged and because power failures leave the plants inoperable for hours at a time (Sengupta 2006).

Having invested in an expensive centralized system of moving water and sewage, institutional structures for repair and maintenance are poor. The city's water supply runs through a 5,600-mile network of battered public pipes, and between 25 and 40% of the water leaks out, so that very little water reaches people at the end of the line (Sengupta 2006). Methods for pricing and metering are so irregular that some of those deprived of water resort to pilfering water by creating leaks in the pipes. Pricing and metering also create water inequities, as the large consumers often pay a smaller price per liter of water than those who require a minimal amount for household consumption and who may even have to purchase water from a tanker.

[21]http://cgwb.nic.in.

6.5 Modernity, Sustainability, and Water

A historical perspective on the cultural landscapes of water in Delhi reveals a substantial transformation in the last 200 years in the sources, availability, and demand for water. Undoubtedly, intensive urbanization has stretched the available resources to bring about the current water crisis in the city. But equally significant are the transformations in the meanings of water, the practices of extraction, use, and distribution, the social relationships surrounding water, and the institutional structures for managing the resource.

The gains to citizens from the modernization of infrastructure provision in the piped supply of potable water are obvious. Under ideal circumstances, when water is plentiful, distribution systems adequate and fair, the quality of water high, and sewage removal efficient and clean, municipal provision of these services to all its citizens would, no doubt, be an achievement. However, prevailing discourse on demand and supply of water obscures the loss and reinterpretation of features in the hydrological landscape through modernity and colonialism and the more recent trends in globalization and hyper-modernity. Current municipal efforts at water provision in Delhi do not question the premises of modern infrastructure provision. Even in the cities of Western Europe and North America, where water and sewage connections are provided to all residents, officials have in recent years questioned the sustainability of such provision. Studying the cultural landscapes of water through a historical perspective gives a window into alternative views, technologies, interpretations, and practices that worked well once. This perspective gives us an opportunity to examine whether they can be modified to work well again. Such a cultural view of water management also allows us to reflect on the transformations in its premises and as such, reframes discussions of water in megacities and our responses to it.

The most obvious loss is in the dereliction of the structures themselves. The canals, *qanat*, *hauz*, *baoli*, and wells all are in a state of disuse. They have either gone dry due to the drop in the water table or the water in them is too polluted to be used. The *baoli* and wells are also affected by the accumulation of silt and vegetation. Less evident is the loss of an understanding of their interconnections and flows, and the hydrological logic of the structures and the terrain. The local knowledge of those who designed and built them is lost to us, as are the inherited practices of their use and maintenance, and the knowledge of local meteorology, geology, and hydrology embedded in these practices. Modern urban planning and water supply systems disregard years of accumulated knowledge on ways to predict and counter nature's bounty in floods and excessive rainfall as well as droughts. Vanished also are the institutions that monitored and maintained the structures: the wealthy philanthropists who built the structures, the customs, beliefs, and mores that governed their use, the ordinary people who complied with these customs and cared for the sources of water, and the *bishti* who delivered water to the streets and households from a static source. *Dhobi* for instance, were a community of washermen who washed and dried clothes in specific places along the river or canals assigned as *dhobi ghats*. While pit latrines undoubtedly posed health hazards and created a stratified society with the cleaners and their head-loads at the bottom of the social pyramid, the *mehtar* who collected the night-soil from houses also had in place a long-standing system of composting of night-soil in the outskirts of the city to convert it into organic fertilizer for farmers.

Modernity and changing world views have gradually brought about a reinterpretation of the activities and meaning of water. Before the introduction of piped water supply, sources of water in the city were celebrated places and landmark features in the city. Public interaction and social connection, especially among women, happened over the daily acts of washing and collecting water. Water sources played a significant role in defining community identity, not only in the gardens laid out on the *char bagh* principles of the Mughal, but also in public places. Of the landmarks of the old city, a substantial number had to do with water: Chandni Chowk, Faiz Bazar, Lal Dhiggi, Phuvvara, Khari Baoli, and Hauz Khazi; outside the walls lay Hauz Khas, and further away, Suraj Kund, and of course, the river Yamuna. Corresponding to the city's public spaces was a hierarchy of visible water places: the river *ghats,* the public *baoli* and *dighi*, the neighborhood stepped wells, and the household wells.

With the supply of piped water, consumption of water became a private activity to be carried out in the privacy of one's home. Water from the river and canals was first piped to a filtration plant and then in underground conduits to households. These processes rendered the sources of water largely invisible. The waterworks or filtration plants with their ungainly machinery were tucked away from public view, outside the city.[22] The disconnection between source and use had several implications. The amount of water available, the condition of the source, and its care were no longer matters of public concern. The state's promise of a limitless supply of water on the condition of payment led to much carelessness and waste in its use. The aesthetic, religious, and social significance of water sources in Delhi diminished and largely vanished through the twentieth century. Although Edwin Lutyen's design for imperial Delhi included ponds as an element of its

[22]Today these are within the city itself, but remain hidden from view.

landscape, for the ordinary citizens, water was to be hidden in pipes. Ideally all the sewage was to be collected from individual homes and businesses through underground pipes, taken to a treatment plant, and then released as clean water into rivers or canals. But the reality of inadequate sewage connections, leaking sewer lines, and overburdened treatment plants resulted in the release of raw sewage and toxic wastes.

The pre-modern landscapes of water made no pretensions to equality: royalty and the nobility had special ducts that brought plentiful water into their bathing tanks and gardens, while the poorest trudged to the river's edge with their washing or were limited to the use of specific wells. Since modern technologies of infrastructure provisions were premised on egalitarian principles, their failure to address the needs of all residents equally, is a failure. After all, in cities in North America, Western Europe, Australia, and Japan, all households in the urban areas have water connections and continuous water supply.

The failure in Delhi is not that of merely failing to reach an ideal of egalitarianism, but of further exacerbating inequities and the exploitative extraction of natural resources. It is also the failure of a single centralized system of infrastructure delivery to address the needs of a vast population that falls outside the legal framework. Those on the margins of the system include at one end, expensive developments established on the promise of legalized infrastructure provision and at the other end, vast landscapes of squatters without civic status. While the first group provides water for itself through large-scale extraction of groundwater using technology for deep drilling, the latter groups are forced to resort to whatever drains or water channels are available in the vicinity for cooking, washing, drinking, as well as waste disposal. When municipal water connections or hand-pumps are not available nearby for water collection, mysterious leaks in passing water lines provide the much-needed source. The indiscriminate extraction and use of precious resources pose health hazards for the entire region.

In recent years, an increasing global pressure to move towards sustainability has brought prevailing practices of water management under scrutiny, including issues of scarcity, pollution, and exploitation of water resources. The need to augment existing sources, prevent pollution, stabilize the shrinking water table, accurately meter water connections, fix leaks, and create new waterlines are among the range of issues that agencies struggle with independently within the boundaries of their mandate. Yet a connection between water and urban development remains largely unexamined, as are the relationships with the natural terrain and geology of the region and its vegetation.

Having brought about the destruction of customary relationships with the environment and of community institutions of place-making, the forces of modernism have finally acknowledged the unsustainability of present modes of development everywhere. Urban development in Delhi has involved a four-part trajectory; first, the rejection of locally inherited knowledge about geography, terrain, and the built environment in the name of modernization; second, a history of exploitative policies and unsustainable urban development imposed in the colonial period; third, continuing unsustainable practices in the post-colonial period seen as necessary for modernization and competing in global markets; finally, having destroyed and lost local knowledges, Delhi, like other cities in Asia, is now compelled to find "green" technologies for urban development.

One response would be to consider small-scale efforts along with the grand schemes. A cultural landscape approach to water would give back its symbolic, social, and ritual significance in people's everyday lives in Delhi. This approach implies that planners and policies would nurture continuities in the institutional and administrative apparatus by involving and empowering communities in managing both supply and demand. The quantitative microanalysis of water issues in isolation from its historical and cultural context has meant that water is no longer seen in relationship to built form. The state has not identified topography, paving texture, shady courtyards, and the community ownership of stepped wells as significant in addressing the water crisis in Delhi. So the kind of rigid interventions proposed will continue to fall short.

From this perspective, if we were to legitimize a diversity of "alternative modernities" rather than privileging the singular experience of cities in the developed world as the universal model of modernity, we would also be recognizing varying cultural interpretations of nature as a crucial dimension of sustainability. This means accepting local adaptations of global modernity. In the actualization of universal agendas in a particular place, *indigenous modernities* reconcile the uniqueness of a region and its history with the "universals" of science (Hosagrahar 2005).

The implications for using a historical perspective on the cultural landscapes of water are numerous in modern Delhi. First, a comprehensive planning and integrated approach would be called for that would include understanding the terrain and the geological and hydrological landscape, including vegetation; local meteorology; the economics of supply, demand, and pricing; the technologies of filtering, treating, and transporting clean and waste water; and institutional and governance mechanisms. Second, water would be made a *visible* element of the landscape rather than hidden in underground pipes and consumed in private. Making water sources visible, aesthetic, and public is likely to encourage a sense of community, identity, and collective responsibility, and help in keeping water sources visibly clean. Third, the ideal of having running water in the home 24 h a day may be called into question, since only a minority of homes now have that provision. For instance, using tankers with hygienic water, regular delivery to neighborhoods may actually make it easier for larger numbers of households to have access to stored water, rather than allowing only a few households to have running water.

Finally, households, neighborhoods, and developments could earn "water points" or "water credits." Rather than minimizing the *use* of water, the emphasis here would be on each household, building, street, or neighborhood augmenting *sources* of water. Water harvesting, water recycling, vegetation cover added or maintained as well as activities for maintaining existing water structures (for instance cleaning or desilting wells) would earn water points either towards purchasing more water or a relief from taxes of some sort. Such financial incentives to generate and protect a public good might be one way to blend the community responsibility of customary water management with the idea of a modern infrastructural service.

With New Delhi slated to host the Commonwealth Games in 2010, the government proposes to remake Delhi's waterfront with a sports and recreation complex. Rather than exploiting the riverfront only for its views, this could be an opportunity to explore alternative relationships to water by educating, engaging, and empowering different groups of people, and allowing for and re-introducing a variety of flexible and responsive relationships to water as more than simply a utilitarian good.

Acknowledgement

Damien Carriere ably assisted with the bibliography and references.

References

Arnold D (2000) Science, technology, and medicine in colonial India. New Cambridge history of India, vol. 3, part 5. Cambridge University Press, Cambridge

Bosch C (2005) Integrated safeguards datasheet, concept stage. World Bank report

Delhi Development Authority (2005) Draft master plan for Delhi 2021, Part 14: Physical infrastructure. New Delhi

D'Souza R (2006) Water in British India: the making of a "colonial hydrology." History Compass 4(4):621–628

Energy Resources Institute (no date) How Delhi makes the sprightly Yamuna a "dead river." TERI report, Habitat, UN. Accessed May 2010 at http://www.unhabitat.org/content.asp?typeid=19&catid=460&id=2170

Greathed WH (1852) Report on the drainage of the city of Delhi and on the means of improving it. Agra

Gupta N (1981) Delhi between two empires, 1803–1931: society, government and urban growth. Oxford University Press, Delhi

Hill CV (2008) South Asia: an environmental history. ABC-CLIO, Santa Barbara, CA

Hosagrahar J (2005) Indigenous modernities: negotiating architecture and urbanism. Routledge, London

Hosagrahar J (2007) Indigene moderne: Über Architektur und Ambivalenz in Indien. ArchPlus:33–35

Kumar D, Habib I (eds) (1982) The Cambridge economic history of India. Orient Longman, New Delhi

Noe SV (1989) Shahjahanabad: geometrical bases for the plan of Mughal Delhi. In: Singh P, Dhamija R (eds) Delhi, the deepening urban crisis. Sterling Publishers, New Delhi

Prakash G (1999) Another reason: science and the imagination of modern India. Princeton University Press, Princeton, NJ

Prashad V (2001) The technology of sanitation in colonial Delhi. Mod Asian Stud 35(1):113–155

Raychaudhuri T, Habib I (eds) (1981) The Cambridge economic history of India. Cambridge University Press, Cambridge

Report of a Committee on the Classification of Public Works Expenditures, (1858), as quoted in Cambridge Economic History of India by Dharma Kumar and Irfan Habib, 2007, 692. Calcutta: Printing SoG

Sengupta S (2006) Thirsty giant: teeming India, water crisis means dry pipes and foul sludge. New York Times

Sharma A, Gupta M (no date) Reducing urban risk through community participation. Sustainable Environment and Ecological Development Society (SEEDS), published on website of the Geospatial Research Portal

UN/WWAP (United Nations/World Water Assessment Programme) (2003) 1st UN World Water Development report: water for people, water for life. UNESCO and Berghahn Books, Paris, New York and Oxford

Véronique D, Ramanathan U (2007) Du traitement des slums à Delhi: Politique de "nettoyage" et d'embellissement. In: Véronique D, Heuzé DG (eds) La ville en Asie du Sud: Analyse et mise en perspective. Purushartha 26, École des hautes études en sciences sociales, Paris

Zérah M-H (2000) Water: unreliable supply in Delhi. Manohar and Centre de Sciences Humaines, New Delhi

7. Bangkok's Urban Evolution: Challenges and Opportunities for Urban Sustainability

Sidh Sintusingha

7.1 Introduction

This chapter investigates Bangkok's urban evolution from its inception as a "water-based" city shaped by and in harmony with natural processes, to its current domination by environmentally insensitive global forms and practices. Also investigated are the official visions, plans, and measures to counter the negative impacts of uncontrolled market-driven urbanization, characteristic of Bangkok's expansion over the past 4 decades. Based on these investigations, the chapter proposes reorganization on the scale of "superblocks" – the units of expansion of suburban Bangkok – as a practical pathway towards sustainability.

Girardet has noted the difficulty of making cities of over a million in population sustainable (1999: 61–62). However, these large cities are a present reality. The more apt and practical response towards such a pressing problem could be the mitigation of the socio-environmental effects of these cities – considering alternative and specific approaches towards sustainability, tailored to the variables inherent in places and cultures.

Cities with expanding economies and populations reinforce the inherent conflict manifested within the concept of "sustainable development," which Rist (1997) has described as an oxymoron, since "sustainability" mainly advocates decreased consumption, while "development" advocates economic and population growth. In this unresolved conflict, climate change and other environmental issues are prodding society to negotiate effective compromises.

The downside of the narrow focus on particular, albeit pressing, environmental issues, and the resultant preference for market responses (emissions trading) and technology fixes (renewable fuels and increased

A. Sorensen and J. Okata (eds.), *Megacities: Urban Form, Governance, and Sustainability*,

fuel efficiency), are apparent,[1] and developmental pathways that more broadly address the city's complexity are needed. This chapter argues that in order to move towards the goal of urban sustainability, the on-ground realities of urban development, including its specific history and cultural practices, need to be investigated and addressed, and that innovative sustainable retrofits are desirable. The specific narratives of each city and parts of cities must be integral in the sustaining trajectory of the city's future development (Sintusingha 2006: 21).

This chapter investigates these issues for Bangkok, a mega-city of over ten million people, beginning with an overview of the broader, abstract cultural practices at work. The paper then investigates the city's physical evolution and transformation from an indigenous water-based to modern land-based material culture and the problem this poses for contemporary sustainability. The paper concludes with both proposed formal and speculative solutions to Bangkok's urban phenomenon.

7.1.1 Sustaining Bangkok, Sustaining Thailand

Bangkok has always been a primate city – a city that dominates the rest of the country economically, socially, and culturally. It is the "world's pre-eminent primate city" according to Sternstein (1982: 109).[2] This is even more apparent today after Thailand, an ardent participant in globalization, experienced decades of unprecedented economic growth.[3] The majority of that growth materialized in the capital city in the form of intense urbanization that spread (and is still spreading) into adjacent provinces (Hamilton 2000: 461).

[1]The increase in demand for bio-fuels has in turn resulted in the transformation of productive and ecologically sensitive lands to supply the energy sector – one cause of the current global inflation of food prices.

[2]Using the "disparity" in size between Bangkok and the next largest city as the measuring criterion (Bello et al. 1998: 95–96). Bangkok began with clear comparative advantages over the rest of the country as it was located in the richest rice-growing area with, then, the only deep-sea port in the country (Vichit-Vadakan and Nakata 1976: 8).

[3]This growth began with commercialized agricultural production and industrialization in the late 1950s "under the influence of the World Bank-USAID ideology of developmentalism" (Bello et al. 1998: 144), starting with a phase of import-substitution, followed by export-oriented growth fueled by foreign direct investments (FDI) particularly from Japan in the 1980s, and the liberalization of the financial sector in the early 1990s (Bello et al. 1998: 6–7).

This growth has come at high social and environmental cost, as the city not only invaded the surrounding rural farmlands and plantations, but also replaced the pre-existing agrarian lifestyles with the industrial. It exploited resources, natural and human, throughout the kingdom and the much poorer neighboring countries. The environmental and social impacts are not limited to the city and its physical sprawl. Bangkok's impact is national, even supranational. Thus, the sustainability debate in Thailand must address activities and practices in Bangkok. It is here that environmental deterioration is at its worst (Douglass and Zoghlin 1994: 172; Bello et al. 1998: 74). Beside the generic phenomena of large modernizing cities are many specific factors that need to be identified, investigated, and addressed.

7.1.2 The Thai Cultural Frame: Culture as "Flow" and the Formal/Informal Dichotomy

Anthropologist Neils Mulder (1992: 147) suggested that traditionally one defining characteristic of Thai culture[4] is its ability to import foreign cultural products, usually divorced from and devoid of their original meaning, and integrate those products into the local context. The cultural flow (*wadthanatham*[5]), which selects products based on their "usefulness," is designed to ensure "continuity" (Mulder 1992: 146–147). This practice applies to both tangible objects and abstract ideas. Often the original terminology of the imported cultural product fails to fully describe its Thai form.[6] Seen through this cultural framework, Bangkok's urbanization and suburbanization[7] processes can be better comprehended.

---

[4]The culture manifests itself both positively and negatively in the ever-shifting narratives of traditionalism versus progress and development.

[5]"The Thai concept of *Wathanatham* is more comprehensive than the Western concept of 'culture' in that it expresses a more dynamic concept of 'The Way of Life.' And in Oriental, like in Heraclitian thinking 'Way of Life' is like a stream, or a road (Tao). It encompasses all aspects of life and is moreover open for change, and surprise, good or bad" (Alting Von Geusau 1989: 1, as quoted by Aasen 1998: 7). The fact that the word was coined as recent as the early 1930s (Barme 1993: 160) to define Thai culture reflects this dynamic attitude to "culture."

[6]Given the problems of translating Thai forms and cultural concepts into another language, the question arises – is English, the dominant language of academia, limiting or liberating?

[7]Practices which continued from the previous capital at *Ayutthaya*, that "...regularly absorbed, and made the best use of the considerable talents of, a heterogeneous population of great cultural, ethnic, and linguistic variety" (Wyatt 2003: 120).

" 'Informal mechanisms, in which powerful interests move where they wish... have a strong influence over the development of the landscape,' with the result that 'central administrations are unable to dictate what development is appropriate where, and master plans and zoning are largely a hollow exercise' " (Bello et al. 1998, from Ross 1993: 5).

Bangkok is the physical manifestation of the "formal" and the "informal," of both private developers as described by Bello and of the urban poor, of systems and patterns of socio-economic development – the separation between the formal and informal being often ambiguous.[8] Although the two systems are intertwined at many levels, the relationship has been an uneasy one as it maintains uneven development patterns and unequal wealth distribution. At the same time, the "informal" is further eroded with the increasing global participation of the country. Paradoxically, the relationships are complementary – preventing social/class tensions or conflicts by being inclusive of all in the process of development in the hierarchical socioeconomic system while providing a structure for upward social mobility.[9]

Viewing the formal/informal dichotomies as cause–effect relationships, every "formal" action, so defined, would acquire a patina of the "informal" over time. This occurs as the planning infrastructure is relatively weak and there are no follow-up policies or controls in place to coordinate growth and change at the finer scale. From an urban design or planning perspective, there has been a clear lack of an intermediary agency to coordinate coherent, desirable growth. At the same time, this approach leaves space for "informal" developmental mechanisms on the lower tiers of power. Referring to Mulder's statement, forms are introduced devoid of meaning – which is left open for local interpretations. The "planned/designed" and the "unplanned/undesigned," reveal multiple layers of authorship (with or without formal authorization) and a palimpsest of development on the ground.

In Bangkok, there is a constant change of the roles of author and authored, formal and informal through, and alternating in, time and space: government in the provision of roads (*thanon*s) and urban utilities; private

[8]Evers and Korff (2000: 33) prefer to use the description "urban subsistence production" as they argue that "the social economy of the poor urban masses is neither a market of subsistence economy, nor does it neatly fall into the formal or informal sector."

[9]Hence its tolerance by governments and policymakers, although Farrell (2004) maintains that informality's benefits "are...greatly outweighed by its long-term negative impact on economic growth and job creation."

developers in the provision of housing and sideroad access (*sois*[10]); and the inhabitants of those times and spaces. Consequently, everyone has the capability to effect change, varying in scales. With these local cultural and practical frames in mind, the spatial processes on the ground can be better understood (Sintusingha 2002: 139).

7.1.3 A Laissez-Faire Attitude Towards "Planning": The Self-Organizing City and the City in Need of Reorganization

"Consequently, the city is the expression of the needs and wants of international and economically powerful forces using the city as their playing field. Such a city is not planned and designed for people according to traditional principles, based in collective values; in any case, we are advised that 'there is no such thing as society' and so everybody is on his or her own. Such a city just happens" (Frey 1999: 1–2).

Based on the cultural practices described above, it could be said that Bangkok's growth from 1960 to the early 1990s was laissez-faire, dictated by and responding to local and global market forces. The planner's or bureaucrat's hand seemed almost absent[11] – in fact, Bangkok did not have an official urban plan until 1992 (Webster 1995: 41).

This self-organizing, "organic" growth may have characterized many traditional human settlements historically. However, pre-industrial urban growth was responsive to the physical and environmental constraints or "carrying-capacity" of the settlement's immediate surroundings, as well as the physical limits of the human body – which cannot be said of the present form of growth.

---

[10]Iamworamate's (1989: 105) Thai-English Dictionary gives a relatively fine classification of *Thanon*: *Thanon* – "road, avenue, street"; *Thanonsoi* – "side-road; side-street"; *Thanonmain* – "main road, main street"; *Thanonyuthasart* – "strategic highway"; *Thanonhonthang* – "road; way; path; street; avenue"; *Thanonwongwhaen* – "ring road"; *Thanonluang* – "highway"; *Thanonyai* – "main road; main street", which corresponds to Western classifications. Interestingly, for *soi* he gave only "lane; alley" (295). I would argue that the Thai typologies are more specific, their use is often more diverse than the translation implies.

[11]To the point that the location of those investments was left up to foreign investors, which, due to better infrastructure, concentrated their industrial and manufacturing heavily in the Bangkok Metropolitan Region (Bello et al. 1998: 117).

Urban growth changed radically with the introduction of fossil fuel technologies applied indifferently worldwide. Environmental constraints have been disregarded, resulting in the deterioration of the urban and peri-urban environment. Although there are similarities in patterns of industrialization, urbanization (Wright 1999: 7, from Yeung 1992: 265), and environmental decline, Western cities grew in tandem with the development of fossil fuels and the automobile – while Asian cities, later adopters of these technologies, struggle with their impacts as the technologies were usually introduced piecemeal and superficially imposed and absorbed while those cities expanded at exponential rates. Such patterns of development necessitate the restructuring of self-organized urban environments through planning for sustainable future growth – a significant challenge, but not without opportunities, considering pre-existing practices.

7.2 Bangkok's Urban Evolution

How did Bangkok arrive at its current unsustainable state? This is a highly complex phenomenon that encompasses every field of study – political, economic, social, and cultural. In the pre-colonial era, the physical environment was a major influence on the form of indigenous settlements. As the hegemonic global economic order instigated by the Industrial Revolution, advancement in fossil fuels, and later communications and electronic technologies increasingly exerted itself throughout the mid nineteenth to twentieth centuries, the city's development became increasingly divorced from its environmental patterns and sensibilities.

This section briefly traces the formal evolution of Bangkok, from its roots as a "water-based"[12] settlement with very "public" rivers and canals as its lifeline and with floating houses or houses on stilts as its collective form, to its heavily mechanized present, with very "private" roads, spaghetti-like expressways raised above highways as its lifelines, and the ubiquitous shophouses, gated communities, highrises, and malls as its current collective form.

[12]Jumsai (1997) in the seminal work *Naga: Cultural Origins in Siam and the West Pacific,* examines the water-based foundations of Thai culture. This chapter adopts Jumsai's terminology – "water-based" and "land-based" – to describe the phenomenon of Bangkok's transformation.

7.2.1 The Indigenous City (Rama I – Rama III, 1782–1851)

Bangkok,[13] capital of Siam since 1782, was at its inception a water-based city responsive to the seasonal swelling of the Chao Phraya that empties into the Gulf of Thailand. The city was tied together by an intricate system of canals or *khlongs*,[14] both natural and dug, relying on water from these aquatic networks to sustain a predominantly agrarian lifestyle. The extensive *khlongs*, plantation irrigation ditches, and the low-lying rice paddies also functioned as drainage and water catchments, alleviating serious flooding (Vichit-Vadakan and Nakata 1976: 27).

Dwellings were amphibious, raised on stilts or floating on rafts, and highly suitable to the aquatic environs (DTCP 1999: 95). "The center of the population, as it had been right from the outset, was the Chao Phraya River itself which, together with the canal network, was said to contain some 7,000 floating houses or a floating population of 350,000[15] people" (Jumsai 1997: 169).

Indigenous Bangkok was thus the manifestation of a literally fluid city[16] – a city that changes with the natural currents, the daily and seasonal rise and fall in the level of the river, and also with the whims of its inhabitants where "a troublesome neighbour may be ejected and sent floating away to find another site for his habitation. A tradesman, too, if he finds an opposition shop taking away his customers, can remove to another spot with very little difficulty" (Sternstein 1982: 16).[17]

---

[13]The city was recorded on a Dutch navigation chart as early as 1642 as "*Banckock*" (Ginsburg 2000: 20) – otherwise known locally to Thais as *Krungthep*, the abbreviated version of a much longer sacred name. The capital, established on the site of a former farming and fishing village and trading post, was built to stabilize and restore the former glory of the Siamese polity, shocked from the razing of the former center of over 400 years at *Ayutthaya* (1350–1767) by the Burmese in 1767 (Wyatt 2003: 129–130). This discrepancy in name reflects the deliberate perceptual gap that is geared differently towards locals and foreigners.

[14]Henceforth referred to as *khlongs*, a specific local urban-rural typology, not Iiamworamate's literal translation of "canal" (1989: 157).

[15]Although many "seemingly trustworthy" sources provide varying numbers (Sternstein 1982: 93) – one of the first censuses in 1882, instigated by the commencement of the postal service, gave a much lower number of 169,000 (Sternstein 1982: 77). The numbers may have also varied according to where the boundary of the city was drawn.

[16]This fluidity also characterized the broader indigenous notion of the sovereignty of ambiguous borders, centered at the city, its influence expanding and contracting in relation to competing polities and shifting alliances (Winichakul 1994).

[17]Sternstein (1982) is an anthology consisting of accounts from 15 eyewitnesses between 1821 and 1855.

This was an organic city synchronized with its natural location,[18] its settlement patterns, architecture, and building technologies designed to mitigate the hot, humid climate for the inhabitants (Dick and Rimmer 1999: 310). However, change was hovering at Bangkok's doorstep, as the European colonial powers sought to impose their influence in the region – politically and economically. These developments were to have profound effects on the urban characteristics of Bangkok.

7.2.2 The Transition City (Rama IV – Early Rama IX, 1851–1946)

Contact with European colonial powers and their "superior" land-based culture and industrial technologies signaled the beginning of a permanent transformation.[19] The advent of roads and eventually automobiles heralded the new land-based era in Siam – with the first road for vehicles, Rama IV, opened to the public in 1857 (Jumsai 1997: 170; DTCP 1999: 95–98) instigating a schism with water-based urban practices.

Hoche, a western observer, noted that "The two towns, the nautical and the land-based, badly sewn together, contradicted one another strangely and duplicated each other's functions, especially now that the centuries have separated their realities…" (Hoche 1898: 132, translated by Jumsai 1997: 170). These dual, duplicating realities were also manifested in the private realm. "At home, the wealthier Thai entertained Europeans in quarters wholly European, but lived in their traditional way in quarters wholly Thai" (Sternstein 1982: 21).

Earlier on, vehicle usage was limited to the upper classes with a light rail service introduced for the public in 1887 (Jumsai 1997: 170). However, the road and rail system was not extensive and most people still relied on the *khlongs* to travel and commute. In fact, earlier roads were usually built alongside the canal system, but as preference shifted ever more towards land-based settlement patterns, canals began to get filled for road construction. The

[18]Similar to pre-industrial European towns, which were shaped by the "physical constraints of the land," water supply, and food sources (Hough 1995: 10–11).

[19]The event also heralded the conception of the Siamese modern nation-state of clear political boundaries defined with European surveying technology (Winichakul 1994). In fact, the constitutional monarchy form of government was adopted in 1932, making Siam one of the first Asian countries to adopt Western democracy – at least in form, as it would take many decades more before "democracy" began to take root in practice.

increased traffic reduced the city's drainage capacity and led to the eventual loss of an attractive traditional open space typology (Sternstein 1982: 87). Land-based architectural typologies, such as the shophouses, introduced by the Chinese, and mansions on the ground, bought in by the Europeans, began to hold sway over the traditional aquatic counterparts (Jumsai 1997: 170–171).

While the replacement of *khlongs* with roads occurred within the core city, during the reign of Rama V a vast system of canals was dug to open up the hinterland for agriculture – a direct effect of the Anglo-Siamese Bowring Treaty of 1855, which opened the kingdom to free trade[20] (Bunnag et al. 1982: 45; DTCP 1999: 72–73). Land tenure,[21] which further encouraged land-based settlements, was allowed for the first time on either side of the *khlongs*. This change launched the city into its first bout of market-driven "sprawl" – not of urban land, but rather of agrarian, mainly water-based settlements into the hinterland (Wyatt 2003: 200–201).

While the aforementioned "cultural experience" in mitigating and assimilating differences may be an important factor in the ability of the Siamese to negotiate with Western imperialism "constructively and forcefully" (Wyatt 2003: 165), this does not apply to the assimilation of land-based urban practices, manifested in split, multiple realities.

"Banking facilities, hotels, a hospital and a nursing home, a university and several secondary schools, a library and a museum, one of the finest race-courses in the East, and a number of social-cultural-athletic clubs were among the amenities provided for 'modern' living. Still, the majority of the half-million people of Bangkok lived a very much less-than-modern life" (Sternstein 1982: 23).

7.2.3 The Modern City (Rama IX, 1946 – Present): Capital and Technology-Led Change

"The megalopolis, for that is what Bangkok has become, appears as an alien organism unrelated to its background and surroundings, a great concrete

[20]Or pried it open at the behest of western colonial powers. Trade before that consisted of monopolies run by the nobility through the indigenous hierarchical "patron-client" system (Vichit-Vadakan and Nakata 1976: 7; Wyatt 2003: 168).

[21]At the time, "Title deeds were nonexistent; courts of law lacked jurisdiction, so that people defended their claims as best they could. Any occupant of land without a protector was in danger of being dispossessed" (Hanks 1972: 94). It was not until the Land Law of 1901 that private landownership "as a category distinct from usufruct" was institutionalized (Bello et al. 1998: 138–139).

pad on partially filled land which despite all its land-based pretences must succumb to the flood every year" (Jumsai 1997: 171).[22]

"The construction of railways has not only the greatest influence upon the development of a country but is also the most striking evidence of that development... By furnishing rapid and easy means of transportation, it adds materially to the value of the land and its products... The railway wherever it goes carries with it enlightenment and encourages the growth of that national feeling which is so important an element in the welfare of a country" (King Chulalongkorn, quoted in Sternstein 1982: 32).

King Chulalongkorn's description of the railways parallels contemporary Thai perceptions of modern roads that herald *garn patthana* and *kwamcharoen* (literal translations of the verb "to develop" and the noun "development"[23]) and its subordination of the "traditional" *khlongs* that prevails today.[24]

After 1945, the postwar reconstruction boom worldwide fueled urban growth in the modern form of highways and concrete box buildings. Bangkok's growth conformed to those tendencies, aided by American know-how and financial assistance through the decades of the Second Indo-China War (1959–1975). With the roads, the newly established real-estate market pushed outward into agrarian lands, failing to make up for lack of central planning and resulting in "...a great many of the city's problems" that "stem from the dramatic failure of the government to discipline and channel the energies of the private sector" (Bello et al. 1998: 95; see Fig. 7-1 for a representation of Bangkok's expansion from the 1950s to the 1990s).

By the late 1990s, with the completion of many expressway projects and the first phase of the Bangkok Mass Transit System (BTS) skytrain, Jumsai's earlier prediction had been fulfilled – the city's population at the turn of the century edged closer to ten million (counting both official residences and those from dormitory suburbs in adjacent provinces[25]). Except for the older parts of the city – Rattanakosin Island and the surrounding areas – Bangkok's public realm has become little different from any other

[22]Consistent with Nicholson-Lord's (1987: 17) description of the city as "artificial islands floating in a natural sea, having little or nothing in common with the surrounding folk culture."

[23]From Sethaputra's (1970: 385), definitions 3 and 4.

[24]There is even a saying, "*toi lung lhong khlong*" or "to back into the *khlong,*" meaning to reverse into the now denigrated, obsolete state or past.

[25]Such as *Nonthaburi* to the northwest, which grew 50-fold in population from 1947 to 2000 (Wyatt 2003: 302).

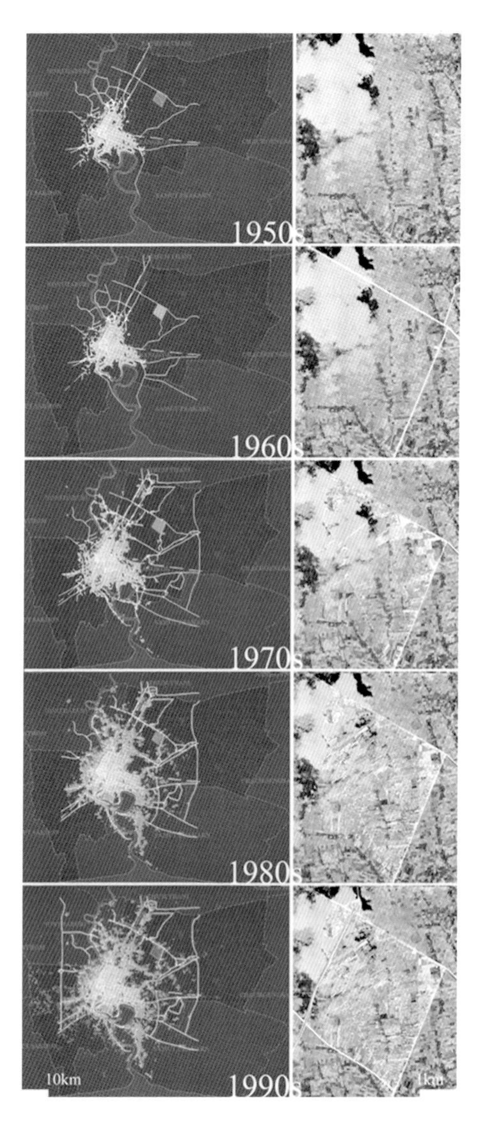

Fig. 7-1. Bangkok's urban expansion from the 1950s to late 1990s. The *left column* represents Bangkok's built-up area superimposed on the city's administrative boundaries (*dark grey*) and the main *khlong* network. The *right column* represents the expansion pattern of a superblock northeast of the city (*light-grey square* in left column) through the corresponding period with built-up areas superimposed on a 1950 aerial photograph (when the area was predominantly rice paddies defined by linear villages lining the *khlongs*)

developing ASEAN[26] city's agglomeration of concrete, steel and glass high-rises, highways, and elevated expressways, experiencing the same sprawl of suburban gated communities, malls, factories, and industrial estates that invade prime agricultural lands. These are the characteristic of the homogenized modern city favoring the global middle-class lifestyle, ignorant of pre-existing environmental, social, and cultural contexts (Dick and Rimmer 1999: 305).

For Bangkokians, now addicted to this land-based existence, annual flooding has become an enormous nuisance to everyday life. In response, the city administrators erected concrete dykes to keep the waters off the city's "great concrete pad." By doing so, the city not only rejected its (former) environmental constraint by literally overwhelming that constraint, it subjects the surrounding countryside and settlements outside the dykes to more severe flooding (Na Ranong 2002; Kemgumnerd 2002).

With the advent of air-conditioning technology, the ignorance of the environment has become more extreme. Middle- and upper-class citizens can now live in their cool, air-conditioned houses, cars, offices, shopping malls "in climate which is much closer to colleagues in Europe or North America than to ordinary people in the same city" (Dick and Rimmer 1999: 321). In fact, the microclimate of the external environment has worsened due to the use of heat-absorbent and -reflective building materials, often without sun-shading devices, the paving of large areas of the cities to create roads and car parks with the associated loss of shade, and the exhalation of hot air from the air-conditioning units. All these factors, coupled with pollution from motorized traffic and industry, contribute to heat islands, which raise the microclimate of the city by several degrees day and night (Dick and Rimmer 1999: 321). People of lower incomes, who cannot afford – but now aspire to – these technologies of private car ownership and air-conditioning, have no alternative but to tolerate the additional heat generated by modern urban practices.

City planners, realizing the acute problems associated with road-based development, have since advocated mass-transit systems, which are now guaranteed vote-winners for politicians. The city is on the verge of a new metamorphosis, adding to the previous water- and land-based stages of evolution with skytrains and subways. In the inner parts of the city, this transformation to the global city is nearly total. Beyond that area, the urban colonization of the rural lands and the *khlong* network, instigated over a century ago, continues unabated.

---

[26]The Association of South East Asian Nations (ASEAN), established in 1967 in Bangkok.

7.3 Bangkok's Superblocks

7.3.1 Patterns of Lateral Expansion: Fragmentation Through Time, Space, and Scales

"Road development accelerated rapidly in the 1950s. This marked the beginning of the 'superblock' mode of road/land development, a pattern which continues to the present, extending 30–40 km from the original city center. 'Superblocks' can be as large as 20 km^2. Superblocks are the product of the fact that most side roads (*sois*) dead end within large rectangular areas bounded by a few major roads... BMA has indicated that reducing the number of dead end *sois* to alleviate the superblock problem is a major priority" (Kaothien and Webster 2000: 29).

Bangkok, like other cities, did not develop in isolated, unrelated phases and the erasure of preexisting settlements by newer patterns of development has never been coherent or total. One effect of the typical pattern of transformation from the system of *khlongs*, serving the water-based city, to the system of roads as the transportation lifeline serving the land-based city, is the fragmentation of the city. Water-based lifestyles have been retained where the road system is weak, such as at older settlements along the Chao Phraya River and the *khlongs* west of the river (FangThon). But where the road system is strong, such as areas planned and constructed during the early road/automobile period of Old Bangkok, there is a densely settled urban grid once supported by the earliest form of public transport, the trams. Further away from the urban core, the road system weakens and the city becomes spatially fragmented, characterized by leapfrog developments along road corridors defining the edges of the superblocks[27] with empty tracts of land locked between and within (see Fig. 7-1). These superblocks characterize Bangkok's urban growth pattern and make up the majority of the Metropolitan Region area.

At the finer scale within the superblock, the physical evolution, as at the broad scale, is constantly changing and fragmenting. "The city decomposes and rebuilds itself every day. In the 1960s, four- or five-story 'rowhouses'

[27]As distinct from the "superblock" in the "Radburn planning" idea that originated in the United States after the First World War, where "Areas known as superblocks, containing a complex of houses, shops, schools, offices, etc., around a central green or pedestrian space, are ringed by roads from which cul-de-sac service roads provide access," in which "the main object of the plan is the complete segregation of traffic and pedestrians..." (Fleming et al. 1999: 468). The "superblock" in Bangkok's context is an unplanned phenomenon.

were built for a population beginning to burgeon … Thousands live in the interstices between vast high-rise glistening offices and apartment buildings fronting the main roads. Inside, narrow laneways and alleys wind in accordance with the accidents of building-time, something built here, demolished there, leaving a space and a new passageway" (Hamilton 2000: 464).

This fragmentation is not just spatial but also social. The middle- and upper-class lifestyles of private cars, suburban housing enclaves, high-rises, and malls are closely integrated with the road networks. The urban poor, without the luxury of choice, are often compressed into crowded, poorly ventilated settlements next to the now-putrid canal systems, used as sewage conduits for the better-off settlements.

7.3.2 Patterns of Movement: From Fluid *Khlongs* to Clogged Roads

Bangkok's road network and its winding patterns of *thanons* and *soi*s are derived from the organic patterns of the *khlongs* feeding water into agricultural lands (rice paddies and plantations) with the main system feeding into a root-like system (*khlongsoi*, *khu* – smaller irrigation channels) that terminates in dead ends. This pattern was designed for traditional paddleboats and the agricultural lifestyle in which long-distance travel is rare. Vehicles run on fossil fuels at speed on roads that enable and encourage much longer trips. The *khlong*-replicating road network was not designed for vehicular traffic where cars, reversing against the irrigation flow of traditional *khlongs*, travel from dead-end *soi*s into the limited main road network. Bangkok lacks the complementary secondary road systems of cities designed and planned for the automobile, which provide alternative routes through the city; as a result, Bangkok's main roads always come to a standstill in peak periods of travel.[28]

"Most of the privately built secondary and tertiary road network consists of narrow, winding, unconnected streets and cul-de-sacs. Secondary roads, which generally serve to link main arterials with local lanes (*soi*), are all but absent from many parts of Bangkok in both the urban core and the outer peripheries because responsibility for planning and building them has been relegated to the private sector. With no great incentive to do anything,

[28]In 1993 the Bangkok Metropolitan Administration (BMA) hired a traffic management team from the Massachusetts Institute of Technology to produce a development plan for Bangkok. The team determined that the city may have the worst traffic congestion compared to cities of similar size (Bello et al. 1998: 98).

private developers have largely failed to provide an adequate secondary road system." (Robinson 1995: 98).

Responding to the traffic problems on land, the *khlongs* are once again being used for mass transportation, with the introduction of "long-tail" boats in 1990 (BMA 1999: c4–c79). Bangkokians who are willing to brave the foul water at least halve their traveling time in and out of the urban core. The *khlongs* have the potential to provide a much lower-cost alternative for an extensive mass transit system than the heavy-duty elevated or underground rail systems. They are currently viewed as a complementary mass transit system for the road networks and land-based mass transit systems (BMA and MIT 1996: 60). Although the loud long-tail boats are viewed as a nuisance by those who live beside the *khlongs*, with proper planning, better boat technologies, and investment, this transportation mode could contribute to the revival of the *khlong* network.

Once the planned sewage treatment plants are fully functioning,[29] there is great potential to revitalize the *khlongs* through coordination with urban settlements and road developments. The *khlong* typology once formed the public realm that made Bangkok unique and livable and could be re-invoked, recreated, and re-interpreted to regenerate the public realm.

7.3.3 Patterns of Suburbanization: Villages in the City

Seen broadly, the process of urbanization and suburbanization – or urban sprawl – is a global phenomenon, characteristic of the period since the mid twentieth century. The pattern of urbanization mirrored that of American cities after the Second World War, and the promotion of the American Dream. "Sustained economic growth, cheap home mortgages, affordable private cars, and federally subsidized highways – all touted on big screens and small – made that dream house with its own yard, quiet neighborhood, local school, and nearby shopping possible for millions of families" (Rusk 1995: 6).

[29]As of 2002, many wastewater treatment facilities have been completed, but due to the "over reliance on high-end technology that requires centralised management and high operational costs" (instead of low-tech wetland treatment), many of the facilities are inoperable (Techawongtham 2002). Other facilities, such as at Khlong Dan, face more complex issues. Billions of baht were invested on the wastewater treatment plant at Khlong Dan which was almost completed, but then became mired in controversy amidst allegations of corruption and a lack of transparency on the part of officials, politicians, and funding bodies such as the Asian Development Bank – issues long raised by villagers, with assistance from NGOs, affected by the project (Janchitfah 2002).

However, cities that took centuries to evolve have an urban/rural tradition that predates the current global archetype. For many such cities, developments are negotiated in varying ways between the existing and the new – the result yielding unique characteristics in each place. The imposition of twentieth-century suburbs on agrarian foundations (as illustrated in Fig. 7-1), however, is problematic, as Sheer contends: "Suburban growth develops in patterns that are strongly conditioned by pre-urban fabric, such as farm roads and fields. These patterns can generate extremely scattered and disordered suburban environments, which are difficult to plan or change because they are structurally flawed" (Sheer 2001: 28).

The modern city rapidly sprawls into the urban-unfriendly rural framework along road corridors slicing through agricultural fields and villages. The rural becomes the city. T.G. McGee's (1991) *desakota*, a term that juxtaposes two *Bahasa Indonesia* words for "village" and "city," characterizes urban patterns in ASEAN cities, where direct foreign investments fuel industrialization and factories are located in densely populated rural areas to take advantage of the local work force. This pattern of industrialization competes with middle- and upper-class gated suburban communities (and associated functions of golf courses and commercial activities) in transforming rural land.

"Operating in Asia is the emergence of what can be described as region-based urbanization, as opposed to city-based urbanization. Rather than drawing a population from rural areas to a city, region-based urbanization utilizes an in situ population in the extended metropolitan region as well as drawing migrants from other rural areas … As Chinese geographer Zhou has put it, 'These are the people who live in villages but work in cities' (Zhou 1991: 97)" (McGee 1991, 10).

The economic benefits of this decentralization of industry and associated urbanization are obvious and thus encourage the rush to modernize and develop (Bello et al. 1998). Apart from providing affordable housing for the expanding middle class, these trends contribute to rising household incomes and increased employment opportunities, especially for young women of rural backgrounds. An increasing proportion of housing, factories, and population is located in these dynamic regions, forming an integral part of the nation's economic health (McGee and Robinson 1995: x). However, serious negative social and environmental implications are generally associated with sprawl, so that the specific problems of the extended metropolises of Asia are "compounded by a lack of effective land-use and environmental controls and other institutional machinery necessary for managing the new urban complex" (McGee TG 1995).

Environmental deterioration has also compounded the problems of spatial inequality on the basis of microclimate. It is often people from the lowest income bracket (often rural, and more recently foreign economic migrants) who live in the least desirable areas of the city (Douglass and Zoghlin 1994: 172). But as McGee (1991, 22) has noted, this richly mixed spatial and functional diversity may also provide unexplored opportunities to create viable, more "sustainable" settlements through reorganization.

7.4 Urban Plans and Visions for Bangkok's Development and Sustainability

"The newly developing Asian cities like Bangkok are the worst off; they are putting a high proportion of their wealth into old-style American freeways just as the US are recognising the error of their ways and going for 'smart growth' in transit-oriented villages, brownfields redevelopment and growth management at the fringe" (Peter Newman in Yencken and Wilkinson 2000: 142).

Dictated by the whims of globalization's market forces, Bangkok's pattern of urbanization, driven by road networks[30] rather than by land use regulations or development controls, through the years followed in the footsteps of Los Angeles, "the world city of the future: a generic, technologically driven, futuristic urban region that transcends identification with North or South, with any particular culture, or with any specific level of economic development" (Webster 1995: 33). In recent years, the increasingly extensive expressway system has greatly contributed to low-density, corridor-aligned sprawl (Kaothien and Webster 2000: 23). As a result of that physical growth and sprawl, mega-cities of Bangkok's size and expanse prove difficult sites for the application of sustainable development practices, as acknowledged by Girardet (1999: 62). This is largely due to the magnitude of its problems. In the less affluent cities of developing countries, the problems seem to be multiplied.

However, a mega-city inhabited by millions of people is Bangkok's present reality and the likely scenario is that city will continue to expand in both size and population. As a whole, the problems seem insurmountable; however, in the absence of an effective strategic comprehensive plan, implementation, and management approach for the city region, smaller-scale, coordinated, incremental sustainability plans can and should be developed and tailored to

[30]Encouraged by the unofficial, but highly influential Greater Bangkok Plan 2533 proposed by the American team Lichtfield and Associates in 1960 (Bello et al. 1998: 97).

specific areas of the city. Societal preference towards rail-based mass transit is already a positive step and further transit-oriented development should be explored. On the other hand, within the existing urban fabric, practices, such as urban agriculture, must be explored in light of the threats of climate change and peak oil.

"It has been suggested, however, that such regions are extraordinarily difficult for planners to handle. The mixture of activities often creates serious environmental, transportation, and infrastructural problems, particularly if such regions are treated with conventional city planning… On the other hand, the very mixed, decentralized, intermediate and small scale of economic organization and the persistence of agriculture in these Extended Metropolitan Regions (EMRs) offer exciting prospects for recycling, use of alternative energy sources, and so on, which are difficult to introduce into conventional city space" (McGee 1995, 22).

7.4.1 Decentralized-Concentration Vision for Bangkok

"That Bangkok will retain its status as the 'beau ideal' of a primate city is certain, however, … despite government's efforts to implement the national policy of 'decentralized urbanization' – formulated in the facc of the evident deterioration of the metropolitan milieu" (Sternstein 1982: 107).

At the broadest scale, planners have long acknowledged the merits of a decentralized polycentric spatial form to discipline Bangkok's indiscriminate growth (Sternstein 1982: 118, 121). This plan also extends to the adjoining provinces (particularly Nonthaburi, Pathum Thani, Samut Prakan, Samut Sakon, and Nakorn Pathom) that are directly affected by Bangkok's urbanization. But in the 3 decades since the first unofficial plan "Greater Bangkok Plan 2533"[31] prepared by Lichtfield Whiting and Brown in 1960 for the National Economic and Social Development Board (DTCP 1999: 116) together with the setting up of Department of Town and Country Planning (DTCP) in 1961 (Sternstein 1982: 113) to Bangkok's first official master plan in 1992, the reality of urbanization on the ground – characterized by uncontrolled environmentally degrading sprawl – has remain inconsistent with the plans.

Planners and public officials face a dilemma: "They need to make their planning and management tools not only strong enough to prevent ecological

[31]What was produced was basically a strategic land use plan with mosaics of different functions divided by access ways (*khlong*s, roads, rail lines) to cater for population and industrial growth up to 1990 (the year 2533 in the Buddhist calendar) (Sternstein 1982: 109).

and environmental deterioration and the other negative consequences that accompany settlement of these fringe areas but also flexible enough to permit the areas to develop in a healthy and socially responsible manner" (Robinson 1995: 104).

This is the classic development conflict (Campbell 1996: 297–298) – how to expand the economy concurrently with the conservation of natural, ecological, and agricultural resources. The latter component is often lacking in the various plans produced since the 1960 plan. In 1971, DTCP produced the "First Revised Metropolitan Plan," which essentially confirmed Lichtfield's 1960 plan, with the difference that there were no lands zoned for agricultural use, whereas two-fifths of the land was earmarked for such use in the previous plan, suggesting an "empty" countryside in to which the city could sprawl (Sternstein 1982: 111). This approach reflects the fact that the plans were directed by private growth rather than directing it, and local planners were practical accomplices of private-sector driven realities on the ground.

At around the same time, in 1969, the "Greater Bangkok Plan 1943" was published by the local City Planning Division in the Municipality of *Krung Thep*[32] (Bangkok) using "near identical means to gain near identical ends" with DTCP's plan reflecting the frequent overlap between the roles of government agencies which "is aware of but does not acknowledge the activities of the other" (Sternstein 1982: 113–14). "Attesting to the ascendancy of developers…" who resisted public planners' intervention (Bello et al. 1998: 107), the plan met the same fate as its DTCP versions, in that it never became official.

7.4.2 Official Visions Vs. the Reality on the Ground

The polycentric city preceded and generally corresponds to characteristics of the decentralized concentration model (Frey 1999: 26, based on Breheny 1992: 22) as the appropriate model to address the megacity's sprawl. The polycentric or multinucleated spatial form's "underlying principle is the close integration of residences and places of work in centers and subcenters, each developed around and near a transportation node and containing a mixture of retail, commercial, light manufacturing, and relatively dense

[32]Today known as the Department of City Planning of the Bangkok Metropolitan Administration (BMA), which officially produces and revises Bangkok's master plans with the DTCP (now DPT), which is responsible for settlements in the rest of the country, part of an effort to decentralize planning responsibility to local administrative bodies.

residential areas. This pattern usually results from conscious governmental planning and/or control and is not a common occurrence in either developing or developed countries" (Robinson 1995: 85). Most Asian cities, recognizing the advantages of polycentricity, have polycentric city plans as part of official government policy, but often lack the means and will to implement and enforce them.

"The form and types of public intervention have often impeded an efficient process of polycentered development, as planners have ignored pricing information conveyed by the private land and estate markets. Population projections in the master plans were far off the mark, and in general the plans were too rigid and inflexible to meet the changing conditions. Finally, there has sometimes been too much reliance on the private sector, or else the political will to act has not been sufficient to overcome the opposition of special interests" (Robinson 1995: 89).

Despite these barriers, Bangkok's master plans recognized that the city needs to evolve into a polycentric city (see Fig. 7-2, modified from BMA's 1999 master plan) in order to be more sustainable in the long term, particular in view of past and current patterns of sprawl. Bangkok's influence extends far beyond its boundaries – both physically and economically – and requires strategic plans and political bodies to manage the mega-urban region's development and growth, while at the same time the city needs local, political bodies to handle more localized issues. Current political reforms are heading in this direction, albeit slowly.[33] However, implementation has proved to be consistently problematic (due to *realpolitik*[34]) and what has transpired, through the decades, has been decentralization in the form of uncontrolled sprawl rather than the aimed-for polycentricity (Robinson 1995: 92). Newly formed local elected administrative bodies (at the *tambon* or municipal level, resulting from the 1997 constitution), more often than not, respond to the electorate's desires and advocate road-led urban-type developments in their jurisdiction.

[33]There are many proposals mooted for the decentralization of the city's administration, such as one to divide the city into 12 zones, each with its own elected mayor, the ability to collect taxes, and participation in planning issues. Citywide administration would be under a governor, and state services within the city, such as electricity, tap water and telephones, normally separately administered by differing agencies, under the city's jurisdiction, as well as traffic police and building safety inspectors (Santimatanedol and Changyawa 2003). However, it is not yet clear whether this administrative decentralization is coordinated with physical decentralization.

[34]Compounded over the past few years, when opposing parties occupied the national and BMA governments.

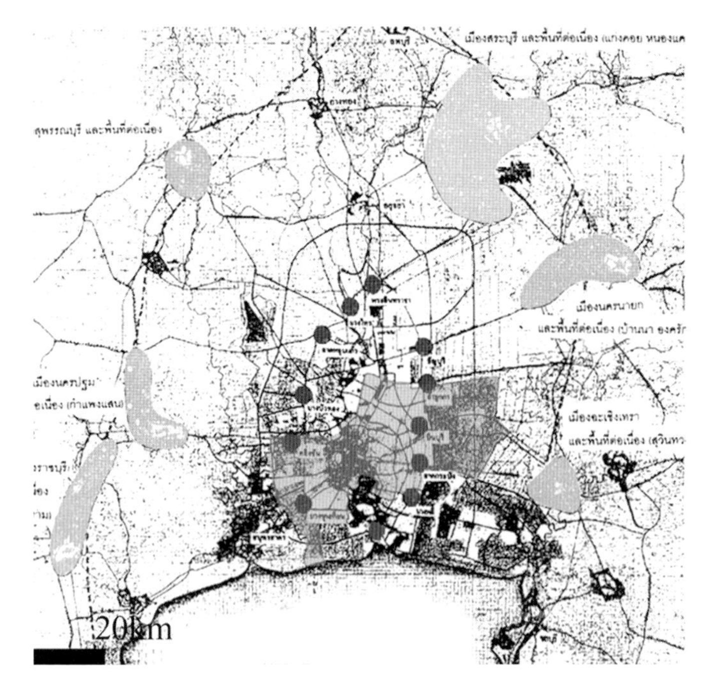

Fig. 7-2. The planned six satellite cities and 11 urban nucleuses (*darkened circles*) around Bangkok Metropolitan Administration (*shaded area* in center. Modified from BMA (1999: c6–c8) from DTCP (1999)

7.4.3 Alternative and Speculative Visions

The environmental responsiveness of past water-based settlements may be considered by some to be too utopian and inapplicable to Bangkok's current and projected future land-based state. However, without change, Bangkok will continue to be subjected to seasonal flooding and the city cannot afford to ceaselessly sprawl into the limited fertile agricultural land of the Chao Phraya River basin. Moreover, the possibility of rising sea levels due to climate change will exacerbate the problem.

Cognizant of these issues, Sumet Jumsai, a Thai architect and urban planner, foresees the necessity of the expansion of Bangkok southward over water onto the Gulf of Thailand within the next century, when he projects the population will reach 30 million. He proposes revisiting the traditional concept of a floating city or a city on stilts using multiple sources of clean energy (Jumsai 2003) – a bold return to the water-based, amphibious forms,[35] not on greenfields, but on the "bluefields" of the sea.

[35]More in the typology of oilrigs or even floating giant tankers than the land-reclamation schemes of land-scarce Tokyo, Hong Kong, or Singapore.

On a smaller scale and tailored to the present, his proposed floating parks could solve Bangkok's lack of green open space next to the Chao Phraya River, as most land along both banks of the river is privately held. Instead of reclaiming costly private land, he suggests building parks on floating pontoons that rise and fall with the tidal or flood level of the river (Jumsai 2003), taking a cue from the floating house/city typology of the past. Addressing planning on land, he also proposed that new settlements could be inserted sensitively on pre-existing rural and hydrological patterns (Jumsai 2003) – building on greenfield sites.

In contrast, the superstar architectural firm OMA proposed the classic high-rise typology, characteristic of many high-density Asian metropolises, as the solution for Bangkok, stating that "Bangkok is a city on the edge of the tolerable… a city ripe for experimentation." OMA proposed a 1,000-m tall "hyperbuilding…a city in a building, a self-sustaining indoor metropolis for a population of 120,000" (Koolhaas 2004: 420–425) on Bangkok's green lung of Bangkrajao opposite Khlongtoey port.

Practical lessons for sustainable development could well be drawn from the many "compact" mixed-used slums. They are the results of spatial, social, and economic stratification, usually located where environmental deterioration is at its worst (Herbert and Thomas 1997: 52). However, they represent a model because, out of "necessity and poverty"[36] the inhabitants have coordinated efforts to address the environmental challenges that form part of their everyday reality – as vernacular settlements such as the floating houses had to.

If the characteristics of sustainable settlements were to be applied to any communities or urban typologies in Bangkok, these slums would likely exhibit more sustainable characteristics than those settlements of higher socioeconomic brackets. For example, Douglass and Zoghlin's study of the *Suan Phlu* community in the Bangkok slums revealed that the inhabitants used community-based environmental management routines (1994: 174) such as:

- Compact settlements, in which most community services are within walking distance of most houses
- Employment in or near the community
- Social capital and the exchange of favors in the construction of houses, the provision of childcare, and other services
- Relatively strong awareness of environmental issues and their relation to livelihood – with assistance from external agencies (involving

[36]"Necessity and poverty" also influenced European vernacular settlements in contrast to the great parks and gardens that came about as the result of artistic efforts (Hough 1995: 12).

networking and the sharing of lessons and experiences from other communities), and activism
- Out of necessity, the efficient use of energy and resources
- Recycling of building materials and waste

Unfortunately, these lessons are not easily transferable to middle- and upper-class settlements without fundamental changes in values and lifestyles. What these dense communities also highlight is the strong public realm and social connectivity in contrast to the tendency to retreat to the comforts of the private in settlements of households in higher income brackets. At the same time, it is also important to acknowledge that slums have serious social problems, higher crime rates, and greater levels of engagement in underground or informal economies. In the slums, "low incomes and a deteriorating environment combine in their most debilitating forms" (Douglass and Zoghlin 1994: 171). Furthermore, the social bonds may be tenuous – especially in times of strife, such as during the economic crisis of 1997 (Bello et al. 1998: 5, from the World Bank 1998).

At the intermediate scale between the strategic regional level and individual neighborhood enclaves, there are also opportunities to address Bangkok's sustainability through the city's pattern of lateral expansion via the superblocks.[37] Using the proposed tool of "land readjustment"[38] (DTCP 1999: 173–176) Bangkok's generic and specific problems can be addressed:

- Urban sprawl
- Lack of urban infrastructure – roads, rapid transit systems, sewage treatment, green urban space for both recreation and increase natural stocks, biodiversity; etc.
- Urban environment degradation
- Land subsidence

[37]The author has published a detailed planning and design review of a superblock in Bangkok in an earlier paper, "Sustainability and urban sprawl: Alternative scenarios for a Bangkok superblock" (Sintusingha 2006).

[38]The bill was proposed in 1987 with JICA's support, but failed to get passed due to both resistance from interest groups and parliamentary mishaps (Thansettakij 2004). The recent protest by Buddhist organizations over the inclusion of temple property in the bill came from misunderstandings, miscommunications, and mistrust that the land could be used as the (business-oriented) government saw fit (Bangprapa 2004; Thairath 2004). While Sorensen (2000, 2007) has noted high expense as a barrier to successful application of this tool, the mainly empty centers with depressed land prices of Bangkok's superblocks provide opportunities for a more cost-effective application of the land re-adjustment process.

- Flooding
- Social and spatial inequalities and divides
- Local accessibility to mitigate land wastage

Within the superblock, the mixture of activities and the specific forms of *khlong*s, now much degraded, and empty tracts of land,[39] leave many unproductive and waiting to be infilled with real estate developments. Yet superblocks can be re-adjusted and revitalized to reintroduce "biodiversity" (the definite forms that they take can be prescribed by inclusive societal processes[40]). The *khlong*s and empty tracts form broad networks, both continuous and fragmented, throughout Bangkok and her surrounds, varying physically in relation to settlement densities and corresponding tract sizes and shapes, as well as particular social, economic, and cultural contexts associated with location (Sintusingha 2004: 144–145).

There are opportunities to retrofit this network into a viable ecological and agricultural framework that counterbalances and provides a complementary system to Bangkok's hegemonic pattern of expansion through road corridors of different scales – the intensely urban, lived-in streets and *sois*. The resuscitated network could provide potential respite, in the form of natural and agricultural sanctuaries, from the concrete suburbs as well as reserving land for urban agriculture – both for subsistence and for the markets, partially addressing the economic and social dimensions of "sustainability." Urban transportation along the highways also needs to be reorganized towards more efficient public transport and the rationalization of nodes and linkages feeding secondary systems within and between superblocks. Built forms and functions of buildings should not only respond and relate to these streets and highways, but also the proposed natural/rural systems of *khlongs*, ponds, urban forests, and agricultural land – being of higher densities (intense commercial and high-density residential) along major transportation arteries, progressively reducing settlement densities (to local-scale commercial and low- to medium-density residential uses) closer to the green–blue arteries, with easy access to both – particularly by a formalized pedestrian, bicycle, and vendor routes.

[39]Hough (1995: 6) refers to the "ignored landscape," but of a different nature to those in superblocks. This is the more generic "landscape of industry, railways, public utilities, vacant lands, urban expressway interchanges, abandoned mining lands and waterfronts" (which is consistent with Parham/OECD, 1996).

[40]The author concurs with Hough (1995: 20) that human actions and ecological evolution in the city are inexplicably linked. It calls for natural processes to be "internalized into human activities" (Hough 1995: 27).

This intermediate-scale approach involves investigating and adapting lessons from the "vernacular" – often ignored by city administrators (Sintusingha 2004: 146–147) – which here refers not only to traditional forms and patterns of the past, but their contemporary manifestations such as *thanons* and *sois* which, it has been argued, can trace their lineage to the *khlongs* and *khlongsois* as much as the carriageways and roads introduced in the mid nineteenth century. They are typologies in themselves, even if more by local habit and evolution than by planned intervention. The "formalization" of superblocks, *thanons*, *sois*, and *khlongs* (coupled with innovations in typologies) into finer categories could form part of a strategy to increase Bangkok's sustainability (Sintusingha 2006).

These forms can be implemented incrementally, but must be orchestrated by broader sustainable plans and participatory practices. Together they could help fulfill the sustainable principle of self-sufficiency. For example, food and other agricultural products can be produced near or within the locality, while water and wastes from the urban settlements can be recycled to sustain the agricultural plots and urban parks. Retrofitting natural and rural areas into the city, and integrating both realms as part of urban inhabitants' everyday life also addresses a fundamental principle of sustainability – that of educating and raising awareness of ecological processes at the finest unit of the individual, bridging that mythical divide between humans and nature perpetuated by the modern city.

7.5 Conclusion

Bangkok is an Asian megacity with complex, compound problems that seem beyond resolution, even without considering the obligations of "sustainability." Many are systemic issues that need to be addressed at the strategic city-regional planning and design level (Frey 1999: 20). Essentially, environmental and ecological sustainability can be sufficiently tackled at this scale – particularly air and water quality, which, according to Robinson (1995: 104), "involve external diseconomies by their very nature and can only be adequately dealt with by managing the entire airshed and watershed."

But what of the finer scales, the fragments, the local typologies and superblocks that constitute Bangkok – surely they must play a role in order for the broader strategy to work? Past and present master plans were preoccupied with scales far above the everyday life of the inhabitants – arguably the crucial scale that "sustainability" can establish root and prosper.

"However, even the best laid and best backed of master plans will 'gang agley' if it does not plan at a human scale... Each of the master plans for Bangkok was pre-occupied with the grand scheme of things, with networks, layouts and overall order. Although each plan was loudly dedicated to the improvement of the lot of the people of Bangkok, this was a soft nothing since the inhabitants of the city were not considered first or directly" (Sternstein 1982: 117).

References

Aasen CT (1998) Architecture of Siam: a cultural history interpretation. Oxford University Press, Kuala Lumpur

Bangprapa M (2004) Temple property exclusion agreed. Bangkok Post. http://www.bangkokpost.com/News/29May2004_news19.php. Accessed 29 May 2004

Barme S (1993) Luang Wichit Wathakan and the creation of a Thai identity. Institute of Southeast Asian Studies, Singapore

Bello W, Cunningham S, Poh LK (1998) A Siamese tragedy: development and disintegration in modern Thailand. Zed Books Ltd, London

BMA, MIT (1996) The Bangkok plan: a vision of the Bangkok metropolitan administration area 1995–2005 (draft plan). Bangkok Metropolitan Administration, Bangkok

BMA (1999) Pang Muang Ruam Krungthep Mahanakorn (Bangkok Masterplan 1st revision) (in Thai). Department of City Planning, Bangkok Metropolitan Administration, Bangkok

Breheny MJ (ed) (1992) Sustainable development and urban form. Pion, London

Bunnag P, Nopkhun D, Thadaniti S (1982) Canals in Bangkok: History, changes and their impact (1782 A.D.–1982 A.D.). Research Affairs Office Chulalongkorn University, Bangkok

Campbell S (1996) Green cities, growing cities, just cities? Urban planning and the contradictions of sustainable development. J Am Plann Assoc 62(3): 296–312

Dick H, Rimmer P (1999) Privatising climate: first world cities in South East Asia. In: Brotchie J, Newton P, Hall P, Dickey J (eds) East west perspectives on 21st century urban development: sustainable eastern and western cities in the new millennium. Ashgate, Aldershot

Douglass M, Zoghlin M (1994) Sustaining cities at the grassroots: livelihood, environment and social networks in Suan Phlu, Bangkok. Third World Plann Rev 16(2):171–300

DTCP (1999) Karn Pungmuang nai Ratchasamai Phrabatsomdej Phrachaoyuhua Bhumiphol Adulyadej (Urban Planning in the Reign of King Bhumiphol Adulyadej) (in Thai). Department of Town and Country Planning, Bangkok

Evers H, Korff R (2000) Southeast Asian urbanism: the meaning and power of social space. Lit Verlage, St. Martin's Press, Institute of Southeast Asian Studies, Munster, New York, Singapore

Farrell D (2004) The hidden dangers of the informal economy. McKinsey Quarterly. http://www.mckinseyquarterly.com/article_page.aspx?ar=1448&L2=7&L3=10. Accessed 3 June 2004

Fleming J, Honour H, Pevsner N (1999) The Penguin dictionary of architecture and landscape architecture. Penguin, London

Frey H (1999) Designing the city: towards a more sustainable urban form. E & FN Spon, London

Ginsburg H (2000) Thai art and culture: historic manuscripts from western collections. University of Hawaii Press, Honolulu

Girardet H (1999) Schumacher briefing no. 2 creating sustainable cities. Green Books, Devon

Hanks LM (1972) Rice and man: agricultural ecology in southeast Asia. University of Hawaii Press, Honolulu

Hamilton A (2000) Wonderful, terrible: everyday life in Bangkok. In: Bridges G, Watson S (eds) A companion to the city. Blackwell, Oxford, pp 460–471

Herbert DT, Thomas CJ (1997) Cities in space: city as place. David Fulton, London

Hoche J (1898) Le Siam et les Siamois. Paris

Hough M (1995) Cities and natural process. Routledge, London

Iamworamate T (1989) A New Thai English dictionary. Ruamsasna, Bangkok

Janchitfah S (2002). The good fight. Bangkok Post. http://www.bangkokpost.net/en/Outlook/10Jul2002_out01.html. Accessed 10 July 2002

Jumsai S (1997) Naga: cultural origins in Siam and the West Pacific. Chalermnit Press and DD Books, Bangkok

Jumsai S (2003) Floating city – Bangkok 1550–2100 (lecture) in a design-research workshop: floating city (11–16 October 2003) at the Faculty of Architecture, Building and Planning, University of Melbourne

Kaothien U, Webster D (2000) The Bangkok region. In: Simmonds R, Hack G (eds) Global city regions: their emerging forms. E & FN Spon, London

Kemgumnerd T (2002) Dykes worsen problem as river heads for record. Bangkok Post. http://www.bangkokpost.com/021002_News/02Oct2002_news05.html. Accessed 2 October 2002

Koolhaas R (2004) Content. Taschen, Cologne

McGee TG (1991) The emergence of Desakota regions in Asia: expanding a hypothesis. In: Ginsburg N, Koppel B, McGee TG (eds) The extended metropolis: settlement transition in Asia. University of Hawaii Press, Honolulu

McGee TG, Robinson IM (1995) (eds) The mega-urban regions of Southeast Asia. UBC Press, Vancouver

Mulder N (1992) Inside Thai society: an interpretation of everyday life. Duang Kamol, Bangkok

Na Ranong J (2002) Overflowing dams increase flooding threat downstream. Bangkok Post. http://www.bangkokpost.net/280902_News/28Sep2002_news05.html. Accessed 28 September 2002

Nicholson-Lord D (1987) The greening of the cities. Routledge & Kegan Paul, London

Rist G (1997) The history of development: from western origins to global faith (translated by Patrick Camiller). Zed Books, Atlantic Highlands, NJ

Robinson IM (1995) Emerging spatial patterns in ASEAN mega-urban regions. In: McGee TG, Robinson IM (eds) The mega-urban regions of Southeast Asia. UBC Press, Vancouver

Rusk D (1995) Cities without suburbs. Woodrow Wilson Center Press, Washington, DC

Santimatanedol A, Changyawa P (2003) Elected mayors may answer to governor. Bangkok Post. http://www.bangkokpost.net/News/19Feb2003_news08.html. Accessed 19 February 2003

Sattha C (2002) Discharges planned from swollen dams: run-offs unlikely to affect Bangkok. Bangkok Post. http://scoop.bangkokpost.co.th/bkkpost/2002/sep2002/bp20020921/news/21Sep2002_news10.html. Accessed 21 September 2002

Sethaputra S (1970) New Model English–Thai dictionary library edition (4th edition in two volumes). Thai Watana Panich, Bangkok

Sheer BC (2001) The anatomy of sprawl. Places 14(2):28–37

Sintusingha S (2002) *Muang*, *Khlong*, and *Thammachat* (city, canals, and nature): ingredients for "sustainable" Bangkok. Modernity, tradition, culture, water. In: Proceedings of an international symposium, Bangkok, October 2002. Kasetsart University Press, Bangkok

Sintusingha S (2004) Bangkok: sustainable sprawl? NaJua J Fac Arch Silpakorn Univ 20(2003–2004):139–148

Sintusingha S (2006) Sustainability and urban sprawl: alternative scenarios for a Bangkok superblock. Urban Des Int 11(3/4):151–172

Sorensen A (2000) Conflict, consensus or consent: implications of Japanese land readjustment practice for developing countries. Habitat Int 24(1):51–73

Sorensen A (2007) Consensus, persuasion, and opposition: organizing land readjustment in Japan. In: Hong YH, Needham B (eds) Analyzing land readjustment: economics, law, and collective action. Lincoln Institute for Land Policy, Cambridge, MA

Sternstein L (1982) Portrait of Bangkok. Bangkok Metropolitan Administration, Bangkok

Techawongtham W (2002) Billions of baht flushed away. Bangkok Post. URL address unknown. Accessed 26 April 2002

Thairath (2004) 41 Ongkorn Phuddhasasna karn kormor jadrhubteedin (41 Buddhist Organizations protest Land readjustment Bill). Thairath. http://www.thairath.co.th/thairath1/2547/educat/apr/08/edu1.php. Accessed 27 May 2004

Thansettakij (2004) Perd jai Sawang Srisakhun pud "muang mai nai fan" yark ying gwa khen krok kun phukhao (Interview with Sawang Srisakhun: it is extremely hard to build a new city). Thansettakij. http://203.107.133.147/than2000/1905/columninterview4.htm. Accessed 19 May 2004

Vichit-Vadakan V, Nakata T (eds) (1976) Urbanization in the Bangkok Central region. Thai University Research Associate, The Social Science Association of Thailand, Bangkok

Webster D (1995) Mega-urbanization in ASEAN: new phenomenon or transitional phase to the "Los Angeles World City"? In: McGee TG, Robinson IM (eds) The mega-urban regions of Southeast Asia. UBC Press, Vancouver

Winichakul T (1994) Siam mapped: a history of the geo-body of a nation. University of Hawaii Press, Honolulu

World Bank (1998) Social aspects of the crisis: perceptions of poor communities. Draft Report

Wright TJ (1999) Characteristics of design for sustainable urban settlement. Faculty of Architecture, Building and Planning, University of Melbourne, Melbourne

Wyatt DK (2003) Thailand: a short history. Yale, New Haven

Yencken DGD, Wilkinson D (2000) Resetting the compass: Australia's journey towards sustainability. CSIRO Publishing, Collingwood, Australia

Zhou Y (1991) The metropolitan interlocking region in China: a preliminary hypothesis. In: Ginsburg N, Koppel B, McGee TG (eds) The extended metropolis: settlement transition in Asia. University of Hawaii Press, Honolulu

Vichit-Vadakan V, Nakata T (eds) (1976) Urbanization in the Bangkok Central region. Thai University Research Associates, The Social Science Association of Thailand, Bangkok

[illegible]

8. Urban Dualism in the Jakarta Metropolitan Area

Haryo Winarso

8.1 Introduction

The growth of the Jakarta Metropolitan Areas (JMA) has been very rapid and intense, particularly in the last three decades. Jakarta began as a tiny town named *Sunda Kelapa* in 1527 with a population of less than 100,000. It has since grown to become one of global cities in Asia with a total population of over 21 million in 2007 in an area that includes four other administrative regions (or *Kabupatens*) – Bogor, Depok, Tangerang, and Bekasi – and is widely known as *Jabodetabek*[1] (Fig. 8-1).

After a steady and slow development for almost 450 years, Jakarta experienced a spatial transformation during the last three decades.[2] It started with the economic boom in Indonesia between 1972 and 1990s, when housing development soared. During this time, the number of registered land development companies almost tripled, from 907 companies in 1990

[1] *Jabodetabek* was formerly known as *Jabotabek*, based on a plan which was initially developed with the assistance of the Dutch Government in 1970. (The concept of *Jabotabek* was coined by a Dutch consultant in 1970.) The planning concept was inspired by the model of *Randstad* in the Netherlands (Giebels 1986). The concept includes self-contained growth centers. Two main models were introduced, one concentric and the other linear. Since then, the plan has been reviewed three times; however there has been no significant alteration to the basic concept, except for updated forecasts of population growth. The last review, conducted in 1992, reiterated the plan for development along east-west and north-south axes. The plan, however, is not legally binding.

[2] Silver (2008) noted that the spatial change actually started after the 1900s with the colonization of Batavia.

A. Sorensen and J. Okata (eds.), *Megacities: Urban Form, Governance, and Sustainability*,

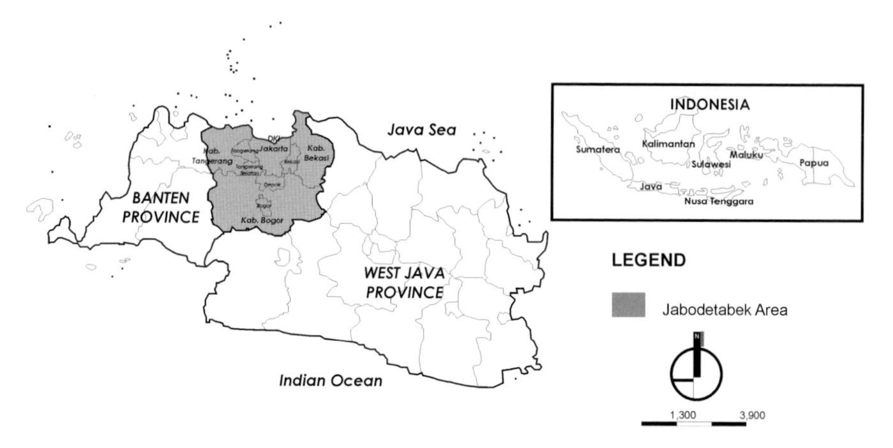

Fig. 8-1. Jakarta metropolitan area

to 2,312 companies in 1997 (Simanungkalit 2002).[3] During the 1990s, the private sector in the JMA developed more than 15 large-scale housing estates on 16,600 ha of rural land, selling more than 25,000 housing units annually. In the absence of sound planning and regulations, this development, which was supported by the more liberal economic policies of the Suharto regime, created sprawl and presented the duality of both planned and unplanned urban forms.

The transportation systems are also under stress, particularly those connecting the newly developed areas to the core of the JMA. More than 1.2 million cars enter the core of the JMA everyday, creating congestion in the core area and contributing to air pollution. Water services are inadequate: less than 70% of the JMA's population is connected to piped water.

Yet, despite these problems, JMA has contributed significantly to the economic development of the country and represents the most modern city in Indonesia, with heritage conservation areas and public and commercial areas that rival those of other modern world cities. Nevertheless, the urban dualism of formal–informal, planned–unplanned, rich–poor characterizes the JMA. There are "villages" close to sophisticated residential estates; informal commercial areas adjacent to modern malls and shopping centers; and *kampungs*[4] surrounded by modern office buildings, apartments, and condominiums.

This paper describes the development of the JMA in three broad phases of change – the colonial period, the post-colonial period, and the modern

[3]In 2008 the companies registered as members of REI was 1,900 (interview with REI President, March 2008).

[4]*Kampung* is an Indonesian word for an informal and incrementally developed settlement in an urban area.

period – emphasizing the changes that took place in the modern period. The modern period has brought social and economic and spatial transformation, creating a multi-faceted city: modern in some areas, traditional in others, with both sophisticated residential areas and slums, both formal and informal developments.

The dualism of the city spaces create a unique urban form, in which some areas are extremely densely populated, mostly by low-income people, while adjacent to these lie wealthy neighborhoods. Although the spatial segregation created by this dualism may be dangerous for social cohesiveness (Leaf 1996; Winarso 2005), the urban form produced by this dualism could also be seen as a way to sustain city life and thus create a sustainable urban form.[5] This paper argues that the urban dualism in the JMA can be viewed in one of two ways. On the one hand, it may ease the tensions of modernity associated with fast, expensive, individualistic ways of life; on the other hand, segregation can exacerbate social disparities because it simultaneously insulates the bourgeoisie and sharpens and mobilizes class and racial conflicts.

This paper traces the spatial restructuring of Jakarta from the tiny town of *Sunda Kelapa* to its emergence as a large metropolitan area, explaining the urbanization processes involved, the development of the private sector, and how urban spaces have been shaped over time.

8.2 A Brief History of the JMA: The Formation of Social Dualism

8.2.1 Colonial Urbanism: The Beginning of Dualism in Jakarta's Urban Form

Social dualism in a city is not new; many articles have discussed the phenomenon. Leaf (1996), for instance, has documented his view on the social dualism in the metropolitan region of Jakarta. Borrowing from Wertheim (1956), Leaf suggests that dualism has been used to describe the separation of colonial elites and indigenous groups, or the feudal classes in a city. Leaf further argues that recently social dualism has been manifested in the formal and informal sectors of the economy.

[5]The concept of sustainable urban form has been much debated recently; see for instance Williams et al. (2000). Borrowing from their work, urban form is taken to be sustainable if it "enables the city to function within its natural and man-made carrying capacity; is 'user friendly' for its occupants; and promotes social equity."

Urban social dualism is also seen in the formal and informal development of Third World cities. Segregation may be caused by the uneven distribution of urban space based on ethnicity, social status, or origin (Barbosa 2001). Spatial segregation is therefore associated with the spatial concentration of certain groups (Bolt et al. 2006). This phenomenon is seen in the JMA. Although in the kingdom era, the city had been divided between the royal quarter and the areas where the common people lived, social dualism in the city was even stronger under the Dutch administration.

Jakarta, the core city of the JMA, originally called *Sunda Kelapa*, was founded in the 1300s as a small trading port at the mouth of the Ciliwung River. After the triumph over the Portuguese in 1527 by the Sundanese ruler, *Sunda Kelapa* was named *Jayakarta*, which means victory.

In the early 1600s the Dutch took command of the city and administered it under the United East Indies Company (*Vereenigde Oost Indische Compagnie* or VOC) after its founding in 1602. The city was renamed Batavia in 1618. By 1799, the VOC possession of Batavia was transferred to the Dutch Crown. This marked the beginning of the colonization of the country. The administration of the country by the Dutch Colonial Government brought many changes to the city's social, economic, political, and physical structures, particularly economic exploitation under a policy known as *cultuurstelsel*.[6] Batavia became the center of a colonial system the purpose of which was to administer the appropriation of agricultural surpluses.

William Daendels, the first Governor General of the Colonial Government, in 1808 ordered the development of a new residential area in suburban Batavia (Surjomihardjo 1977), commonly called *Weltevreden* (Silver 2008). In 1811 Batavia's population consisted of 552 Europeans and another 1,455 persons legally recognized as Europeans; other Asian citizens numbered only 45,000 (Marcussen 1990).

By the 1900s the population had increased to around 500,000. The Europeans living in Batavia enjoyed the European quarter at *Menteng*[7], while the native local people lived in the surrounding *kampungs* and in traditional villages. This urban form of European mansions surrounded by *kampungs*

[6]*Cultuurstelsel* was a system enforced by the Dutch colonial government whereby peasants were required to grow export crops on a certain percentage of their land or, alternatively, to work for a number of days annually on state plantations or other state projects (Marcussen 1990).

[7]Menteng is an expensive housing area in the centre of Jakarta now. This area was a European quarter just at the end of the old Batavia.

reflected the urban socio-economic dualism of the city (see, for example, Leaf 1993), and marked the beginning of social dualism in urban Batavia.

8.2.2 Post-Colonial Urban: A City to Reflect National Pride

After the Second World War, the new government of Indonesia brought changes to the social and physical structures of the city. In 1950 when the Republic of Indonesia was recognized internationally, Batavia was renamed Jakarta and became the capital of the new nation. Kusno (2000) portrays Jakarta under Sukarno, the first president of Indonesia, as a city that represents both modernism and tradition, "constructed out of a complementary contradiction of identity and difference, of juxtaposing local tradition and global modernity."

President Sukarno's agenda for urban development stressed city beautification in keeping with the idea that the capital of a nation is a reflection of the country and therefore must express the power and centrality of the state. Jakarta would be compared to New York and Moscow as the "portal of the country" and a "beacon of the emerging nation" (Kusno 2000).

In the 1950s, Sukarno wanted to make Indonesia and Jakarta the center of what he described as the '*New Emerging Forces*' of the world. A Central Business District (CBD) was constructed around the main square close to the presidential palace, and a National Monument was erected in the square. The CBD and the square were designed in the manner of an *agora* with a network of freeways to the southwest, connecting the central square to *Kebayoran Baru*. Along the road, high-rise buildings and a huge complex for the Asian Games were later constructed. All of these efforts reflected Sukarno's desire to show off the pride of Indonesia.

During this period *Kebayoran Baru*[8] became an area of middle- and high-income residences in Jakarta. Several other residential developments followed, of which the most prominent was in *Slipi*, the first housing in Indonesia developed by a real estate company. It was created by a government-owned company, PT[9] Pembangunan Jaya, under the chairmanship of Ir. Ciputra[10] (Properti Indonesia, February 1994: 101). The first

[8]*Kebayoran Baru* is a new town in the south of Jakarta, planned by Thomas Karsten, a prominent architect involved in the creation of the first planning act in Indonesia in 1945, and planner for several other cities in Indonesia.

[9]*Perseroan Terbatas* means Limited Company.

[10]Ciputra became the most prominent person in land development in Indonesia. He was the president of the International Real Estate Federation (FIABCI), and owns several of the largest real estate companies in Indonesia.

residence built by a foreign company in this period was probably Pertamina's[11] housing complex, developed by Tosho Sangyo, a Japanese company, in the late 1960s (Properti Indonesia, February 1994: 16–17).

The transformation from a colonial society to a free nation was not an easy process. In 1965, pressured by high inflation and mass political action, Sukarno's government collapsed. Before this collapse, foreign and domestic investment had decreased because of Sukarno's anti-capitalist policies. These socio-economic conditions were reflected in the development of Jakarta.

The first Master Plan for Jakarta, prepared in 1952, which envisaged an urban area with a ring road as the limit and surrounded by a greenbelt, following the principles of Ebenezer Howard's Garden city, had never been actualized. At that time the population had already reached 1.5 million, more than double that in 1945. By 1961, Jakarta's population had reached 2.9 million, which made it one of the largest cities in the world. Most of its population, however, still lived in dense *kampung* areas with poor infrastructure. Public transportation systems were largely neglected. This situation indicated the contradictions of urban development, where public spaces designed to express national pride co-existed with deteriorating *kampung* settlements.

8.2.3 Modern Urban: The Excitement of Property Development and the Economic Crisis

Since 1965, Jakarta has transformed itself from a city of three million people to a city-region of more than 15 million people, emerged as a center of development, and come to dominate the economic activities of the country. Its development goes beyond Jakarta's administrative boundary to encompass a vast urban and peri-urban region; an expansion that has caused social and environmental problems (Firman and Darmaphatni 1994; Hudallah et al. 2007; Mattingly 1999; Sari and Winarso 2007).

Rapid economic development during this period was instrumental in the emergence of private-sector property developers who have played

[11]Pertamina is the only state oil company which had an important role during the first decade of the Suharto's administration. Ibnu Sutowo, the president of the company, acted as the president's political financier (Winters 1991). In an interview with Winters, Sutowo is reported to have said: "You can't find a single road or school or hospital that wasn't at least partly funded by the money I borrowed through Pertamina." Winters's dissertation on the political economy in Indonesia gives a good picture of the role of Pertamina at that time.

important roles in the creation of spaces in JMA (Winarso 1999; Leisch 2002). Starting with *Pondok Indah* in south Jakarta in the 1970s, which transformed 720 ha of rubber plantation into the first planned residential area for middle- and high-income Indonesians after independence, hundreds of new residential areas were developed in JMA together with modern public facilities (Winarso 1999, 2002). Between 1987 and 1989 Indonesia, and Jakarta in particular, experienced the first boom in property development (Winarso 1999). The second boom in 1995 was even higher; coming after a period in 1991–1992 when the country's economy overheated (Winarso 1999; Winarso and Firman 2002).

In conjunction with flourishing housing development came the construction of modern malls and shopping centers, which created new urban spaces in Jakarta. A prominent property analyst reported that in 1997 the supply of new malls and shopping centers in JMA reached 290,204 m^2 (Simanungkalit 2002), the highest single-year increase ever recorded in the region. Meanwhile, the development of large-scale residential areas in the form of new town development also was at its height.

During this 10-year period of rapid economic growth, more than 20 new towns were developed (Winarso 1999). Most of the new towns in JMA were gated communities with high-security perimeter defenses, separated from the low-income *kampungs* or villages in the surrounding areas – reinforcing spatial dualism and segregation (Winarso 2005; Winarso and Saptono 2008).

When the value of the Rupiah fell against the dollar[12] in 1997, development in JMA slowed down. The economic crisis hit Indonesia especially hard (Winarso et al. 2001); the number of poor people increased,[13] as did the poverty level.[14] In December 1998, the number of poor people (living in urban and rural areas) reached 49.5 million (24.23% of the total population), or 27 million more than the number before the crisis. This figure was reached within a mere 18 months.

[12]The Rupiah depreciated from approximately 2,500 Rupiah per US$1 in 1995 to approximately 10,000 Rupiah per US$1 in May 1998.

[13]In 1976, the number of poor people was 54.2 million (or 40.08 % of total population). The number had decreased to about 22.5 million (11.34 %) in 1996, just before the crash.

[14]The increasing number of people living in poverty was due to a rise in the level of the poverty line, from Rp. 42.220 (US$4.20) in 1996 to about Rp. 96.959 (US$9.60) in 1998 in urban areas and from Rp. 31.141 (US$3.15) to Rp. 72.780 (US$7.20) in rural areas. The shift in the poverty line was the result of substantial changes in relative prices.

Within a very short period of time the gap between the haves and the haves-not widened considerably. This condition increased tensions between groups in the region. This situation, combined with the collapse of the banking industry, triggered an economic crisis in Indonesia (Winarso and Firman 2002) and culminated in the social–political turmoil of the country in 1998. The housing and commercial property markets collapsed. Slowly, the property market began to recover and in 2004 the supply of and demand for office space in Jakarta CBD was increasing.

8.3 Urbanization in JMA: The Birth of a Megalopolis

From 1961 to 1971, Jakarta underwent massive urbanization. The urban population almost doubled, from 2.9 million to 4.6 million, with an annual growth rate of 5.8%. This was the fastest urban population growth in the country and the fastest in Jakarta's history (see Table 8-1).

This rapid urbanization was a result of the rapid economic growth of the country. Between 1967 and 1970, the economy grew at the rate of 6.6% per year, while domestic as well as foreign investment grew rapidly as well (Hill 1996). Particularly noticeable in Jakarta was the development of international hotels and the banking sector, and the expansion of the civil service. Physical infrastructure systems were also rehabilitated, road transport capacity was expanded, and a growing number of inexpensive commercial vehicles contributed to greater mobility. During the 1970s economic conditions further improved, with an average growth rate of 7.7% per year (Hill 1996), and by the end of 1980, the population of *Jabotabek* reached more than 11 million, making JMA the biggest metropolitan area in Southeast Asia.

The rapid urbanization of Jakarta was not without problems. The vast majority of the migrant population was housed in *kampung* areas with very limited infrastructure. A 1969 survey revealed that 65% of all houses had no private toilet facilities, 80% had no electricity, and 90% had no piped water (Sivaramakrisnan and Green 1986:196–197). Meanwhile, as a result of increasing foreign investment in the city, the conversion of land uses became unavoidable. It became obvious that the urban area was expanding beyond its original administrative boundaries to include the adjoining districts or *Kabupatens*. Thus in 1967 a second master plan, covering the period of 1965–1985, was introduced to deal with massive new development in the area.

In general, the area of the JMA can be classified into three zones: core, inner zone, and outer zone (Gardiner and Gardiner 2006). The core is the Special Region of Jakarta. The inner zone is the adjacent areas within *Kabupaten* Tangerang, *Kabupaten* Bekasi, and *Kabupaten* Bogor. The outer

Table 8-1. Population in Jabotabek (000's)

	Population				Annual growth (%)		
Region	**1961**	**1971**	**1980**	**1990**	**1961–1971**	**1971–1980**	**1980–1990**
Jakarta	2,905	4,579	6,503	8,254	5.8	4.7	3.0
Bogor	1,303	1,662	2,494	3,736	2.8	5.6	5.5
Bogor municipality	146	196	247	272	3.4	2.9	1.1
Tangerang	848	1,067	1,529	2,765	2.6	4.8	9.0
Bekasi	690	831	1,144	2,104	2.0	4.2	9.3
Botabek	2,987	3,756	5,414	8,877	2.6	4.9	7.1
Jabotabek	**5,892**	**8,335**	**11,917**	**17,131**	**4.1**	**4.8**	**4.9**

Note: Botabek is the combination of Bogor, Tangerang, and Bekasi
Source: Winarso and Kombaitan (2001)

Table 8-2. Composition of population growth in Jabotabek

Area	Jabotabek Population in '000s 1980	1990	Annual growth rate (%)
Urban	7,337	13,050	5.8
Rural	4,558	3,946	(1.4)
Total	11,895	16,996	3.6
Core Area			
1980 Urban	7,337	9,220	2.3
Expansion	1,730	3,830	7.9
1990 Urban	9,067	13,050	3.6
Rural	2,828	3,946	3.3

Source: Gardiner and Gardiner (2006) in Winarso and Hudallah (2006) based on extensive reconciliation of 1980 and 1990 data sets at the *desa* level to account for boundary, code, and name changes

zone consists of areas further away from Jakarta, but still in the jurisdiction of the above three *Kabupatens*.

The inner zone and the outer zone constitute the peri-urban area of the JMA. Looking at these three zones, one notices the transformation in the JMA. Annual urban population growth in *Jabotabek*, the JMA, is about 5.8%, while the rural population has been shrinking at an annual rate of 1.4%. In the core urban areas, annual growth is about 2.3%, while in the expanding outer areas, population growth was much higher at 7.9% (see Table 8-2). These outer areas have contributed 41% to overall population growth in the metropolitan region[15] (Gardiner and Gardiner 2006).

The JMA is characterized by sprawl. The JMA consists of the core, in which land uses are undergoing a transformation from residential to commercial uses as the consequence of increasing land prices, and the peri-urban area, where new settlements or new towns are located. As shown in Table 8-3, the population in the core area is declining, showing a high

[15]This information is based on statistical data which defines urban as *functionally* urban. "Urban" in Indonesia has two definitions: one is by function, and the other is by administrative area. According to the functional definition, each of the smallest administrative units (*desa or kelurahan*) is accorded a functional urban or rural status based on its characteristics. BPS (Indonesia's Statistical Bureau) defines urban by function and this definition can be changed over time as areas become more densely populated or less agricultural, or as they gain urban facilities and services (Gardiner and Gardiner 2006).

Table 8-3. Area, population, and density of Jabotabek metropolitan area 1997, 2000, and 2003

		Population			Density (people/km²)		
Area	**Area (km²)**	**1997**	**2000**	**2003**	**1997**	**2000**	**2003**
Kabupaten/District							
Bogor	2,237	2,862,292	3,060,618	3,097,409	1,279	1,368	1,385
Bekasi	1,065	1,544,900	1,330,389	1,556,278	1,450	1,249	1,461
Cianjur	2,639	1,812,936	934,409	2,066,787	687	354	783
Tangerang	1,098	2,594,084	2,258,244	2,187,512	2,362	2,056	1,992
Total	7,040	8,814,212	7,583,660	8,907,986	1,252	1,077	1,265
Municipality							
JakartaI	660	9,373,900	7,798,679	7,356,456	14,199	11,813	11,143
Bogor	109	673,882	691,421	748,353	6,183	6,344	6,867
Bekasi	210	1,471,477	1,294,258	1,170,458	7,022	6,176	5,585
Tangerang	305	1,765,819	1,506,757	837,056	5,782	4,934	2,741
Depok	212	834,556	949,207	953,121	3,932	4,472	4,491
Total	1,496	14,119,634	12,240,322	11,065,444	9,436	8,180	7,395
Jabodetabekjur	8,536	22,933,846	19,823,982	19,973,430	2,687	2,322	2,340

Sources: Jawa Barat Dalam Angka 1997, Podes 2000 and 2003, Jabodetabekjur includes: Jakarta, Bogor, Depok, Tangerang, Bekasi, Cianjur

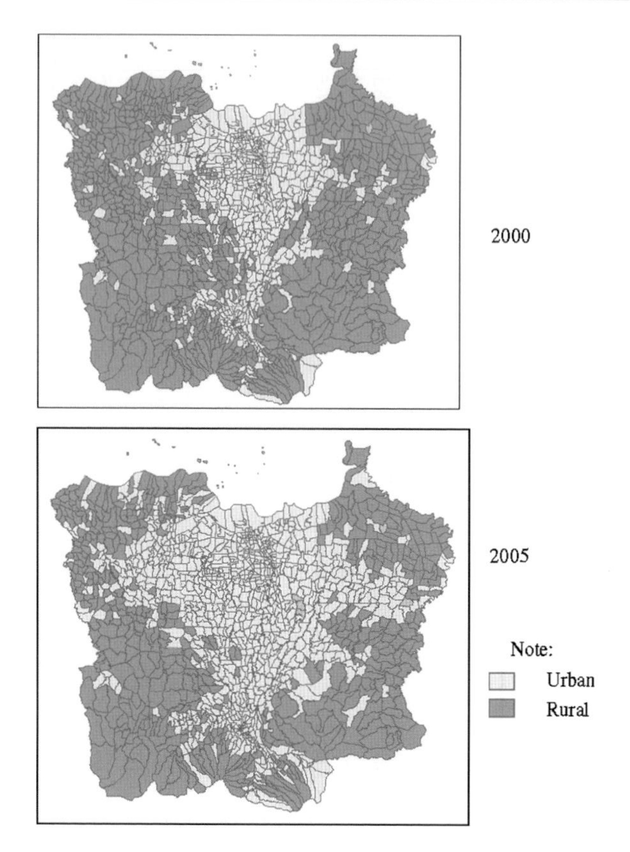

Fig. 8-2. The expansion of urban areas in JMA (2000–2005). Source: Winarso et al. (2007): Based on Village Data 2000 & 2005

Table 8-4. Land use change in *Jabotabek*

No.	Land use	1992 (ha)	1992 (%)	2001 (ha)	2001 (%)
1	Open land	142,718.9	19.94	169,276.8	23.65
2	Agriculture	104,186.4	14.55	104,108.9	14.54
3	Mixed vegetation	176,614.7	24.67	183,534.8	25.64
4	Forest/farmland	197,792.0	27.63	64,084.1	8.95
5	Settlements	68,169.2	9.52	139,684.1	19.51
6	Other use	26,351.6	3.68	55,144.4	7.70
	Total	715,832.9	100.00	715,832.9	100.00

Source: Satellite interpretation LAPAN (Direktorat Jenderal Penataan Ruang Dep. PU 2004)

level of out-migration; while the population in the peri-urban is increasing because of in-migration.

Urbanization consists not only in the movement of people from rural to urban areas, but also the transformation of rural land uses into urban land uses. In the JMA, urbanization is also clearly shown by the penetration of urban development into formerly agricultural land, first at the periphery of the city and then in the areas beyond, in some cases as far as 45 km from Jakarta (Fig. 8-2), and the conversion of land from agriculture to urban uses (Winarso 2007). Table 8-4 shows that the settlement area has increased significantly from 68,351.6 ha in 1992 to 139,684.1 ha in 2001, while forest and farm land decreased from 197,792 ha in 1992 to 64,085.14 ha in 2001.

Within the metropolitan area of Jakarta, 16,600 ha of rural land far away from the built-up area have been converted to urban land uses and private-sector housing developers sell about 25,000 housing units annually (Winarso and Firman 2002). This development is undoubtedly creating environmental problems, particularly affecting groundwater and air quality (Cybriwsky and Ford 2001; Firman and Darmapatni 1992; Mattingly 1999). Transportation and housing problems are also emerging (JICA and BAPPENAS 2001; Winarso 2002).

The total area of the JMA is about 617,000 ha. Although a good transportation system is needed to serve such a large area, the JMA cannot provide such a system. A current research report (JICA and BAPPENAS 2004), shows the uneven distribution of per capita roads and toll roads (Table 8-5).

Jakarta's inner city, the core of the JMA, attracts many commuters from peri-urban areas. A recent transportation study (JICA and BAPPENAS 2001) maintains that there were 17 million trips per day within Jakarta, and more than 1.3 million trips from the peri-urban area (the *Bodetabek*) into Jakarta. Some commuters travel more than 100 km per day. Out of the total trips, 44% were made using private vehicles, either a car or motorcycle, and 56% were made on public transportation. This ratio shows the lack of public transportation in the JMA, and the increase in the number of private cars (Fig. 8-3).

8.4 The Creation of Spaces in the JMA: Reinforcing Spatial Segregation

Scholars have examined the processes of spatial restructuring taking place in Jakarta and argued that these processes relate to the process of economic development in Indonesia (see, for example, Leisch 2002; Winarso 1999;

Table 8-5. Per capita road and toll road

Administrative area	Population	Road length (km)	(%)	Per capita (km/ 1,000 population)	Toll road length (km)	(%)	Per capita (km/ 1,000 population)
DKI Jakarta	7,610,349	6,548.4	58	0.9	113.0	52	0.02
Kota/Kab. Bogor	4,212,605	1,762.7	16	0.4	23.9	11	0.01
Kota/Kab. Bekasi	3,280,810	1,450.1	13	0.4	34.2	16	0.01
Kota/Kab. Tangerang	4,093,174	1,357.7	12	0.3	36.4	17	0.01
Kota Depok	n.a	245.0	2	n.a	7.8	4	n.a
Total	19,196,938	11,363.9	100	2.0	215.3	100	0.05

Source: SITRAMP (2002)

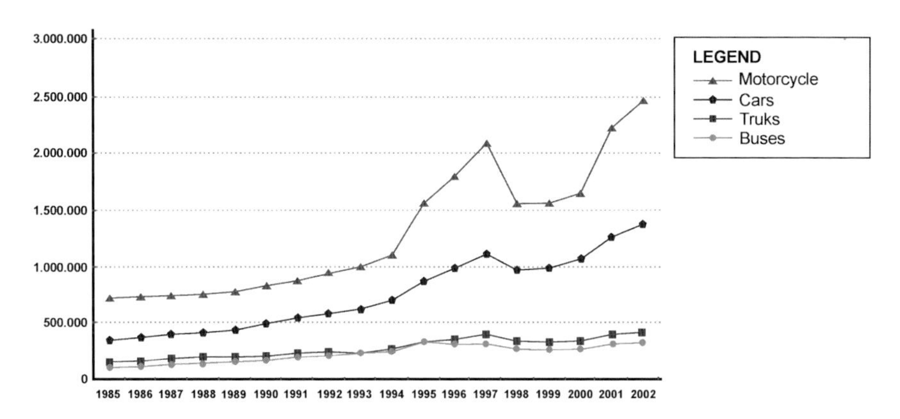

Fig. 8-3. Number of registered vehicles in Jakarta 1986–2002. Source: Polda Metro Jaya quoted by JICA and BAPPENAS (2001)

Winarso and Saptono 2008). Spatial restructuring creates urban spaces that on the one hand lead to social segregation, but on the other hand allow the development of ultra modern urban spaces that can be compared with modern spaces in cities in the world.

Spatial segregation in modern cities has been much documented (Barbosa 2001; Knox 1989). It is widely accepted that segregation in urban areas is mostly caused by the uneven distribution of land uses, particularly in residential areas, usually called residential differentiation. Spatial segregation may also mean the social division of space, through the spatial concentration of certain groups (Bolt et al. 2006). Taste and lifestyle differences may also lead to segregation. Scholars agree that spatial segregation can be voluntary, involuntary, or for ecological reasons (see, for example, Schwab 1992; Knox 1989). Voluntary segregation creates little conflict, while involuntary segregation usually has the potential to spark community conflicts.

The following section discusses the creation of new spaces and spatial segregation in new residential areas, vernacular residential areas, malls, apartments and offices, and heritage conservation areas in the JMA.

8.4.1 New Residential Areas: Creating Centers

In the JMA, spatial segregation is particularly visible in recently developed areas in which property markets are booming and private-sector firms compete to develop housing, malls, offices, and other forms of real estate. The creation of new urban spaces in the JMA has been intense. By 1997 more than 50 residential areas (known also as new-town developments) were developed; out of these, about 30% were large-scale residential developments of more than 500 ha (see Table 8-6). Most of these residential areas were developed with sophisticated facilities, usually arranged around a *cul de sac* with a guard at the main entry. One example of this type of residential development is *Pondok Indah* (which translates to “beautiful home”), which became a symbol of a wealthy residential area in Jakarta. The price of land in the area was skyrocketing and in 2005 it reached Rp. 20 billion (US$200,000[16]) for a house of 500 m^2, while in 1975, when the project started, the same types of houses were being offered at less than Rp. 100 million (US$10,000) (Winarso 1999). The plan was inspired by new town development in the United States, complete with expensive social facilities, such as schools and malls.

One of the new towns is *Bumi Serpong Damai* (BSD), developed by the same developers who created *Pondok Indah*. BSD was designed to house 600,000 people by 2005 in an area of 6,000 ha. However, by late 2004, only 1,466 units had been built (BSD City 2004). If the average household size is 4.3[17] and only 90% of the units were occupied, the number of inhabitants in BSD would be 61,644. Thus the density is 38 persons per hectare, which is very low compared to Jakarta (average 1,243 persons per hectare).

In 2002, BSD, which was built by a consortium of ten developers, was taken over by *Sinar Mas Group*[18] (*Properti Indonesia*, March 2004) and renamed BSD City. In order to meet demand, BSD City is now developing more gated residential enclaves, complete with commercial areas for malls and international trade centers. These new facilities have boosted the price of houses in the area. For example, as reported by *Property Magazine*, a house of 36 m^2 on a 72-m^2 plot sold at Rp. 53 million (US$5,300) in 1997; the same type of house was being marketed at Rp.114 million (US$11,400) in 2004, an increase of more than 115% (*Properti Indonesia*, March 2004).

[16]An exchange rate of Rp. 1 million = US$100 is used throughout this article.
[17]Winarso (2002) notes that average household size in new towns in *Kabupaten Tangerang* is 4.3, lower than the figure for Jakarta (4.7) or for Indonesia (4.5).
[18]Sinar Mas Group is owned by Muchtar Wijaya, an Indonesian real estate tycoon.

Table 8-6. Large-scale residential developments (>500 ha)

No.	Name	Area (ha)	Location	No.	Name	Area (ha)	Location
1	Milik PT Pembangunan Delta Bekasi	1,500	Kab. Bekasi	19	Taruma Resort	1,100	Kab. Bogor
2	Milik PT Lippo City Development	780	Kab. Bekasi	20	Talaga Kahuripan	750	Kab. Bogor
3	Milik PT Pura Delta Bekasi	1,500	Kab. Bekasi	21	Kota Tenjo	3,000	Kab. Bogor
4	Cikarang Baru	1,400	Kab. Bekasi	22	Milik PT Bangun Jaya Triperkasa	500	Kab. Bogor
5	Bekasi Matra Real Estate	500	Kab. Bekasi	23	Maharani Citra Pertiwi	1,679	Kab. Bogor
6	Milik PT Dwigunatama Rintisprima	850	Kab. Bekasi	24	Milik PT Banyu Buana Adhi Lestari	500	Kab. Bogor
7	Kota Legenda (Bekasi 2000)	2,000	Kab & Kot. Bekasi	25	Kotabaru Tigaraksa	3,000	Kab. Tangerang
8	Milik PT Sinar Bahana Mulia	800	Kab. Bekasi	26	Puri Jaya	7,145	Kab. Tangerang
9	Pantai Modern	500	Kab. Bekasi	27	Citra Raya	3,000	Kab. Tangerang
10	Lippo Cikarang	3,000	Kab. Bekasi	28	Lippo Karawaci	2,000	Kab. Tangerang
11	Harapan Indah	800	Kab. Bekasi	29	Gading Serpong	1,500	Kab. Tangerang
12	Bukit Jonggol Asri	30,000	Kab. Bogor	30	Alam Sutera	700	Kab. Tangerang
13	Citra Indah	1,000	Kab. Bogor	31	Bumi Serpong Damai	6,000	Kab. Tangerang
14	Kota Taman Metropolitan	600	Kab. Bogor	32	Bintaro Jaya	2,321	Kab. Tangerang
15	Kota Wisata	1,000	Kab. Bogor	33	Kota Modern	770	Kab. Tangerang
16	Bukit Sentul	2,000	Kab. Bogor	34	Kota Wisata Teluk Naga	8,000	Kab. Tangerang
17	Rancamaya	500	Kab. Bogor	35	Kota Jaya	1,745	Kab. Tangerang
18	Resort Danau Lido	1,700	Kab. Bogor	36	Pantai Indah Kapuk	800	DKI Jakarta

This price is very expensive for most people, and the magazine suggests that only a household with a monthly income of more than Rp. three million (US$300) could buy this house.[19] This is well above the average monthly income in Jakarta (Rp. 255,463 or US$25.50) or in the Province of West Java (Rp. 151,618 or US$15.10),[20] and above the monthly income of all urban households in Indonesia (Rp. 234,000 or US$23.40). Studies of the age, family size, education, employment, and annual earning of the population in the new cities suggest that most urban residents are young professionals working in the private sector (Winarso 2002; Leisch 2002). One study also indicates that the consumers of new housing in the region belong to the middle- and high-income segments of the Indonesian population and are of Sino Indonesian descent (Leisch 2002). These characteristics are not unique to the population of BSD City, but are also found in the other "new cities" and high-income residential enclaves in the area. A recent study (Winarso and Saptono 2008) found that the development of BSD City has created segregation within and around the new city, spatially and socially.

Other centers in the region provide offices, shopping centers, and major public amenities in their projects, and counteract the centripetal pull of the core city of Jakarta. The provision of these public facilities and amenities elsewhere in the region has reduced the number of household trips to Jakarta for daily activities, as members of the household are no longer forced to make such a trip (Winarso 2002).

8.4.2 Kampungs: Vernacular Urban Residential Settlements

Adjacent to the large-scale, modern developments are many informal settlements known as *kampungs*, which are unplanned, incrementally developed areas, frequently associated with slums. The word *kampung* originally meant a village with rural characteristics, but as the city expands, many of

[19]In Indonesia, where the total population reached 206.6 million in 2000 (BPS 2000) those living in urban areas in 2000 made up 42.0% of the total population (BPS 2000). Almost 71% of the urban population consisted of those from moderate- and low-income groups. The current median monthly household incomes (50th percentile) for urban areas within and outside DKI Jakarta are Rp. 950, 000 and Rp. 892, 000, respectively. The median household income in rural areas is Rp. 579,300 (Hoek-Smit 2001). Only about 15% of the urban population can afford to buy a better house. The large majority, 45%, can buy only simple houses and require loans or subsidies to do so.

[20]These figures are from BPS (1994). The inflation rate is not calculated.

these traditional settlements have been "trapped" in an urban setting. Some of them have been transformed into urban villages that retain certain rural characters, such as an informal way of living, and minimal infrastructure and services. Borrowing Turner's (1968) argument about the "bridge-headers" or rural migrants who hope to make their fortune by coming to a city and living in inner-city areas close to the available jobs, *Kampungs* are the first place these migrants stay, because of the informal characteristics of the lifestyle and the housing. Because of this migration, the *kampungs* have become very dense. In some cases, the density can reach more than 1,000 persons per hectare.

In 1969, *kampungs*, for the first time, received formal attention from the Governor of Jakarta, then Ali Sadikin, who launched the first *Kampung* Improvement program (KIP). This program was a success and was replicated in other cities in Indonesia. The KIP also received acknowledgement from the World Bank. The KIP in 1969 was an enhanced version of the 1920s Dutch Colonial scheme of *kampung* improvement. The program involved making improvement to basic infrastructure to enhance health and sanitation (Silver 2008). Ali Sadikin himself received an honor from the World Bank in 2004 for his achievement in improving *kampung* conditions city wide.

Conditions in *kampungs* in Jakarta, the core of JMA, are not as bad as they were before the 1990s, but because the density is so high and infrastructure is limited, they are still considered slums. The general characteristics of a *kampung* include a lack of public facilities, small alleys and footpaths, a limited clean water supply, poor management of solid waste, and inadequate drainage. Nevertheless, *kampungs* offer an affordable place to live close to the city center for those working in the informal sector or for low-income employees working in offices or malls in the CBD. *Kampungs* in peri-urban areas provide housing for service workers, domestic workers, and other employees in the informal sector upon whom residential estate dwellers depend (Leaf 1996; Winarso and Saptono 2008).

Not all *kampungs* are in bad condition. Some are considered vernacular urban space, since the built heritage is associated with the indigenous inhabitants of Jakarta – the *Betawi* – and other ethnic groups closely associated with the *Betawi*, including the Arabs, Chinese, and Portuguese. Jakarta's vernacular urban space can be classified in the following way:

- Coastal *Betawi*: vernacular settlements located in coastal areas, i.e. Kampung Luar Batang and Marunda in northern Jakarta.
- Urban-*kampungs*: vernacular settlements located adjacent to "colonial" activity centers, e.g. Kampung/Desa Tugu (Portuguese), Kampung Koja (Arab and Chinese), and the Glodok area (Chinese). These areas are located in northern and western Jakarta.

- Hinterland *Betawi*: vernacular settlements in former agricultural areas characterized by *Betawi* cultural heritage, e.g., Condet and Srengseng Sawah. These areas area located in eastern and southern Jakarta.

One example of this type of urban space is Condet in eastern Jakarta, which has been preserved as a fruit-growing village. In 1975, Condet was planned as an agricultural village, and was listed as an area of Betawi Cultural Heritage in 1976. One of Condet's famous fruits, salak (*Salacca edulis*), is the symbol of Jakarta. In this area, one can still find traditional modes of transportation, fashion, architecture, landscape, art and crafts, fruit and vegetable markets, medicine, culinary traditions, and language (Bahasa Indonesia spoken in the *Betawi* dialect).

The Condet conservation plan covered an area of 700 ha; 50% of this area was agricultural land.[21] The Government of DKI Jakarta planned to preserve the *kampung*, particularly the Balekambang district, bordered by the Ciliwung River. By preserving the environment and restoring some of the *Betawi* vernacular houses, this plan encouraged tourism. The "*Betawi* village" is designed to be a tourist destination that is unique in the context of the modern development of Jakarta.

8.4.3 Malls, Apartments, and Office Buildings: Modern Urban Space

A survey by the *Asian Retail Property Review* (2006) lists a number of new developments of malls and shopping centers (Table 8-7), although there are already more than 15 high-end malls and shopping centers in the JMA (see Fig. 8-4). One is the mall known as *Pondok Indah*, one of the most prestigious malls in Jakarta; the price of a kiosk in the mall in 2004 was about Rp. 75,000 (US$7.5) per square meter per month (Alexander 2004). About 40,000 people visit the mall every weekday and about 80,000–100,000 people visit on weekends (Alexander 2004). This mall offers many kinds of branded (that is, expensive) goods.

The latest development, which puts together malls, apartments, and office buildings, is *Kelapa Gading* in northeastern Jakarta. In the 1970s, this area

[21]At least three conservation plans for Condet were prepared in the 1990s by Dinas Tata Bangunan & Pemugaran (Building and Conservation Office), Dinas Kebudayaan (Culture Office), and Dinas Tata Kota (Urban Planning Office) in DKI Jakarta.

Table 8-7. Shopping centers in Jakarta

Shopping center	Location	Marketing scheme	Status
Gajah Mada Square	Central Jakarta	Leased	Under construction
Plaza Pondok Gede 2	Bekasi	Strata	Finishing
Pulo Gadung Central Business	North Jakarta	Strata	Finishing
Sentral Grosir	Cikarang Bekasi	Strata	Finishing
Plaza Dua Raja	Bogor	Strata	Finishing
Kelapa Gading Mal Phase 4	North Jakarta	Leased	Under construction
Mall Of Indonesia (Kelapa Gading Square)	North Jakarta	Strata	Finishing
Pluit Junction	North Jakarta	Leased	Under construction
Pusat Grosir Cililitan 2	East Jakarta	Strata	Under construction
Emporium Pluit (CBD Pluit)	North Jakarta	Leased	Under construction
Grand Indonesia	Central Jakarta	Leased	Finishing
CBD Ciledug	Tangerang	Strata	Under construction
Pamulang Square	Tangerang	Strata	Under construction
Summarecon Mal	Tangerang	Leased	Under construction

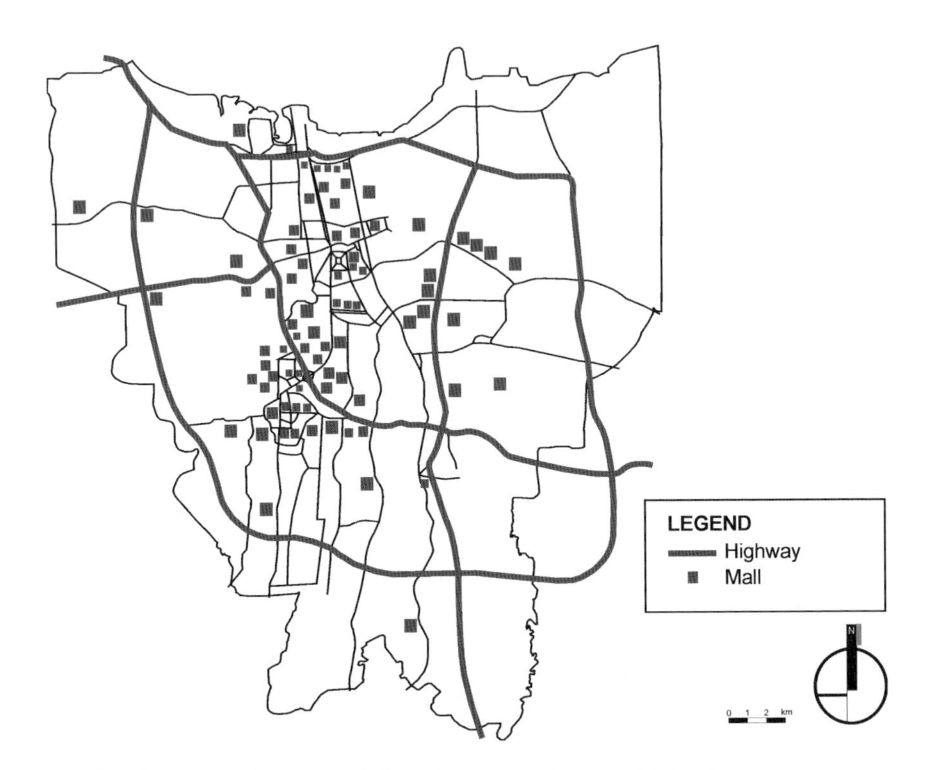

Fig. 8-4. Location of malls and shopping centre in central Jakarta

was rural and some of the areas were swampy. Today, this 1,800-ha area has been transformed into a new town with expensive public facilities. There are apartments, condominiums, office buildings, and one of the biggest malls in the JMA. One prominent newspaper reported that *Kelapa Gading* has 3,500 traditional-style shophouses and 500,000 m^2 of mall space (Sinar Harapan 2003). Property prices in this area are increasing; in 1983 the price of a high-quality house was Rp 7.5 million (US$7,500). In 1990 the price of the same type of house reached Rp 750 million (US$75,000), an increase of ten times within 10 years (Sinar Harapan 2003). This type of urban development most likely will be repeated in the coming years as the property market is still promising in Jakarta. Recent reports from Colliers International Indonesia (2006) show that cumulative supply and demand for office space is still increasing.

These newly developed malls, apartment buildings, and condominiums are creating modern urban spaces adjacent to the old ones, including some dilapidated *kampung* areas (Table 8-8).

8.4.4 Conservation of Colonial Heritage: Remembering the Orderly Past

In 2001, the Governor of Jakarta Special Capital City issued a decree to preserve the old city of Jakarta and make the old historic city a cultural tourism destination that would boost heritage conservation values and provide an economic benefit. Kusno (2004) has argued that this policy was intended to help change the image of Jakarta as a city of "chaos, and hectic, inhuman traffic jams," and that it was not so much tourism that was the goal as the desire of the urban elite to instill order and authority.

The conservation plan focused on the following points.

- Conservation and spatial restoration of the traditional block pattern of Kota (old Batavia), including canals and streets.
- Protection of the outer "hard" edges with strict building regulation (height, profile, scale). Block infill inside the edges can be allowed to develop more freely as "soft" infill (*kampungs* and warehouses).
- The use of trees and plants to reinforce, support, and articulate the urban space (both linear and central) in canals, streets, and squares.
- Making visible, as part of the [old] townscape, the historical axis of the eastern town, the oldest historic district of Kota, including a reconstruction of the shape of *Benteng* (Fort) Island and the restructuring of the northern stretch of the river as a tourist center.

Table 8-8. Retail in Jakarta (2004–2006)

No.	Retail	Location	GLA (m^2)	Operation year	Anchor tenant
1	Jakarta City Center Hyperstore	Central Jakarta	200,000	2006	Hypermart
2	Senayan City	Central Jakarta	76,000	2006	Debenhams Department Store
3	Pondok Indah Mall 2	Southern Jakarta		2006	Sogo Department Store
4	Cityloft Retail	Central Jakarta	20,000	2007	Fashion boutique
5	Grand Indonesia Shopping Town	Central Jakarta	150,000	2007	Seibu Department Store
6	Shopping Center at Pacific Place (Sudirman CBD)	Central Jakarta	40,000	2008	Fashion boutique
7	Pasar Senen (Phase 2)	Central Jakarta	250,000	2008	Carrefour
8	Plaza Indonesia 2	Central Jakarta	25,386	2008	Sogo Department Store
9	Blok M Square	Southern Jakarta	200,000	2008	Carrefour
10	Shopping Center Gandaria	Southern Jakarta	80,000	2008	Metro Department Store
11	Kemang Village Shopping Center	Southern Jakarta	10,696	2008	N/A
12	Kota Casablanca Shopping Center	Southern Jakarta	132,000	2008	Sogo Department Store

Source: Colliers International Indonesia, Research Department, 2006

- Re-designation of historically valuable building complexes, such as warehouses and shophouses.

Adaptive reuse is needed to maintain the old historic district as an attractive urban center. All this effort may go to waste if there is no positive impact to the community, as it will only reinforce social dualism and segregation. This will occur if, because of the high cost of maintaining the buildings, only wealthier groups can use the space, while other, less fortunate groups, usually those in the informal sector, could get the benefit of the conservation. As Mertokusumo (2006) has noted, if conservation is only seen as a romantic evocation of the orderly past, it does nothing to present alternative solutions for present and future problems.

8.5 Concluding Remarks: Urban Dualism and Sustainable Urban Form

Jakarta has experienced a massive transformation from a tiny settlement into a vast metropolitan area with a population of more than 20 million people, within less than 500 years. During the colonial period, social dualism emerged; the European quarter for the Dutch and *kampungs* for native Indonesians.

The JMA spatial structure shows the creation of urban spaces that include mixed land uses and high-density development, not only in the vernacular, *kampung*, residential areas, but also in certain superblock developments containing high-rise condominiums and apartments in a relatively small land area. At the same time, there are acute transportation problems created by increasing commuting using private cars and a lack of adequate public transportation systems to transport the population. One solution that is becoming a trend for private developers, is developing a center that mixes residential, commercial, office, and recreational space. This trend is turning the JMA into a polycentric metropolitan region.

High density and mixed use development in a compact planned city is believed to be one of the requirements of a sustainable urban form (Williams et al. 2000). Some of these requirements are present in the JMA, in centers that combine housing, workplaces, and amenities. But how dense is dense? Most Third World cities are more densely populated than those in developed countries. Jakarta has an average population density of 7,600 people per square kilometer, and ranks second in the world for its number of population according to *Demographia* (2009). This is certainly more than

London 5,100 people per square kilometer (rank 29 in the size of urban population) or Paris at 3,400 per square kilometer (rank 22 in the size of urban population). What makes it dense is not the high-rise buildings, but the *kampung* areas, some of which have more than 10,000 inhabitants per square kilometer. Gardiner and Gardiner (2006) argue that the decreasing population density in the central area observed in the last decade is mostly caused by the conversion of *kampung* areas into modern malls, offices, and recreational amenities.

Centers in the JMA are incrementally developed in a mixed use fashion, with modern buildings side-by-side with traditional *kampung* areas. This apparent dualism is, to a certain degree, creating mutual symbioses. A low-wage worker can live in a nearby *kampung* and work in an apartment or office in the area. Also, in many ways, people living in this *kampung* area are better off, compared to those living in rural areas. Young people are closer to education institutions and have opportunities for greater freedom of expression (Gardiner and Gardiner 2006). Employment opportunities are also better in the JMA, compared to the rural hinterlands. The dependency ratios (the ratio between the population aged 0–14 and 65+ over the population 15–64 years) is also lower in the urban area compared with rural areas of metropolitan regions.

However, the urban spaces created in the JMA are not supported by adequate transportation systems and show a spatial mismatch of workplaces and homes. The compact mixed-use centers that are supposed to reduce the number of commuting trips are not achieving the goals set for them. As there is no proper mass rapid transportation system, people use private cars to go to work; resulting in traffic jams in most of the city roads during peak hours.

Even worse, the modern development of Jakarta as a global city has reinforced urban dualism and segregation. The exclusivity of some malls, apartments, and condominiums in the last decades has threatened the cohesiveness of the community. There is a potential for social conflicts between the urban communities, a potential aggravated by the segregation of the city.

As Johnston (1984, quoted by Knox 1987) puts it, "Because changes to the urban fabric introduce new sources of positive and negative externalities, they are potential generators of local conflicts. … Alterations in land use are needed if investors are to achieve profits, and if the losers in the conflict over changes are the less affluent, then the price paid for those changes is substantially carried out by them. Local conflicts are part of the general contest between classes within capitalist society."

Some of the modern spaces created are only for the upper classes, because only they can afford to buy expensive houses in areas with high-quality facilities. If this trend continues, a sustainable urban form for the JMA cannot be achieved.

Acknowledgements

The author would like to thank Rina Priyani, Yudi Saptono, Maulen Khairina Sari, Ardy Maulidy Navastara, and Ivan Kurniadi, all research associate at the Urban Planning and Design Research Group, for their help in preparing data for this article.

References

Alexander HB (2004) "City walk, town square, walk around, and soon ……". In: Properti Indonesia, p 14

Barbosa EM (2001). Urban spatial segregation and social differentiation: foundation for a typological analysis. In: Conference paper. Lincoln Institute of Land Policy

Bolt G et al. (2006) Immigrants on the housing market: spatial segregation and relocation dynamics. In: Paper for the ENHR conference "housing in an expanding Europe, Sloveni

BPS (1994) Population statistics for Indonesia. Available at http://www.bps.go.id

BPS (2000) Population statistics for Indonesia. Available at http://www.bps.go.id

BSD City (2004) Development progress report

Colliers International Indonesia (2006) Quarterly Research Report: Jakarta. Colliers International, Indonesia

Cybriwsky R, Ford LR (2001) City profile: Jakarta. Cities 18(3):199–200

Demographia (2009) Demographia world urban areas & population projections. Available at http://www.demographia.com/db-worldua.pdf

Firman T, Dharmapatni IAI (1994) The challenges to sustainable development in Jakarta metropolitan region. Habitat International, 18(3), pp. 79–94

Gardiner P, Gardiner MO (2006) Ecology of population dynamic in Indonesian metropolitan areas. In: Winarso H (ed) Metropolitan in Indonesia, fact and challenges for spatial planning. Directorate General for Spatial Planning, Ministry of Public Works, Jakarta

Giebels LJ (1986) Jabotabek: an Indonesian–Dutch concept on metropolitan planning of the Jakarta-region. In: Nas PJM (ed) The Indonesian city. Foris Publication, Dordrecht

Hill H (1996) The Indonesian economy since 1966. Cambridge University Press, Hong Kong

Hoek-smit (2001) Effective demand for low and moderate income housing, homi project, Kimpraswil, Government of Indonesia

Hudallah D, Winarso H, Woltjer J (2007) Peri-urbanisation in East Asia: a new challenge for planning? Int Dev Plann Rev 29(4):503–519

JICA and National Development Planning Agency (BAPPENAS) 2001 The study on integrated transportation master plan (SITRAMP) for the Jabodetabek phase 1. Final report. PCI and ALMEC Corporation, Jakarta, Republic of Indonesia

JICA and National Development Planning Agency (BAPPENAS) 2004 The study on integrated transportation master plan (SITRAMP) for the Jabodetabek phase 2. Final report. Technical report. PCI and ALMEC Corporation, Jakarta, Republic of Indonesia

Johnston RJ (1984) Marxist political economy, the state, and political geography. Progr Hum Geogr 8:473–492

Knox P (1989) Urban social geography: an introduction, 2nd edn. Longman Scientific & Technical, New York

Kusno A (2000) Behind the postcolonial: architecture, urban space and political cultures in Indonesia. Routledge, London

Kusno A (2004) Whiter nationalist urbanism? Public life in governor Sutiyoso's Jakarta. Urban Stud 41(12):2377–2394

Leaf M (1993) Land rights for residential development in Jakarta, Indonesia: the colonial roots of contemporary urban dualism. Int J Urban Reg Res 17(4):477–491

Leaf M (1996) Building the road for the BMW: culture, vision, and extended metropolitan of Jakarta. Environ Plann A 28:1617–1635

Leisch H (2002) Gated community in Indonesia. Cities 19(5):341–350

Marcussen L (1990) Third world housing in social and spatial development: the case of Jakarta. Avebury, Aldershot

Mattingly M (1999) Institutional structures and processes for environmental planning and management of the peri-urban interface. In: Strategic environmental planning and management for the peri-urban interface. University College London, London

Mertokusumo W (2006) Urban heritage conservation and "the modern project": critical notions on urban conservation and heritage management. Paper presented the 6th international conference: our modern re appropriating Asia's urban heritage, Tokyo, Japan, 1–5 November 2006

Properti Indonesia (1994) Menjual Superblok Dengan Kepercayaan (Selling Superblock with Trust), pp 16–17

Properti Indonesia (1994) "Bekasi dan Tangerang Akan Jadi Incaran Utama" (Bekasi and Tangerang Will be the First Choice), p 101

Properti Indonesia (2004) Legenda Midas A la Sinar Mas (Midas Legend A la Sinar Mas), p 10

Sari MK, Winarso H (2007) Transformasi Sosial Ekonomi Masyarakat Peri-Urban di Sekitar Pengembangan Lahan Skala Besar: Kasus Bumi Serpong Damai. Jurnal Perencanaan Wilayah dan Kota 18(1)

Schwab WA (1992) The sociology of cities. Prentice-Hall Inc, Englewood Cliffs

Silver C (2008) Planning the megacity: Jakarta in the twentieth century. Routledge, London

Simanungkalit P (2002) Prospek Pasar Perumahan Nasional dan Bisinis Properti Jabotabek Tahun 2002 (The Prospect of National Housing Market and Property Bisnis in Jabotabek). Jurnal Properti Indonesia VIII

Sinar Harapan (2003) Properti di Kelapa Gading Tak Kenal Krisis. Harga Melonjak Ditopang Lingkungan Tertata Baik

Sivaramakrisnan KC, Green L (eds) (1986) Metropolitan management: the Asian experience. Oxford University Press, Oxford

Surjomihardjo A (1977) The growth of Jakarta. Djambatan, Jakarta

Turner JC (1968) Housing priorities settlements pattern and urban development in modernising countries. AIP J

Wertheim, W.F. (1956) Indonesian Society in Transition, A Study of Social Change. W van Hoeve, The Hague

Williams K, Burton E, Jenks M (eds) (2000) Achieving sustainable urban form. E & FN Spon, London

Winarso H (1999) Private residential developers and spatial structure of Jabotabek. In: Chapman P, Dutt AK, Bradnock RW (eds) Urban growth and development in Asia. Ashgate, Aldershot

Winarso H (2002) Access to main roads or low cost land? Residential land developers' behaviour in Indonesia. Bijdragen tot de taal-, land- en volkenkunde. J Humanit Soc Sci Southeast Asia Oceania 158(4)

Winarso H (2005) City for the rich. Paper presented at APSA 8th international conference, Penang

Winarso H (2007) Large scale land development and the peri-urban transformation of Jakarta Metropolitan area: the case of tangerang regency. Paper presented at the international conference on New concepts and Approaches for Urban and Regional Policy and Planning. Leuven, 2–3 April 2007

Winarso H, Firman T (2002) Residential land development in Jabotabek, Indonesia: triggering economic crisis? Habitat Int 26:487–506

Winarso H, Hudallah D (eds) (2006) Metropolitan in Indonesia, fact and challenges for spatial planning. Directorate General for Spatial Planning, Ministry of Public Works, Jakarta

Winarso H, Kombaitan B (2001) The large scale land development process in Indonesia: the case of Jabotabek. Paper presented at the World Planning School Congress, Shanghai, 11−15 July 2001

Winarso H, Saptono Y (2008) Large scale land development and spatial segregation in Jakarta peri-urban areas: the case of land development in and around BSD. Paper presented at the Asia and Pacific metropolitan development forum, held by the China executive leadership academy Pudong (CELAP), 2–3 November 2008

Winarso H, Argo TA, Pangaribuan I, Prima M (2001) Energy, poverty and sustainable livelihood: the case study of Jakarta, Indonesia. Research report for DPU-DFID

Winters JA (1991) Structural power and investor mobility: capital control and state policy in Indonesia, 1965–1990. Unpublished Ph.D. dissertation, Yale University, New Haven

Part II
Europe and North America

9. Strategic Planning for London: Integrating City Design and Urban Transportation

Philipp Rode

9.1 Introduction

Over the last decade, London has reformed strategic planning more than any other mature western city of similar size. In 2000, the U.K. government created the Greater London Authority (GLA), including a directly elected mayor, ending a 15-year period without any citywide government. As a consequence, urban planning and transport have been upgraded by a strategic citywide plan, the London Plan, and a multi-modal transport agency, Transport for London. Both offer an interesting example of how a city that had abandoned citywide planning is rediscovering strategic planning as an important tool for sustainable urban development. The city's congestion charge is as much part of this strategy as are more progressive approaches to implement higher residential density levels. This essay examines London's current urban development strategies, which aim to achieve greater integration of urban planning, design, and transportation and offers reflections on the successes and problems that have emerged since implementing this important reform.

The quest for greater integration is neither new nor particularly groundbreaking and tends to be an updated version of the well-established agenda of coordinating policymaking and synchronizing public administration (Pollitt 2003). More recently, however, the rhetoric of "holistic," "joined-up," or "integrated" policymaking has not only increasingly dominated political debates, but has left recognizable marks within government structures, decision-making, and planning processes. And indeed, the global environmental challenge, coupled with increasing difficulties for governments at all levels to respond to new sets of interdependencies, has elevated the universal need for simple coordination to a far more ambitious strategy for integrated governance (Brundtland 1987; UN 1992; Lafferty and Hovden 2003).

A. Sorensen and J. Okata (eds.), *Megacities: Urban Form, Governance, and Sustainability*,

These new forms of interconnected governance are of particular relevance to megacities with their rapidly increasing complexities and entwined dependencies. Aggravated by the negative social consequences of modernist city visions and the dramatic anti-urban results of decisions taken in sectoral silos, many cities had already adopted integrated approaches prior to the introduction of the sustainability agenda (Gehl 1987; Kelbaugh 1989). Early on, increasing urban sprawl, fragmentation, and social exclusion demanded a more balanced cross-sectoral recognition of the environmental, social, and economic components of growth. In fact, urban development is often featured as the ultimate testing ground for greater policy integration and has already produced many of the most innovative practices. In recent years, well-documented integrated policy has emerged from cities as diverse such as Barcelona, Johannesburg, Bogotá, Kolkata (Calcutta), London, and Berlin. Furthermore, it is the exceptional interdependence of spatial development and transport that for long has pushed the pair to the forefront of an agenda for greater integration (Jenks et al. 1996; DETR 1999; Rogers and Power 2000; Burdett et al. 2005; Busquets 2004). Again, it is in cities that this relationship is most pronounced and in dire need of consistent policy integration.

Despite these pressures, decision makers and practitioners still find it difficult to give the agreed-upon goal of greater integration more meaning by finding robust strategies that allow for the desired level of policy integration (Cowell and Martin 2003; Meijers and Stead 2004). In particular, as pointed out by Cowell and Martin, there is a sustained naivety about the "tough political decisions about control, resources, organizational design, and (potentially conflicting) policy objectives" that result from shifting towards more joined-up practice. Looking at spatial development, Kidd comes to similar conclusions: "While there is general recognition that integration is an essential feature of spatial planning, understanding of its complexity in terms of spatial planning theory and practice is still emerging" (Kidd 2007).

Clearly, London's latest governance reform and planning policy innovation offer valuable insights to this discourse.

9.2 Greater London

Greater London covers approximately 1,600 km^2 at a gross residential density of about 4,800 people per km^2. However, almost half of this surface consists of open and recreational space. In recent times London, a service-led urban economy with a global orientation, has experienced significant economic growth. Currently its Gross City Product is estimated at US$49,000 per capita, accounting for almost 20% of the UK's national economy with just 12% of the population. The city's booming urban economy has reinforced its status amongst the top three global cities as a financial powerhouse as well as a creative hub. Yet a core of poverty prevails in inner London, particularly in its eastern and southern areas.

Following a long period of population decline between 1940 and 1980, Greater London's population has been growing by an average of 45,000 persons per year over the past two decades and reached about 7.5 million in 2007 (Fig. 9-1). The population increase has accelerated in recent years and in 2005 reached almost 90,000 persons per year (GLA 2006). Projections indicate that the total will reach eight million within the next 10–15 years, and that over the period between 2003 and 2026, an additional 800,000 households will be added to the city (DCLG 2007). London plays a particular role within its national context and is characterized for example by a significantly higher GDP per capita, as well as lower home and car ownership levels.

Amongst cities of similar size and status, London is built at relatively low density levels. More than 50% of its dwelling units are terraced, semi-detached, or detached houses. Typical density levels within residential neighborhoods vary between 40 persons per hectare in Outer London and up to 150 persons per hectare in Inner London. London features one of the

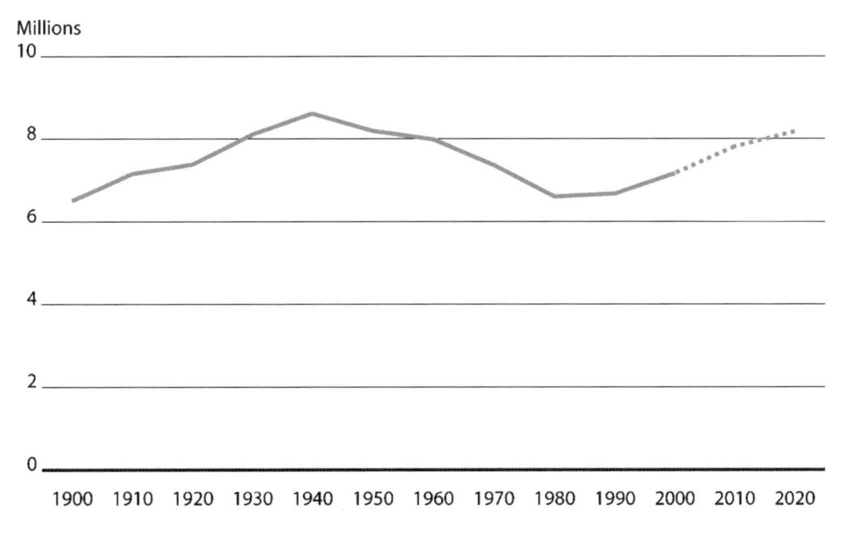

Fig. 9-1. Population growth London (administrative city). Source: Urban Age Programme, based on UN 2005, Greater London Authority (2006)

world's most extensive rail systems. Its Underground lines total 408 km and regional rail within the larger metro region (70 by 70 km) extends a further 1,400 km (Fig. 9-2). Travel patterns are a direct consequence of the city's form and transport system. While relatively high levels of public transport use are guaranteed by the extensive system, low density levels make car use the most dominant means of travel and offer little incentive for walking and cycling (Fig. 9-3).

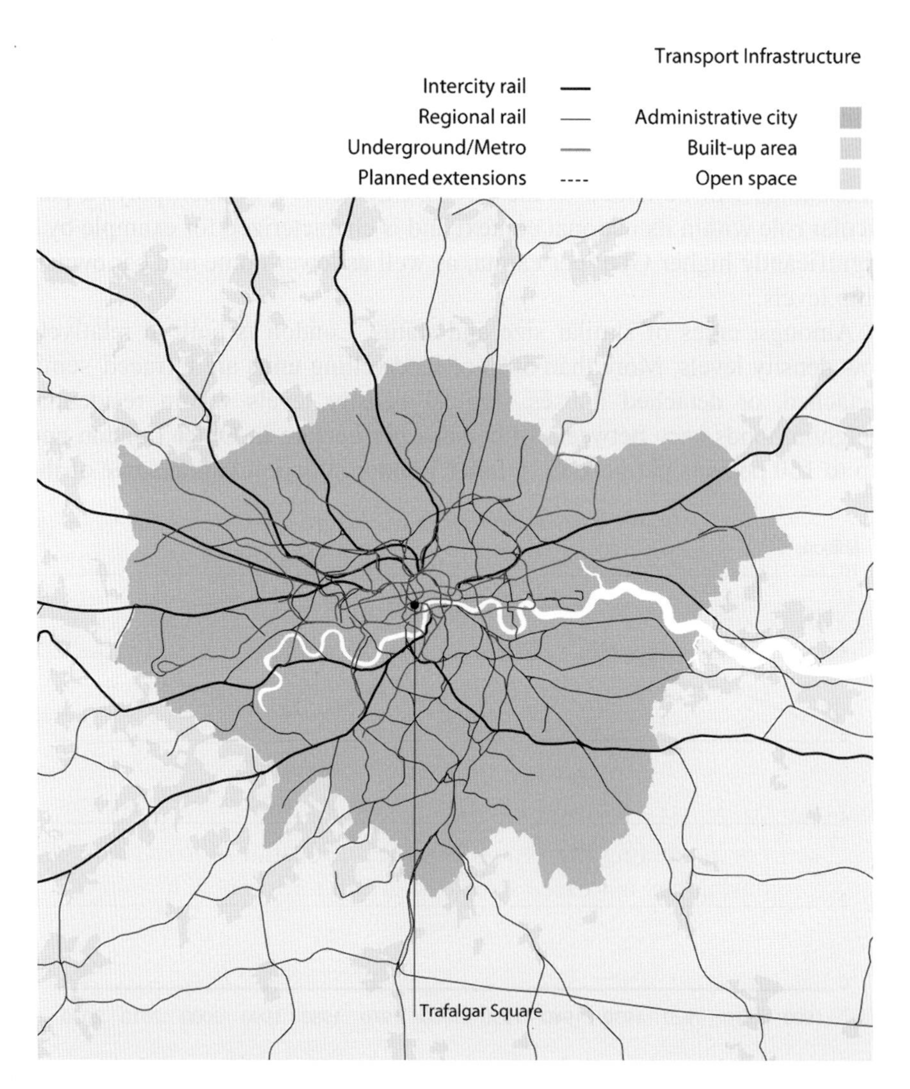

Fig. 9-2. Rail infrastructure in London. Source: Urban Age Programme, based on UK Census 2001; Transport for London (2004)

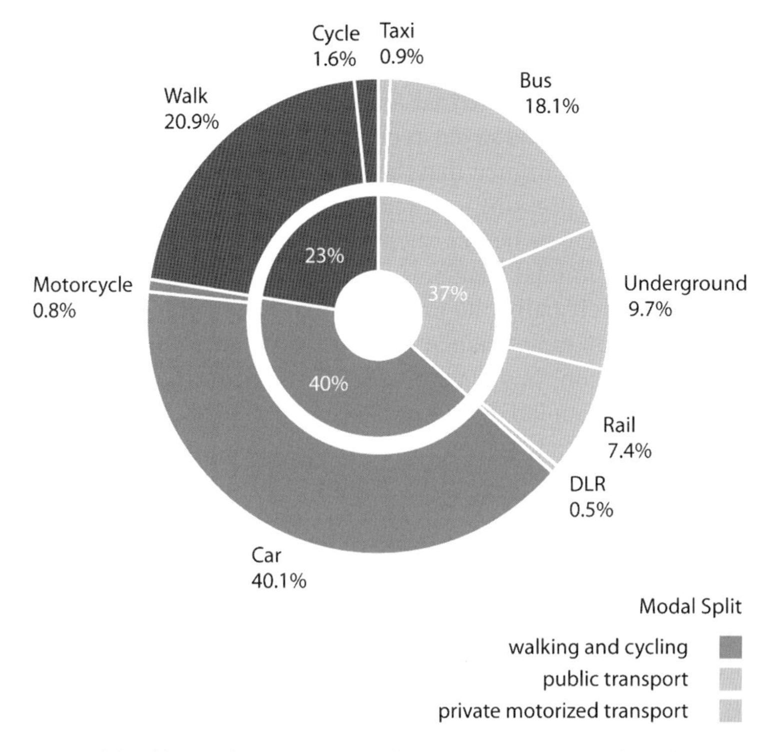

Fig. 9-3. Modal split London. Source: Urban Age Programme, based on Transport for London (2006)

Partly as a result of its success and partly because of structural deficiencies, London continues to suffer from problems. A high cost of living, traffic congestion, a shortage of affordable housing, crime, and problems with transportation are typically referred to most frequently and were confirmed by the public response to the latest London survey (Ipsos MORI 2007). At least three of the five top challenges are directly related to spatial development patterns of the city and highlight the important interface of transportation and city design. So far, policy makers have had little success in tackling the housing crisis. The overall shortage and high cost for housing has not eased and strategies for affordable housing have had only limited success.[1] Experts in London confirm in particular the potential risk of imbalances within the housing market and its regional consequences.[2]

[1]Stakeholder Interview, Senior Officer, London First, 2007.

[2]Expert Interview, Urban Planner, Bartlett School, London, 2007.

Developments in the transportation sector are more positive. Since the Greater London Authority and the Mayor of London were inaugurated in 2000, transportation has emerged as one of the most innovative policy fields through which London has received significant international attention. It could easily be argued that the recognition of urban transportation as one of the most pressing challenges paved the way for progressive demand management strategies such as London's Congestion Charge or new forms of multimodal transport planning facilitated by Transport for London. More specifically, the problems that have led to these responses include the lack of maintenance of large parts of transportation infrastructure,[3] congestion, and severe overcrowding on trains, underground lines, and buses, coupled with poor service quality. The overall transportation system further struggles to cope with a growing metropolitan region[4]; a problem exacerbated by a failure to integrate urban activity patterns and land use.

9.3 Governing Greater London

In 2000, urban governance in London was significantly altered with the introduction of the Greater London Authority (GLA), including a directly elected mayor. Greater London includes all 33 London boroughs and is one of three regions covering 13 counties that form the London metropolitan region, with about 19 million people. Still, the new London government operates within a relatively centralized country. With a contribution of almost a fifth to the UK's GDP, London's economy is essential to the entire country and central government is carefully devolving further power to the city level (Fig. 9-4).

A number of central government departments have responsibilities within Greater London, including the provision of health services, the oversight of commuter railways, and a decisive voice in major planning decisions. Central government also has a degree of control over the GLA and the city's boroughs through regulatory powers.

The creation of the Greater London Authority (GLA) brought with it the integration of formerly fragmented agencies responsible for urban development and transport to a significant degree (Fig. 9-5). The Mayor of London is the elected executive for many citywide services, notably public transport

[3]Stakeholder Interview, Senior Officer, City of London, 2007.
[4]Stakeholder Interview, Senior Officer, Design for London, 2007.

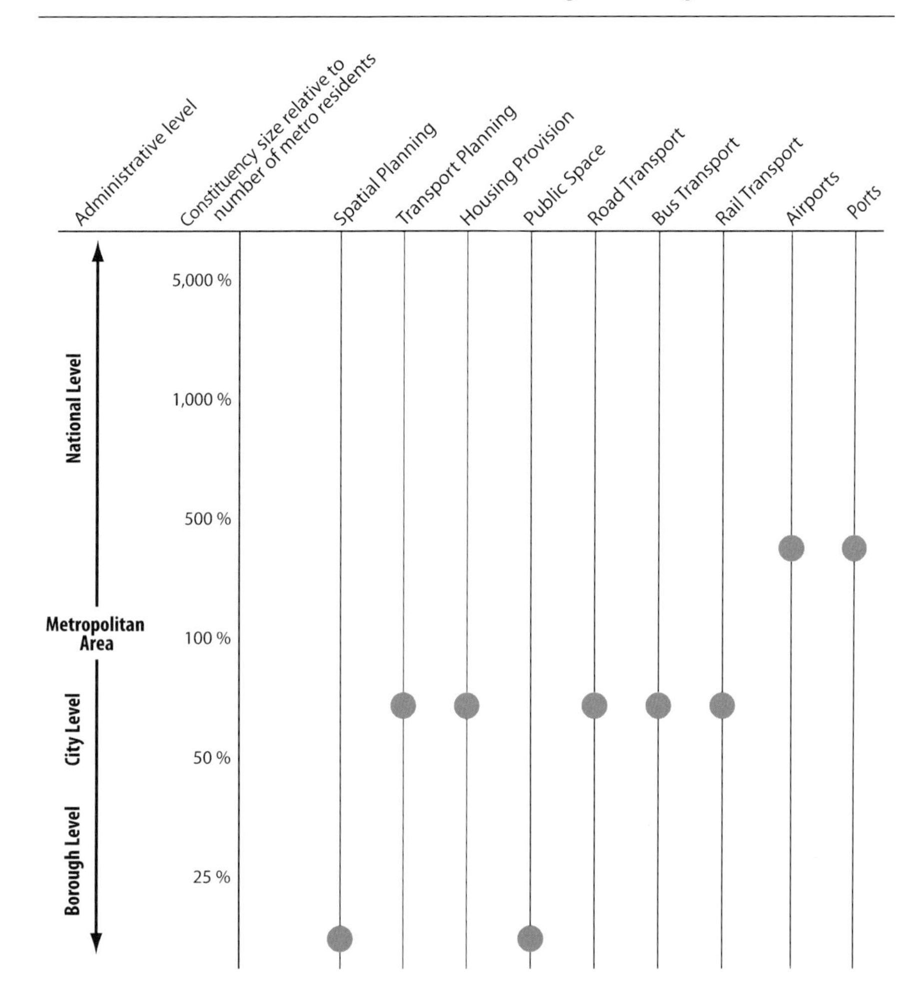

Fig. 9-4. Governance hierarchy: where are the key decisions taken? Source: Urban Age Programme

and spatial planning – the two most important agencies being the London Development Agency (LDA) and Transport for London (TfL). Two other important agencies are the Spatial Planning Group, which is directly associated with the Mayor's office, and Design for London (DfL), a newly created body focusing on design quality.

The executive power of the Mayor of London, who has direct oversight of all four, allows for coordination and synchronization. However, the fact that these bodies have been set up as relatively independent agencies still tends to compromise integration, particularly between transportation and spatial planning. Still, Burnham notes that although the GLA's policy-making was not as integrated as intended by the legislation that had led

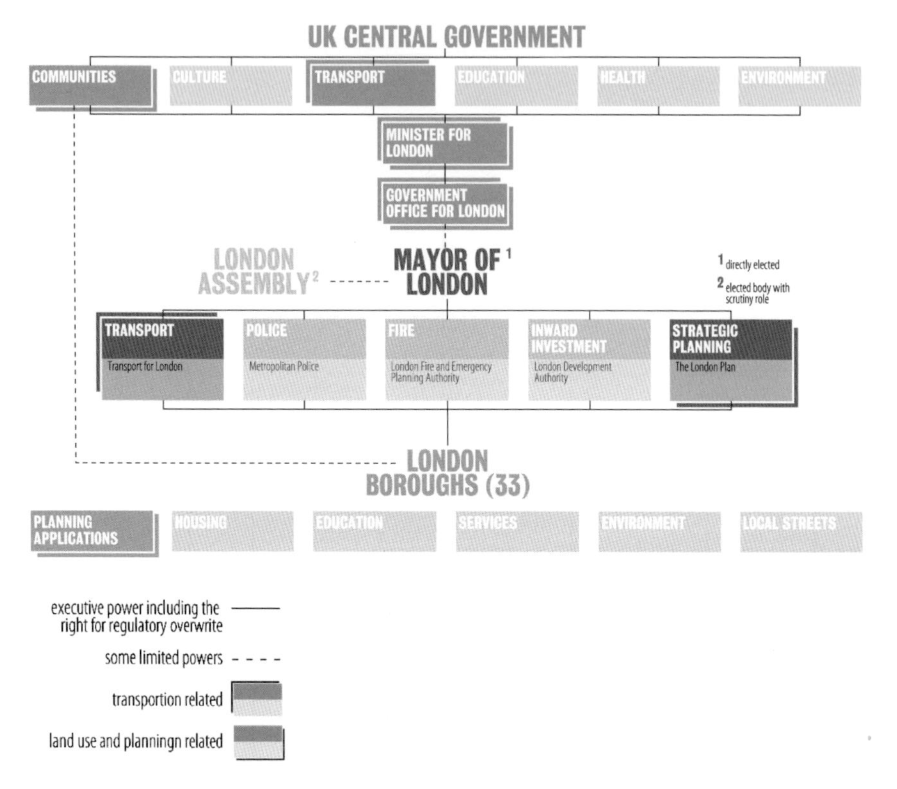

Fig. 9-5. Governance structure. Source: Urban Age Programme

to its creation, "its approach to transport was more integrated than under previous organizational arrangements" (Burnham 2006). In particular, organizational integration in London has been pushed to maximum levels within the area of transport planning and operations through the creation of Transport for London (TfL).

TfL is directed by a management board the members of which are appointed by the Mayor of London, who further acts as the chair of the board. As a unique example of a multimodal transport agency, TfL brings together strategic citywide transportation planning, public transportation operations including rail, bus, and taxi service, traffic management, road maintenance, and efforts to facilitate walking and cycling. As such, TfL combines responsibilities that in most cities are typically dealt with separately by a department of transportation, a department of public works, one or more public transportation agencies, a road traffic management body, and local-level agencies responsible for public space, walking, and cycling. A senior officer of TfL points out that the overriding strength of this organizational structure is its ability to produce truly comprehensive transportation plans that deal with more than just public transportation and are therefore far better suited for strategic planning in cities and have an influence on urban planning.[5]

TfL's success further relies on its regulatory and budgetary powers. With an annual budget of about £6 billion – by far the largest of any GLA agency – it has sufficient regulatory control not only to determine the nature and volume of public transport services, but also to manage travel demand and mobility patterns (GLA 2006). As a senior officer of TfL points out, this combination of powers allowed the successful implementation of London's most innovative transport policy, the congestion charge scheme. "Commercial operators would never produce sufficient public transport as a part of a large scheme to prevent people from car ownership. We could not have done congestion charging without a control over the bus service, which said that we want more buses to operate."[6] TfL's holistic transport agenda also facilitates a clear commitment to reducing overall travel demand. In other cities with less comprehensive organizational designs for transportation planning, this strategic goal is often neglected – if not contradicted by the interests of individual transportation providers.[7]

Improvements in overall transportation efficiency are further seen as a consequence of the strong political leadership of the Mayor of London (Burnham 2006). Combined with the effectiveness of TfL's role in proactive planning for urban transport in London,[8] this leadership has allowed the city to commit to ambitious targets for tackling climate change. By 2025, the 40% reduction in London's CO_2 emissions will include a significant reduction in the ground-based transportation sector of 4.3 million tonnes, or 22% of all reductions. These reductions will be generated by a combined strategy, including further modal shifts, more efficient operations, and infrastructure improvements that all rely heavily on coordinated strategies across transport modes (GLA 2007).

TfL's achievements have been confirmed by independent reviews. In 2004, the Audit Commission rated the agency's performance as "excellent" (Audit Commission 2004). Burnham emphasizes that in part, TfL's success has also relied on the efficiency of its various organizational bodies prior to being combined: "Good outcomes have been delivered because well-managed

[5]Stakeholder Interview, Senior Officer, Transport for London, 2007.
[6]Stakeholder Interview, Senior Officer, Transport for London, 2007.
[7]Stakeholder Interview, Senior Officer, Transport for London, 2007.
[8]Expert Interview, Urban Planner, Bartlett School, London, 2007.

transport organizations were already in place, and have been led since 2000 by transport professionals who were given the political and financial support they needed" (Burnham 2006).

Despite its success, until recently TfL struggled with two particular issues. The first was the public–private partnership scheme for maintaining and upgrading the London Underground network, a scheme pushed through by central government against the mayor's will, which ultimately led to the bankruptcy of the operating company Metronet in 2007.[9] The second is the oversight of national rail operators, which are hugely important for commuting within the metropolitan region and were not initially within the remit of TfL.[10] Both issues are closely tied with the overarching transportation challenge of reducing overcrowding and improving the service quality of public transport. The influence of the central government beyond TfL's control is also built into Crossrail, the £17-billion rail mega-project offering fast east–west service underneath the city.[11]

At a far lower funding level, another agency of the GLA group facilitates integrated urban development for Greater London. Design for London (DfL) operates as a city design agency with the core mission "to support the delivery of well-designed projects across London, and to make sure that the Mayor's commitment to design excellence is reflected within all projects that the mayoral agencies commission or fund" (DfL 2008). A senior officer of Design for London emphasizes that fulfilling this role requires close coordination with agencies across sectors and disciplines. "We are the only organization that bridges across Transport for London, the London Development Agency, and the Greater London Authority… Everything that involves physical development, we see, we comment on, we agree, and sign off their design. For the first time, we are able to see way deep inside the three big agencies in London government in a way that hasn't otherwise happened."[12]

In this way, DfL – set up in early 2007 – promises to operate as catalyst for the greater integration of physical planning and development strategies. Rather than relying, as was previously the case, on ad hoc steering groups and liaison meetings at various levels, DfL attaches itself to various activities throughout the London government. As part of its work, the agency has developed strategic documents such as design guidelines for developing high-density

[9]Metronet – Lessons from a wreckage. The Guardian: Leader. February 9, 2008. http://www.guardian.co.uk/commentisfree/2008/feb/09/leadersandreply.mainsection.
[10]Expert Interview, Urban Planner, Bartlett School, London, 2007.
[11]Expert Interview, Urban Planner, Bartlett School, London, 2007.
[12]Stakeholder Interview, Senior Officer, Design for London, 2007.

housing; policies and best practices for designing green roofs; and the Green Grid, an effort to "create a network of interlinked, multi-functional and high quality open spaces" that will connect with town centers, employment and residential areas, and public transportation nodes (DfL 2008).

Although the Greater London Authority has been successful in advancing more coordinated urban development, the full integration of its various agencies is not yet concluded and requires further adjustments. However, prevailing organizational fragmentation is primarily seen as a result of the particular circumstances under which the London government was implemented in 2000, after decades of neglecting strategic citywide governance.[13]

9.4 Strategic Planning

While London's new governance structure is an essential prerequisite for more integrated urban development, it requires a consistent system of plan making and implementation that together define more positive outcomes on the ground. What follows is an overview and evaluation of two key regulations that together form the basis of London's strategic planning effort. The first is the national green belt policy, which since its introduction in 1955 has become a defining regulation for urban development in the London metropolitan region. The second is the London Plan, the mayor's spatial planning strategy, which came into force in 2004.

9.5 The Green Belt

The London Green Belt – often referred to as the Metropolitan Green Belt – is one of 14 such areas in Britain surrounding the country's mayor metropolitan centers. Within these areas, land use regulation protects open land from being developed and limits each city's expansion into its rural hinterland. London's green belt covers about 4,860 km^2, making it about three times the size of Greater London (Fig. 9-6).

Green belts belong to the category of urban growth boundaries (UGBs), a principal tool for spatial planning in metropolitan regions. In evaluating their applicability, it is important to differentiate a city's expansion on the

[13]Stakeholder Interview, Senior Officer, Design for London, 2007.

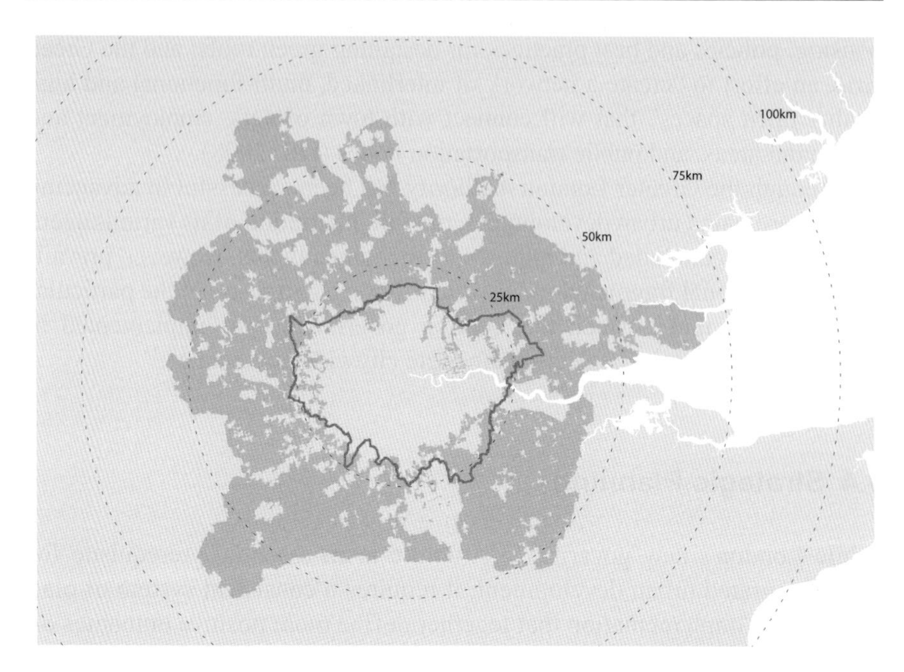

Fig. 9-6. London's green belt. Source: Urban Age Programme, based on Ordnance Survey OS Master Map, Magic

grounds of efficiency gains on the one hand and excessive urban sprawl resulting from market failures on the other (Brueckner 2000, 2001). In the latter case, UGBs are considered a response to negative externalities related to increased travel and commuting times, pollution, congestion, loss of public amenities, and the loss of open space (Cheshire and Sheppard 2002), as well as the opportunity costs of reduced agglomeration effects and urbanity as a consequence of lower densities, the segregation of land uses, and the lost value of public space. In these cases, the benefits of UGBs compared to laissez-faire scenarios of urban growth have been well documented and are widely accepted (Kanemoto 1977; Arnott 1979; Pines and Sadka 1985).

As national policy in the U.K., green belts were first introduced in 1955 following a 20-year-long process of refining the details of London's green belt. The first official proposal referring to a green belt was put forward by the Greater London Regional Planning Committee in 1935 (ODPM 2001). Its proposal to reserve public open space and recreational areas was closely tied to the Garden City Movement, led by Ebenezer Howard. In 1944 the idea first appeared in an advisory Greater London Plan prepared by Patrick Abercrombie, and in the 1947 *Town and Country Planning Act*, the green belt finally gained legal status for London. With minor updates, the overall principle of the green belt policy has been maintained until today.

Its details are regulated by Public Policy Guidance 2 (PPG2) – Green Belts. The guidance states the following core purposes, reflecting the success and overall acceptance of the green belt:

1. To check the unrestricted sprawl of large built-up areas
2. To prevent neighboring towns from merging into one another
3. To assist in safeguarding the countryside from encroachment
4. To preserve the setting and special character of historic towns
5. To assist in urban regeneration, by encouraging the recycling of derelict and other urban land (ODPM 2001)

The primary functions foreseen for green belt land includes, above all, recreational uses for urban dwellers, agricultural and forestry uses, and conservation.

As a national policy, PPG2 is binding on all regional and local planning authorities responsible for making provisions for green belts. Accordingly, land use regulation is established at the local level by development plans following the strategic targets established by structure plans at the regional level, which themselves are scrutinized by the central government. Regulatory details for green belt areas are also dealt with by national policy, which defines new buildings within the green belt boundary as inappropriate unless they are agricultural, forestry or recreational facilities or they represent alterations or replacements of existing dwellings. Further infilling within existing villages and affordable housing projects for existing communities are also acceptable (ODPM 2001). However, exceptions exist and over the last 20 years, some local and regional plans have adjusted green belt boundaries to accommodate universities, business parks, and housing estates (Nathan 2007).

9.5.1 Positive Effects

The U.K.'s green belt policy is widely celebrated as one of the great success stories of strategic spatial planning in the country. Cities with green belts have been able to maintain a degree of compactness and city center activity while containing urban sprawl. Their developments differ greatly from many North American cities, where uncontrolled growth has led to disastrous anti-urban effects such as the creation of "exurbs." In fact, the more recent adoption of green belt policies in the United States appears as a direct consequence of the latter phenomenon (Nathan 2007). In London, the city's green belt was crucial in maintaining a degree of density that proved essential for its global city status and for countering fierce competition from New York and Paris – both cities that have maintained their urban concentration due to physical factors: Manhattan's particular geography as an island and Paris's concentration inside the Périphérique ring road.

Even today, planning experts in London clearly confirm the value of the city's green belt, not only in the way it gives shape to the metropolitan region and contains sprawl, but more importantly in its contribution to the regeneration of more central areas and to strengthening the urban character of the city.[14] Urban growth boundaries were also endorsed by the Urban Task Force Report in 1999 – a central policy paper that gave direction to the U.K.'s urban agenda (DETR 1999). Finally, green belt policies enjoy unusually high popular support and are probably the best-known planning tools in the country (Nathan 2007). Although they limit the individual freedom to develop privately owned land, they have been welcomed partly as a result of the British public's appreciation for nature, coupled with conservationism.

9.5.2 Negative Effects

Despite the success of the green belt, the last few years have seen an emerging debate about the wisdom of the green belt policy in its current form. Policy makers and planners are locked into discussions created by competing agendas and find it increasingly difficult to maintain full support for the current approach. While the broad political consensus of strengthening city and town centers and promoting brownfield development and urban regeneration continues to generate valuable arguments in favor of the current green belt policy, others argue that sharp increases in population and the U.K.'s housing crisis make the need for amendments urgent. More specifically, the following three arguments for adjustment were recently put forward by the Barker Review on Planning (Barker 2006).

First is the general need to release greenfield land. The housing shortage caused by increases in population and the number of households (TCPA 2002) is said to be unsolvable by brownfield development only. In the South East, nearly 1.5 million people are on waiting lists for housing, and in addition to the government's growth area program, the center-left Institute for Public Policy Research suggests that a further 200,000 homes will be needed by 2016 (Nathan 2007). Surveys also frequently point out that only about 2% of the population has a preference for living in flats, the housing form usually associated with inner-city brownfield development (CABE 2004).[15]

Second is the need to review the location of protected land. Evidence suggests that green belts have led to leap-frogging (Fig. 9-7), whereby new

[14]Stakeholder Interviews, London, 2007.

[15]CABE (November 2004) Public Attitudes to Architecture and Public Space: Transforming Neighbourhoods: Final Report. Research Study Conducted for the Commission for Architecture and the Built Environment, 30.

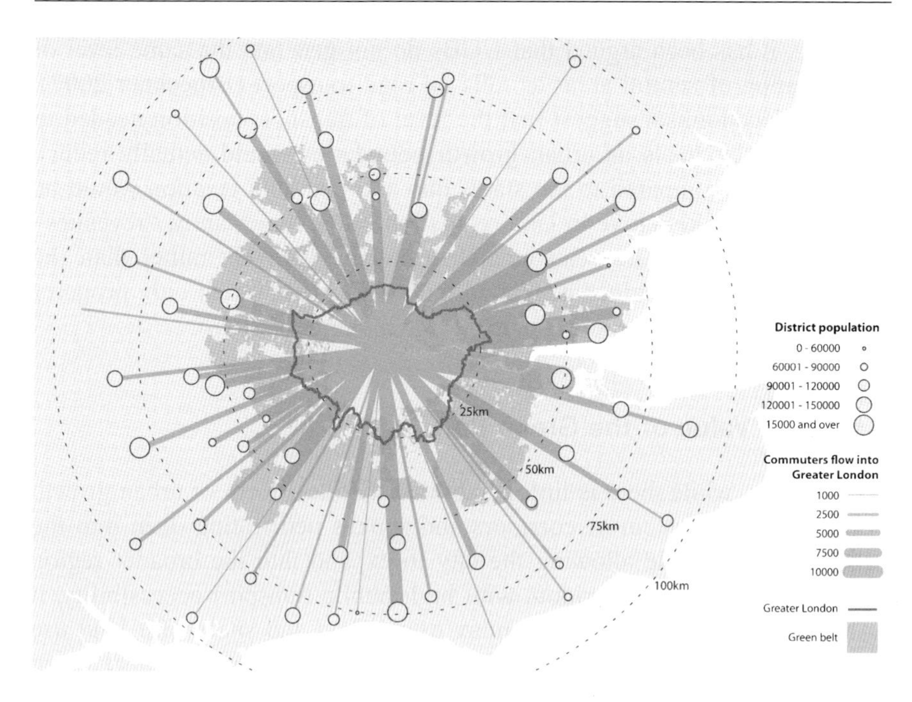

Fig. 9-7. Commuting flows – green belt jumping. Source: Urban Age Programme based on Ordnance Survey OS Master Map, Magic, UK Census 2001

developments occur in the countryside beyond the limits of green belts. This pattern leads to even longer commutes, more congestion, and greater car dependency, and severely compromises the sustainability targets set by governments. The latest U.K. census suggests that green belt jumping includes about 300,000 commuters within the region. The prevailing form of green belts closing in on the city further limits possibilities for the development of mixed-use public transport corridors along major radial rail lines (TCPA 2002). Finally, the vast public support for green belts is said to be based on a misunderstanding, with 60% of the population believing that their purpose is to protect wildlife (MORI 2006).[16] Therefore, it is said to be sensible to review the location of land to be protected.

Third is the need to re-assess regulatory instruments such as urban growth boundaries versus taxation of either transport or land. Economists frequently refer to UGBs as a second-best planning tool, emphasizing their regulatory rather than tax-based character. The primary purpose of any planning policy is to correct markets while increasing overall welfare, in which case instruments based on taxation should be considered first. For

[16] Ipsos MORI poll for the Barker Review of Land Use Planning.

example, it has been argued that UGBs do not generate the same level of densification of central areas as tolls on road transport (Brueckner 2007). However, economists suggest that the level of transport taxation needed to achieve similar goals as urban growth boundaries would actually reduce welfare levels compared to the status quo and that land taxation would be an appropriate alternative to land regulation. Most importantly, "revenues" generated by this policy can be redistributed effectively rather than the increasing property values generated by UGBs, from which only property owners profit (Cheshire and Sheppard 2002; Hepburn 2006).

9.5.3 The Value of the Green Belt

To conclude, while there is little doubt that the ideal form of urban growth boundaries is a system of corridors and spokes penetrating deep into the urban territory while allowing the city to expand into the broader region along established rail corridors with high public transport accessibility, it is both dangerous and naïve to relax established and successful land use protection. Policy experts warn that the implementation of a new green belt policy could prove difficult and would be a risky undertaking (Nathan 2007). Local authorities lack the strategic view to resist private-sector interests and a consistent green belt policy so far has proved effective.

To put it bluntly, it simply should not be a problem to accommodate even another million new residents within the boundaries of Greater London, while still keeping the entire city area at half the population density of New York City. In London alone, more than 450,000 new homes have been set as a development target between 1997 and 2015 (GLA 2005a, b: 6).

Arguably, second-best land use controls are more acceptable than the best tax approaches. They are easy to understand and can be communicated to the public successfully, as their current popular support shows. Finally, strategic land use planning operates with long time horizons and should embrace policies that can sustain themselves over a long period and during different political cycles. Taxation would be far too easy to change for opportunistic reasons in responding to popular demands by the electorate.

9.6 The London Plan

In 2000, the U.K. government's initiative to re-establish a London government paved the way for a citywide strategic planning instrument, the London Plan. The degree to which the London Plan rehabilitated the city's positive attitude to strategic planning in general and integrated plan-led development more specifically can hardly be overestimated. A planning expert notes, "Undoubtedly, the whole structure of the London Plan, the statutory requirement for the mayor, who has the primary responsibility to create, review, and revise the London Plan with a requirement to integrate these different elements, has been the outstanding development of the past decade."[17] The plan was first published in 2004, putting an end to a period of nearly 20 years during which London did not have any strategic plan.

The London Plan is of particular relevance to international planning discourse, considering the difficult circumstances under which it operates. Urban governance, development and fiscal structures differ greatly between London and many European cities that on the whole have a long tradition of strategic planning. First, London does not have a tax base that allows for much financial freedom and its governmental powers at the citywide level remain limited compared to non-U.K. cities. Second, important implementation agencies largely belong to the private sector. And third, London is regarded as a difficult territory for planning because of a prevailing deep mistrust in government as a whole. Together, these factors tend to challenge any strong political visions coming along with a set of physical interventions.[18]

The London Plan is the mayor's spatial development strategy for Greater London. The plan is a legal requirement of the Greater London Authority Act 1999, and The Town and Country Planning (London Spatial Development Strategy) Regulations 2000. The process for setting up this strategic plan was itself heavily influenced by the European Spatial Development Perspective (ESDP) of 1999 (European Commission 1999). The ESDP is less of a master plan for development in the EU than an agreed commitment of all member states to advance its principles and strategies through adjustments to national planning policies. It refers to a central ambition for greater sectoral integration, including transportation and land use, and endorses policies for "Better co-ordination of spatial development policy and land use planning with transport and telecommunications planning" (European Commission 1999: 30).

The London Plan takes up many of the ESDP's recommendations and, while being a spatial strategy, addresses a cross-section of policy fields. Its provisions include sustainable growth, quality of life, economic growth, social inclusion, accessibility, design quality, and climate change adaptation

[17]Expert Interview, Urban Planner, Bartlett School, London, 2007.
[18]Stakeholder Interview, Senior Officer, Design for London, 2007.

(GLA 2004). However, as experts point out, the London Plan has a particular emphasis on housing and responds to the city's core challenge, which is not covered by any other strategy document of similar stature.[19]

The plan was prepared by the Greater London Authority (GLA) and is binding on the GLA family including Transport for London, Design for London, the Police and Fire Departments, the Olympic Development Agency, and the London Development Agency. All are directly placed under the Mayor of London, who facilities overall integration and publishes the London Plan as a holistic vision for the city's future.[20] The plan directly addresses the key challenges facing the city and has accelerated the implementation of appropriate measures.[21]

For boroughs, however, it largely acts as a guiding document, although the Mayor has the authority to veto planning consent given by boroughs when such consent violates principles defined by the London Plan. The plan's rather open-ended specifications for local-level planning are emphasized by its unique character. Despite its spatial focus, the London Plan is a text-heavy, 400-page document setting a strategic vision rather than a plan specifying territorial features or land uses based on a scaled map. In fact, the only maplike representation within the document is the so-called "key diagram" which has to be kept at a schematic level: "No key diagram or inset diagram contained in the spatial development strategy shall be on a map base" (Town and Country Planning Regulations 2000: Part I, 5 (4)). Instead, the key diagram identifies growth corridors, opportunity areas, and areas for intensification at the strategic citywide level. By doing so, it puts forward the principles of accommodating London's future growth on brownfield sites. The specific strategies for these corridors and areas are dealt with in greater detail by the relevant boroughs.

The key diagram of the London Plan further highlights other structural features, including the central activities zone, metropolitan centers, and major transportation infrastructure, as well as metropolitan open land and the green belt. For each feature, it refers to policies that are discussed below. The plan also sets a number of quantitative targets, such as 50% affordable housing for all new development (GLA 2004: Policy 3A.7: 64). This is, however, an aspirational target, as boroughs are merely asked to take this figure into account.

The process leading to the publication of the London Plan includes a statutory 3-month public consultation period. The consultation is based

[19]Expert Interview, Urban Planner, Bartlett School, London, 2007.

[20]Stakeholder Interview, Senior Officer, Transport for London, 2007.

[21]Stakeholder Interview, Senior Officer, Transport for London, 2007.

on a Draft London Plan and is followed by an Examination in Public, a government-appointed panel which tests the strategy for robustness, effectiveness, and consistency with other strategies and government policies. The panel then considers the responses to the consultation and publishes its report to inform the drafting of the Mayor's final London Plan.

9.6.1 Vertical Integration

The English planning system secures for the central government a key role in spatial planning. Its Department for Communities and Local Government establishes guidance for local planning and regional development strategies. There is no spatial plan for all of England. The top hierarchy of spatial plans is assigned to the regional level – the London Plan being one of these. It has a similar status to the Regional Spatial Strategies (RSS) prepared for two adjacent regions, East England and South East England. However, the integration of planning efforts between neighboring regions is limited, because of the general lack of coordination across English regions. The one exception is the London Green Belt, which is fully integrated with the regional strategies of all three regions within the London metropolitan area.

With regards to transportation, crucial powers remain in the hands of central government, given current funding mechanisms and central planning powers: "The system of plan-making (national guidance to the London Plan to Local Development Frameworks) facilitates integration. One difficult anomaly is that although the office of the Mayor has planning powers over major applications, central government reserves the right to 'call in' planning applications and trigger a public inquiry."[22]

Planning permission in London is granted by the city's boroughs, which traditionally have a high degree of control over spatial planning. Besides being the implementation agency for most spatial initiatives, they are responsible for developing so-called Local Development Frameworks (LDFs) that are currently replacing the former Unitary Development Plans. Among other objectives, the reason for introducing LDFs was to improve flexibility, reinforce plan-led development, strengthen community and stakeholder involvement, and ensure that key decisions are taken early in the planning process (ODPM 2004). LDFs have to follow the principles put forward by the London Plan and are tested for conformity before being published (ODPM 2004). Particularly within an international context, it needs to be emphasized that LDFs are by no means binding plans that directly pass on

[22]Stakeholder Interview, Senior Officer, Transport for London, 2007.

rights for development to individuals. For that, the English planning system still requires a planning process in which planning permission is ultimately given on a case-by-case basis.

9.6.2 Horizontal Integration

While the London Plan is the Mayor's central citywide plan, there are seven other statutory mayoral strategies. They include Air Quality, Ambient Noise, Culture, Economic Development (through the London Development Agency), Transport, Biodiversity, and Waste Management. The London Plan is the integrating framework for all the others.

In particular, the plan aims to integrate urban planning, design, and transportation with the main objectives of the Mayor's Transport Strategy, which was published in 2001 – prior to the London Plan. Here, key transportation targets, such as shifts in modal split, are put forward. The Transport Strategy considers the current modal split in central, inner, and outer London, and identifies 20-year targets to improve the balance between private vehicles, pedestrians, cyclists, and public transport. It was this strategy paper that laid the foundation for London's Congestion Charge (GLA 2001).

For the London Plan, this has led to the identification of growth areas based on public transport capacity. In the future, developments with high trip-generation potential must be located at places with high public transport accessibility (GLA 2004: Policy 3C.1: 103–104). The publication of so-called PTAL (Public Transport Accessibility Level) plans, which were prepared alongside the key transport strategy documents, has been highly influential: "Things like PTALs and the ways in which those are being used, scrutinized by the planning system, has meant that there has been a great deal of thought in a scheme-by-scheme basis, which has linked planning, development, land use and transport systems together."[23]

The London Plan's density matrix further sets standards for dwelling densities based on the level of transport accessibility. The better the public transport access, the higher the density level at which the area should be developed. Targets are also set for the reduction of car use in central London and for limiting traffic growth in inner and outer London (GLA 2004: Policy 3C.1: 103–104). The plan suggests that certain forms of developments can lower the need to travel by car and defines standards for the provision of private parking. It also deals with the design of public

[23]Stakeholder Interview, Senior Officer, Design for London, 2007.

space in relation to transportation strategies, and aims to promote walking and cycling.

The overall synchronization of the London Plan with its transport components is facilitated by Transport for London (TfL). "TfL has developed its transport plans in a way which supports the areas where uses are to be intensified. The draft London Plan was tested by TfL to assess whether its proposals could be delivered through the improved transport included in its Investment Plan... So for the plan to be approved, we have to go and say, 'Yes, we can do it.'"[24]

However, proposals put forward in the London Plan remain on a general level. Crucial elements of city design and transport integration, such as a decisive impact on urban form, are still constrained by the U.K.'s planning culture: "In terms of form and design, London is not a city which has traditionally been subject to a rigid set of design guidelines, although conservation is ensured through legislation... Many of the detailed decisions on form and design are taken at a local level by boroughs. Design for London has recently been established by the Mayor to take a strategic view of design."[25]

9.6.3 Success Factors

The London Plan is generally seen as having a positive impact. With its rather loose but inclusive vision, it is welcomed as a new instrument guiding future development in London – a city that has met most planning efforts with great skepticism. "The vision ... from the mayor is a very general and a loose vision, although it is a very strategic vision. This is a vision that most Londoners, who are in a position to improve the city would in some way articulate, even if they didn't realize that it was the mayor's vision."[26]

When looking at its most relevant success factors, it is important to emphasize that experience with the plan is rather limited and its outcomes to date are hard to assess. Particularly its ability to integrate the various sectors of planning remains to be seen. However, several points have already emerged as success factors of the plan. They include the commitment to a clear vision, participation, transport agency backing, site-specific endorsements, strategic alliances, and plan updating.

[24]Stakeholder Interview, Senior Officer, Transport for London, 2007.
[25]Stakeholder Interview, Senior Officer, Transport for London, 2007.
[26]Stakeholder Interview, Senior Officer, Design for London, 2007.

The commitment to a clear vision is regarded as having had a particularly positive impact on follow-up decision making. In the context of its overarching objectives, certain aspects of the plan have become more comprehensible and can be translated more easily to sectoral strategies and to the local implementation scale.[27] As a spatial strategy, the London Plan's clear ideas for compact urban form and brownfield site development have triggered a process of rethinking urban development in the city, particularly for Inner London.

Urban transportation, which for decades has been identified as one of the most significant pressure points in London, is centrally acknowledged by the London Plan and its transport-related strategies profit from far-reaching transport agency backing. The plan's strong commitment to increasing residential density levels and adjusting overall development to transportation accessibility is exemplary. The approval of the London Plan by the city's transport agency is particularly effective, considering that Transport for London has been established as an integrated, multi-modal transportation authority.[28]

Without specifying particular land uses, the London Plan includes site-specific endorsements and crucial location-based considerations. The plan's designation of priority areas for redevelopment can be interpreted at a local level by the boroughs. Since 2004, a number of these areas have been the site of new developments, including Stratford, Greenwich, and King's Cross. In this context, the London Plan is able to successfully combine the interests of the private sector and national policy for more sustainable urban development.

The strategic alliance with national policy further spurs efforts regarding the key development corridors put forward by the London Plan. At the same time, they are part of the core strategy of national government. A planning expert has remarked that the two growth corridors in the London Plan "are remarkably well integrated with national strategies, because they form the start of the two major development corridors under the national 2003 sustainable communities plan."[29]

The way the London Plan has been set up also allows for a further crucial success factor, and that is frequent updating. Experts repeatedly emphasize the importance of operating with a "living document" – a plan that adjusts to changing circumstances: "What you would expect in fact is happening with the London plan. It is being revised and updated in the light of experience and the change in demands. For example, it is being updated to take into account climate change and so forth."[30]

[27]Stakeholder Interview, Senior Officer, Transport for London, 2007.
[28]Stakeholder Interview, Senior Officer, Transport for London, 2007.
[29]Expert Interview, Urban Planner, Bartlett School, London, 2007.
[30]Stakeholder Interview, Senior Officer, Transport for London, 2007.

9.6.4 Critical Comments

As a new strategic planning instrument, the London Plan is far from perfect. Most noticeably, it has little direct power to steer developments on the ground. Furthermore, any agenda for holistic integration of spatial planning from the national to the local level is often exposed to great skepticism by a political system eager to maintain the status quo of power sharing. This is particularly pronounced for London, since it is the country's economic powerhouse.

First and foremost, vertical integration remains largely unsatisfactory. Serious shortcomings of the London Plan's relationship are identified at the regional and national levels, as well as the local (borough) level. Concerns highlight in particular the absence of coordination within the metropolitan region. A planning expert has stated that "There are very serious issues of how the London plan joins up or does not join up with the plans of the regions immediately outside London's boundaries. This, I would say, is one of London's major issues."[31] Missing vertical integration with the local level is even more severe for its actual impact on the ground. Here, the London Plan's fate is a combined result of its own non-binding character for local planning and the limited powers that were given to the Mayor of London to implement a citywide strategy: "If the mayor has been given the job of strategic planning, he has to be given the capability to deliver that plan, even when the boroughs may not agree with him."[32]

These tensions are even more pronounced in relation to housing, where the mayor would like the power to intervene in details such as specific planning applications. Additional risks for integration stem from a lack of funding that prevent desired projects from being implemented. Here, London-wide strategic planning is fundamentally constrained by its dependence on national financing schemes.[33]

A particular struggle to implement the specifications of the London Plan is ultimately related to refraining from binding land use standards. While development may or may not occur in the identified opportunity areas with corresponding public transport accessibility, there is a great risk that ground realities will not follow the compact city standards that were set for London.[34] Similarly, the Plan's quantitative standards for housing, density,

[31]Expert Interview, Urban Planner, Bartlett School, London, 2007.
[32]Expert Interview, Urban Planner, Bartlett School, London, 2007.
[33]Stakeholder Interview, Senior Officer, Transport for London, 2007.
[34]Stakeholder Interviews, London, 2007.

and parking are often not followed by boroughs and developers when implementing actual projects.

An area where many of the problems of the London Plan become evident is the Thames Gateway, the city's most important development corridor along the former industrial land framing the river Thames east of central London. On the one hand, the city's strategy for compact urban development relies heavily on public transport accessibility that can be delivered only by new rail infrastructure financed by central government.[35] On the other hand, local implementation of the plan's general strategy is compromised by a multiplicity of boroughs and agencies within the area.[36] Begg and Gray confirm these problems: "The proposed 'Thames Gateway' development illustrates how difficult it is to integrate policies under current administrative structures" (Begg and Gray 2004: 161).

An often-criticized lack of integration is also highlighted by the London Plan's weakness in setting a clearer agenda for polycentricity. Here the plan follows a strict logic of promoting short-term economic growth by increasing office concentration in Central London. At the same time, it neglects opportunities for strengthening town centers – a spatial strategy with great opportunities for shifting transport behavior towards walking, cycling, and public transport due to shortened journeys.[37] It is further related to orbital transport strategies that focus on radial railway developments – again something that has not been prioritized by the London Plan.[38]

In that sense, the London Plan encourages a zoned city and continues with London's tradition of having a central business district embedded in inner and outer rings of housing. Traditionally, this pattern has resulted in longer commuting distances and times – a crucial issue left unanswered by the London Plan. On the contrary, London continues to struggle with fully breaking the logic of vertical office growth in the city center, along with the horizontal spread of housing. Although frequently referenced, the related issue of small- and large-scale mixed use is not treated in the London Plan as part of a strategy to reduce the need to travel. As already mentioned, by refraining from taking a clear position on citywide land use patterns, the plan neither clarifies the appropriate scale nor the degree of mixing different types of uses. Closely related is the London Plan's struggle to address development patterns in outer London, where town centers

[35]Expert Interview, Urban Planner, Bartlett School, London, 2007.

[36]Stakeholder Interviews, London, 2007.

[37]Stakeholder Interview, Senior Officer, Transport for London, 2007.

[38]Expert Interview, Urban Planner, Bartlett School, London, 2007.

face stiff competition from new shopping centers. The loss of these centers would mean a setback for sustainable city development.

9.7 Conclusion

The creation of the Greater London Authority has clearly improved London's capacity for strategic citywide planning. In particular, a combination of the legacy of the city's green belt, the introduction of the London Plan, and the creation of a multi-modal transport agency has improved the integration of city design and urban transportation. The synergy of these components have further created a clearer agenda for more compact urban form.

However, the improvements also reflect on the far-reaching fragmentation that dominated planning in London during the 1980s and 1990s. Probably no other large European city was confronted with the same degree of incrementalism, whereby spatial planning and transportation were also entirely separated. The initial failure of the Canary Wharf redevelopment project is only the most symbolic outcome of these severe shortcomings; numerous other examples highlight the past lack of integration.

Following years of efforts to amend a system that was entirely developer-led by introducing critical plan-led components, London is still far from many of its European counterparts. Nevertheless, it has successfully combined dynamic private-sector development with an innovative way of managing growth and shaping the city's urban fabric.

The election of a new Mayor of London in early May 2008 will further prove whether London's new institutional arrangements and strategic planning system operate effectively, based on its structure or whether its success relies on the strong political leadership London has been exposed to over the last 8 years.

Acknowledgements

This essay was prepared as part of comparative research on Integrated City Making currently conducted by the Urban Age Programme at the London School of Economics and Political Science (LSE). Urban Age is a joint initiative of LSE and Deutsche Bank's Alfred Herrhausen Society investigating the future of cities.

The author would like to thank all key stakeholders and experts who were interviewed as part of the research. Special thanks also to Julie Wagner, Richard Brown, Christos Konstantinou, Kay Kitazawa, and Richard Simpson for their support and feedback.

References

Arnott RJ (1979) Unpriced transport congestion. J Econ Theor 21:294–316

Audit Commission (2004) Transport for London – initial performance assessment. http://www.audit-commission.gov.uk/Products/BVIR/1A7E1050-3DA6-11d9-A86E-0010B5E78136/TransportForLondonInitialPerformanceAssessment25Nov04REP.pdf. Accessed 27/02/2008

Barker K (2006) Barker review of land use planning; final report – recommendations. http://www.hm-treasury.gov.uk/media/3/A/barker_finalreport051206.pdf. Accessed 26/02/2008

Begg D, Gray D (2004) Transport policy and vehicle emission objectives in the UK: is the marriage between transport and environment policy over? Environ Sci Policy 7(3):155–163

Brueckner JK (2000) Urban sprawl: diagnosis and remedies. Int Reg Sci Rev 23(2):160–171

Brueckner JK (2001) Urban sprawl: lessons from urban economics. Brookings–Wharton papers on urban affairs, pp 65–97

Brueckner JK (2007) Urban growth boundaries: an effective second-best remedy for unpriced traffic congestion? J Hous Econ 16:263–273

Brundtland Report (1987) http://www.anped.org/media/brundtland-pdf.pdf

Burdett R, Travers T, Czischke D, Rode P, Moser B (2005) Density and urban neighbourhoods in London. Enterprise LSE Cities, London

Burnham J (2006) The governance of transport in London then and now. Local Gov Stud 32(3):255–272

Busquets J (2004) Barcelona – the urban evolution of a compact city. Harvard University Graduate School of Design

Cheshire P, Sheppard S (2002) Taxes versus regulation: the welfare impacts of policies for containing sprawl. Williams College, Department of Economics, Working paper 193

Cowell R, Martin S (2003) The joy of joining up: modes of integrating the local government modernisation agenda. Environ Plann C Gov Policy 21:159–179

DCLG – Department of Communities and Local Government (2007) Table 401: household estimates and projections: Great Britain, 1961–2026. http://www.communities.gov.uk/documents/housing/xls/141263. Accessed 27/02/2008

DETR – Department of the Environment, Transport and the Regions (1999) Towards an urban renaissance. Final report of the urban task force

DfL – Design for London (2008) Website, http://www.designforlondon.gov.uk

European Commission (1999) European spatial development perspective: towards balanced and sustainable Development of the Territory of the European Union. http://ec.europa.eu/regional_policy/sources/docoffic/official/re-ports/pdf/sum_en.pdf. Accessed 27/02/2008

Gehl J (1987) Life between buildings: using public space. Van Nostrand Reinhold, New York

Greater London Authority Act (1999) Chapter 29 – arrangements of sections. http://opsi.gov.uk/acts/acts1999/pdf/ukpga_19990029_en.pdf. Accessed 27/02/2008
GLA – Greater London Authority (2001) The Mayor's transport strategy. http://www.london.gov.uk/mayor/strategies/transport/pdf/highlights2.pdf. Accessed 27/02/2008
GLA – Greater London Authority (2004) The London plan – spatial development strategy for Greater London. http://www.london.gov.uk/mayor/strategies/sds/london_plan/lon_plan_all.pdf. Accessed 27/02/2008
GLA – Greater London Authority (2005a) Housing – the London plan supplementary planning guidance. http://www.london.gov.uk/mayor/strategies/sds/docs/spg-housing.pdf. Accessed 27/02/2008
GLA – Greater London Authority (2005b) Housing in London: the London housing strategy evidence base 2005. http://www.london.gov.uk/mayor/housing/evidencebase/fulldocument.pdf. Accessed 27/02/2008
GLA – Greater London Authority (2006) The Greater London authority's consolidated budget and component budgets for 2006–07. http://www.london.gov.uk/gla/budget/docs/0607budget.pdf. Accessed 26/02/2008
GLA – Greater London Authority (2007) Action today to protect tomorrow: the Mayor's climate change action plan. http://www.london.gov.uk/mayor/environment/climate-change/docs/ccap_fullreport.pdf. Accessed 26/02/2008
Hepburn C (2006) Regulation by prices, quantities, or both: a review of instrument choice. Oxford Rev Econ Policy 22(2):226–247
Ipsos MORI (2007) The London survey. Commissioned by the Mayor of London. http://www.london.gov.uk/mayor/annual_survey/2007/als-2007-toplines.pdf. Accessed 27/02/2008
Jenks M, Burton E, Williams K (1996) The compact city: a sustainable urban form? E & FN Spon, London
Kanemoto Y (1977) Cost-benefit analysis and these second land use for transportation. J Urban Econ 4:483–503
Kelbaugh D (ed) (1989) The pedestrian pocket book: a new suburban design strategy. Princeton Architectural Press, New York
Kidd S (2007) Towards a framework of integration in spatial planning: an exploration from a health perspective. Plann Theor Pract 8(2):161–181
Lafferty WM, Hovden E (2003) Environmental policy integration: towards an analytical framework. Environ Polit 12(3):1
Meijers E, Stead D (2004) Policy integration: what does it mean and how can it be achieved? A multi-disciplinary review. In: 2004 Berlin conference on the human dimensions of global environmental change: greening of policies – inter linkages and policy integration, Berlin
Nathan M (2007) UK cities in the world: 2008 and beyond. Centre for Cities. http://www.centreforcities.org/index.php?id=362. Accessed 26/02/2008
Office of the Deputy Prime Minister (2001) Planning policy guidance 2: green belts. http://www.communities.gov.uk/documents/planningandbuilding/pdf/155499. Accessed 26/02/2008)

ODPM – Office of the Deputy Prime Minister (2004) Planning policy statement 12 – local development frameworks. http://www.communities.gov.uk/documents/planningandbuilding/pdf/147429. Accessed 27/02/2008

Pines D, Sadka E (1985) Zoning, first-best, second-best and third-best criteria for allocating land for roads. J Urban Econ 17:167–183

Pollitt C (2003) Joined-up government: a survey. Polit Stud Rev 1:34–49

Rogers R, Power A (2000) Cities for a small country. Faber & Faber, London

TCPA – The Town and Country Planning Association (2002) TCPA policy statement: green belts. http://www.tcpa.org.uk/policy_files/g-beltsPS.pdf. Accessed 26/02/2008

Town and Country Planning (London Spatial Development Strategy) Regulations (2000) http://www.opsi.gov.uk/si/si2000/20001491.htm. Accessed on 27/02/2008

Transport for London (2006) Transport 2025, transport vision for a growing world city. http://www.tfl.gov.uk/assets/downloads/corporate/T2025-new.pdf. Accessed 27/02/2008

UN – United Nations (1992) UN Rio Declaration on the environment and development. http://www.un.org/documents/ga/conf151/aconf15126-1annex1.htm

10. Towards an Ecological Urbanism for Istanbul

Neyran Turan

Istanbul is one of the largest metropolitan areas of the world, a megacity with a population of about 12.5 million and a total area of approximately 5,000 km^2. On the north–south axis, the metropolitan region stretches along the Bosphorus, a 30-km long stretch of water, which acts as a natural frontier between the European and the Asian continents. On its east–west axis, the city has expanded to 100 km in width (Fig. 10-1).

Istanbul grew rapidly in the second half of the twentieth century. The population of the city swelled from 4% of the national population in the 1920s to 17% in 2007 (Fig. 10-2). The city has also been facing an important spatial restructuring in its growth and development over the past two decades. This paper will provide context for the contemporary development of Istanbul and discuss its ecology, sustainability, and terrain as they relate to urbanism.

With the effects of globalization, the implementation of privatization and liberalization policies starting in 1980, and the European Union accession negotiations of Turkey – which have triggered an increase in the amount of foreign investment in the city as well as formal pressures to comply with European standards of environmental regulation – contemporary Istanbul aims to become a new regional node.[1] In parallel, the city is positioning

---

[1]The EU-Turkey relationship started with the Ankara Agreement in 1963 and since then has gone through various stages. The decision of the Helsinki European Council in 1999, seen as a landmark of this relationship, has affected the legal, political and economic structures of Turkey since then. As for the impacts of EU environmental policy on the national policies of Turkey, as early as 1999, the National Environmental Action Plan of 1999 required the adoption of EU environmental standards. The EU, for its part, granted 2.3 million Euros in 2002 for the development of environmental sector in Turkey. For more on the topic, see Izci (2005).

A. Sorensen and J. Okata (eds.), *Megacities: Urban Form, Governance, and Sustainability*,

Fig. 10-1. Istanbul. Satellite (ASTER) image of the central Istanbul in 2000. (Image courtesy NASA and U.S./Japan ASTER Science Team)

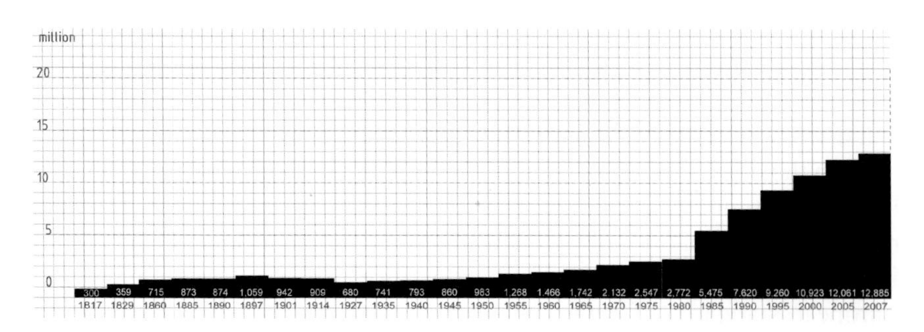

Fig. 10-2. Population growth in Istanbul, 1817–2007 (Diagram by Neyran Turan)

itself as a new service center and has been facing massive urban development projects to expedite this new regional role. Three recent developments exemplify this condition: the Istanbul Spatial Development Plan (2009), large-scale infrastructure projects such as the Marmaray Tunnel Project (Marmara Rail) that goes under the Bosphorus Strait, and the selection of Istanbul as the European Cultural Capital for 2010 (along with Essen,

Germany, and Pécs, Hungary) by the European Union Council. The director of the Istanbul Metropolitan Planning and Urban Design Centre (IMP) declares, "We will be creating a new Istanbul for 2025."

10.1 Sustainable Istanbul

In this context, the terms "sustainability," "environmental protection," "urban regeneration," and "global city" have become pervasive in the urban planning discourse of the city. A recent report prepared by the Turkish Sciences Academy summarizes the priorities for Turkey's "sustainable development" as "environmental awareness, environmental education, water supply networks, coastal management and marine environment, urbanization, treatment of waste, protection of ecosystems, energy policy, emissions of pollutants, environmental health." Meanwhile, the term "world city" appeared for the first time in the 1995 plan of Istanbul, as a concept which guided the city's historical, cultural and natural development and protection.[2]

Considering the popularity of the topic of "sustainability" as well as the city's desire to attract investment and to become an important node in the global economy, Istanbul's attention to the relationship between the sustainable and the urban is not surprising, and typifies many other rapidly growing cities with similar aspirations (see Jonas and While 2007). It should be noted that while urban planning in Istanbul has been going through a rapid restructuring process aiming for an integrated and decentralized system, issues such as environmental protection, "risk management," transportation, and "urban renewal and regeneration" have increasingly been incorporated into its urban planning

[2] For the report of Turkish Sciences Academy, see Tekeli (2002). The first Turkish 5-year development plan to include a section on environmental protection was the plan prepared for 1973–1978, released to coincide with the Stockholm Conference of 1972. The Turkish Ministry of Environment was created in 1991 as part of the process leading to the Rio Summit in 1992. In 2003, the Ministry of Environment and Ministry of Forestry were merged. Early examples of promoting Istanbul as a "global" or "world" city could be seen in a report prepared by TUSIAD (the Turkish Industrialists' and Businessmen's Association) (TUSIAD 1991). The report outlines Istanbul's new role as a service center for Europe and the surrounding region after the dissolution of the Soviet Union. Another early document is a report presented at the 1993 Habitat Conference (held in Istanbul) titled: "Future's Istanbul: A Democratic, Efficient, and Livable Global City." For a more recent account of Istanbul's role within the international economy, its aspirations to be a regional node, and the relation to urban governance, see OECD (2008).

discourse.[3] One of the recent signs of the restructuring process is the change in the administrative boundaries of the Istanbul Metropolitan Area Municipality in 2004 to include provinces previously governed by the central government (the urban area increased from 1,830 to 5,340 km^2) and the establishment of the Istanbul Metropolitan Planning and Urban Design Center (IMP) – a research center created to serve the different directorates in the municipalities.[4]

In an attempt to balance rapid population increases and the city's massive and uncontrolled growth while reinforcing Istanbul's competitiveness within the global economy, the Istanbul Spatial Development Plan was prepared in 2006 and revised in 2009 – the first plan prepared by the IMP. The plan places a strong emphasis on sustainability. The population limit of Istanbul according to the "sustainability principle" is determined as 16 million for 2023 in the Plan, which would mean growth of less than four million people within the upcoming 15 years. To preserve critical water basins and associated forests to the north of the city and keep a check on continued northwards urban growth, the east–west linear development of the macro-form is the main strategy in Istanbul development policies today. Another important emphasis of the plan is a development pattern that includes a hierarchical ranking of sub-centers aligned on the east–west axis as a remedy both to the highly imbalanced structure on either side of the Bosphorus and heavy commuter traffic. To alleviate the fragmentation of the multi-centered metropolitan structure, an extensive subway network is proposed (the first phase of development and construction has already begun). The plan also proposes the decentralization and relocation of the main ports and the industrial zones to the outskirts of the city and the redevelopment of those former industrial areas into education, finance and service areas, hotels, congress, festival and convention centers. While a strong emphasis is given to the development of the service, finance and information sectors, employment distribution is aimed to be 70% service, 25% industry, and 5% agriculture by 2023 (whereas the current numbers are 60%, 32%, and 8%, respectively) according to the plan (see Istanbul Municipality 2009).

---

[3]For a critical review of recent urban renewal projects in contemporary Istanbul, see Candan and Kolluoğlu (2008) and Uzun (2003). The topic of risk relates to the prediction that Istanbul will be subject to a strong earthquake in the next 30 years. The city is in danger because of the North Anatolian Fault, which stretches from northern Anatolia to the Marmara Sea. On August 17, 1999, the Kocaeli earthquake (7.4 magnitude) killed more than 18,000 people, destroyed 15,400 buildings, and caused $10–20 billion damage. The epicenter of the Kocaeli earthquake was about 90 km east of Istanbul.

[4]The law that granted the change is the Municipality Law 5216. The same law also emphasizes sustainability as an expected approach.

Although the plan itself was approved very recently and some of its ideas need to be further discussed and critically re-evaluated, the plan is a symbol of the current aspirations and challenges of contemporary Istanbul. Given EU environmental regulatory requirements, concerns about resource and risk management, and its dream of becoming a regional node, Istanbul's preoccupation with "sustainability" is hardly surprising.

As the "ecological turn" of Istanbul is currently limited to specific managerial perspectives on urban governance – such as "resource management," "environmental risk," or "urban renewal and transformation" – it could be argued that this turn may also be seen as an opportunity to recalibrate certain dialogues regarding much broader interpretations of ecology for the city. Rather than limiting the sustainability discussions to dichotomies of either an uncritical/progressive urban management framework or cynical ignorance of the new challenges that the city will face in the near future, sustainability might provide the necessary framework to build new relationships between various scales of Istanbul's contemporary urbanism (i.e., between the city and its larger geographical setting, as well as between the physical and the social aspects of its urbanism). To elucidate this idea, this paper will review the urban development of twentieth century Istanbul and reflect on the current situation of the city.

10.2 Early Development Until the 1950s

Istanbul was founded in the seventh century BC, and acted as the capital city of the Byzantine (395–1453), and the Ottoman (1453–1923) empires until the founding of the Republic of Turkey in 1923. Until the beginning of the nineteenth century, the urban form of Istanbul was confined to the area within the city walls on the peninsula and some small villages along the Bosphorus. Starting with the 1838 Anglo-Turkish Commercial Treaty, the nineteenth century marked a series of reforms by which Istanbul became an important port city within European commercial networks.

In parallel with the government reforms and the urban legislative developments taking place within the nineteenth century reformist Ottoman Tanzimat Era (1839–1976), the city went through a period of infrastructure development. Although the adoption of the first building codes and regulations date back to 1796, Istanbul would witness most of its important legislative transformations – including the establishment of the first municipal organization, the formation of a road improvement commission, and the first plan or development policy of the city in 1839 – in the nineteenth century. In addition to these legal reforms, a series of important infrastructure projects were undertaken during the same era. The establishment of the first ferry services, the telegraph, the illumination of some public buildings, the commencement of street lighting, and the construction of the first underground railway line all took place during the last part of the nineteenth century (see Çelik 1986).

Mainly due to the growth of the Ottoman economy in the nineteenth century and migration from lost territories in Europe, the population of Istanbul nearly tripled relative to that of the early 1800s and reached one million at the end of the nineteenth century. As economic development spurred infrastructural transformations such as the east–west rail line and ferry services along the Bosphorus, it also brought new institutions (banks, insurance companies, trading firms) as well as new building types (military barracks, train stations, apartment blocks). As its population grew, the city expanded toward the northern bank of the historical peninsula, along the shores of the Bosphorus as well as in an east–west direction along the Marmara Sea shores (Fig. 10-3).

After the collapse of the Ottoman Empire and the inauguration of the Turkish Republic in 1923, when Ankara became the administrative center

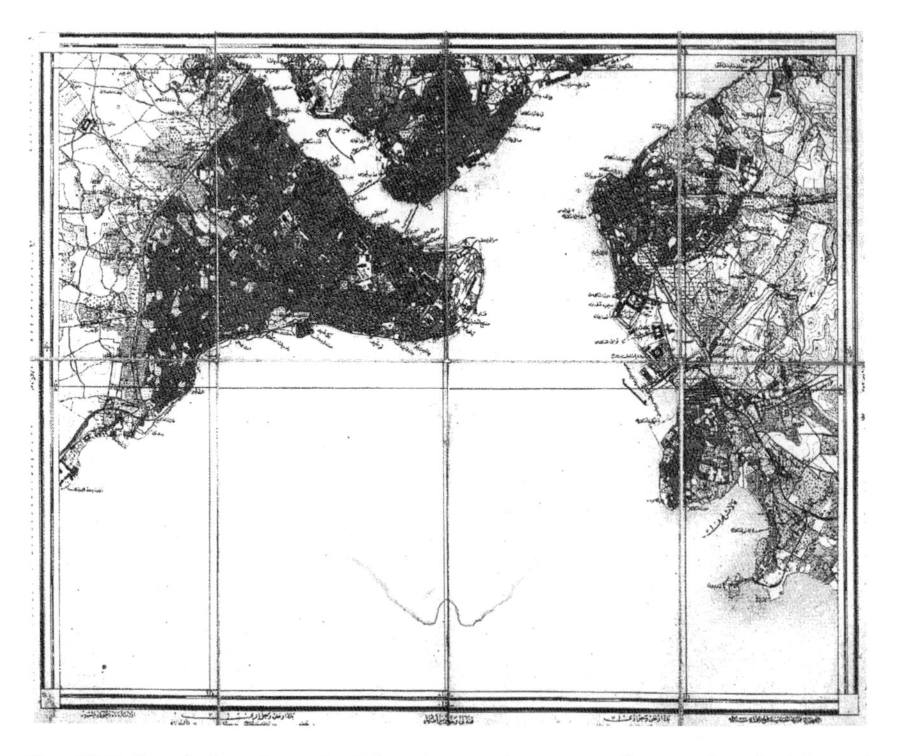

Fig. 10-3. Istanbul at the end of the nineteenth century (Source: Istanbul Ataturk Library)

of the new state, Istanbul's population started to shrink dramatically.[5] The population of Istanbul was 356,653 in 1844; it reached 909,978 in 1914, and dropped to almost half or about 500,000 in 1924. The population decrease during the 1920s was related to many factors: the exodus of higher-income groups, including foreign residents, during the First World War; the migration of populations from Istanbul to Anatolia because of the financial and economic predicaments caused by the war; and the relocation of the bureaucracy, including embassies and military officials from Istanbul to Ankara (Toprak 1992; see also Karpat 1985). The population of Istanbul started to increase again after 1924 and reached 741,148 in 1935. Despite the population decrease, by the late 1930s, Istanbul was still the most populous city of the country (in 1935, the population of the two other big cities, Izmir and Ankara, were 171,000 and 123,000, respectively) and was continuing to grow.

Although the early years of the Turkish Republic focused on the countrywide industrialization and rail network as well as the development of the capital city of Ankara, as early as the mid-1930s, Turkish modernity embraced the development of Istanbul. Henri Prost, the previous chief architect of Paris, who also had planning experience in Casablanca, the Port of Algiers, and Rabat, prepared the first plan for Istanbul. The main features of Prost's 1937 master plan were proposals for new roads and transportation networks (including highways, tunnels, bridges, and viaducts), functional zoning (industrial, residential, and recreational), ports, parks, and public promenades as well as the preservation of the Bosphorus silhouette and the historical peninsula.[6]

After the late 1940s – an era of nationalist and isolationist economic policies, an interventionist economic program based on rural industrial development, and secular authoritarianism – Turkey turned toward policies based on models of "development" and "modernization" followed by economic liberalization.[7] Within the context of the Cold War, Turkey clearly

[5] Istanbul was capital of the Ottoman Empire for five centuries. In the history of transforming the country to a nation-state and its cities to places of modernity, Ankara was chosen as the capital of the newly founded Turkish Republic instead of Istanbul. While some argue that this selection was clearly a result of the search for a real "from-scratch" modernization model for the nation-state, Ankara ultimately became the ground on which the Turkish modernist utopia was established, not Istanbul (see Tekeli 1998). For more on the Turkish modernity project and its relation to modern Turkish architecture, see Bozdoğan (2001).

[6] For more on the work of Henri Prost in Istanbul, see Hautecoeur (1960) and Akpinar (2003).

[7] The era between 1923 and 1945 is regarded as the Republican Era by most scholars of Turkey.

stayed within the capitalist camp, being one of the first countries to join the Bretton Woods system. Loyalty to liberalization and alignment with the West were ensured by American financial aid through the Truman Doctrine and the Marshall Plan, and resulted in Turkey's sending troops to the Korean War, allowing U.S. air bases on its territory, and, finally, joining NATO (see Dodd 1983; Keyder 1987). The Turkish government used the aid especially for the development of industry, mechanized agriculture, and the military sector. In relation to these changes, Istanbul became the engine of industrial development within the country.

Recognizing that urbanization and development were the fundamental challenges to the country, Prime Minister Adnan Menderes, the "honorary mayor of the city," started an extensive urban development plan for Istanbul during the mid-1950s. In contrast to the bureaucratic nature and isolated situation of Ankara, Istanbul was a perfect setting for Menderes's development in an era of economic liberalization. Starting in 1956, similar to, for instance, the work of Robert Moses in New York City in the 1950s and 1960s, Menderes launched the construction of a new highway network for Istanbul (Fig. 10-4a). The implementation of this new highway network was the major component of the "industrial development plan" in Turkey, carried out by the newly founded General Directorate of Highways with the advice of a group of about 50 engineers of the United States Bureau of Public Roads. U.S. Marshall Plan aid remained crucial for the populist political propaganda of the "little America" or "the welfare state."

Although some roads and highways were constructed in Istanbul before the 1950s, what made the operations under the directive of Prime Minister Adnan Menderes remarkable was their more extensive scale.[8] Between 1956 and 1960, following the main features of the previous Henri Prost plans (but with major difference in the width of streets, as Prost's proposals were enlarged by a factor of two or three), and the slogan "This city has a hunchback, let's straighten it," Istanbul embarked up a large-scale urban intervention that resulted in wide avenues being cut through the historical fabric of the city in a Haussmannian fashion. With that and the construction of new highways, Istanbul would experience the most radical urban development in years (Fig. 10-4b).

The rapid urbanization of the 1950s affected the physical and social form of the city in a different way from that imagined in Menderes's plans. Triggered by the widespread mechanization and commercialization of

[8] Expenditure by the Istanbul municipality on highways and bridges increased 334% between 1950 and 1957 compared to spending in the period 1923–1949.

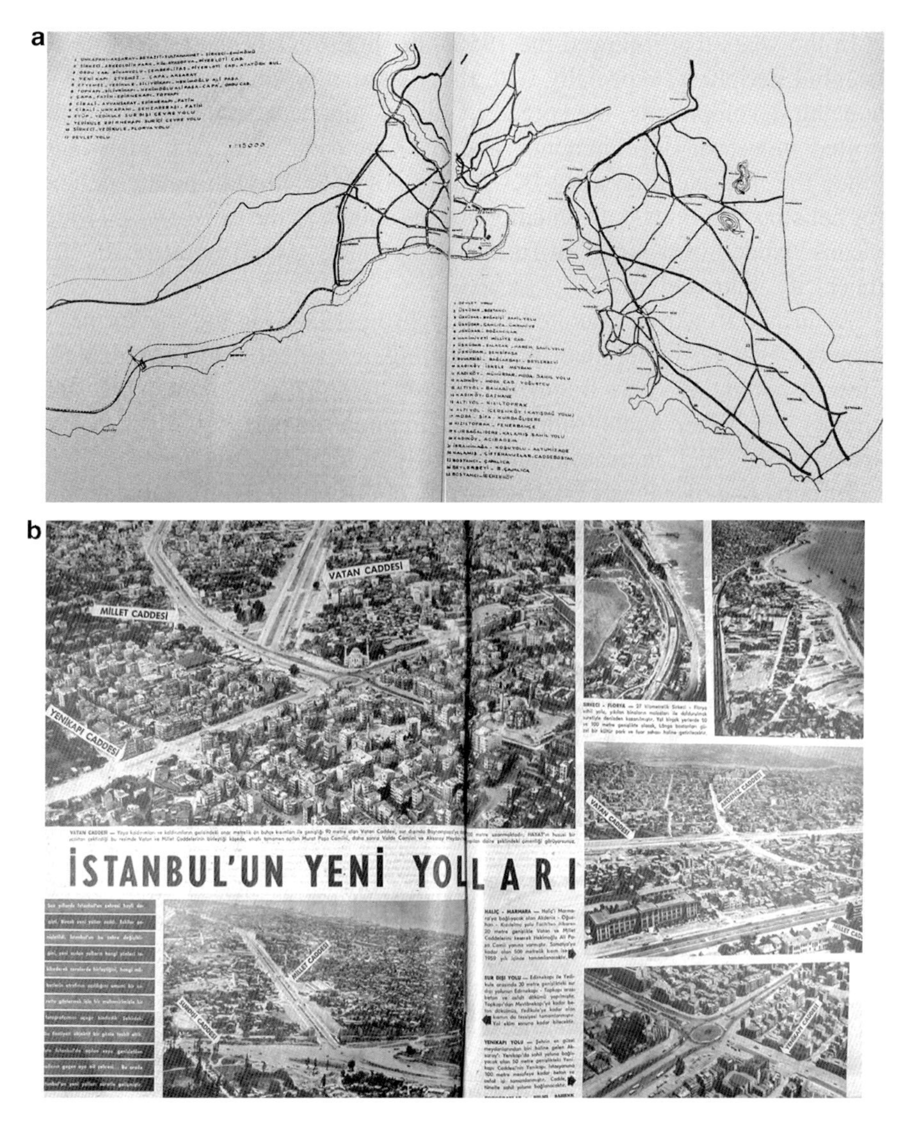

Fig. 10-4. (**a**) New highways of Istanbul as illustrated in a report from the Urban Development Bureau of Istanbul in the 1950s. (Source: *Arkitekt*, 1955). (**b**) New highways of Istanbul as represented in the news. (Source: *Hayat*, 1958)

agriculture, a massive exodus from rural areas during the 1950s overwhelmed major Turkish cities, including Istanbul. In the early 1920s, the population of Istanbul was about 500,000; in 1950 it was 975,000, and in 1965 it reached 2,141,000. Migration to big cities, the emergence of squatter settlements, the increased ownership of motor vehicles, and inner-city industrialization all contributed to extremely rapid urbanization.

In the years that followed the 1950s, the highways began to activate the Istanbul periphery, especially with the construction of upper-middle class housing developments, the spread of illegal squatter communities, uncontrolled industrial developments, and the extension of coastal highways.[9] Since the massive migratory flows were not coupled with public policies for housing, migrants built squatter houses known as the *gecekondus* (which means "landed-over-night" in Turkish) on publicly owned lands mostly near inner-city industrial areas.

As urban growth accelerated following the 1950s, so did the format of growth. That is, rather than accumulating individual buildings, Istanbul grew by adding new "big fragments" – even the squatters settled in big urban chunks – or by the uncontrolled incursion upon the periphery through land speculation, which increased tremendously in the following decades.[10]

Perhaps one of the earliest critical reflections about the fragmentation of Istanbul was an article published by architect Zeki Sayar in 1954, in which he writes about the "artificial expansion" of the city beyond its official boundaries. "Artificial" because, as Sayar argues, the boundaries at the time were generous enough to accommodate population growth, so expansion came about through intensified land speculation. In 1955, the difference between the population within the municipal boundaries of Istanbul and that within the metropolitan boundaries was 50,000; by 1965, this figure had risen to 380,000. Of the total metropolitan population increase of 802,000 between 1955 and 1965, 40% settled in areas outside of the municipality (Istanbul Municipality 1971; Piccinato 1970). Sayar writes:

> There are some parcels that have 1000–2000 divisions. These divisions, because of being outside the Municipality boundaries, are done by land registry office or in the interest of the landowner, and not by any means of urbanism guidelines. Perhaps there are more than 100 or 150 of them now in Istanbul. These parcel islands—disconnected from the city as well as from each other—are able to survive via their sole connection to the waterfront, the highway or the railway (Sayar 1954).

Despite Sayar's critical reflection, in 1950, with a population of one million, Istanbul's urbanized areas extended only 30 km from the center. The population increased to five million in 1980 and doubled to ten million

---

[9]For a further discussion on the development of the periphery and its relation to informality in Istanbul, see Keyder (2000).

[10]In 1948, it was estimated that there were about 25,000–30,000 *gecekondus* in Turkey; in 1953 this number increased to 80,000, and in 1970 to 500,000. Of those, 20% were in Istanbul. See Öncü 1988 and Buğra (1998).

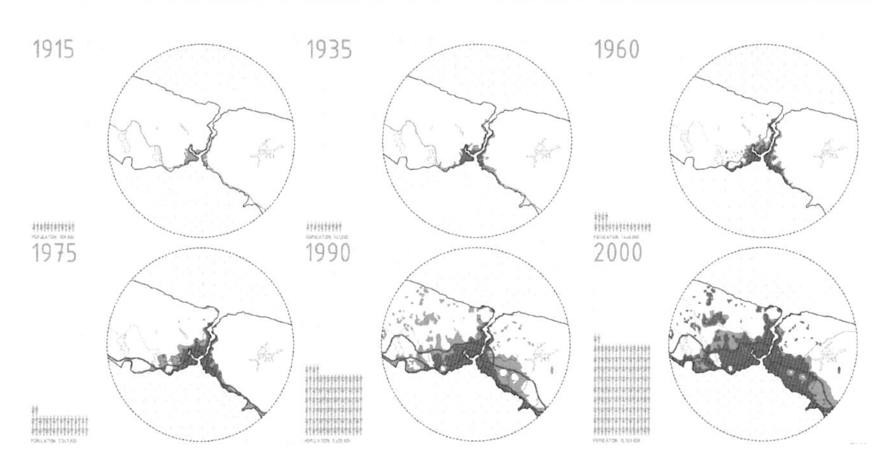

Fig. 10-5. Urban development of Istanbul in the twentieth century. (Diagram by Neyran Turan)

in 2000, while the expanse of the urbanized area grew to 50 km wide in 1980 (Fig. 10.5). Today, Istanbul extends about 80 km to the west of the Bosphorus and 40 km to the east.

10.3 Istanbul After the 1980s

The 1980s marked the era in which neoliberal economic policies opened the national economy of Turkey to world markets – a macroeconomic, social and political restructuring which was very much in line with wider global transformations around the world, including disorganized capitalism, post-Fordism, flexible accumulation, and globalization (Harvey 1989; Lash and Urry 1987). These policies had tremendous effects on the social and spatial form of Istanbul as they did in many other cities around the world (Sassen 1991; Brenner and Theodore 2002; Hackworth 2007). For Istanbul, one of the most important factors in the impact of globalization in the city has been the increase of foreign direct investments. Between 1980 and 1998, foreign direct investments in Turkey increased 320 times, with an even sharper increase after the 1990s (Kaptan and Enlil 2009). As of 2003, 75.4% of foreign direct investment in Turkey was in Istanbul – 2.53% in agriculture, 25.8% in industry, and 71.7% in the service sector (see Özdemir 2002: 249–259).

During the 1980s, integration with the market economy triggered legal, financial, and institutional restructuring in local governance. The newly elected center-right government (ANAP), which aimed to accomplish full liberalization and deregulation for Turkey, saw the urban development of big cities as crucial in attracting international capital (see Keyder 1994). Local governance restructuring was needed to create the necessary setting for ambitious infrastructural investments and urban renewal projects. For instance, the government increased the total tax revenues allocated to municipalities and also passed the Municipality Law of 1984, which allowed the complete decentralization of the metropolitan municipalities of the three big cities (Istanbul, Ankara, and Izmir). The Law expanded not only the metropolitan municipalities' administrative and financial resources, but also the direct control and jurisdiction of various public works agencies, which were previously under the domain of central government ministries. (An example would be the creation of the Master Planning Bureau and the Water Supply and Sewage Authority.) This restructuring led to the privatization of municipal services such as transportation, housing, and natural gas in Istanbul, as well as a series of urban renewal projects administered by the metropolitan mayor Bedrettin Dalan in the late 1980s. Like the urban development projects of the 1950s – such as the Hausmannian boulevards cut into the historical fabric – the large-scale infrastructure projects of the 1980s spurred the uncontrolled development of the city.

In addition to the 1984 Municipal Law, the Act on the Promotion of Tourism (1982) and the Mass Housing Fund (1984) were important pieces of legislation, as they affected the nature of urban growth over the following years. The Act on the Promotion of Tourism designated certain sites in the city as "Tourism Areas," which functioned like free zones in that they were exempt from local planning regulations (for instance, building heights) and eligible for financial incentives such as exemptions from custom duties and tax deductions. Forty areas were declared "tourism and business centers" between 1984 and 1991 in Istanbul (Kaptan and Enlil 2009). High-rise office buildings and luxury hotels were built in these areas, and a financial center developed in the northern part of the city. As for the establishment of the Mass Housing Fund, more than 750,000 housing units were constructed in Turkey by the Mass Housing Administration (MHA) between 1984 and 1999. Of those, more than 100,000 were in Istanbul (Keyder 1994: 402). The MHA is still responsible for one-third of housing starts in Istanbul, mostly units built on government land, and for offering long-term loans (Ayata 2002).

Along with restructuring in governance, the 1980s marked the accelerated fragmentation of Istanbul beyond its original contours. Although the city still retained a relatively compact form until 1980s, the opening of the two Bosphorus Bridges (1970s and 1980s, respectively) and the creation of peripheral ring roads associated with the bridges (the E-5 international highway and the Trans-European Highway respectively), led to massive fragmentation. Unplanned industrial developments and illegal squatter settlements began to appear along the highways on the periphery (Öncü 1988).

The fragmentation of the city occurred at different levels, each of which developed independently while triggering the growth of the others. The main changes were: (1) a dramatic increase in uncontrolled development within the outer limits of the Municipal area; (2) the spread of *gecekondus* (see Keyder 2005); (3) state-initiated high-rise, high-density mass-housing projects on the periphery, developed by the Mass Housing Administration, which ended up serving mostly upper-middle class and higher-income groups; (4) a new financial center toward the north; (5) gated residential developments in the suburbs with easy access to the Trans-European Highway and the northern financial center.[11] These developments not only accelerated uncontrolled urban expansion, they also made the city into a megalopolis, or an archipelago, i.e. dispersed fragments separated by voids (Fig. 10-6).

Fig. 10-6. Archipelago of voids in contemporary Istanbul (Mapping by Neyran Turan)

[11]According to one estimate, there were 650 gated communities in Istanbul in 2005 (see Danış and Pérouse 2005).

10.4 Towards an Ecological Urbanism for the Istanbul Archipelago

> Ecology is guilty of forgetting about society, just as social science and social theory are predicated on the forgetting of ecology (Ulrich Beck, *Ecological Politics in an Age of Risk*, 1995, 40).

Partially created by the impacts of globalization and observed in many other megacities of the world, the archipelago form of the city might at first seem to be the spatial expression of transnational connections, market flows, and expanded infrastructure. However, it is widely argued today that, as much as the archipelago model portrays connections, it is composed of "splintered" and highly differentiated networks with sharply defined enclave spaces where not only the physical attributes or parts of the city are fragmenting, but also the infrastructure and networks themselves (Graham and Marvin 2001).

Broadly speaking, fragmentation is interpreted in the field of urban studies as "dividing," "splintering," or "partitioning" contemporary cities, indicating social and spatial disparities and polarization within income groups as well as in the provision of infrastructure. Although various studies use the term fragmentation to refer to urban structure, urban form, the system of land use, the disjunction of public and private spaces, or the socio-economic and cultural integrity of the city, the most prominent common factor in each example is an uneven, or asymmetrical access to infrastructure and resources. Extremes are critically portrayed in a range of theories about gated communities, gentrification, *laissez-faire* planning, neoliberal economic policies and their effect on the form of the city (see, for example, Davis 1990; Fainstein et al. 1992; Zukin 1995; Caldeira 2000; Graham and Marvin 2001; Marcuse and van Kempen 2002; Bauman 2004).

Although the fragmentation of the city is by no means a new phenomenon, and dates back to the altering nature of the metropolis at the turn of the twentieth century, what seems to make contemporary fragmentation strikingly different from previous instances is the level of autonomy and self-containment reflected by the fragments or the islands of the archipelago as well as their extremely unbalanced access to resources compared to the vast array of infrastructure to which they are connected. Yet as much as the contemporary archipelago poses new urban symptoms and spatial configurations, it also provides a framework to critically examine the form of the city and reflect on the forces that constitute it.

Recent literature on Istanbul (especially in the fields of urban studies and sociology) has examined the fragmented condition of the city in the context of globalization, and provided critical reflections on it (see, for example,

Kurtuluş 2005; Keyder 2005). Although these studies provide an important framework for understanding the contemporary contradictions inherent in Istanbul's urban fragmentation, there is a compelling need for a careful examination of the specific characteristics of this new spatial configuration in the hinterland of Istanbul. In this light, a closer spatial analysis reveals certain important relationships.

In the spatial mappings of the contemporary Istanbul archipelago, a clear relationship between the highway system and fragmentation becomes apparent (Fig. 10-7a). In particular, after Istanbul's accelerated growth during the 1980s, when its transition to a megalopolis took place, one can observe from the mappings that the first spatial transformation was a result of the Trans-European Highway, which spurred an outward leap-frog pattern of growth and sprawl in the form of squatter settlements, industrial developments, financial centers, and gated communities on the outer edge of the city; most of this development was uncontrolled (Fig. 10-7b).

At this point, it could be argued that a second – and rather specific – spatial configuration has been taking form very recently (starting in the mid-1990s). Beginning once more at the edge of the city, this second spatial transformation has again been triggered by the Trans-European Highway; but rather than the leap-frog centrifugal sprawl just described, the second expansion has been more centripetal and has taken the form of intensification and infill. That is, large tracts of land along the Trans-European Highway and its interchanges are becoming crowded with big-box stores, identical high-rise and high-density housing (mostly built on government land by the Mass Housing Administration), and mixed-use office buildings. This has produced a different spatial configuration along the edge of Istanbul, where the city has started to change in its development pattern through differentiated clusters of infill projects (on sites along or with easy access to the highway), most of which are surrounded by existing lower-income or squatter housing developed during the first round of leap-frog developments after the 1980s. Although leaving undeveloped voids could be seen as an efficient pattern of urbanization because of their potential to develop at higher densities later, in Istanbul's case, these developments have proceeded in an unplanned, uncontrolled manner.

At first glance, the previously described configuration on the edge of Istanbul can be likened to a typical "edge city" formation in which increasing concentrations of shopping, entertainment, and business agglomerate at highway intersections (Garreau 1991). However, in contrast to a typical edge city model – where "side-by-side development" occurs near the highways radiating out from the city center – concentric growth tendencies of urbanization in Istanbul are actually balanced by the linear axis of the geography where the hinterland-edge still keeps a level of attachment

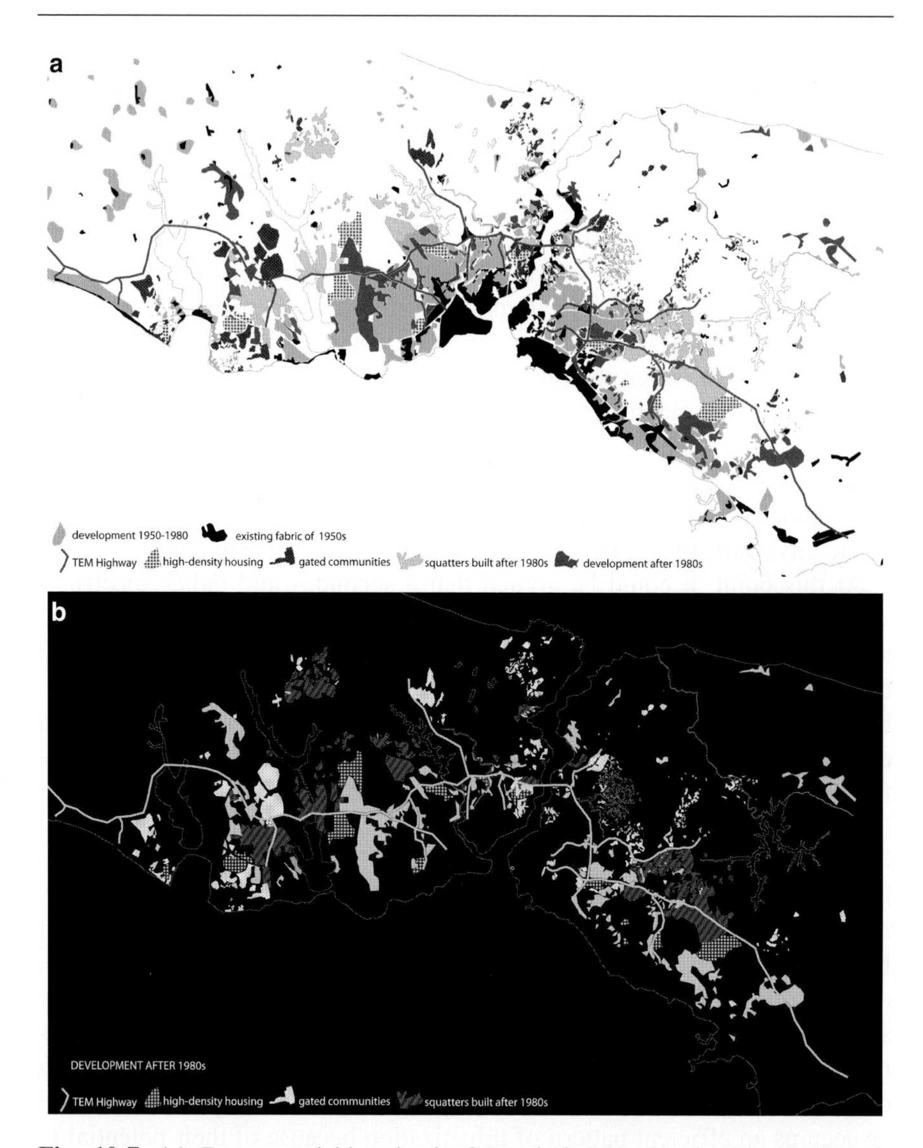

Fig. 10-7. (**a**) Fragmented hinterland of Istanbul (Mapping by Neyran Turan). (**b**) The development of Istanbul after the 1980s in relation to the TEM (highway). The map shows built fabric after 1980 and also depicts high-density housing (mostly developed along the TEM), squatter areas and gated communities. (Mapping by Neyran Turan)

and proximate relationship to the city by infill developments. Therefore, because of its linear yet still concentric form, the continuous hinterland-edge created along the highway still keeps a level of adjacency to the city, rather than radiating away from it.

This proximate but rather active characteristic of the hinterland-edge and its more recent spatial configuration suggest an alternative reading of the Istanbul archipelago. That is, rather than seeing the archipelago in terms of its enclaves or islands (gated communities, shopping malls, skyscrapers, squatter settlements) and focusing on their disparities and differentiated structures, one can focus on the potential of the *archipelago of voids* in Istanbul – the interstitial territories on the hinterland-edge which represent alternative sites for future projections on the city.

Before speculating on the relevance of this spatial configuration further, it might be helpful to contextualize some of the related developments more specifically. The transformations brought about by the new Municipality Laws of 2004 and 2005 are a continuation of the liberalization efforts of Turkey since the 1980s, Istanbul's desire to integrate with international market economies, and accompanying policies to decentralize and strengthen the powers of municipalities.[12] These laws have not only granted additional powers to Istanbul's local government by further expanding its limit of jurisdiction to the metropolitan area, but have also relaxed the rules for public–private collaboration and provided the necessary legal framework for the allocation of new responsibilities to the municipalities in the context of natural disaster management and the implementation of "urban transformation" projects. Some recent examples include large-scale urban projects designed by architects Zaha Hadid and Ken Yeang, controversial port development projects in Galataport and Haydarpaşa, and "urban renewal" efforts to transform squatter housing areas into more livable environments. While the goals as well as the implementation of these transformation projects have occasioned much criticism by advocates of more democratic and transparent policy processes and political discussion locally, the projects represent attempts to stabilize the availability of public and private resources as well as the massive growth of the city with more sustainable forms of urban development. Among the most important challenges that Istanbul will face in the upcoming years are the spatial distribution of urban density and infrastructure, controlling development within the water basins, risk management in relation to future earthquakes, and the impact of these changes on the social structure and the quality of life.

Accordingly, recent governance and policy restructuring, as well as developments such as the Istanbul Development Plan, the Marmaray Tunnel Project, the future subway network, and projects associated with the Istanbul 2010 European Cultural Capital, signal the need for even more

[12]Related laws include Law no. 5366 (Law for the Protection of Dilapidated Historical and Cultural Real Estate through Protection by Renewal), passed in 2005, and the 2010 European Cultural Capital Law, approved in 2007.

active urban governance and project implementation for future Istanbul. This period offers an opening to reconsider the contemporary urban form of Istanbul and speculate on its relation to the city's specific challenges. That is, going back to our earlier discussion on the "ecological turn" of Istanbul – where the idea of ecology is interpreted narrowly from a managerial perspective – it could be argued that the current historical situation of Istanbul is an opportunity for more expanded interpretation of ecology and sustainability in Istanbul.

An example would be the spatial configuration of the urban-edge condition as it relates to recent urban policy changes as well as the ambitions of the Istanbul Development Plan. The expansion of the jurisdictional limits of the metropolitan area would suggest the possibility of a more unified and integrated urbanism. Along with the ambition of local government to take rapid action on implementing these projects, the strong emphasis on ecology and infrastructure development in the recent Istanbul Development Plan creates an opening for a new approach. For instance, in addition to designating specific areas for water basin control, ecological preservation, eco-agriculture, and bio-diversity parks along the edge of the city, the Plan proposes specific areas for new housing developments and public facilities (hospital and health centers, education centers, decentralized "mini-terminals" for transportation) along the hinterland-edge. While all of these areas will be connected by new subway infrastructure (construction has started and the subway is expected to be complete in 2023), the meaning of infrastructure could be expanded to benefit Istanbul's urbanism. For instance, infrastructure need not be limited to transportation networks, but could include public facilities such as housing, health, or education services. Rather than simply limiting sustainability to an urban managerial inquiry, the real question remains: what kind of projections might these new urban policies instigate regarding urban ecology and infrastructure and what do they mean for the livability and the social cohesion of Istanbul?

As answers to such questions will be critical in the following years, at this stage, one could argue that sustainability might offer a framework for building necessary relationships between the city and its environment as well as between the physical and the social aspects of its urbanism. An initial conclusion deriving from this framework is the need to establish a wider understanding of Istanbul's larger metropolitan terrain – through further explorations on the changing spatial configuration of the hinterland-edge, its landscape, and the construction of the subway and other elements of public infrastructure – and the incorporation of that knowledge into Istanbul's urbanism.[13]

[13]For a recent study that aims to historicize this relationship, see (Turan 2009).

Revisiting geographer Matthew Gandy's assertion that "it is perhaps only through an ecologically enriched public realm that new kinds of urban environmental discourse may emerge" (Gandy 2006), a second point would be that sustainability stands as a relevant and significant topic for Istanbul's contemporary urbanism as long as it helps to build new interactions among the city's ecologies, infrastructure, and public realm, ultimately resulting with a more expanded understanding of urban sustainability for the city.

References

Akpınar I (2003) The building of Istanbul after the plan of Henri Prost 1937–1960: from secularisation to Turkish modernisation. PhD dissertation, University College, London

Ayata S (2002) The new middle class and the joys of suburbia. In: Kandiyoti D, Saktanber A (eds) Fragments of culture: the everyday of modern Turkey. Rutgers University Press, New Brunswick, NJ, pp 25–42

Bauman Z (2004) Wasted lives: modernity and its outcasts. Polity Press, Malden

Bozdoğan S (2001) Modernism and nation building: Turkish architectural culture in the Early Republic. University of Washington Press, Seattle

Brenner N, Theodore N (2002) Spaces of neoliberalism: urban restructuring in Western Europe and North America. Blackwell, Oxford

Buğra A (1998) The immoral economy of housing in Turkey. Int J Urban Reg Res 22(2):282–302

Caldeira T (2000) City of walls: crime, segregation, and citizenship in São Paulo. University of California Press, Berkeley

Candan AB, Kolluoğlu B (2008) Emerging spaces of neoliberalism: a gated town and a public housing project in Istanbul. New Perspect Turkey 39:5–46

Çelik Z (1986) The remaking of Istanbul. University of Washington Press, Seattle

Danış D, Pérouse J (2005) Zenginliğin Mekanda Yeni Yansımaları: Istanbul'da Güvenlikli Siteler. Toplum ve Bilim 104

Davis M (1990) City of quartz: excavating the future in Los Angeles. Verso, New York

Dodd CH (1983) The crisis of Turkish democracy. Eothen Press, Huntingdon

Fainstein S, Gordon I, Harloe M (eds) (1992) Divided cities: New York & London in the contemporary world. Blackwell, Oxford

Gandy M (2006) Urban nature and the ecological imaginary. In: Heynen N, Kaika M, Swyngedouw E (eds) In the nature of cities: urban political ecology and the politics of urban metabolism. Routledge, London, pp 63–74

Garreau J (1991) Edge city: life on the new frontier. Doubleday, New York

Graham S, Marvin S (2001) Splintering urbanism: networked infrastructures, technological mobilities and the urban condition. Routledge, London

Hackworth J (2007) The neoliberal city: governance, ideology, and development in American urbanism. Cornell University Press, Ithaca

Harvey D (1989) The condition of postmodernity: an inquiry into the origins of cultural change. Blackwell, Cambridge

Hautecoeur L (1960) l'oeuvre de Henri Prost: architecture et urbanisme. Academie d'Architecture, Paris

Istanbul Greater Municipality Urban Planning Directorate (2009) 1/100.000 Ölçekli Istanbul Çevre Düzeni Planı. Istanbul Büyükşehir Belediyesi, Imar ve Şehircilik Daire Başkanlığı, Şehir Planlama Müdürlüğü, Istanbul

Istanbul Municipality (1971) Greater Istanbul master plan report of 1971

Izci R (2005) The impact of European Union on environmental policy. In: Adaman F, Arsel M (eds) Environmentalism in Turkey: between democracy and development? Ashgate, Aldershot, pp 87–100

Jonas AEG, While A (2007) Greening the entrepreneurial city: looking for spaces of sustainability politics in the competitive city. In: Krueger R, Gibbs D (eds) The sustainable development paradox: urban political economy in the United States and Europe. Guildford Press, New York, pp 123–160

Kaptan H, Enlil Z (2009) Istanbul: global aspirations and socio-spatial restructuring in an era of new internationalism. In: Sarkis H, Turan N (eds) A Turkish triangle: Ankara, Istanbul, and Izmir at the gates of Europe. Harvard Design School, Cambridge

Karpat K (1985) Ottoman population, 1830–1914: demographic and social characteristics. University of Wisconsin Press, Madison

Keyder C (1987) Political economy of Turkish democracy: 1950–1980. In: Schick IC, Tonak EA (eds) Turkey in transition: new perspectives. Oxford University Press, New York, pp 27–65

Keyder C (1994) Globalization of a third-world metropolis: Istanbul in the 1980s. Review 17:383–421

Keyder C (2000) Liberalization from above and the future of the informal sector: land, shelter, and informality in the periphery. In: Tabak F, Crichlow M (eds) Informalization: process and structure. Johns Hopkins University Press, Baltimore

Keyder C (2005) Globalization and social exclusion in Istanbul. Int J Urban Reg Res 29(1):124–134

Kurtuluş H (2005) Istanbul'da Kentsel Ayrışma: Mekansal Dönüşümde Farklı Boyutlar. Bağlam Yayıncılık, Istanbul

Lash S, Urry J (1987) The end of organized capitalism. University of Wisconsin Press, Madison

Marcuse P, van Kempen R (eds) (2002) Of states and cities: the partitioning of urban space. Oxford University Press, Oxford

Organization for Economic Cooperation and Development (OECD) (2008) OECD Territorial reviews: Istanbul, Turkey. OECD Publishing, Paris

Öncü A (1988) The politics of the urban land market in Turkey: 1950–1980. Int J Urban Reg Res 12(1):38–63

Özdemir D (2002) The distribution of foreign direct investments in the service sector in Istanbul. Cities 19(4):249–259

Piccinato L (1970) Istanbul Metropoliten Alan Planlama Çalısmaları. Mimarlık 70(5):55–78

Sassen S (1991) The global city: New York, London, Tokyo. Princeton University Press, Princeton

Sayar Z (1954) Istanbul ve Civarı II. Arkitekt 267

Tekeli I (1998) Türkiye'de Cumhuriyet Döneminde Kentsel Gelişme ve Kent Planlaması. In: Sey Y (ed) Bilanço'98: 75 Yılda Değişen Kent ve Mimarlık. Tarih Vakfı Yayınları, Istanbul

Tekeli I (ed) (2002) Türkiye için Sürdürebilir Kalkınma Öncelikleri: Dünya Sürdürülebilir Kalkınma Zirvesi için TUBA'nin Görüşü. TUBA, Ankara

Toprak Z (1992) Tarihsel Nüfusbilim Açısından Istanbul'un Nüfusu ve Toplumsal Topoğrafyası. Dünü ve Bugünüyle Toplum ve Ekonomi 3

Turan N (2009) Geographic Istanbul: episodes in the history of a city's relationship with its landscape. PhD dissertation, Harvard University, Cambridge, MA

Türk Sanayicileri ve İş, Adamları Derneği (TUSIAD) (1991) Towards the 21st century: a development strategy oriented to the future. TUSIAD Publications, Istanbul

Uzun N (2003) The impact of urban renewal and gentrification on urban fabric: three cases in Turkey. Tijdschrift voor Economische en Sociale Geografie 94(3):363–375

Zukin S (1995) The cultures of cities. Blackwell, Cambridge

11. Toronto Megacity: Growth, Planning Institutions, Sustainability

André Sorensen

11.1 Introduction

During the last 50 years the Toronto region has grown from a small city of 1.3 million in 1955 to a sprawling metropolitan region of about six million today. Although most of this growth took place as the use-segregated, automobile-oriented, suburban tract development often considered characteristic of suburbanization in North America, Toronto has a distinctive urban form, which is quite different from the U.S. model, and poses different sustainability challenges.

The main distinguishing features are that Toronto's suburban areas have been developed at relatively high densities, and urban growth in the post Second World War era has been accommodated with relatively little unregulated development, and in a contiguous pattern without significant leapfrog development or large-lot estate development. A recent study, which measured average population density of the full contiguous built-up area of entire metropolitan regions on a consistent basis, found that the Toronto region had an average population density of 27 people per hectare, the same as Copenhagen, and slightly higher than Stockholm (26/ha). This is much higher than similar-sized U.S. cities such as Chicago (15/ha), Washington (13/ha), Houston (11.4/ha), or Atlanta (6.8/ha) (see Sorensen and Hess 2007). This chapter is about the entire Toronto metropolitan region, that includes both the current City of Toronto (known as Metropolitan Toronto before amalgamation in 1998), and its contiguous suburbs in Halton, Peel, York, and Durham Regions, an area often referred to as the Greater Toronto Area (GTA) (see Fig. 11-1).

The distinctive urban form of the Greater Toronto Area (GTA) is a product of the actions during the last 50 years of a robust set of planning and development control institutions. Suburban land development has been

A. Sorensen and J. Okata (eds.), *Megacities: Urban Form, Governance, and Sustainability*,

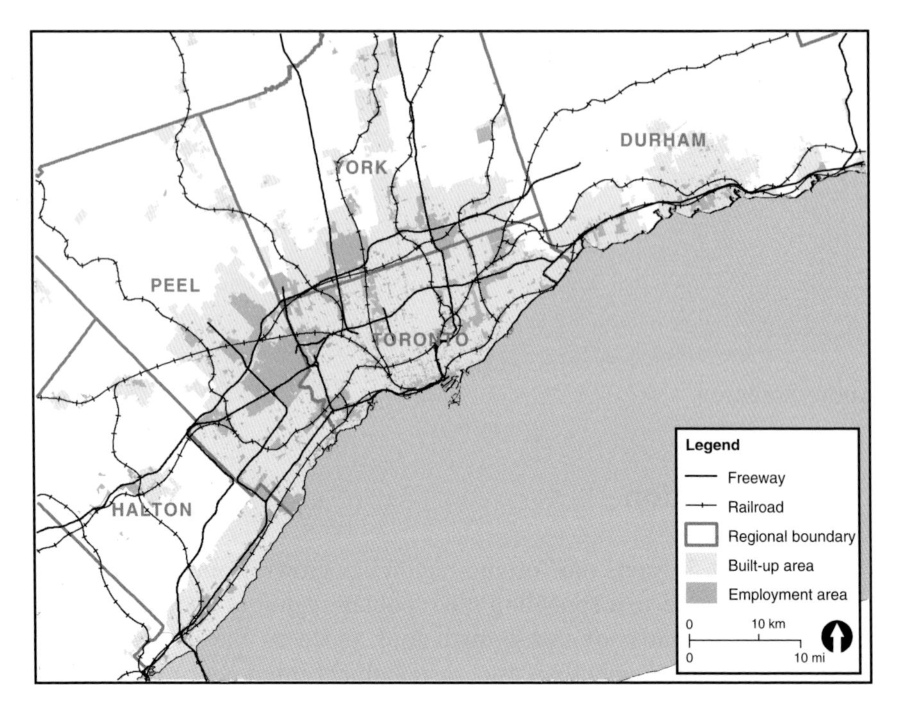

Fig. 11-1. Land use and urban structure of the Greater Toronto Area

tightly linked to municipal investment in the infrastructure of water supply and sewer systems, primarily to manage the timing of construction and achieve efficiencies of scale, thereby reducing costs. Development control ensures that local services such as roads, sidewalks, and sewers are paid for by developers, who must also provide local park space and set aside lands for natural heritage protection and schools. In combination with local Conservation Authorities established to prevent the recurrence of flood damage caused by Hurricane Hazel in 1954, this development control regime has achieved significant protection of natural heritage features, including green buffers flanking most rivers and streams, an extensive regional parks network, and large protected green areas. In short, Toronto's development control regime has resolutely achieved the modernist vision of suburbanization and in the process has created a highly planned and relatively compact metropolitan region that is quite different than most US cities.

This description of the Toronto region as highly planned and tightly regulated seems at odds with the views of many urban observers of the last 10 years, who have depicted Toronto's postwar suburban growth as urban sprawl and criticized the rapid consumption of high-quality farmland, destruction of wildlife habitat, and the conversion of a planned greenbelt into a utility and expressway corridor (Wheeler 2003; Winfield 2003; Solomon 2007;

Sewell 2009). The conventional planning wisdom is that although the original City of Toronto and the Regional Municipality of Metropolitan Toronto (Metro) achieved considerable planning success, after the early 1970s planning at the scale of the region was largely abandoned, just at the moment that growth passed beyond the boundaries of Metro Toronto (Wronski and Turnbull 1984; Filion 2000; Frisken 2007; White 2007). This view has been succinctly and famously summarized in the description of the Toronto region as "Vienna surrounded by Phoenix" (Cervero 1998; Filion 2000; Wheeler 2003), an exaggeration on both counts. Nonetheless it contains a measure of truth in identifying Toronto's dualistic urban form, with a high-density mixed-use transit-oriented core in the prewar City of Toronto, surrounded by much lower-density, segregated-use, auto-oriented suburbs.

The suggestion that regional planning was largely abandoned also contains a measure of truth, as there is no longer a planning agency responsible for the region as a whole, but as this chapter will show, that that does not mean that the Toronto region is unplanned and unregulated. Rather, the core planning, development control frameworks, and infrastructure provision strategies established during the 1950s and 1960s to regulate development in the region have continued to function, and have even strengthened, allowing an accelerating build-out of the postwar vision of efficient, planned suburbanization, even as explicit regional-scale planning waned.

In part, this confusion is a result of the multiple meanings of the term "planning." Although explicit "regional planning," which attempted to achieve a pre-ordained urban form for the Toronto region, was largely abandoned after 1970, as many have argued, the machinery of development control, municipal regulation, and environmental management at the municipal scale has continued to evolve and even strengthen over the last four decades. It is the product of this planning system for regulating suburban development that is the focus of this chapter.

It is also worth distinguishing between three scales of planning activity: (1) regional strategic planning, which attempts to shape patterns of growth for the urban region as a whole, (2) municipal scale land-use planning through zoning and infrastructure building, and (3) design and regulation of the development of individual land parcels or subdivisions through secondary plans, site plan control, and subdivision control. In Canada, the federal government plays almost no direct role in urban affairs.[1] Local government

[1]The federal government does, however, have enormous influence on the scale and speed of urbanization through its control over immigration policy, which has encouraged high levels of immigration. Most immigrants settle in the three major metropolitan regions (Toronto, Montreal, and Vancouver), and about half the total choose to settle in the Toronto area.

and urban planning are a provincial responsibility, and municipalities have no independent constitutional status, but are merely the creations of provinces, and are closely regulated and supervised by them. Regional strategic planning has been inconsistently applied in Ontario, while municipal planning and site planning have been applied with considerable consistency.

Before the Second World War, there was little large-scale urban planning in Ontario at all, and almost no attempt to shape regional growth patterns (Gomme 1984; Harris 1996). This changed with the passage of the *Planning Act* in 1946, and especially with the creation of Metropolitan Toronto (Metro) in 1953. As Richard White has convincingly shown, Metro was the de facto regional planning agency from 1953 until the mid to late 1960s, when the province became increasingly active in devising plans for the region (White 2007). During the 1950s and 1960s Metro included both the existing built-up area and the suburban growth areas, and was responsible for planning and building the large-scale infrastructure of roads, public transit, and pipes that shaped patterns of growth.

After 1970, most greenfield growth was taking place beyond the edge of the Metro political boundary, but instead of expanding the Metro area, the province created four new two-tier regional governments in the suburbs surrounding Metro Toronto. Regional planning became much more fragmented and competitive, the political will to plan for the whole region diminished, and the political power of the suburbs increased (Gomme 1984; Walks 2004; Frisken 2007: 141). Issues of regional urbanization patterns and infrastructure needs and costs resurfaced periodically, but most commentators agree that from 1970, until the resurgence of regional scale planning in the early years of the twenty-first century with the creation of the Greenbelt and Places to Grow plans, there was little explicit regional planning for the GTA.

On the other hand, development in the region has been carefully planned and managed at the local scale, largely by the municipal governments that are responsible for local official plans, zoning, subdivision control, secondary plans, and infrastructure management. As this chapter will show, those efforts have faithfully reproduced much of the conception of "good urban form" established by Metro in the 1950s, and have reinforced the development management institutions established at that time, even though the suburban forms generated by those institutions have since been widely criticized. Municipal institutions and patterns of development management have also been structured by the large-scale infrastructure building and land-use planning frameworks established by the province and Metro in the 1950s and 1960s, including the expressway system, the major employment areas, sewer systems, and natural heritage preserves.

This pattern of urban development has significant positive elements as discussed below, but as the Toronto region's population pushed past the five million mark, the flaws in this planning vision became more apparent. The most important of these flaws is undoubtedly the extreme auto-dependence of the postwar suburbs, which are highly use-segregated, with large mono-functional areas, so that even with relatively high population densities they are difficult to serve with high-quality public transit. Even with a robust expressway and arterial roads system, road congestion has become endemic, especially in the suburbs, where the roads are most extensive. Air pollution is a serious and steadily worsening problem that causes some 440 extra deaths in the City of Toronto each year according to the city's Department of Public Health (Winfield 2003; Toronto Public Health 2007). Automobile dependence produces both high levels of congestion and high levels of energy use per capita.

Perhaps most problematic in the long run is the highly inflexible urban form that has been created, which for multiple reasons examined below is likely to be much more difficult to adaptively re-use and re-design than the urban areas created in the prewar period. In particular, the units of land development, and the size of mono-functional areas has steadily increased, so land uses are less mixed, and there has been a spread of urban forms that are designed to prevent change over time.

During the last 15 years, this critique of the problematic patterns of urban growth of the GTA has become increasingly influential and has played a major part in shifting public opinion against "suburban sprawl." The change in attitudes has been a major factor behind recent Provincial government initiatives, including the protection of the Oak Ridges Moraine, the creation of the Greenbelt, and the Places to Grow regional plan discussed below.

This chapter traces the evolution of the Toronto growth management and regional planning paradigm and examines the characteristic patterns of urban form it has produced. Part 2 examines the creation of the major institutions of land development control and infrastructure planning during the 1950s, grounding those innovations in an analysis of the major urban problems of the 1920s and 1930s that they were designed to prevent. Part 3 describes and analyses the patterns of urban form that have been produced during the last half-century. Part 4 summarizes the major characteristics of the Toronto megacity's urban form, discusses the relationship between urban form and sustainability in the region, and suggests that the dominant urban forms created during the last 50 years will make it difficult for current intensification policies to contribute to greater sustainability.

11.2 The Emergence of a New Development System

The robust and enduring institutional framework that has structured the creation of today's Greater Toronto Area was a product of major legislative reforms and governance innovations of the 1940s and 1950s, and the emergence of a large-scale development industry that specialized in suburban land development. The development system established during these years was a direct response to the serious urban problems created during the 1920s and 1930s, especially haphazard urban sprawl, shortages of municipal infrastructure in growth areas, and the severe fiscal problems of suburban municipalities, many of which went bankrupt in the 1930s.

A pivotal issue in the creation of the postwar Toronto growth management regime was thus the vexing question of the high costs of servicing urban growth – more precisely, who was to pay? As increasingly high standards of municipal infrastructure and building regulations were advocated and achieved, the cost of providing infrastructure for rapidly growing urban areas had grown exponentially, but the question of how to regulate suburban development and to finance infrastructure remained unresolved, creating major problems for both municipal and provincial governments.

A second major factor impelling action was the surprisingly rapid urban and economic growth experienced during the 1940s and early 1950s, which was concentrated in the Golden Horseshoe region at the western end of Lake Ontario, stretching from Oshawa through Toronto to Hamilton. The resumption of urban growth in the 1940s after a decade and a half of depression and war created a crisis for Toronto region urban policy-makers, who agreed that the existing system of planning and governance was failing and that a new arrangement was necessary.

In Toronto planning, the late 1940s represent a critical juncture of precisely the sort described by institutional theorists such as Katznelson (2003). Established institutions and governance arrangements for regulating the growth and development of the metropolis were found to be inadequate, and had lost legitimacy as a framework for interpretation and action, creating the need to develop new institutions, and presenting opportunities for new actors and ideas to gain influence. The institutions created during this critical juncture are a direct response to the critique of the failings of existing arrangements, so an analysis of that critique is important for understanding the particular institutional innovations that were implemented.

The main issue was how to pay for the urban infrastructure necessitated by urban growth. Until 1912 the city of Toronto had grown through regular annexations of new territory, often in advance of significant development. After 1912, however, the City Council decided against further annexations, primarily because of political controversy over the high costs and the extra taxes associated with extending public services to the annexed areas (Harris 1996: 151; Frisken 2007: 55). The last major annexation had been North Toronto, where the city found itself obliged to rebuild at great expense an inadequate sewer system in which some of the pipes ran uphill. By 1918 the voices opposing further annexation had gained the ascendancy, with the Toronto housing commissioners declaring "For the City to embark on any such schemes would not only involve improperly risking the ratepayers' capital and credit, but would unquestionably greatly increase the municipality's already heavy debt" (cited in Harris 1996: 151). The direct result was that during the 1920s, large areas were developed in unincorporated rural townships outside the city boundary. Several new municipalities were eventually incorporated in these areas.

Those new municipalities lacked the financial resources and planning expertise to build municipal infrastructure such as roads, schools, water mains, and sewers, and did not enforce requirements for sanitary hookups or expensive building standards, whereas Toronto required connections to water and sewer systems, and brick construction for all dwellings to prevent fire (Harris 1996). Water supply outside the city was provided by inexpensive wells, and where they existed, sewer systems provided only basic treatment before effluents were released into nearby rivers and streams.

These suburbs became a relatively cheap place to own a home, allowing large numbers of working people and new immigrants to build their own inexpensive houses in "shacktowns" outside the city. Starting with a tarpaper shack, homeowners gradually improved the structure as time and money allowed.[2] Such development patterns were a disincentive for the city to annex these areas, as it was very expensive to service them retroactively, and their property taxes could not cover the investment. Not surprisingly, during the Depression of the 1930s, many of these same municipalities went bankrupt, and the province was obliged to assume their debts.

Rapid economic growth in the 1940s, and pent-up housing demand dating from the 1930s combined to produce a development boom outside the City of Toronto that demonstrated the inadequacy of the existing planning framework. The major problems with the existing planning system were clearly summarized by the first Chairman of the Municipality of Metropolitan Toronto, Frederick Gardiner, in a 1953 speech to the Empire Club in which he sets

[2] Harris (1996) has documented the high rate of owner-building in the Toronto area, praising the access this provided to working-class homeownership, while criticizing the lack of planning that contributed to widespread foreclosures, municipal bankruptcies, and retrenchment in the 1930s.

out the arguments in favor of Metropolitan government, referring specifically to problems associated with growth in the 1940s and early 1950s:

> In North York, there are over 15,000 septic tanks built in clay which has neither the qualities of absorption nor evaporation. No comment is necessary with respect to the unsatisfactory nature of that condition. Some municipalities were able to finance the services which their residential development required, others were not. The issuance of building permits was stopped or held up on account of the inability of some municipalities to provide the services required. One municipality boasted that it had the finest educational system in Canada. Others were unable to provide their children with a minimum standard of education except with the utmost financial difficulty. Nothing approaching a system of arterial highways accompanied this tremendous development. This was because no agreement could be arrived at on a cooperative basis between the thirteen municipalities as to where the arterial highways should go and how they would be paid for. All agreed that expressways and parkways were necessary so long as they ran through some other municipality and someone else paid for them. … The Toronto and York planning board, of which I was chairman for five years, lined its walls with plans for the development of the whole area. We knew what needed to be done but in the absence of power to tax the constituent municipalities and to take expropriation proceedings, none of the essential works could be undertaken. … There was a crying need for housing. The city had no room for a housing development program and the suburbs could not finance the necessary services. Maps, plans and theoretical discussions accomplished nothing. We had to be driven by intolerable inconvenience and the threat of financial difficulty before steps were taken to solve our problems. When some of our municipalities had difficulty in selling their bonds it was evident that a major operation was necessary (Gardiner 1953).

The major operation undertaken by the provincial government in response to this crisis was the creation in 1953 of the Municipality of Metropolitan Toronto (Metro). Although the City of Toronto had finally applied in 1950 for amalgamation with its 12 suburbs, that proposal encountered strong resistance from the suburban municipalities, and the Ontario Municipal Board[3] (OMB) rejected the application (Milner 1963: 261). Instead the

[3]The OMB is a quasi-judicial adjudicative tribunal established by the Province of Ontario to settle disputes over land-use planning, development charges, land expropriation, and municipal finance (www.omb.gov.on.ca/english/home.html).

province commissioned an inquiry into regional governance and planning, that recommended a two-tier system of government, with a metropolitan-level government to provide regional planning and infrastructure investment, while the 13 local municipal governments were left in place, and retained local planning and zoning powers and responsibilities for service delivery. Metro would plan, build, and sell wholesale services to the municipalities, and they would retail them to users.

Some enduring characteristics of Ontario's planning culture are visible here, including the concern for the efficient deployment of public investment, the desire to facilitate continued growth, the recognition of the need to supply housing at a price working people could afford, and a concern for "fairness" among municipalities in bearing a share of the costs of metropolitan services. The fact that the poorer municipalities often had the worst services and highest tax rates, while affluent suburbs had lower taxes and excellent services was widely seen at the time as a serious social equity problem (Frisken 2007).

11.2.1 The Metro Development Control Regime

The urban development priorities and planning approaches of Metro emerged directly from the context in which Metro was created, and the problems it was meant to solve. First and foremost, Metro was created to build the major public infrastructure of water supply and sewers, roads and public transit, schools and other educational facilities to permit the continued growth of the region, which the small and fragmented suburban municipalities had been unable to do, both because of coordination problems, and because of financial constraints. Metro, with an integrated planning, development, and financing machinery, could overcome the problem of coordination and, drawing on the rich tax base and excellent credit rating of Toronto, finance the needed investment in the most cost-effective way.

Efficiency and cost-effectiveness were major planning values for Metro, and were achieved in part through economies of scale, and in part through coordination that eliminated duplication, but especially as a result of the decision to build a single integrated Lake Ontario-based water supply and sewer treatment system for the whole region. This eliminated well-based water systems and the disposal of wastes into the region's small rivers and streams. The 1946 Ontario *Planning Act* had permitted municipal governments to deny permissions for residential and industrial development based on small-scale septic tanks for wastewater, effectively tying development to the provision of municipal plumbing systems. The Act also required registered plans of subdivision approved by municipal officials and the Minister for all land subdivision in designated urban development areas, giving municipal planners considerable leverage to negotiate the standards and design for new subdivisions (Gomme 1984: 104).

A closely related planning priority for Metro was to ensure compact, contiguous development, without leapfrogging over undeveloped land. This priority followed directly from the decision to use integrated lake-based water and wastewater systems. While the globally dominant metropolitan planning paradigm in the 1950s and 1960s was the creation of satellite towns separated by greenbelts, following the London model, Toronto opted for compact, contiguous peripheral growth. It simply didn't make sense to build satellite towns that would require pipes from the Metro system to cross a greenbelt. As White (2007: 17) puts it, "The Board's overall 'vision' of the region was thus as much a product of engineering as planning."

The achievement of contiguous development was also made possible by the fact that the Metro Toronto Planning Board (MTPB) was given planning authority over an area three times the size of Metro, and used this authority to prevent most developments outside Metro until the Metro area was almost fully built out, ensuring that investment in infrastructure was paid back through full use of built capacity. As Frisken shows, Metro proved a cost-effective way of providing infrastructure, saving the Provincial government considerable money by allowing a reduced share of Metro's infrastructure costs to be paid directly through provincial grants (2007: 86).

Another of Metro's priorities was to ensure an adequate supply of land for housing to provide access to homeownership for the majority of the population, and employment lands to make space available for industrial investment. This role, which was seen as essential to ensure that land prices were not pushed up by lack of supply, followed directly from the Metro mandate of facilitating planned growth. However, the huge investments in infrastructure, and the restrictions on unplanned development, also provided powerful incentives for the provision of sufficient land in sites where services had been supplied. Land supply for housing further required both the agreement of local governments to rezoning, and the willingness and ability of developers to subdivide and develop land and housing.

A key institutional innovation of the postwar planning regime was the requirement that services internal to developments be entirely supplied by developers as a condition of the permit to subdivide. As of 1954, the standard subdivision agreement in Metro required the subdivider to install roadways (including asphalt surfacing), watermains, sanitary sewers, storm sewers, sidewalks, street lighting, and street signs. Agreements also specified existing and final grades and contours, land for municipal purposes (schools and parks), and drainage works, and contained provisions for financial arrangements with the township, and registration of the subdivision agreement (Milner 1963). Municipalities increasingly levied development charges that the developer paid on a per-acre or per-lot basis for capital infrastructure required by the development, but external to the actual site, such as sewer systems, pumping stations, new schools, etc. Most of the upfront costs of urban growth were thus transferred from municipal governments to developers, who in turn passed along the increased costs to house buyers. Many suburban municipalities in this way became dependent on a continuing stream of development charges from greenfield development as a major part of their revenues.

One consequence was that large, highly capitalized private developers became essential to the growth of Metro as a planning and infrastructure-building juggernaut. The prototype was Don Mills Development Limited, which designed and built Canada's first comprehensive privately built suburb. Don Mills was the creation of E.P. Taylor, one of Canada's most successful and richest businessmen, who had made his fortune brewing beer. He started buying land north of Toronto in 1947, and by 1952 had assembled a tract of 2,063 acres (835 ha) (Sewell 1993). Taylor assembled a talented team of designers and planners, and in Don Mills they created an approach to development that incorporated the latest planning ideas. The main planning principles were: complete segregation of land uses and housing types into their own areas, neighborhood units centered on public schools, an abandonment of the street grid in favor of discontinuous, looping road systems with many cul-de-sacs and T-intersections, and extensive green spaces (Fig. 11-2a shows Don Mills today).

Such design concepts for new residential areas were subsequently actively promoted by the Community Planning Branch of the Ontario Department of Planning and Development. The traditional "gridiron" layout was criticized as boring, wasteful of land, and producing the maximum of dangerous intersections. Best-practice examples of the "Planned Neighbourhood: Good Curvilinear Pattern" were provided, that demonstrated a road pattern with less land used by roads, many fewer cross-intersections, more private residential lots, more multiple dwelling units, higher overall population densities, and more land area for parks, schools, churches and other community facilities (Milner 1963).

Most significant in the context of the present discussion were Taylor's innovative approaches to infrastructure finance. Although municipalities around Toronto were gradually adopting the practice of requiring subdividers to build infrastructure internal to the subdivision, such as local roads and piping, there were still significant off-site costs for water supply, sewage

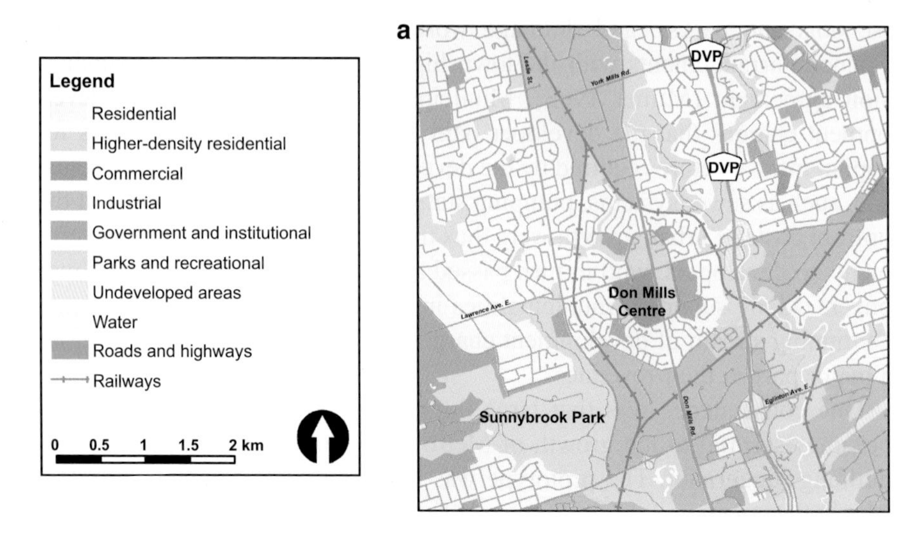

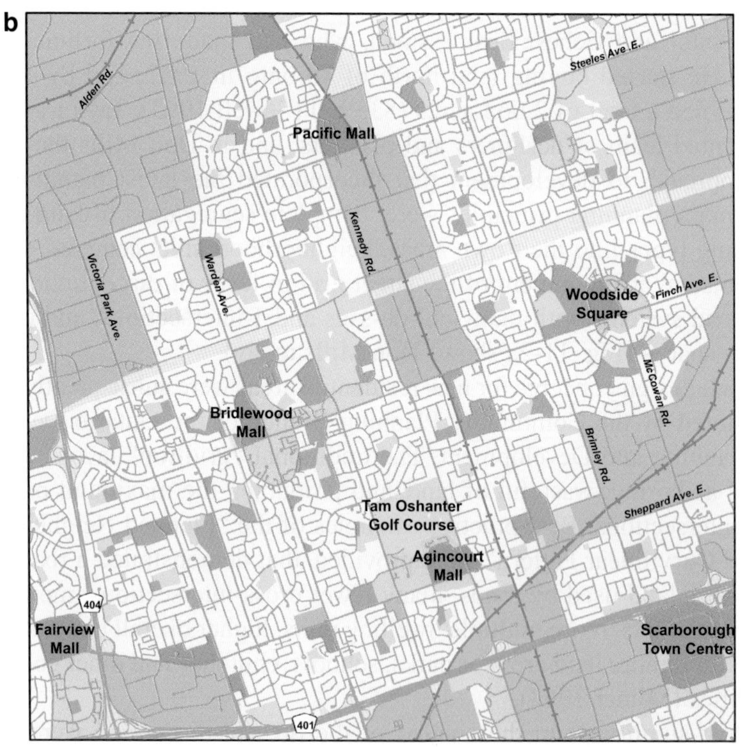

Fig. 11-2. (**a**) Don Mills and (**b**) North Scarborough

treatment plants, and schools. Municipalities had to shoulder these costs, creating a risk that local property taxes in the new development would not be sufficient to cover them. To speed up approval by a hesitant North York council, Taylor offered to pay for the off-site infrastructure himself. As Sewell puts it:

> Quite simply, Taylor agreed to assume almost all the servicing costs. The financial risks were taken off the shoulders of the municipality and borne by the developer. The municipality's role of providing services was eschewed for one of simply being a planning regulator. Since the municipality bore little risk, it had little reason not to permit the developer to do exactly as he saw fit. In one simple stroke, Taylor had totally changed the rules of development. Now, the only developers municipalities need concern themselves with were those large enough to provide funds for all services demanded by the municipality (Sewell 1993: 95).

Another reason for the emerging preference for large-volume, integrated development firms was the widespread concern about the rising cost of housing. Housing experts believed that a shift to mass production of housing would allow significant economies of scale compared to the existing practice in which most houses were built individually by small builders (Harris 2004: 121).

Taylor's successful Don Mills set a template for large-scale land development that was widely copied throughout the GTA and Canada. Segregated land uses, hierarchical road systems with major arterials for through traffic and looping disconnected local distributors, neighborhood units based on primary schools, extensive park space – all became standard features in the years to come, as did the reliance on developers to finance both on-site and off-site infrastructure. Don Mills Developments built a second, even larger development West of Toronto called Erin Mills on over 6,000 acres (2,400 ha), which has since become a core part of the city of Mississauga. In Erin Mills, as in Don Mills, the plan was distinguished by an ambitious approach to comprehensive town development, including the creation of a commercial center, employment areas, and a mix of housing types from detached houses to mid-rise apartments.

This model, in which Metro and the Province of Ontario built regional infrastructure, and developers designed and built local infrastructure, proved extremely robust, and provided a template for development that became the business-as-usual pattern of land development and urban growth in the Toronto region for the next half-century. The MTPB insistence that developers contribute land for schools, parks, and other public purposes was consistently upheld by the OMB (Kaplan 1982: 727). This approach relieved municipalities of most of the financial burden of urban growth, but tended to make them dependent on further growth to supply a steady stream of development charges to finance other municipal infrastructure and spending.

11.2.2 The Metro Concept of Urban Form and Mobility

The draft Metropolitan Toronto Official Plans of 1959 and 1965 set out in detail the proposed urban form for the region, a form that was largely implemented, even though Metro's official plan had no legal status until it was finally approved by Metro Council in 1980, by which time virtually the whole Metro area was already built up.[4] The basic principle was that urbanization would be linear, along the north shore of Lake Ontario from Oshawa in the east to Hamilton in the west, allowing lake-based services throughout the metropolitan area. The only exception was to be a corridor heading north along Yonge Street. The central business district of Toronto would be strengthened and intensified, continuing to function as the regional employment centre, accessible from all parts of the metropolitan area by mass transit (Metropolitan Toronto Planning Board 1959: S4). Secondary employment areas were dispersed throughout the planning area near railway and road facilities, so that there would be more than enough employment land to provide location choices for industry.

According to Frisken (2007: 89), Metro plans repeatedly endorsed a consistent set of planning principles throughout Metro's history: a relatively compact regional urban structure, with well-defined urban boundaries, a strong core with most commercial, cultural, and institutional activities; large amounts of central city housing in high-rise forms in redeveloped inner-city neighborhoods; and commercial areas away from the core in the form of huge shopping centers located at major transportation nodes surrounded by high-density housing. The goal of having many employment districts distributed throughout the new suburban areas was to enable people in the suburbs to live near their work if they chose. This, combined with the proposal for a comprehensive mass transit system, was designed to prevent congestion: "While the proposed scheme thus maximizes opportunities for commuting, it is proposed to minimize the need for commuting by reserving ample areas for industry in each major section of the area. The residents of all sections will have a choice between local employment and employment in the central area" (Metropolitan Toronto Planning Board 1959: S5); (see also Frisken 2007: 89).

[4] As both Frisken and White explain, although the draft plan was for many years not submitted for approval by Metro Council, it served as a guide for the development of the region.

A new pattern of roads was sought that could handle much larger volumes of traffic and prevent the sort of congestion that had begun in the 1920s when increasing private automobile traffic had overwhelmed the downtown grid. The basic principle of the roads system was to build a three-level hierarchy, with limited-access expressways to carry long-distance and through trips across the region, a large-scale grid of arterial roads of two or three lanes in each direction to carry traffic around the city, and local distributor roads within the arterial grid squares to bring traffic to individual houses or businesses. Through traffic was to be diverted away from local roads by curved and discontinuous roads, T-intersections, and cul-de-sac layouts within large grid squares. Although public opposition resulted in the cancellation in the 1970s of parts of the planned expressway system in the already built-up areas of the former City of Toronto,[5] the majority of the system outside the existing built-up area was rapidly built out, with about 218 km of the current 315 km completed by the late 1960s (Filion 2000: 169).

The basic road network in Toronto's postwar suburbs, however, is based on the old rural concession divisions that were surveyed when Ontario was first settled by the British colonial government at the end of the eighteenth century. The grid was 100 chains (1 chain = 66 feet) between concession roads, forming square blocks of 100 chains by 100 chains (1.25 miles by 1.25 miles or about 2 km by 2 km), with a 1-chain right-of-way separating each concession block that contained about 1,000 acres or 400 ha of land (Taylor et al. 2008). In the first Metro plan, these grid squares became the basic building blocks of urban form, and the concession roads were widened into an arterial road grid with a standard right-of-way of 120 feet (36.6 m). The 400-ha grid squares also came to be seen as an appropriate scale for neighborhood units, with their own public schools and parks.

A fundamental principle of the first Metro plans was that land uses should be separated, with some areas for residential use, others for employment uses, and major shopping centers for retail, reflecting the conventional planning wisdom of the time. As Harris (1996: 171) notes, Toronto land subdividers in the early decades of the twentieth century had gradually realized that buyers were willing to pay a premium for lots in areas where noxious uses were prohibited. This led to a growing practice during the 1920s of large developments that were promoted as exclusively residential, sometimes protected by deed restrictions and with housing standards that ensured exclusivity. Housing-only developments ensured that noisy and

[5]The success of the opposition movements, led by downtown residents including Jane Jacobs, is often credited as being a turning point in protecting the vitality and liveability of central Toronto (see Nowlan and Nowlan 1970; Sewell 1993).

noxious industrial plants and associated traffic were kept out, and more important, single-use zones were seen as better protected against change, which was equated with eventual decline and loss of property values.

As Filion points out, this development pattern requires very little coordination between monofunctional zones, as long as each was buffered by arterial roads and/or green space. Individual 4-km^2 concession blocks were usually internally carefully designed and planned, but the overall pattern needed little coordination, as interzone integration is provided by the road system (Filion 2000: 171). Development could proceed according to market demand on a block-by-block basis. Whereas early comprehensive developments such as Taylor's Don Mills and Erin Mills attempted integrated plans for "complete communities," and Metro had a similar overall vision for the Metro area, those ambitions gradually devolved into concession block sized development of a greatly simplified "neighborhood unit" concept of housing with a local school and local green space bordered by arterial roads, and sometimes a local retail area on a designated corner or along an arterial road. Critically, outside the Metro area the contiguous areas of monofunctional use became much larger, with many adjacent concession blocks of almost purely residential uses, and enormous employment areas.

Local governments also developed sophisticated methods to ensure unified development of whole 2 ha concession blocks, even in areas where multiple owners owned separate tracts of land, as was often the case. Because municipal governments had some discretion about the timing of development, and could prevent leapfrogging by delaying development of a particular block until main services were available, developers had a powerful incentive to cooperate. A system evolved in which each developer contributed proportionately to space allocated for parks and schools and other public facilities, even if the secondary plan established by the municipality meant that most of that space was actually on one developer's land, in which case that developer would be compensated with developable parcels contributed by other developers. This system solved the problem of land assembly for developers, who no longer needed to assemble huge sites, as in Don Mills and Erin Mills. And of course, the assembly of a site such as Erin Mills soon became virtually impossible, as most developable land within the two-to-four-decade development horizon had already been bought or optioned by the end of the 1960s.

11.3 Toronto Urban Form 1954–2006

A remarkable aspect of development patterns in the Toronto region since 1954 has been the very consistent urban form that has been produced. Despite recurring concerns and debates about regional patterns of urban growth, the urban development and design strategies pioneered in the 1950s still provide the basic template for greenfield development, even as regional conditions have changed greatly. This section summarizes briefly the major urban form characteristics produced by Toronto's postwar suburban development regime, positive and negative, and reviews the factors that have tended to produce continuity in regional development patterns.

Perhaps unsurprisingly, the main successes of this development regime relate directly to the problems identified in the postwar crisis, and the solutions proposed in response. A major achievement was the efficient development of large-scale physical infrastructure systems, particularly water supply, sewers, arterial roads, and expressways, but also local roads and parks, and public facilities such as schools (Rose 1972: 99; White 2007: 17). Regional infrastructure systems allowed the efficient and rapid build-out of huge new urban areas, with significant regional coordination and little duplication of functions. Tying land development to provision of municipal water and wastewater systems made infrastructure construction more cost-effective and virtually eliminated leapfrog development, as municipal governments were able to insist on contiguous, phased land development.

Equally important, the system required land developers to build high-quality local infrastructure, provide land for local parks and schools, and set aside land for regional greenspace and natural heritage systems. This meant that most of the cost of new development, including the public infrastructure associated with it, was internalized into the development process and included in the cost of new housing, instead of being paid out of general tax revenues. This had the effect of ensuring that house buyers paid for much of the costs of infrastructure upfront, thereby increasing private debt instead of public borrowing. An extensive parks and green space system was created (based primarily on existing rivers, creeks and valleys), as well as local parks and school playgrounds. It seems certain that the parks system thus created is larger and better connected than it would have been if municipal governments had simply bought land for parks on an ad hoc and occasional basis, as was the case in prewar Toronto. Similarly, the local road system of high-capacity arterials and low-capacity distributors is robust and comprehensive, and built almost entirely on existing rights of way and land contributed at no cost by developers.

A major advantage of the system is that there is a relatively long pipeline of land development. Development companies purchase urban fringe land and hold it for many years before development is permitted, so there is sufficient time to create coordinated development plans even where there are multiple landowners. And when the housing market periodically picks up, developers can supply large numbers of new homes relatively quickly in areas where plans have already been approved. Although the early vision of balanced "complete communities" was gradually abandoned and worries are frequently voiced that the costs of housing are increasing faster than incomes, compared to suburban areas in the United States, Toronto's suburbs are built at relatively high densities, with a significant proportion of higher-density housing forms, including duplex housing, townhouses, and particularly in the Metro area, many high-rise housing units. Huge amounts of good-quality housing have been produced, at a range of prices, in desirable and well-serviced neighborhoods.

The continuity in development patterns during the last 50 years is documented in a recent research project that examines the evolution of urban form in the Toronto region during the twentieth century. A major finding is that both dwelling unit densities and population densities have declined over the last 40 years (Taylor et al. 2008: 35). During the same period, the provision of road space, parks, schools and other public facilities has been quite consistent, indicating that design standards developed during the 1950s have continued to be applied with few changes, although the amount of park and greenspace on a per-person and per-dwelling unit basis has increased (Taylor et al. 2008: 50).

The burst of institutional reform and innovation in the 1940s and 1950s in the way cities are planned and built in Ontario set a template that structured the next 50 years of development. This model evolved over time, however. For early comprehensive developments such as Don Mills (Fig. 11-2a), the concept was of a new town with a commercial center, higher-density housing in a mix of styles near the center, surrounded by neighborhoods of lower-density single-family homes and employment lands near the railways on the edges of the site. It is important to note the small scale of Don Mills (originally only the area within the railway lines), yet it had its own town center, higher-density housing, and employment areas. Metro planners replicated the Don Mills pattern of commercial centers, nearby higher-density housing, and medium-sized industrial areas in north Scarborough, built within Metro in the 1960s (Fig. 11-2b). This area looks like nothing so much as five linked Don Mills, which together produce a much larger scale of suburban development.

By the 1980s much of the early vision of "complete communities" had been abandoned in favor of the regional patterns of mobility that universal car ownership made possible. It became the norm to develop new concession blocks with purely residential uses, associated schools and parks, and perhaps some commercial space at a corner. Areas of residential-only development grew larger and more uniform, and there was little attempt to establish "town centers" or nearby industrial areas. While there were smaller, scattered industrial areas within Metro, outside Metro there are just a few vast employment areas (see Fig. 11-1). The scale of urban form gets much larger, with huge areas of purely residential and employment use.

Two examples of more recent development are shown in Fig. 11-3a Richmond Hill, north of Toronto, and Fig. 11-3b Meadowvale, to the west of Toronto. As these two areas are both located at the newly developed fringe of the built-up area, the pattern of urban development by concession block is apparent, with the edge between urban and rural following arterial roads, and partly built-out blocks visible in both examples. In Richmond Hill a linear area of mixed use remains along the old highway known as Yonge Street, but apart from that and some older industrial areas along the railway, development is purely residential. This pattern is particularly visible in the newest developments between Bayview and Leslie, and the partly built-out block west of the Richmond Hill Golf Club.

Figure 11-3b shows the western edge of urban development of the Toronto region, in Mississauga. The area to the north and east of Winston Churchill Boulevard was designed and developed starting in the 1970s as part of Erin Mills, while the areas south and west of Winston Churchill have been developed since the 1990s. The newer grid squares are purely low-density residential, with some schools and a few neighborhood commercial areas, while the earlier development included town centers, areas of higher density housing, and employment areas.

So the Toronto model has, despite considerable success, produced several serious urban form problems. Key here is that the urban pattern is premised on universal automobile ownership and use, and a highly auto-dependent urban form has been created, so that virtually all trips in the outer urban area are made by car. Whereas in central Toronto, 33% of all trips are made by transit, and in the rest of Toronto the proportion is 21%, in the rest of the GTA only 6% of trips are made by transit (Miller and Soberman 2003: 24). This finding reflects the fact that mono-functional urban zones have become much larger, indicating a virtual abandonment of the earlier ideal of "complete communities" that integrate housing, employment zones and neighborhood retail centers, and allow walking and cycling for some trips.

Mono-functional areas are extremely hard to service with high-quality public transit, although housing densities are fairly high in many neighborhoods. Auto-dependent urban forms, combined with medium densities, have created a congestion crisis that is much worse in the suburbs than it is in the old central city, where the roads are not as good but more than half of trips are made by transit, walking, or cycling. In the long run, even more troubling is the virtual elimination of mixed-use areas from the suburban fabric, apart from a few older villages that were enveloped by new development.

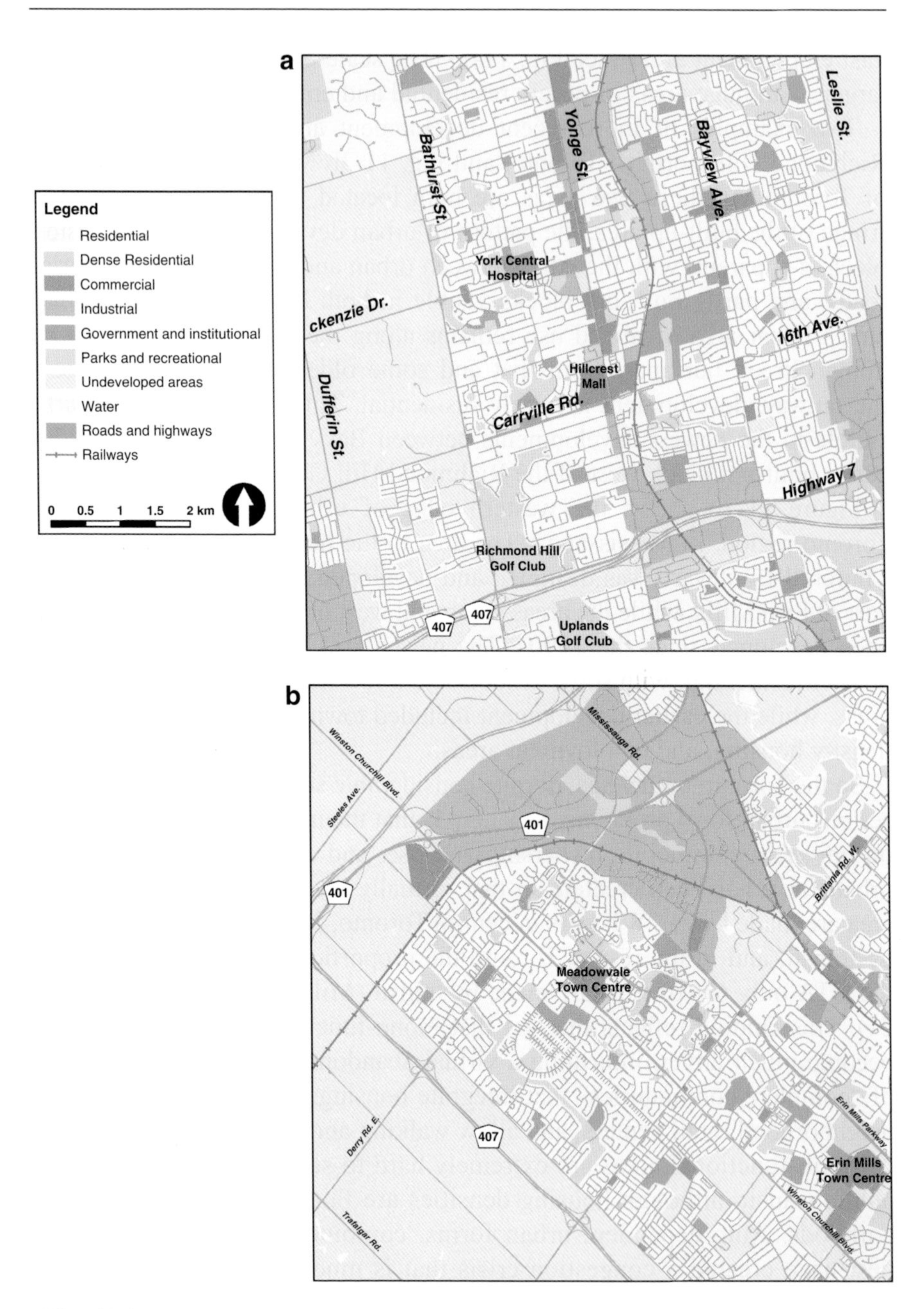

Fig. 11-3. (**a**) Richmond Hill, and (**b**) Meadowvale

This creates two serious problems. First, the design and land-use patterns of newly developed lands are not just highly segregated, but also highly inflexible. Large residential areas in particular are designed in a way that makes future mixed use almost impossible: road systems prevent through traffic and make walking and bicycling difficult, single-use zones are designed to be unchanging, many houses back onto arterial roads that might be logical routes of public transit systems, preventing redevelopment into Main Street style boulevards with a mix of shops, employment, and residential uses. The adaptive re-use of buildings and districts that is occurring downtown will be very difficult in areas outside Toronto. Second, the processes and institutions for building mixed-use areas have been lost, as none have been built for 50 years. Even though provincial plans are premised on the development of high-density mixed-use nodes throughout the region, it is not clear that this will be possible within existing institutional frameworks. The development of new nodes will be made even more difficult by the recent dispersion of retail to big box centers scattered around the region in auto-only locations (Jones and Doucet 2003; Buliung and Hernandez 2009).

Multiple factors tend to support continuity in what Bourne has described as the "culture of development" (Bourne 1996: 705). Perhaps most important is the central role of large developers. A major product of the new planning system was the creation of a large-scale development industry. The building of roads, parks, sewers, and other community facilities for integrated developments required a scale of capitalization previously unknown in the Ontario land development industry. Huge development companies, with extensive land banks and long pipelines of development projects (from initial land purchase through design, planning, approval, servicing and eventual house marketing) tend naturally towards conservatism of design, and prefer a stable regulatory approach. By the late 1960s these companies had built up their land banks through purchase and options on most of the developable land in the region, a strategy that squeezed out smaller players. Major development companies require an ongoing pipeline of projects to provide a return on their land investment, so are routinely designing and obtaining subdivision permits 5–15 years in advance of construction. Their design conservatism is shared by risk-averse investors, insurance companies, and mortgage holders who want consistent, safe products (Bourne 1996; Grant 2002; Harris 2004).

The preference for continuity is shared by municipal and provincial governments. They invested in regional infrastructure systems that had to be conceived and planned decades in advance of demand, and once built required customers (that is, new residents) to be able to pay back the investment. Suburban municipalities also quickly became dependent on the revenue stream of development charges from new land development projects. The emergence of comprehensive zoning plans as the standard practice from the late 1940s greatly reinforced this trend, as zoning was premised on large stable areas of single land use. Equally, consumers tend to be risk-averse, and the new style of large mono-functional developments is attractive to home-buyers. The standard pattern of suburban development emerged almost fully formed from the first major projects of Don Mills, Erin Mills, and Bramalea. Segregated land uses, arterial roads defining neighborhood units, discontinuous looping distributor roads within those units, local parks, and school systems all became synonymous with "good residential environments" and "good investment." Harris describes these trends towards standard forms of development, consistent housing products, and standardized consumption practices as a form of "creeping conformity" engendered by the shift to suburban lifestyles (Harris 2004).

Thus multiple factors promote continuity in the patterns of greenfield development in the Toronto region. Although "new urbanist" and "smart growth" ideas have been influential in changing residential street patterns towards modified grids instead of loops and lollipops layouts, and densities are inching higher, pushed in part by higher land costs, most urban-edge development today still consists of large mono-functional areas of residential or employment lands that are even more auto-dependent than those of the 1980s, as transit service is poorer and they are even further away from the central city and its high-quality transit facilities.

11.4 Toronto Megacity Sustainability

The most striking aspect of this story is the fact that in response to an urban growth crisis in the 1940s and 1950s, a new suburban planning and development regime was established that has structured the development process until the present day. That solution has been, in many respects, highly successful, by guaranteeing a careful, planned process of suburbanization in which most of the costs of public infrastructure are internalized into the development process, large quantities of good housing have been produced at affordable prices, and the extremely low-density exurban development and gated communities common in the U.S. have largely been avoided. There is no doubt that the Toronto region and its citizens have benefited greatly from many of the institutions established in the 1950s. As Bourne puts it, Toronto "continues to provide a relatively high quality of life for most of its citizens" (Bourne 2001: 44).

For those concerned with metropolitan region sustainability, perhaps the most important message here is that transformative change of governance structures can happen. The critical juncture of the 1940s and 1950s in Toronto, when new institutions of regional governance, land development control, and infrastructure finance were established, shows clearly that it is possible to create new and effective institutions to harness urban growth processes for the production of a higher quality of life and better urban environments. A range of factors made that transformation of the planning system achievable. These include:

- A clear and widely shared analysis of the then-current development pattern as unsustainable in the sense of posing significant long-term added costs and risks
- A suite of solutions and reforms, that while not necessarily agreed by all, were well-known and based at least in part on known precedents
- A mainstream tradition of provincial and municipal reform governments that had tackled and achieved governance improvements in the past (see Kaplan 1982)
- Robust economic growth
- A shared sense that planning, and government intervention more generally, is a legitimate activity that, although not without costs, must still be cheaper and more efficient than inaction

The Toronto planning regime largely achieved the core ideas of the "growth management/smart growth" movement in the United States: compact and contiguous development, integrated infrastructure and land development processes, regional greenspace networks, and affordable and high-density housing integrated into suburban residential areas (see Porter et al. 2002). As the region continued to grow, however, car ownership rates increased, land developers became larger, governance became more fragmented, and ever-larger mono-functional areas were produced. The result is that residents of the Toronto region have grown increasingly auto-dependent in their daily lives, and many see the resulting combination of high-energy consumption, worsening roads congestion, and serious air pollution as the key challenges facing the region. The Toronto experience suggests that the growth management/smart growth conception of sprawl prevention is inadequate to tackle serious problems of urban sprawl and automobile dependence, and that a more ambitious vision is required to create more sustainable cities in future.

The most important shift over time in the urban form that the Toronto development regime has produced has been that from the original idea of "complete communities," such as Don Mills, which had their own commercial centers, flanked by higher-density housing and employment areas, to the current practice of completely residential grid squares within large monofunctional areas. Developers argue that their housing customers prefer homes in purely residential areas, and that retail businesses and other uses that might create "mix" have no interest in locating in residential areas.

This problem is related partly to the lack of controls over or clear regional policy on retail location, and partly to the emergence of "office parks" that took high-density white-collar jobs out of central cities and moved them to employment lands amid surface parking lots. And perhaps worse, most significant public facilities such as hospitals, senior-care facilities, and government buildings have for many years been located in stand-alone suburban locations, instead of in mixed-use walkable centers. Further, although planners have embraced the concept of mixed-use development, most homebuyers prefer homogeneous developments. As Grant suggests, "People want security, predictability, and tranquility in their environments. They fear mix" (Grant 2002: 80). She argues convincingly that this culture of single-use suburbs is powerful and not easily overcome.

Yet the Toronto case shows clearly is that it is quite impossible to build a road network that can handle 100% of all trips without generating serious congestion problems. The Toronto suburbs have a robust arterial road system, on a 2-km grid, with three lanes of traffic or more in each direction, and a larger grid of limited-access expressways on a roughly 10-km grid. Yet that road system generates serious congestion in the suburbs, where there has been a steady increase in the number and the length of trips per person. As building a road system with even greater capacity seems hardly possible, the only solution appears to be to build cities in which a significant proportion of trips can be made without cars. If we add to that challenge rising energy costs, heavy pollution burdens, and global warming, the conclusion is clear: automobile-oriented transport systems don't work for megacities. The problem is that for public transit systems to work well, they need not only higher residential densities than the normal suburban pattern permits, but also the high-density mixed-use clusters of jobs and services that provide concentrated destinations for transit riders.

The major question this paper raises about the current policy is whether such high-density mixed-use nodes are achievable. Despite periodic bouts of concern with urban sprawl, particularly since the mid-1980s, despite the significant influence of New Urbanist ideas reflected in the design of major areas of suburban development outside Toronto since the mid-1990s, and despite a widespread acceptance of "smart growth" concepts over the last decade, little has really changed in the urban form being produced. The overwhelming majority of new housing is still being built in exclusively residential tracts, entirely separate from employment and retail areas. And there are major obstacles to the adaptive re-use of much of the suburban fabric developed during the last 30 years in particular. It will not be enough simply to raise population densities. Most areas are too use-segregated, and have been carefully designed specifically to *prevent* future land-use change. It will be difficult to achieve the kinds of intensification and reurbanization required to create more sustainable urban form in such areas (Bourne 1996). Yet the Places to Grow policy cannot work without the high-density mixed-use nodes and corridors patterns of development it envisions.

It is clear that from the point of view of urban sustainability challenges, the institutional frameworks of land development and planning and the cultures of development and homeownership are crucial. In Toronto those institutional frameworks are largely the product of an intense period of institutional innovation during the 1940s and 1950s, which have since become deeply embedded in Ontario planning and development culture. Changing those institutions is certain to be more difficult than drawing a tighter urban growth boundary, or the creation of a greenbelt and incentives for more intensive land use and intensification of existing areas.

The solutions to one urban crisis can sow the seeds of the next crisis. We can only hope that the capacity for transformative institutional and governance responses seen in the 1940s and 1950s is still available to deal with this next generation of urban form challenges.

References

Bourne LS (1996) Reurbanization, uneven urban development, and the debate on new urban forms. Urban Geogr 17(8):690–713

Bourne LS (2001) Designing a metropolitan region: the lessons and lost opportunities of the Toronto experience. In: Freire M, Stren R (eds) The challenge of urban government: policies and practices. World Bank Institute, Washington, DC, pp 27–46

Buliung R, Hernandez T (2009) Places to shop and places to grow: power retail, consumer travel behavior, and urban growth management in the Greater Toronto Area. Neptis Foundation, Toronto

Cervero R (1998) The transit metropolis: a global inquiry. Island Press, Washington, DC

Filion P (2000) Balancing concentration and dispersion? Public policy and urban structure in Toronto. Environ Plann C Gov Policy 18:163–189

Frisken F (2007) The public metropolis: the political dynamics of urban expansion in the Toronto region, 1924–2003. Canadian Scholars' Press, Toronto

Gardiner F (1953) Metropolitan Toronto. The empire club of Canada speeches 1953–1954 (Toronto, Canada: The Empire Club Foundation, 1954). Empire Club of Canada, Toronto, pp 52–65

Gomme T (1984) Municipal planning in Ontario. Plan Canada 24(3/4):102–114

Grant J (2002) Mixed use in theory and practice – Canadian experience with implementing a planning principle. J Am Plann Assoc 68(1):71–84

Harris R (1996) Unplanned suburbs: Toronto's American tragedy, 1900 to 1950. Johns Hopkins University Press, Baltimore

Harris R (2004) Creeping conformity: how Canada became suburban, 1900–1960. University of Toronto Press, Toronto

Jones KG, Doucet MJ (2003) The big box, the flagship, and beyond: impacts and trends in the Greater Toronto Area. Can Geogr 45(4):494–512

Kaplan H (1982) Reform, planning, and city politics: Montreal, Winnipeg, Toronto. University of Toronto Press, Toronto

Katznelson I (2003) Periodization and preferences: reflections on purposive action in comparative historical social science. In: Mahoney J, Rueschemeyer D (eds) Comparative historical analysis in the social sciences. Cambridge University Press, Cambridge, pp 270–301

Metropolitan Toronto Planning Board (1959) Official plan of the metropolitan Toronto planning area. M. T. P. Board, Municipality of Metropolitan Toronto, Toronto

Miller E, Soberman R (2003) Travel demand and urban form. Neptis Foundation, Toronto

Milner JB (1963) Community planning: a casebook on law and administration. University of Toronto Press, Toronto, 1971

Nowlan DM, Nowlan N (1970) The bad trip; the untold story of the Spadina expressway [by] David and Nadine Nowlan. House of Anansi, Toronto

Porter DR, Dunphy RT et al (2002) Making smart growth work. Urban Land Institute, Washington, DC

Rose A (1972) Governing metropolitan Toronto: a social and political analysis, 1953–1971. Published for the Institute of Governmental Studies [by] University of California Press, Berkeley, CA

Sewell J (1993) The shape of the city: Toronto struggles with modern planning. University of Toronto Press, Toronto

Sewell J (2009) The shape of the suburbs: understanding Toronto's sprawl. University of Toronto Press, Toronto

Solomon L (2007) Toronto sprawls: a history. University of Toronto Press, Toronto

Sorensen A, Hess PM (2007) Metropolitan form, density, transportation. Regional comparisons. Retrieved June, 2008, from http://www.neptis.org/atlas/show.cfm?id=60&cat_id=29

Taylor Z, Van Nostrand J et al (2008) Shaping the Toronto region, past, present, and future: an exploration of the potential effectiveness of changes to planning policies governing greenfield development in the Greater Golden Horseshoe. Neptis Foundation, Toronto

Toronto Public Health (2007). Air Pollution Burden of Illness from Traffic in Toronto. Toronto Medical Officer of Health. Toronto, Toronto Public Health

Walks RA (2004) Suburbanization, the vote, and changes in federal and provincial political representation and influence between inner cities and suburbs in large canadian urban regions, 1945–1999. Urban Aff Rev 38(4):411–440

Wheeler S (2003) The evolution of urban form in Portland and Toronto: implications for sustainability planning. Local Environ 8(3):317–336

White R (2007) The growth plan for the Greater Golden Horseshoe in historical perspective. In: Neptis Papers on Growth in the Toronto Metropolitan Region. Neptis Foundation, Toronto, http://www.neptis.org/library/show.cfm?id=84&cat_id=13

Winfield M (2003) Building sustainable urban communities in Ontario: overcoming the barriers. The Pembina Institute, Toronto

Wronski W, Turnbull JG (1984) The Toronto-centred region. Plan Canada 24(3/4):126–134

12. Los Angeles: Urban Development in the Postsuburban Megacity

Dana Cuff

12.1 Introduction: The Need for Postsuburban Reinvention

Los Angeles, a dynamic megacity of booms and busts, is on the cusp of an era of a significant transformation. Dubbed the birthplace of sprawl, it is slowly reinventing itself as a postsuburban metropolis. This sea change is sparked by both top-down and bottom-up strategies, and while large-scale plans have been important forces for change, tactical incremental changes have been even more significant.

Los Angeles is a megacity by virtue of its suburban extent; it can only become sustainable with postsuburban reinvention. Here, I use the term *postsuburban* to mean infilling and retrofitting existing city fabric, rather than constructing new residential development at the urban periphery. The extant city is a laboratory for next-generation planning, in which master plans give way to transformative tactics suited to the specifics of current circumstances, development opportunities, and collective problems.

The Los Angeles landscape is punctuated with large projects instigated by private interests and developed as enclaves in relative isolation from any larger urban vision. This practice has produced a multi-centered city, along with policies that reinforce that fragmentation. LA's resulting architectural and urban form manifests a creative diversity at the expense of systemic plans. Combined with horizontality and privacy, generally considered hallmarks of LA's identity, coherent planning has eluded Los Angeles since its founding.

Now, issues of infrastructure and the environment are putting pressure on civic leaders to find new ways to transform the city. LA has had intermittent success with regional strategies such as the freeway system, coastal access, and smog abatement. We can draw lessons from these examples in the

A. Sorensen and J. Okata (eds.), *Megacities: Urban Form, Governance, and Sustainability*,

context of current conditions to address the inherently collective problems of sustainability, which include densification, traffic and public transit, lack of open space, and housing affordability. Recent legislative bills, innovative projects, and creative policies point to an emerging direction for a postsuburban Los Angeles as well as its sprawling relations worldwide.

This essay examines the Los Angeles region of California from the perspective of its planning and design – that is, the social production of the built environment. Housing, transit, open space, environmental resources, suburban sprawl, and urban density comprise a palimpsest of LA's historical evolution in material form. Like other megacities, Los Angeles is less a city than a region, which makes coherent plans difficult, if not impossible, to enact, yet paradoxically all the more necessary. Any number of narratives describe how this paradox plays itself out in the everyday landscape of LA. Recent legislation is a good place to begin, since it represents popular desire to shift the development course of California and Los Angeles.

12.2 The Los Angeles Region

In 2008, Arnold Schwartzenegger, Governor of the State of California, signed into law landmark legislation dubbed the "Anti-Sprawl Bill" (State Bill 375). For the first time, land use policy and climate change policy were knitted together. Implementation begins with the state's setting of ambitious regional targets for reducing greenhouse gas emissions. Each region must develop planning scenarios, or Sustainable Communities Strategies, that link housing growth projections with reductions in vehicle miles traveled, among other tactics. The anti-sprawl legislation is paired with the *Global Warming Solutions Act* of 2006 (Assembly Bill 32), which rolls back the state's greenhouse gas emissions significantly. Critics of the anti-sprawl bill argue that it has no enforcement teeth, and depends instead on incentives to push regions to comply. Those incentives reward *projects*, by making state transit funds available and by streamlining the arduous process of environmental quality review (Fulton 2008; *Planning Report* 2007; State of California 2009).

Alongside these important statewide measures, in 2008 California voters passed an initiative supporting high-speed rail construction throughout the state, and Los Angeles voted to increase its sales tax to pay for a wide range of traffic relief projects, including a large number of public transit solutions (California High-Speed Rail Authority 2009; *Los Angeles Times* 2008).

It is noteworthy that at a time characterized by widespread unwillingness to raise taxes, a politically effective electorate voted to tax itself for public transit. If Angelenos think they have the worst traffic in the United States, they are right – and by a large margin. Estimates of congestion costs for LA in 2007 topped $9.3 billion, followed by the New York region at $7.3 billion; but of the 14 largest urban areas, the rest averaged just $2.3 billion (Texas Transportation Institute 2009). At the end of 2008, when oil prices skyrocketed, the portion of LA's citizens taking public transit increased by double digits. Although ridership dropped thereafter, it did not return to its former levels. Commentators have long argued that Angelenos would never separate from their cars or their single-family homes, but if they are wrong, where better than Los Angeles to retrofit sprawl into new forms of urbanism?

Forty-nine percent of the state's population is concentrated in the six-county area that includes Los Angeles, called the Southern California Association of Governments. Growing at a rate of 2% a year, in 2007 the region included 18.2 million people, nearly a third of whom are foreign-born. The population is diverse: 44% Hispanic, 36% White, 12% Asian, and 7% African American (US Census 2007). Those 18 million people own more than 14 million registered vehicles, so it comes as no surprise that three-quarters of the population drives alone to work each day (Southern California Association of Governments 2007). It will take more than new subways and high-speed trains to wrench people from their cars, although better public transit is sorely needed. To get Angelenos to lead more sustainable lives, as the new Anti-Sprawl legislation seeks, will require creating new places within the city that have a higher quality of life than the suburbs.

While the average person travels just under 30 min to work, there are also many "extreme commuters" who travel 90 min or more each day. If you drive out of Los Angeles at 4 a.m. on a weekday, you will be greeted by an eerie sight: a continuous river of headlights coming into town. From the northeast, for example, more than 20,000 residents of the relatively rural Antelope Valley stream 65 miles (105 km) into Los Angeles every morning and return every evening. They leave early to minimize the commute time; at 4 a.m. the drive might take just over an hour and a half, but by 7 a.m. it would take twice as long. The Los Angeles region has two of the top five extreme commute areas (Howlett and Overberg 2004).

The primary reason for long commutes is housing affordability in the LA area, where median house prices in West Los Angeles are as much as twice those in the remote Antelope Valley. The interrelation of driving distance, commute times, and home prices is inherent to the sprawl model of urban growth that characterizes Los Angeles. While most cities are known by a landmark (Paris and the Eiffel Tower), a great public space (the Zócalo in Mexico City), the downtown (Shinjuku in Tokyo), or the natural setting

Fig. 12-1. Aerial photograph of Lakewood, a classic LA subdivision, under construction in 1950. Credit: William A. Garnett, © Estate of William A. Garnett

(Istanbul and the Bosporus), we rarely think of a city in terms of its residential landscape, the places where its citizens actually live their everyday lives. The exception to that rule is Los Angeles, known around the world as the mother of sprawl from the countless aerial photographs portraying vast landscapes of monotonous suburban houses (see Fig. 12-1).

It is difficult to imagine sprawling Los Angeles transforming itself into the birthplace of the postsuburban city. Not only will a reduction in vehicle miles traveled be necessary, but that change must be accompanied by the creation of higher-density residential districts and the addition of concentrated commercial activity.

12.3 Postsuburbanity

Los Angeles is a study in contradictions, starting with the idea that it is becoming a *postsuburban city*. Urban historians argue that Los Angeles arose from uniquely fragmented social, cultural, and political origins, without any unifying civic identity (Fogelson 1967: 1). The urban environment reflects and exacerbates that fragmentation, with multiple "centers," neighborhoods, districts, and a downtown in name only. This has made Los Angeles difficult to comprehend as urban space, and as a result, difficult to design and plan.

Plenty of contemporary cities are characterized by recent growth that makes them difficult to comprehend: Beijing, Mumbai, or Dubai, for example. Los Angeles is unintelligible for its own unique reasons. Formal patterns are obviously missing, though Herculean efforts permit one to see traces of the plaza and grid of the Spanish Law of the Indies imposed on the original pueblo of the 1780s. Chicago School models of concentric rings emanating outward from a central downtown have been replaced by Los Angeles School formulations of a centerless city governed by hinterlands (Dear and Flusty 2002). "Downtown" is no more a magnet than any of a number of other centers in the polynucleated urban fabric.

By contrast, the architectural critic Reyner Banham (1971) sought to clarify perceptions of LA when he wrote his famous tract on its four ecologies. He managed to capture the dynamic blend of geography and urban form in the freeways, beach towns, ritzy hillside developments, and monotonous plains of the R1 (areas zoned for single-family, detached dwellings – the classic suburb). These he called autopia, surfurbia, foothills, and the plains of Id, respectively. But Banham, for all his insight, merely "rezoned" the city, as if it could be ordered with new but equally broad brushstrokes. Even if his was a plausible description when the book was published in 1971, it overlooks the region's raucous growth politics and offers little in the way of generative or projective guidance. How can "surfurbia" maintain its idyllic populist status in LA geography when all but the wealthiest real estate investors are being priced out of the market?

Current theories of urban form are inadequate to understand Los Angeles. Modern LA can be tracked in the careful separation of land uses and the beautiful clarity of its freeways and boulevards. But LA is missing modernism's essential political agenda, because it was built almost entirely, like most North American cities, by profit-seeking real-estate interests.

"Everyday urbanism" (cf. Chase et al. 1999) is a school of thought that has its roots in LA where there is much to support a bottom-up theory of emergence amid ad hoc citizen action and pockets of vibrant, messy streetscape. But everyday urbanism is mainly a way to read the city, not to generate it, and what it reads best are small-scale interventions by non-designers. This reading also misses Los Angeles's primary mechanism of transformation: the myriad unconventional forms of development that are in some way "top-down," deliberate rather than ad hoc, and relatively large scale. For example, a number of the most important projects in LA today – from the Disney Concert Hall and Los Angeles County Art Museum to the stalled downtown revitalization on Grand Avenue – are spearheaded by one single individual: billionaire philanthropist and housing developer Eli Broad.

What is happening in Los Angeles does not easily fit any existing urban theory, be that modernism, everyday urbanism, or Koolhaas's (2004) junkspace, which some might see as a more appropriate description of the city. If we are to develop theory to fit LA, it should be a politico-projective theory of the city – one that reads the city not only in terms of *what* is made, but *how* it is made – in order to generate and evaluate subsequent practice. In other words, if we think of LA as a city-making machine, what drives its postsuburban operation?

Anyone who reads a newspaper in Los Angeles would answer that local politics have a stronger influence on the region than citywide planning. Neighborhoods, homeowner associations, small commercial districts, and the like – these entities with almost no municipal representation matching their perceived boundaries are some of the most powerful counterforces facing down the private development industry and thus helping shape the next Los Angeles. Perhaps more ironically, facing down LA's regional planners are a distributed, unallied network of planners for each sub-city, sub-region, and community. The City of Los Angeles has its planning department, but the Mayor has his own planning deputy and so do each of the seven powerful city council members. The six-county region is organized by its own planning agency, and within the region are no fewer than 187 cities, each of which does its own planning. Under those conditions, private and public interests alike favor tactical over strategic approaches to development (Fig. 12-2).

One form of urban practice espoused by developers, progressives, and conservatives alike is "smart growth," with its pedestrian, mixed-use, village-like orientation. While adopted as a politically astute brand of development across the LA Basin, it remains not-so-smart in one key way: no one seriously suggests abandoning the car. One earnest version, the "transit-oriented development" (TOD), will become a more common punctuation at nodes where Los Angeles has transit to orient itself around, given the benefits provided by the anti-sprawl bill. At present, Metrorail operates about 73 miles (118 km) of rail and 62 stations in Los Angeles County, where TODs make some sense. Yet popular opinion in Los Angeles still decries "density," as if any transformation to the R1 model of detached single-family homes is an attempt to "Manhattanize" LA.

Some critics suggest that "free parking" available across LA actually has a high cost (Shoup 2005) and gets in the way of smart growth. To reform our parking practices would in turn reform driving, and thus restructure the cityscape. Rethinking infrastructure like parking or development around transit stations requires municipal planning intervention, a tricky business,

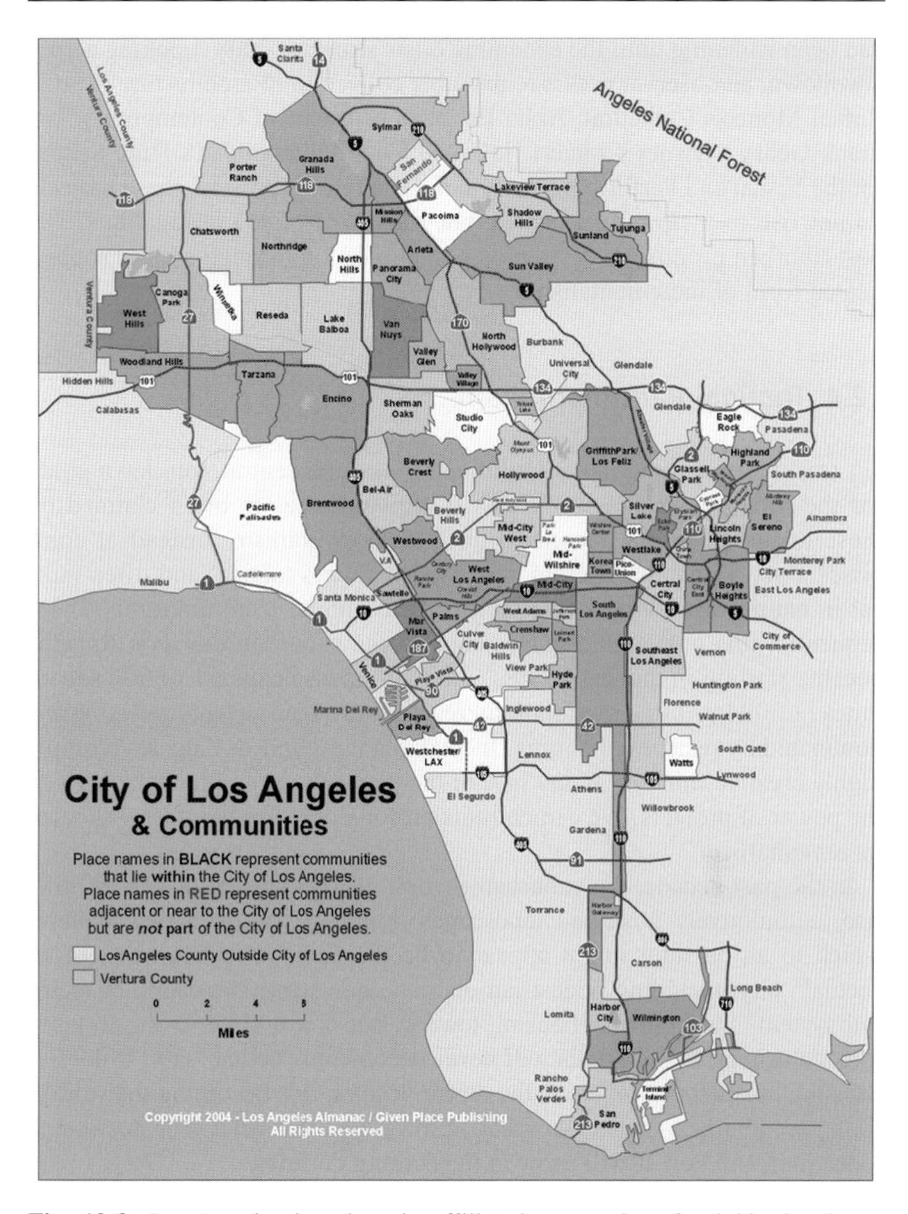

Fig. 12-2. Los Angeles is a loosely affiliated geography of neighborhoods, as evident in this map. Credit: Los Angeles Almanac, Given Place Publishing

since the Los Angeles way of city-making tends to emasculate planners while lionizing private developers.

Los Angeles has always been more "architected" than planned, more project-oriented than plan-driven, more tactical than strategic. This imbalance had been widening until the economic crisis struck in 2008. Looking across downtown, an observer sees a remarkable collection of architectural works: Rafael Moneo's Cathedral, Arata Isozaki's Museum of Contemporary Art, Frank Gehry's Disney Concert Hall, and Coop Himmelblau's High School for the Visual and Performing Arts, to name a few. At present, these projects do not rise to metropolitan status, but stand as isolated destinations. The postsuburban promise is to overcome that isolation through a more sophisticated form of incrementalism.

12.4 Tactical Incrementalism

LA was never planned in the traditional sense of a central, top-down guide for the urban environment. Nor is it unplanned, as is often claimed by those disturbed by its unconventional cosmopolitanism. Instead, it comprises a set of planned increments that are always tactical and often radical in nature, from large-scale upheavals to minute local tinkering. These sequential bits of planning gave shape to the suburban city Los Angeles became starting in the late 1930s, with its immense expanse of 500 square miles (1,300 km^2) in a metropolitan region more than seventy times larger, dominated by residential zoning. Indeed, planning in Los Angeles requires highly creative thinking if any part of the plan is to be implemented, given the power of projects. We can call this prototheory of urban form "tactical incrementalism."

In the past decade, the suburban rhythm of low-density, dispersed, low-rise, automotively governed landscapes is giving way to a new pattern, which to an outsider might appear to be the first low-grade signs of an "actual" city, including pedestrian districts, downtown street life, a metro rail system, and high-rise housing towers. But it would be wrong to jump to conclusions: Los Angeles will never become an "actual" city; it doesn't have the bones for it, let alone the desire. Rather, it is becoming the world's first postsuburban megacity. What follows explains what that is, what it looks like, and how it will grow in the coming decades.

Postsuburbanism is variously defined, but must start with a general notion of suburbia. American suburban development, according to Dolores Hayden (2003), has its historical beginnings in the early nineteenth century. Its most consistent, pervasive, and stereotyped phase is what she calls the "sitcom" suburbs of the postwar period. Here is where we catch Los Angeles in its prime. In vast residential subdivisions that predate the legendary Levittown, Los Angeles began in earnest in the late 1930s to convert its agricultural outskirts into mass-produced housing restricted to white households.

While geography, demographics, and the regional economy played significant roles in this early suburbanization, so did the regional emergence of a residential real estate "industry" that took over from small homebuilders (Cuff 2000; Hise 1997). The postwar subdivisions built in the Los Angeles basin created the template for suburbs everywhere: single land use, detached dwellings for middle-class homeowners, automobile-dependent, built on the urban periphery, and thus requiring commutes to other parts of the city for employment. Even while suburbs have been growing more socially diverse since the Second World War, their physical pattern has remained the same. The Great Depression ushered in new lending policy in the form of long-term, low-downpayment mortgages. The middle and working classes rushed to purchase homes with monthly payments lower than the rents they were already paying.

Postsuburbanism often refers to new types of *suburban* growth: regional growth after the postwar boom that is spatially consistent and extends suburban patterns in forms variously known as edge nodes or ex-urban growth. This is more accurately called "neosurburbanism" rather than postsuburbanism, since it is a variation on the suburban theme: there is a spatial decentralization of the core to a multi-centered form, coupled with a reduction in suburban outcommuting and an increase in suburban employment (cf. Lucy and Phillips 1997). Antelope Valley, the home of the extreme commuters, is a form of neosuburbia, where houses are built at the metropolitan frontier. Orange County, just south of Los Angeles, is often considered the poster child of neosuburbia, where densities remain low, single-family homes predominate, automobiles are essential, and private domesticity is distinct from a more public life of consumption that occurs primarily in regional shopping malls. Yet Orange County is also postsuburban, meaning it is not just decentered, but multi-centered, with some of its growth organized around districts or specialized centers that can range from a shopping mall to a theme park (Kling et al. 1991).

In Los Angeles today, neosuburbia is in decline, while a veritable postsuburbanity is on the rise – that is, a form of metropolitan transformation that redefines the urban–suburban dichotomy and restructures the suburban pattern. Postsuburbia, compared with its source, suburbia, is uneven. Most distinctly, postsuburbia grows inward rather than outward, and in its purest forms, creates urban infill in the suburbs themselves. That infill can be large or small, piecemeal or planned. Such interventions tend to preserve and extend some of the key qualities of suburban form, at least in LA, where postsuburbia acknowledges the importance of the garden, privacy, and identity. Compared to the suburban past, it has higher densities and more mixed land use, reduces dependency on the car without eradicating it, and produces increased ethnic and income diversity.

As important as any of the physical or economic conditions that mobilize postsuburbanity, contemporary local politics shape it. Those politics are centered on local interests, resistance to change, the preservation of property values, and skepticism about the planning profession as well as most political frameworks (such as municipal or regional politics). Thus, in the postsuburban metropolis, enclaves and communities create their own plans, reinforcing an already fractured political and physical geography. In one area, through traffic is curbed with barriers and speed bumps. Another neighborhood successfully garners historic district status. The next community defeats the proposed construction of a gas station.

The history of Los Angeles sets the stage for postsuburbanity, and in particular, for its characteristic feature: tactical incrementalism. Los Angeles was founded in the 1780s, and since that time grew by sporadic leaps, in a series of population, economic, and real estate "booms." In 1850, there were 1,610 residents; by 1930, there were 1.2 million and it was the largest settlement on the West Coast, the fourth-largest city in the United States in terms of population and the second-largest in terms of area (Fogelson 1967). Population booms and municipal boosterism resisted hierarchical governance, producing instead a notoriously fractured city, governed by a weak mayor and 15 strong council districts, as well as five county supervisorial districts. Beyond that, the city contains some 70 neighborhood councils, and the county has about 90 cities and ten million people (2000 census). At the six-county scale, the extent of the megalopolis goes beyond coherent imagining, to 38,000 square miles (98,419 km^2), compared to Tokyo's 239 square miles (619 km^2) with approximately the same population. In this historically open framework, myriad tactics have evolved in recent years to build out the metropolitan region.

New kinds of development are evident in some of the recent policies and projects in the LA Basin. If the city is imagined not as a physical product but as a process, it might be seen as a kind of machine with set operations and procedures that produce patterns of material conditions particular to Los Angeles. Its postwar operations included land subdivisions (which unleashed suburbia), zoning, general plans, and freeway construction. Parking requirements, particularly in residential zones, often determined the organization of the building on a lot as well as how large it could be. The city-making machine that is Los Angeles has acquired a few new operations today. These operations of tactical incrementalism make more Los Angeles, replace older means of more systemic city-making, and are inherently more sustainable – economically, socially, and ecologically – than their suburban-era correlates. Each relies on market economies of real estate rather than public subsidy, and the best projects utilize multiple operations. For example,

rather than zoning or master plans, targeted policies are intentionally partial, fragmented, and heterogeneous. The operations themselves are small but they catalyze larger effects. A few examples will serve to illustrate what is meant by tactical urban development.

The best of the target regulations of postsuburban Los Angeles is the Adaptive Reuse Ordinance (1999), permitting historic buildings in the downtown area to be rehabilitated as housing without meeting current parking requirements. Private developers saw, for the first time, a profitable means to create lofts by restoring existing tall buildings. After several years of success downtown, the ordinance was expanded to other parts of LA, and over an 8-year period, more than 10,000 units of new housing were built using this target regulation (Los Angeles Conservancy 2002) (Fig. 12-3).

Another example illustrates the shift in the scale of projects from the suburban to postsuburban era. Architects and planners have long preferred to organize large, coherent segments of the urban fabric, such as the Docklands in London or Gehry's Atlantic Yards proposal for Brooklyn. In Los Angeles, Playa Vista is just such a grand planning effort, taking over 40 years to bring to fruition. In this sense, Playa Vista is a suburban-era project not unlike the 10,000 suburban, detached homes in adjacent Westchester built in the 1950s (Cuff 2000). In postsuburban LA, opposition to mega-projects has made them nearly impossible to implement, redirecting the city-making machine toward smaller projects. The Small Lot Ordinance (2004), for example, changed the zoning code to permit ownership of smaller, more affordable lots for rowhouse-like construction. Although an incremental approach can lead to architecture without urbanism, the best efforts catalyze their surroundings, preparing the ground for the next small project.

A case in point is the series of Camino Nuevo schools by Daly Genik Architects in the largely immigrant neighborhood around MacArthur Park. An elementary school created from an abandoned mini-mall was followed by a middle school and pre-school in rehabilitated industrial buildings. Later, more land was purchased for a playground. Together, the schools are seeding the neighborhood with local institutions, including adult education and a health clinic on the middle school's ground floor (Fig. 12-4).

A final example of new ways that Los Angeles is transforming itself is the resurgence of local commercial areas. The first-ring suburbs, quite conveniently located, have an older housing stock that is somewhat more affordable as well as adjacent retail zones. As a younger generation moves to neighborhoods like Silverlake, Los Feliz, or Atwater Village, new businesses follow and the housing stock is improved. The process of gentrification in these communities is slow and uneven, producing attractive identities that mix the old and new.

Fig. 12-3. Metro 417 is an example of the Adaptive Reuse Ordinance. The building, originally the Subway Terminal Building (1925) was rehabilitated to create more housing in downtown LA while preserving its architectural heritage. Photo Credit: Casey Benito (flickr)

Fig. 12-4. A converted retail shopping center, or mini-mall, by Daly, Genik Architects is now an academically challenging school for the surrounding Central American residents. Photo Credit: Tom Bonner

12.5 Conclusion

Los Angeles is creating a new model of urban transformation: postsuburbanity. Postsuburbanity, a distinct urban practice compared with new urbanism, smart growth, transit-oriented districts, everyday urbanism, or ad-hoc urbanism, engenders a new way of theorizing the city, as well as new strategies for designing within it. The qualities of this new development model that characterize LA's postsuburbanism include increased density, strategic infill, project-by-project planning, architectural innovation, environmental awareness, an attention to landscape design (or a rethinking of the natural/artificial distinction), recycling the existing city fabric, hybrid uses, and what might be called the exploitation of micro-identities.

There are many indications that the suburban era is behind LA, even as the postsuburban era has yet to be defined, or for that matter, confidently ushered in. The legislation discussed at the start of this essay is a demonstration of widespread, general desire for the region to grow more sustainably. But there are more particular actions aimed at projects necessary to reinforce the general sentiment. Returning momentarily to the drivers streaming out of the Antelope Valley at 4 a.m., there is new evidence that the suburbs, as well as the neosuburbs, are dead. In March 2008, LA's City Council reached an unprecedented decision to reject an immense exurban development in the Antelope Valley, expressing the need to stop urban sprawl, the traffic it generates, and the ecosystems it destroys (Zahniser 2008). In what will prove to be the first of many powerful rulings, Los Angeles recognized the necessity of decreasing rather than expanding the scale of the city.

National stories concur that the mortgage debacle that erupted in 2007 followed by deepening economic recession turned some suburbs into slums, as former homeowners are forced out by foreclosure. In the Antelope Valley, apocryphal stories circulate about whole subdivisions of foreclosed homes being converted into city-owned low-income housing. At the same time elsewhere, Los Angeles was planning downtown high-rise housing towers, including one that would be the tallest residential building (76 stories) west of Chicago, adding to a downtown population that doubled in the past decade to 34,000 (DiMassa 2008).

The problematics of infill sites, along with the complicated political and regulatory contexts, makes slipshod development less viable than ever before. With the economic collapse, postsuburban development tactics will be all the more important as a means to solve increasingly dire problems such as inadequate infrastructure, public service, housing, and schools. These tactics will surgically repair specific problems of the metropolitan body.

While the modernist city was the planners' domain, the postsuburban metropolis is immune to their former ideals. To be successful, the solutions will be created by teams that include experts and stakeholders representing the complexities of the problems themselves. Los Angeles is a case study that demonstrates what this means.

References

Banham R (1971) Los Angeles: the architecture of four ecologies. Penguin, New York

California High-Speed Rail Authority (2009) Website. http://www.cahighspeedrail.ca.gov/ (accessed March 29, 2009)

Chase J, Crawford M, Kalisky J (eds) (1999) Everyday urbanism. Monacelli, New York

Cuff D (2000) The provisional city: Los Angeles stories of American architecture and urbanism. MIT Press, Cambridge

Dear M, Flusty S (2002) Los Angeles as postmodern urbanism. In: Dear M (ed) From Chicago to L.A.: making sense of urban theory. Sage, Thousand Oaks, CA, pp 55–84

DiMassa C (2008) New downtown has shaky pillars. Los Angeles Times, Section 1: 1, p 11

Fogelson RM (1967) The fragmented metropolis: Los Angeles, 1850–1930. University of California Press, Berkeley

Fulton B (2008) SB 375 is now law – but what will it do? California planning and development report. http://www.cp-dr.com/node/2140

Hayden D (2003) Building suburbia. Pantheon, New York

Hise G (1997) Magnetic Los Angeles. Johns Hopkins University Press, Baltimore

Howlett D, Overberg P (2004) Think your commute is tough? USA today. http://www.usatoday.com/news/nation/2004-11-29-commute_x.html

Kling R, Olin S, Poster M (eds) (1991) Postsuburban California: the transformation of postwar Orange County, California. University of California Press, Berkeley

Koolhaas R (2004) Content. Taschen, Cologne

Los Angeles Conservancy (2002) Housing conversion in downtown Los Angeles. http://www.laconservancy.org/initiatives/housingsurvey.pdf

Los Angeles Times (2008) Yes on measure R. http://www.latimes.com/news/opinion/editorials/la-ed-measurer9-2008oct09,0,2413553.story

Lucy WH, Phillips DL (1997) The post-suburban era comes to Richmond: city decline, suburban transition, and exurban growth. Landsc Urban Plann 36(4):259–275

The Planning Report (2007) SB 375 connects land use and AB 32 implementation. http://www.planningreport.com/tpr/?module=displaystory&story_id=1257&format=html

Shoup D (2005) The high cost of free parking. APA Planners Press, Chicago

Southern California Association of Governments (2007) Regional pocket guide. www.scag.ca.gov

State of California (2009) Official California legislation information. http://www.leginfo.ca.gov/

Texas Transportation Institute (2009) 2007 Urban mobility report. Urban mobility information, Texas A&M University. http://mobility.tamu.edu/ (accessed February 3, 2009)

US Census Bureau (2007) More than 300 counties now "majority–minority."http://www.census.gov/Press-Release/www/releases/archives/population/010482.html

Zahniser D (2008) L.A. stops 5,553-unit home plan. Los Angeles Times, Front Section: 1, p 14

Part III
Latin America

Part III
Latin America

13. Mexico City: Power, Equity, and Sustainable Development

Alfonso Valenzuela-Aguilera

13.1 Introduction to the Post-Apocalyptic City

In the summer of 2002, a failed attempt to build a $2.5-billion international airport in the outskirts of Mexico City caused social upheaval. Originally framed as a sound environmental decision to replace the old and limited infrastructure in the central city, the project was later marketed as a way to boost the real estate market. When the affected peasants of the municipality of Atenco realized that the airport project would generate more than a $100 billion in business revenues and increase the land value up to 500%, the $0.65 per square meter offered by the government for their land seemed inconsistent with the projected profits. The economic model behind the project was characterized by Harvey (2003) as a process of "accumulation by dispossession," since the venture followed extensive privatization the financialization of the economy, the management and manipulation of crises, as well as state redistribution of wealth. The model had been challenged since the insurgency of the Zapatistas in 1994, and Atenco's mobilization followed a similar resistance to the concentration of power and wealth.

This chapter argues that the concept of sustainability in Mexico has been extensively used to justify political agendas that have maintained traditional authoritarian rule and preserved the prevalent socioeconomic structure. Interestingly, this approach has been used by both the right-wing federal government in Mexico and the left-wing government of the capital city, since public policies at each level still ground their legitimacy on the social control of the population. Therefore, by recognizing the political use of sustainability as a broadly supported – and desirable – model, it is possible to challenge the official discourse that imposes an agenda set by a "global consensus" which frames the model as the single means to attain development.

A. Sorensen and J. Okata (eds.), *Megacities: Urban Form, Governance, and Sustainability*,

However, the official discourse on sustainable development still has to answer questions on how decisions are made and priorities established. For instance, we should be asking: What scale of intervention makes sense when framing environmental policies in developing countries? Are there alternative options for development and are they being considered? Does framing sustainability in specific ways benefit certain interest groups? Are the chosen policies addressing root causes that hinder development? Is sustainability part of a broader aim to "save" the planet or is it just a strategy to justify development in more "reasonable" terms? How has sustainability been framed by different and competing groups and which are their underlying motivations? And finally, *what* should be sustained and which alternatives exist to attain the desired outcomes?

13.2 Framing the Sustainable Cities Discourse

Even when sustainability has been presented as the basis of a consensus for policy development in Mexico City, competing interest groups have redefined the concept to suit their own agendas (Andrews 1997). Nevertheless, some critics argue the impossibility of reconciling the existing economic model with the preservation of nature, stating that "the current model of development destroys nature's wealth and hence it's un-sustainable" (Kothari 1990). According to this rationale, sustainability as the solution to such a paradox has been called into question because of its structural limitations. Moreover, the assumption that nature can be framed in terms of sustainability underestimates the limits of growth, rendering nature both manageable and negotiable. The paradox has been addressed by the Brundtland Report (WCED 1987) not by questioning the production model itself, but rather by framing sustainability as the maximum growth which still guarantees the regeneration of the environment. However, critical scholars suggest that a more comprehensive approach, which includes broader questions of social needs, equity, welfare, and economic opportunity, is needed (Agyeman et al. 2002). Even when international organizations try to introduce concepts of equity, freedom, and participation in their agendas as well as in sustainable human development reports (UNDP 2002), Polese and Stren (2001) are more explicit in highlighting the importance of democratic and inclusive urban management for redistributive ends as well as responding to cultural conflicts, social inequality, and political fragmentation in order to achieve social sustainability.

Within the international conversation on sustainable cities, the role of dense urban patterns and a more efficient public transport system may convey a powerful building rationality. However, in the case of cities in developing countries, the question of sustainability relies not only on the efficiency of land use regulations, but on unequal access to the benefits of the city. Therefore, urban form in places such as Mexico City is often the product of contrasting socioeconomic conditions more than an articulated policy to achieve an intended urban outcome. How can a city be subject to regulation when at least one-third of its population lives in substandard housing, subject to volatile informal labor practices and extra-legal arrangements of land tenure, infrastructure, and basic services?

More recent global sustainability initiatives, such as the *Rio Declaration* or *Agenda 21*, have attempted to integrate management and decision-making in the international agenda. Furthermore, globalized discourse is stressing partnerships, cooperation, and "the commitment to address root causes." Critical views of this position claim that reframing local environmental problems as global issues advances the interests of the most powerful actors involved, and consequently strengthens prevailing socioeconomic structures (Shiva 1993). However, international conferences have been moving towards structural socioeconomic concerns, expressed for instance in the World Summit on Sustainable Development in Johannesburg in 2002, where it was acknowledged that "poverty eradication, changing consumption and production patterns, and protecting and managing the natural base for economic and social development are overreaching objectives of, and essential requirements for, sustainable development" (WSSD 2002).

Even when key issues have been raised, the international power structure is always present in definitions of *what* is to be sustained. Also, these broader goals are monitored, evaluated, and coordinated through an elite group of development banks, international agencies, and other organizations, largely through undemocratic and technocratic decision-making practices (Sachs 1992, 1993). In the case of Mexico City, local communities are often deprived of their right to participate democratically in the decision-making process of defining what kind of environment and lifestyle they wish to pursue. This authoritarian rule replicates the "civilizatory practices" of the nineteenth century, which supposedly brought "barbaric" cultures into the path of (sustainable) development and progress.

According to critics of the industrial model of development, sustainability has been framed to blend injury with therapy within the same "solution," and usually ends up blaming the victims of the economic system (Sachs 1992; Shiva 1993). Therefore, if development generates poverty, then sustainability is compromised in its task to reconcile the creation of misery with the abolition of economic distress. Moreover, the rhetoric of healing-while-violating the environment would frame sustainability only as an endless reservoir for political propaganda.

The real issue is that global initiatives face the risk of becoming instruments of oppression. According to Sachs (1992), the survival of the planet "is well on its way to becoming wholesale justification for a new wave of state interventions in people's lives all over the world." Moreover, it is appalling that the institutions that traditionally promoted hard-core development schemes (such as the World Bank, the IBD, or the IMF), are now eager to address the full range of environmental needs. In this way, the exploitation of nature and the developmental rationale will remain intact, while interventions are framed or downsized into a more tolerable channel. Finally, ecology today is at risk of being reduced from a social concern into a set of managerial strategies aimed to deal with efficiency and risk management.

13.3 Key Environmental Issues

The Metropolitan Zone of Mexico City (MZMC) is made up of 16 administrative units within the Federal District, plus 58 municipalities in the adjacent State of Mexico. It occupies more than 1,250 km^2 and is home to 19 million people, or 18% of the total population of Mexico. It generates 34% of the country's gross domestic product and offers 33% of the employment opportunities in the country. The city has been growing at a rate of 4.4% per year and the population's density is slightly higher than that of Tokyo, double that of metropolitan New York, three times that of Paris and four times that of London (Ward 1990).

Between 1940 and 1970 the city grew by almost seven times and until recently, was still receiving about 500,000 immigrants per year (see Table 13-1). As in other large, rapidly growing cities, most of these new residents settle in makeshift, marginally illegal communities outside the

Table 13-1. Physical expansion of Mexico City, 1950–2000

Year	Population (inhabitants)	Population growth rate	City extension (ha)	Physical growth rate	Density (inhabitants x ha)
1950	2,952,199	5.85	22,989	–	128
1960	5,125,447	5.52	47,070	10.47	109
1970	8,623,157	5.20	68,260	4.50	126
1980	12,994,450	4.10	107,973	5.82	120
1990	15,274,256	2.64	130,549	2.10	117
2000	18,396,677	0.84	176,965	3.56	104

Source: GDF/COLMEX. INEGI (2000), *XII Population Census*

traditional, formal realm of government regulation and service provision. Consequently, many of Mexico City's residents, especially the poor, do not have adequate housing or basic services, and the city itself puts ever greater stress on an environment which is already suffering from pollution and overuse. Traffic congestion and atmospheric pollution are two related examples of environmental problems. Access to a clean, safe, and sustainable environment is a key measure of the quality of life of the population. However, it is not clear who is responsible for guaranteeing that the public domain is not violated, occupied, invaded, abandoned, or ignored.

Although the Federal District is not growing any more, population and physical expansion are central matters, since the metropolitan municipalities are growing at rates of over 2% a year. Nearly all demographic increases and urban sprawl will occur in the municipalities of the State of Mexico. The distribution of public resources is also an issue that has hindered the two governments from cooperating, since historically the Federal District has been favored with federal investments and educational subsidies that the State of Mexico has not received.

Transport and air pollution are issues with higher possibilities of reaching metropolitan agreements, as proved by programs such as *Monitoreo Atmosférico*, *Hoy no Circula*, *Placa Metropolitana*, and *Proaire*. Still, there is a lack of political will to face the problem of air pollution and, above all, to develop a metropolitan policy of traffic and transport linked to policies of general metropolitan development.

13.3.1 Sustainable Transportation and Air Quality

Carbon monoxide is still the main contaminant in the atmosphere, reaching a yearly 1.8 million tonnes, mainly produced by vehicles (cars, taxis, trucks, buses, etc.). However, in 1991 Mexico began producing cars with catalytic converters to minimize emissions and address growing concerns about air pollution. Also, the government established strict legislation on emission controls in taxis, trucks, minibuses, and private cars, while Pemex, the state-owned oil company, started to produce lead-free gasoline.

In an attempt to reduce air pollution caused by Mexico City's four million vehicles, the government instituted in 1989 a policy to restrict the use of the automobile known as *Hoy No Circula* Program (1 day without a car). The strategy stressed a reduction in the use of private automobiles, and introduced new regulations for cargo trucks and public transport. Nevertheless, the automotive industry continues to be the one of the most important industrial and manufacturing sectors in Mexico. The industry grew from 1.6 million cars produced in 2005 to over 2.1 million cars in 2007, ranking the region among the top ten largest producers of automotive vehicles in the world (United States Department of Commerce 2008). As Lefebvre has explained: "Owners of private cars have a space at their disposition that costs them very little personally, although society collectively pays a very high price for its maintenance. This arrangement causes the number of cars (and car-owners) to increase, which suits the car-manufacturers just fine, and strengthens their hand in their constant efforts to have this space expanded" (Lefebvre 1991).

Transportation infrastructure is representative of the problems that urban development without systematic integration of spatial planning and transportation system development can generate. The fact that about 83% of the total number of trips are undertaken in low-capacity vehicles (cars, taxis, and minibuses) is significant, particularly when combined with the sheer number of trips (over four million intra-metropolitan trips per day). The relative level of private car use is rather low for a major city, but this is somewhat offset by having 58.6% of the total number of single trips carried out in public transport vehicles with very low capacity, such as minibuses and "combis."

The metro system is well-used, but it is mostly based in the Federal District. While metro lines extend out to heavily populated municipalities in the State of Mexico, other MZMC residents living outside the Federal District must first take minibuses to metro stations and then take the metro elsewhere. Given the increasingly long distances involved as the metropolitan region expands, the lack of effective train linkages and the reliance on relatively inefficient low-capacity buses is a significant handicap for commuters.

Commuting distances and travel times have increased significantly since 1987 as a result of both expansion of the urban economic area and, probably, slower traffic flows caused by congestion. Significant differences in the quality of transport services across the metropolitan area tend to produce self-reinforcing disparities in terms of access to employment and levels of investment. These changes in the MZMC's urban form and functions entail the need for significant new investment in citywide public transport infrastructure. The ability of the region to meet these infrastructure demands will depend on the ability of the public authorities to coordinate effective provision of strategic infrastructures in a context of extreme fiscal constraint.

Two contrasting projects embody the divergent courses of action that are being taken by transport policy in Mexico City today. Over the past few years, more than half of the budget allocated to transport was used for road construction, with the most prominent project being a double-decker system of elevated highways over the ring road. As for investment in public transport, the most innovative initiative has been the *Metrobus*, a bus rapid transit system based on the *Transmilenio* model from Bogotá. The new *Metrobus*, which replaced more than 260 mini buses, consists of an initial stock of 80 articulated buses covering a distance of 19 km along Insurgentes Avenue, a main north–south axis of the city. The buses have a dedicated lane and make predetermined stops at elevated stations from which passengers can board swiftly, having already paid their fares on the ground.

What these two projects show is that transport planning still oscillates between old biases and newer efforts to break with the past and transform Mexico City into a city that responds to the needs of the majority of its population who rely on public transport (see Table 13-2).

The impressive dynamics of the car industry has been translated, for the MZMC, into an explosive growth of new vehicles, which, at the end of the 1990s, was calculated at between 250,000 and 300,000 additional vehicles on average per year. During this period, the population growth index for the MZMC was just 1.5% per year on average, so the growth rate of the number of cars in the city is four times that of the population. After nearly 15 years during which no major roads were constructed and with an estimated 25% deficit in transportation coverage, the current Federal District Government (GDF) decided to push forward a rapid-transit road program, as part of the Transportation sector's Integral Program, which has been complemented by several public transportation measures.

13.3.2 Land Conservation

The principal feature of the expansion of the MZMC is not so much the rate of growth in settlement areas as the level of organization and control exerted by the public authorities over the growth process. Controls on urban development have always been relatively weak in Mexico, but these weak structures came under pressure over the past two decades. Land for development within the Federal District became saturated, while at the same time the legal framework for urban development in other areas was reformed, making it somewhat easier for land to be converted from non-urban to urban usage.

The controversial reforms of articles 27 and 115 of the Political Constitution of Mexico and of the *General Act on Human Settlements* in the early 1990s had a detrimental effect on the availability of land for

Table 13.2 Commuting distances and times by public transportation

1987				**2000**		
Mode of transport	**Length of trip (km)**	**Speed (km/h)**	**Average time per trip (min)**	**Length of trip (km)**	**Speed (km/h)**	**Average time per trip (min)**
Buses	3.5	16.8	12.5	5.6	16.7	20.1
Trolleybus	2.4	14.0	10.3	4.1	14.6	16.8
Minibus	n.a.	21.0	4.9	15.7	18.7	n.a.
Metro	7.1	39.0	10.9	9.0	36.0	15.0

Source: Adapted from Molinero Ángel, Taller de Expertos, Revisión del Programa de ordenación de la Zona Metropolitana del Valle de México, Programa Universitario de Estudios de la Ciudad, UNAM, November 2002

urbanization purposes for the low-income population.[1] Nevertheless, the reforms also promoted a more decentralized system whereby municipalities exercised greater controls over land use and authorization of new real estate developments. In addition, simplification of the process of the sale of *ejido* (communally owned) lands opened up for development large tracts on the urban periphery that had hitherto been difficult to commercialize because of contested titles or complicated multiple ownership structures. Overall, these reforms promoted a more fluid land market, but also created a fragmented system favoring a patchwork rather than coordinated pattern of suburbanization and reduced the available land supply for the poor.

Special attention is paid to the conservation land in the southern part of the Federal District. These areas permit the main aquifer to recharge its sources as well as preventing climate change on a regional scale. The aquifers provide water for 70% of Mexico City's demand, but an insufficient recharge rate is resulting in a progressive desiccation of the sources.

Between 1990 and 2000, an 18% increase in population was accompanied by a 31% increase in the city's land area. As the structure of Mexican families evolves, with family size decreasing and people moving into their own accommodation at an earlier age, demand for housing units will continue to grow. Moreover, evidence from other megacities demonstrates that as the population becomes wealthier, demand for larger living spaces will also increase. All this means that the rate of outward expansion of the metropolitan area is unlikely to slow, despite changing demographics.

Estimates of the demand for land for housing and infrastructure vary according to the plot size used in the calculations. Thus, estimates for the growth in land area of the MZMC range from about 20 to 40% between 2000 and 2020, demonstrating that even in situations in which population growth is relatively modest, the expansion of the urban area can be rapid, posing significant challenges for infrastructure development and the provision of public services. Existing high-intensity infrastructure in the Federal District must be maintained to cope with the estimated 3.6 million people who come into the centre to work each day. Moreover, whereas in the past the process of changing residential patterns was characterized by increasing pressure in central areas and a spilling out into adjacent peripheral areas, now further growth is sprawling on the conservation land in the south of the city. Thus the strain on infrastructure and public service provision is felt not only by the central areas, since each additional development on the periphery requires infrastructure and service links necessary to maintain its viability.

[1] In fact, the social production of housing (mostly informal) was possible due to the availability of communally owned agricultural land.

13.3.3 Waste Management

Mexico City produces over 10,000 tonnes of waste and 200 tonnes of industrial toxins every day, most of which are dumped into open pits, landfills, and illegal deposits. It is estimated that at least one-quarter of Mexico City's solid waste is dumped illegally or remains on the streets, and even waste that is disposed of legally is rarely monitored. This vast quantity of mismanaged waste has dire consequences for the city's water supply. Residents receive 60% of their water from the local water table, which is being increasingly contaminated by toxic substances produced by illegally dumped or poorly monitored solid waste. As a result, the water used for drinking and food preparation in Mexico City contains high levels of cadmium, chrome, and iron – metals that cause genetic diseases and cancer in humans. Furthermore, of all the residual water produced, 50 m^3 per second is reused in the city and the remainder is pumped back into the ground where it threatens to infect the water being extracted. Over three million residents lack basic sewage and drainage infrastructure, and those who are connected to the municipal system suffer from inadequate and outdated service. The system for solid waste disposal is overtaxed as well. Sewage treatment plants are unable to cope with the quantities produced, and the sewage itself is poorly collected through a drainage system that needs to be repaired, replaced, and extended.[2]

Fortunately, the problem of solid waste is somewhat ameliorated by widespread recycling. The city government boasts that Mexico City has the largest informal recycling system in the world. Everyday household waste can be given to the garbage collection service with glass, aluminum, paper, and cardboard already separated. (This system has helped keep solid waste from domestic sources at 37.2% of the city's total.) Waste collectors generate most of their income by selling these products to private recycling industries. Despite the success of the private recycling system, it does not recycle plastic, a major source of solid waste. Waste collection has become a highly unionized and powerful industry resistant to change or governmental regulation.

As the largest city in Latin America, Mexico City has great difficulty protecting its environment, providing basic services to its residents (see Table 13-3), and ensuring suitable living standards as well as economic opportunities for the poor. The issue of organic waste disposal and sewage touches upon all these problems. Many residents in Mexico City lack basic

[2]The wastewater is pumped out of the city by giant machines, and estimates indicate that in the event of a general failure, the city would be under several feet of raw sewage within hours.

Table 13-3. Access to basic services in the MZMC, 2000 (percentage of the population)

	Water supply (%)	Sewerage (%)	Electricity (%)
Federal District	94.74	96.00	97.33
State of Mexico	86.51	85.95	91.48
State of Hidalgo	86.72	83.85	89.69
Total MZMC	90.36	90.64	94.21

Source: INEGI (2000). Figures for the States of Mexico and Hidalgo include only those municipalities that are part of the MZMC

sanitation service and are not connected to the municipal sewage system. The resulting pollution causes health hazards in the communities themselves and threatens to poison the entire city's water supply.

13.3.4 The Sustainability of Water

Among the biggest challenges for an urban area is the provision of a safe and reliable water supply for its inhabitants. Often the availability of water for human consumption competes with the water needs of industry. The case of Mexico City is instructive, because it is one of the first megacities in a developing country and one of the first major cities to experience problems with the provision of water.

Experts estimate that the Basin of Mexico is now reaching not only its ecological limits, but also its technological and social limits to substitute or import needed resources. Mexico City is an acute example of uncontrolled urban expansion and environmental deterioration, but is certainly not unique. The combination of natural resource constraints, environmental impacts, and the incapacity of governments to solve complex problems can be found in both developed and developing countries.

The Mexican Constitution of 1917 entrenched water resources as a public domain under the control of the federal government. Water management in Mexico, as in many other countries, is highly centralized. In 1989, in an effort to make federal management more efficient, the government created the National Water Commission (*Comision Nacional del Agua*, or CNA) as the sole federal authority to deal with water management. The CNA operates as an autonomous agency within the Ministry of Environment and Natural Resources (SEMARNAT). The CNA is responsible for implementing Mexico's *National Waters Act* (1992), as well as the operation of an extensive hydraulic infrastructure for the delivery of bulk water supplies.

The Federal District and the State of Mexico, which are responsible for providing drinking water, and for wastewater collection and the disposal within their jurisdictional boundaries, share management of water and wastewater within the Metropolitan Zone of Mexico City.

Mexico City receives 70% of its water as groundwater from the aquifer system that has supplied the population of the basin for hundreds of years. Natural springs and the runoff from summer rains from the sierras and mountains surrounding the city are the main source of water to the aquifer. This source is so bountiful that water was not a scarce resource in Mexico City until about 35 years ago, when the population reached over six million people. Today, however, Mexico City faces a serious water deficit. As a result of increased demand from consumers and industry, and the rapid deforestation in the surrounding hills that have served as the aquifer's recharge areas, more water is now leaving the system than entering it. It is estimated that 63 m^3/s of water is needed to support the potable and agricultural irrigation needs of Mexico City's population. The main aquifer is being pumped at a rate of 55.5 m^3/s, but is being replaced at only 28 m^3/s, or about half of the extraction rate, leaving a shortfall of 27.5 m^3/s. The Rio Magdalena, one of the last small surface water sources in Mexico City, supplements 2% of this shortfall, but this river is increasingly contaminated by urban pollution.

While engineering strategies have been explored to find a solution to the water shortage, the damaging consequence of the aquifer's overexploitation is alarmingly visible to the inhabitants of the capital, whose city is literally sinking beneath them. This sinking, or subsidence, is caused by the depletion of water volume and pressure from the lowering of the aquifer, which causes the clay soils below the city to consolidate and the land that rests on top to collapse. Subsidence has been a problem since the early 1900s as an effect of the diversion and draining of lake water from the basin floor.[3]

Subsidence not only threatens the foundations and structure of Mexico City's many historic buildings, but also causes serious damage to the city's water supply and sewage infrastructure. Water pipes crack or break as the city sinks, causing leaks and enabling potential contaminants to enter the city's distribution system. The dense clays that overlie much of the aquifer were previously considered an impervious barrier to the downward migration of water and contaminants, but when the soil sinks, the dry clay becomes fissured and allows waste from the city above to seep into the water table below. Because of this infiltration, the water quality of the aquifer has become as large a concern as the quantity of water in the aquifer.

[3] Since this time, some areas in downtown Mexico have sunk about 9 m. Today, Mexico City is sinking between 5 and 40 cm a year.

Subsidence has also exacerbated Mexico City's enduring flooding problem. Flooding has always been a seasonal concern in Mexico City, but continued subsidence has required the construction of dikes and a deep drainage canal, as the city has sunk below the natural lake basin. The situation is now so serious that it takes numerous pumping stations, which run 24 h a day all year long, to keep the summer rains from washing sewage and runoff back into the city. Water has been on the public agenda for decades. Apart from increasing its supply, there is not a viable metropolitan hydraulic project taking advantage of technological opportunities, which would reduce risks of supply outages and infrastructure deterioration.

13.4 Planning Environmental Sustainability in Mexico City

Following the shift to a more free-market economy and the withdrawal of the state on public welfare issues that started in the early 1980s, Latin American cities dismantled their planning systems during the 1990s. At the same time, an important shift occurred, from acknowledging social problems in urban settings as a main target of public policy to addressing the extreme effects of the policies. Even when there is no easy resolution of the root causes of the structural inequity inherent in the economic model, trade-offs between important and deeply held values are being contested and discussed.

In Mexico City, the newly elected Mayor, Marcelo Ebrard (2006–2012), is implementing sound environmental policies, such as furthering the Rapid Transit Bus System across the city, building and promoting pedestrian and cyclist transport systems, and building temporary public spaces (public ice rinks and beaches).[4] The reaction to these initiatives has been mixed. On the one hand, these popular initiatives may pave the way for Ebrard's presidential candidacy, and on the other, environmental policies need to be framed within a broader context, namely securing coordination among the Federal District, the State of Mexico, as well as with other bordering states such as Hidalgo.

In the General Program of Development 2007–2012 of the Federal District (Ebrard 2007a), Ebrard and his administration framed sustainability as a long-term strategy. Its main goal is "to grant opportunities for

[4] Nevertheless, the mayor has also undertaken harder measures, such as removing street vendors from the historic center or expropriating areas in the city where criminal activities thrived. Although these actions appear to be a natural way to restore order, they have also revealed the authoritarian side of the current administration.

everyone to achieve their projects and aspirations." However, the pervasive contradiction of wanting to preserve the natural environment while at the same time guaranteeing the "efficient and sustainable management of natural resources" remains a paradox (Ebrard Op. Cit.). Moreover, the official manifesto expresses its unconditionality to international dictates and Ebrard vows Mexico City will become "a city which is to be ruled by international standards, agreements and cooperation on environmental issues in order to reaffirm our solid engagement with humankind." In this sense, Ebrard embraces the global warming framework and assumes his responsibility to mitigate the 1.5% that the city contributes to it on a global scale. Although at the local level Mexico City contributes only 5.5% of national carbon emissions, the city's estimates reveal that in the next couple of years this amount may double (Ebrard Op. Cit.). To prevent this from happening, Ebrard's approach is not only to change the trend, but to set new standards for the developing world: "Mexico City contributes to global warming in a significant manner. This is both a responsibility and an opportunity to position Mexico City as a key factor in attaining the *Millennium Goals*. That is, incorporating within programs and public policies the principles of sustainable development contained in *Agenda 21*. Also to reverse the loss of environmental resources [and to] address the immediate needs of the present while sustaining the resources for the future" (Ebrard 2007a).

The current administration of the Federal District has sworn "to incorporate principles of sustainability in a cross-cutting way and in every action, public policy, and in decisions regarding expenditures and investments" (*Programa General de Desarrollo 2007–2012*, Ebrard 2007a). The comprehensive approach is meant to address everybody's interests – particularly those of the underprivileged – even when the procedures leave ample margins where powerful stakeholders profit from them. However, in the *Programa*, the promotion of "collaboration" and "participation" is still on the broadest terms, and even when the cost to the next generation's welfare is thoroughly emphasized, the decision-making mechanisms are still unclear.

Among the key objectives of the 2007–2012 Program is to improve monitoring systems for various environmental indicators as well as reducing emissions and pollutants. No deadlines or hard numbers are mentioned to frame the endeavor, but at least it is mentioned that a general strategy is imperative for the whole Regional Area of the Valley of Mexico. For instance, the Federal District alone produces more than 12,000 daily tonnes of solid waste, half of it generated by households. Due to the highly recyclable nature of the waste produced (43% organic and 40% potentially recyclable inorganic), the program points to a strategy to collect, select, and recycle most of it.

13.4.1 The Green Plan

Ebrard's environmental plan is synthesized in the *Plan Verde* for the Federal District (a green plan), which has the ultimate goal to "humanize the city" (Ebrard 2008). The plan includes the construction of 94 km of cycling routes and 240 km of rapid transit bus routes (*Metrobus*) a year over 6 years, privileging public transport within a strategy of mobility. Ebrard aims to follow the ongoing conversation among urban planners on the importance of scale and the sense of place of urban life. For Ebrard, cars are responsible for the alienation of citizens, acknowledging that "we had never been as isolated as in the civilization of the automobile" (Ebrard, Op. Cit.). Explicitly informed by urban strategies set in motion in Barcelona and Paris, Ebrard expects to build cycle-stations where people would be able to leave or borrow bicycles in a more flexible way.

For the first time in the recent history of Mexico City, a mayor is attempting to undertake a comprehensive strategy of mobility with measures such as compulsory school bus transportation, new ordinances for trucks, and intensifying public transport use. The bottom line – or at least what the Government of the Federal District is proclaiming – is that "every measure that we are taking can be summarized in two issues: sustainability and [a better] quality of life for our city" (Ebrard, Op. Cit.). Improving the quality of life and acting against global warming are the main targets of Ebrard's government. Recently, during the celebration of the International Year of Planet Earth in Mexico City, he endorsed the global call, framed both as a personal and an institutional promise for his government. At the meeting he launched an urgent call "to undertake the necessary steps to guarantee our survival, the city's sustainability and contribute to the sustainability of our planet" (Ebrard, Op. Cit.).

Ebrard conducted a "green consultation" (known as *Consulta Verde*) where – allegedly – a million citizens expressed their views on ecology, energy, and the management of natural resources.[5] According to the *Consulta*, a vast majority agreed to change patterns of behavior such as reducing their water consumption, using public transport more often, and participating in waste recycling. However, while public policies need to be endorsed by citizens, in Mexico City even basic forms of consultation such as referendum are not available as viable tools to comply with broader democratic needs. In the city's budget, Ebrard's major investments went to the 245 km of *Metrobus* system and the construction of 22 km of underground trains lines (*Metro*) linking the southern part of the city from East to West. Also, an experimental

[5] However, the real value of "public consultations" has been called into question since they have been used to legitimize policies that would not be approved in a referendum.

Public Transport Corridor with Zero [Carbon] Emissions in Eje Central will be constructed, as a prototype for the rest of the city. Even when "zero-carbon" emissions and the use of hybrid technologies in taxis is always laudable, the transformation of a significant proportion of the four million automobiles on the roads is still a long way ahead.

13.4.2 Preliminary Results: The First Address to Citizens

In his first *Informe* (Ebrard 2007b), the major annual address in which the Mayor reports what has been accomplished regarding the general program that was presented at the time of taking office,[6] Ebrard explained that the *Plan Verde* (Green Plan) embodied the fundamental guidelines for the sustainable development of Mexico City. The Plan included a combination of strategies and actions aimed to move towards "sustainable development" over 15 years. The Plan, which includes provision for a coordinating team of the main offices within the city's government as well as a board for assessing and evaluating the outcomes, is expected to inform the environmental policies put in place.

The Green Plan is meant to be ambitious and encompasses the following issues: land conservation, livability and public space, water, mobility, air quality, waste, energy, and climate change. The issues have been a critical concern for past administrations and represent a long history of inadequacies and shortages. For instance, the strategy for *land conservation* aims to achieve "zero growth" in the urbanization of protected land, which is an ambitious goal for a city that has been created over an estimated 60% of formerly agricultural grounds (Ward 1990), and has rarely created land reserves for the low-income groups. *Livability* refers to the creation and recovery of public spaces – a strategy inherited from the Barcelona model[7] – which is presumed to inherently generate conviviality, thriving social encounters, and "social cohesion" (which is not always the case, as in areas with a high incidence of crime). Moreover, and still following the Catalonian school, the creation of structural projects around public spaces are framed as "granting social equilibrium, protecting the environment as well as the natural resources" (Plan Verde 2008).

[6] Even if a year in office is not enough to evaluate the reliability of a city government, it provides the framework of policies to come in the next years.

[7] Barcelona has long been the poster child of politically correct urban planning for Latin America. Former Barcelona officials such as Jordi Borja, Joan Busquets, and others had been hired as consultants for several cities such as Bogotá, Buenos Aires, Mexico, and Santiago, promoting public spaces and environmental quality.

Even if the quest for integration, inclusion, and redistribution of benefits plays a major role in this strategy, the objective of overcoming inequalities through physical interventions in the city is not a proven strategy and its success depends on the scale of and social support for such interventions.

Water is also a key issue for Mexico City because the cost of pumping water to the city continues to increase as the city draws on increasingly distant sources. As the mayor has observed, "we are already importing more than half of the water we consume in Mexico City" (Ebrard 2008). Nevertheless, the Government of Mexico City (GDF) recently inaugurated a water recycling plant and expects to build another three in Iztapalapa, Coyoacan, and Santa Fe. However, distribution is still a key issue, since affluent districts consume 900 l per person per day, while other parts of the city have to cope with only 35 l per person per day. The problem relates to inequity and redistribution beyond the culture of waste. Ebrard seems to be targeting the latter, with his recent remarks that "Water will no longer be free [or cheap], it will no longer be an unlimited resource and the city, that is, us, will have to use it differently" (Ebrard 2008). The strategy for water is based in reducing consumption (following Antanas Mockus's example in Bogotá), improving maintenance and efficiency (preventing leaks), and recycling water. More ambitious projects, such as renovating infrastructure, constructing alternative drainage systems, and creating lake parks are mentioned, but not addressed.

Another instrument designed to promote a comprehensive environmental policy is the *Programa de Acción Climática de la Ciudad de México 2008–2012* (Secretaría del Medio Ambiente del Distrito Federal (2008). The plan endorses the use of energy-efficient technologies, clean fuels, and alternative sources of energy. Financing from the Global Environmental Fund (GEF) has been used to launch the Rapid Transit Buses named *Metrobus* as well as for "harmonizing fragmented policies dealing with environment, urban development and transport" (Ebrard 2007b). Once again, the adoption of green technology is framed as a problem-solver capable of transforming the environment. The requirement of 30% of solar panels to heat swimming pools or establishments employing more than 51 employees is only partially addressing the environmental impact of 22 million people in an urban agglomeration. More significantly maybe, will be the estimated reduction of 300,000 tonnes of carbon monoxide with the construction of the 230 km of *Metrobus* programmed for the next 5 years.

The strategy for waste recycling seems to be struggling, considering the scale of the problem. In Ebrard's first year in office, 76,333 tonnes of construction wastes were reportedly recycled. However, that figure must be compared to the annual 4,380,000 tonnes of general waste reported. The

Informe also noted that 50% of the plans in the urban planning department had been completed, which indicates the assumption that planning is foremost a technical endeavor, in which land uses or future projects do not need to be publicly discussed or brought to consensus.

13.5 Final Remarks

After a decade of left-wing mayors endorsing progressive agendas, Mexico City has experienced a record of uneven results. Even when more attention has been paid to improving the environmental quality of the city, the strategies intended to achieve sustainability have been largely dictated by political agendas as well as the circumstances at the time. In recent years, decisions on major urban projects in Mexico City have been made on the basis of international "success stories" undertaken in comparable cities (i.e., *Transmileno*'s bus rapid transit system in Bogotá), as a response to anticipated major catastrophes (such as floods or earthquakes), or addressing inescapable threats such as global warming and climate change. Therefore, the sense of urgency and fatality has fueled the imposition of a political agenda not only on the local scale, but also on a national basis.

Decision-making over developments, priorities, and instruments continue to be made in a vertical, hierarchical, and nonconsensual way in Mexico City. Paradoxically, progressive mayors still favor allegedly technical and scientific expertise instead of assuming the contradictions that highly political decision-making generates whenever urban enterprises are undertaken. As Lefebvre (1991) claims, "As tools of formal knowledge, all such concepts have a precise aim, which is to eliminate contradictions, to demonstrate a coherence, and reduce the dialectical to the logical. Such an intent is immanent to a knowledge that aspires to be 'pure' and 'absolute' while remaining ignorant of its own *raison d'être*, which is to reduce reality in the interest of power."

Nevertheless, when decisions diverge from the citizens' will, or whenever democracy fails to guarantee the public interest, riots, demonstrations and social upheaval have filled the gaps of legitimacy and have resulted in the abrupt ending of such unpopular initiatives. Thus Atenco, Tepoztlan, and the Alameda Project in downtown Mexico City were abandoned after their poor conception, lack of political *savoir-faire*, and ineffective negotiation skills were revealed. Nevertheless, the battle between public interest and political and economic powers in Mexico City is defined on a daily basis. For instance, major unpopular projects have been built despite social mobilizations, such as a Costco store built on the grounds of the historic hotel known as the *Casino de la Selva* (in Cuernavaca) and elevated highways serving affluent areas of the city. The *Bando 2* – an ordinance to prevent any new construction outside the central city which benefited developers and tenants – has further reduced optimism about events to come.

Gifford Pinchot, the steward of Theodore Roosevelt's Conservation Program, asserted in 1910: "Conservation means the greater good for the greatest number for the longest time" (Pinchot 1910). However, the real challenge hides in the details, as instruments and priorities are often subject to negotiation. The challenge of deciding which is the "greater good," which is the "greatest number [of people]" and which is the best path of development, are still central for the social sustainability discourse.

References

Agyeman J, Bullard RD, Evans B (2002) Exploring the nexus: bringing together sustainability, environmental justice and equity. Space Polity 6(1):77–90

Andrews RN (1997) National environmental policies: the United States. In: Jaenicke M, Weidner HJ (eds) National environmental policies: a comparative study of capacity building. Springer, New York, pp 25–43

Ebrard M (2007a) Programa General de Desarrollo 2007–2012. Gobierno del Distrito Federal, Mexico

Ebrard M (2007b) Primer Informe de Gobierno del Distrito Federal 2007. http://www.df.gob.mx/jefatura/jefe_gobierno/primer_informe/index.html. Accessed May 6, 2008

Ebrard M (2008) Presentación del Proyecto de Red de Ciclovías del Distrito Federal. Antiguo Palacio del Ayuntamiento

Harvey D (2003) The new imperialism. Oxford University Press, Oxford

INEGI (2000) XII Censo General de Población y Vivienda 2000

Kothari R (1990) Environment, technology and ethics. In: Engel JR, Engel JG (eds) Ethics of environment and development – global challenge, international response. University of Arizona Press, Tucson, pp 27–49

Lefebvre H (1991) The production of space. Blackwell, Oxford

Pinchot G (1910) The fight for conservation. Doubleday, Page, NY

Plan Verde (2008) http://www.planverde.df.gob.mx/. Accessed on July 21, 2008

Polese M, Stren R (eds) (2001) The social sustainability of cities: diversity and management of change. University of Toronto Press, Toronto

Sachs W (1992) Environment. In: Sachs W (ed) The development dictionary. A guide to knowledge as power. Zed Books, London, pp 26–27

Sachs W (1993) Global ecology and the shadow of development. In: Sachs W (ed) Global ecology. A new arena of political conflict. Zed Books, London, pp 3–20

Secretaría del Medio Ambiente del Distrito Federal (2008) Programa de Acción Climática de la Ciudad de México 2008–2012. Gobierno del Distrito Federal, Mexico

Shiva V (1993) The greening of the global reach. In: Sachs W (ed) Global ecology: a new arena of political conflict. Zed Books, London, pp 149–156

UNDP (United Nations Development Programme) (2002) Human development report 2002: deepening democracy in a fragmented world. Oxford University Press, New York

United States of America, Department of Commerce/U.S. Commercial Service (2008) http://www.buyusa.gov/mexico/en/automotive_manufacturing.html. Downloaded on April 27, 2008

Ward P (1990) Mexico city: the production and reproduction of an urban environment. Belhaven Press, London

WCED (World Commission for Environment and Development) (1987) Our common future. The Brundtland Report. Oxford University Press, Oxford

WSSD (World Summit on Sustainable Development) (2002) Report of the world summit on sustainable development, Johannesburg, South Africa

14. Bogotá's Recovery Process

José Salazar Ferro

14.1 Introduction

This chapter presents the recent evolution of urban management and planning in Bogotá, Colombia, conceived as part of a region-wide transformation of the city that has occurred in the last 15 years in order to promote sustainable urban development. This process implied profound changes in governance and civic culture, in financial arrangements and the strength of social cohesion, as well as an increase in the capacity of public planning. These elements, which are strongly related, produced positive results in Bogotá's urban dynamics and were vital in overcoming the crisis in which the city's development had been trapped since the 1980s.

The chapter is divided into four parts. The first presents a synthesis of Bogotá's urban development and growth patterns. The second describes the city's crisis during the 1980s and early 1990s, and what has happened during the last decade. The third presents the city's institutional framework and its planning structure. The fourth describes the programs and projects that triggered structural changes, resulting in the reversal of the crisis and the beginning of a development process that continues today.

14.2 Urban Form and Sustainable Development in Bogotá

14.2.1 A Rapid Urban Development

At the beginning of the twentieth century, Bogotá had 100,000 inhabitants and occupied slightly less than 2% of the city's present area. An area of 570 ha – as opposed to the 39,000 ha that the city covers today – was

A. Sorensen and J. Okata (eds.), *Megacities: Urban Form, Governance, and Sustainability*,

sufficient for the activities of the capital city of a country characterized by relative economic backwardness and incipient industrial development. Over the following 100 years, more than 35,000 ha of residential neighborhoods, industrial zones, administrative zones, recreation zones, and service areas were added to accommodate the activities of a city of seven million inhabitants, whose growth was triggered by internal migration and the improvement of the population's living conditions.

Thus, Bogotá has become the capital city of a highly urbanized country, where more than 75% of the population lives in cities, whereas 30 years ago, only 30% did so.

14.2.2 Urban Development in the Twentieth Century

Initially, the city developed on the flat soil of the Bogotá River's eastern basin. The old city includes the city's growth until the end of the nineteenth century, product of a constant transformation process (densification, redevelopment, the enlargement of roads, and the destruction of forests and agricultural lands) and a moderate growth of the original nucleus over almost four centuries. The old city is the present historical center, built on a grid of roads without any apparent morphological hierarchy; a model with a high compact and dense urban fabric, created through the subdivision of property.

Population growth generated the need to expand the urban area. At the end of the nineteenth century and up to the 1920s, new neighborhoods were created, disconnected from the existing city, forming an addition to the old city. These residential neighborhoods were developed on an open and hierarchical grid with plentiful public spaces, including parks and special areas for education, health, and sport facilities. The city's development until the 1950s and 1960s constitutes the present central zone.

The 1950s saw the extension of the periphery with residential subdivisions and informal neighborhoods, and the development of new zones for industrial or service uses. This period marks the first phase of the city's accelerated expansion: the city's population was 1.7 million in 1960 with a 6.8% growth rate (1951–1964), one of the world's highest (see Fig. 14-1).

During this period, a hierarchical road system started to develop, designed independently from the shape of each neighborhood and the urban shape as a whole. This network, which marked the city's accelerated growth on its periphery, was constructed over the existing city to ensure the whole city's interconnection. Although this is a city of residential neighborhoods, each one is thought of as an individual piece, connected in different ways to

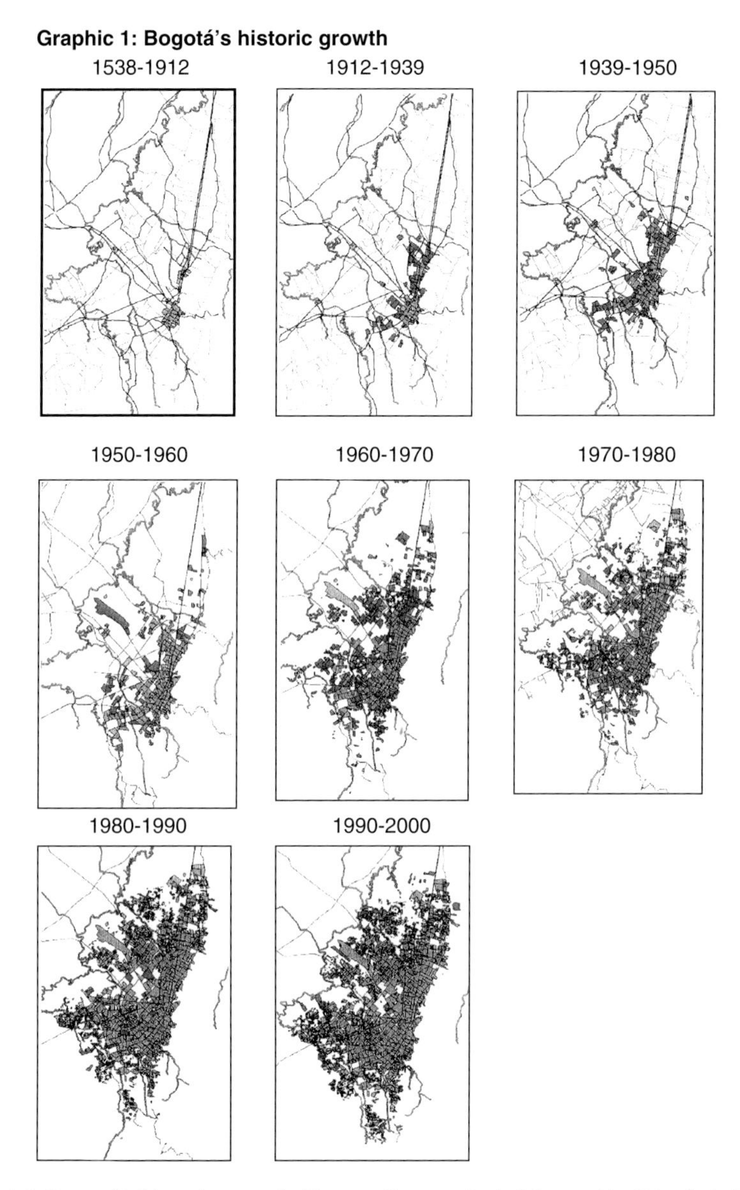

Fig. 14-1. Bogotá's historic growth (Source Secretaría de Planeación Distrital, 2002)

the road network. The city is characterized by discontinuities in the urban fabric and great differences among neighborhoods. Some affluent neighborhoods resemble low-density American suburbs, with generous public space provisions; others, designed for the middle classes, have smaller lots and

row housing; finally, the "working class" neighborhoods have much higher densities, leaving less room for roads and open spaces. They form isolated neighborhoods, large "marginal areas" that will eventually be joined to the rest of the city.
During the last three decades, the following three development tendencies have changed the city:

- The location of informal settlements in zones with geological problems, making it difficult to bring in roads and services because of the loss of land and the occupation of the eastern and southern hillsides, as well as low-lying river zones
- The densification (through redevelopment) and transformation of the urban structure through the location of commercial activities and services in old residential neighborhoods, consolidating activity nodes
- The expansion of both economic activity and housing over the plateau's municipalities, producing dispersed, heterogeneous, and unbalanced urbanization in the 1,500 km^2 of the flat zone to the west of Bogotá and the overflowing of the municipal region as a result of the annexation of six nearby municipalities in 1954 (Cortés 2006)

14.2.3 The Effects of Accelerated Urban Development

This accelerated growth did not generate a parallel institutional and technical framework capable of operating and controlling the city effectively. Economic and technical resources were insufficient to solve the growing demands for goods and services of the population; social cohesion deteriorated.

This situation worsened during the 1980s, and led to an inevitable urban crisis that affected all spheres of human life and the district administration. In the early 1990s, the city was considered ungovernable and unsuitable for investment; confidence in its institutions was extremely low.

At the same time, the urban agglomeration outside the municipal region had no institutional organization; each of the 12 contiguous municipalities[1] took (and still takes) autonomous decisions.

[1] The municipalities of: Soacha, Mosquera, Funza, Madrid, Cota, Chía, Cajicá, La Calera, Sopó, Zipaquirá, Tabio, Tenjo y Facatativá.

14.2.4 The Changes of the 1990s

The 1990s brought important changes in support of urban development in Colombia. A new legal, institutional, and technical framework for urban development was created: it started with the decentralization process in the second half of the 1980s, and continued with the new 1991 Political Constitution, which gave more autonomy to the city.

The Constitution adopted the principle that land ownership is not absolute, but also entails social and ecological duties, and included municipalities in the distribution of capital gains generated by urban development. It served as the basis for the promulgation of laws on environmental and regional planning and legislation, which support a new approach to urban planning.

At the same time, the country's main cities underwent a generalized decline in urban growth rates. Bogotá's growth rate dropped from 6.8 (1953–1964), to 2.6% (1993–2005). Although in absolute terms, the population growth rate was still high, in relative terms it was decreasing: now, the city is preparing for a 20% population increase over 12 years, while in previous decades it had expected that its population would double during that same length of time.

In the context of big urban transformations, the trends marking the international agenda of the 1990s appeared in the country: economic globalization, sustainable development, and the United Nations Millennium Development Goals.

14.2.5 Urban Development and Sustainability

Three key development paradigms have transformed urban development in the cities over the last 15 years:

- The creation of a "competitive platform" capable of attracting foreign investment, which gave the city a role in the global "flow networks" (Borja and Castells 1997), produced by structural changes in international commerce and capital and information flows
- Sustainable development (Río Earth Summit 1992), which led to new ideas about the city's development, and requires the conservation of water, land, and energy and reductions in pollution and the emission of greenhouse gases
- The fight against poverty and inequalities ("Habitat" Agenda 1997; the Millennium Summit), which combine the goal of sustainable development with short- and medium-term local action to improve urban residents' lives

These three trends are not completely compatible in a city located in a developing country such as Colombia. Although huge efforts have been made to bring the city into the globalized economy through "efficiency recipes," these efforts have not produced the desired effects. Corrections have had to be made in development to reduce poverty and social and spatial inequities, and to respond to the new challenge of sustainable development.

Thus, Colombian cities face a double challenge: (1) readying themselves to compete in the international market and attract investment and (2) extending the access of a growing urban population to urban goods and services (Balbo 2003). Other forces call for controlling the effects that these processes have had on the world's environment, making the second challenge even more complex and harder to achieve.

The practical application of sustainable development programs has been very slow (Ardila 2003), for they have clashed with the exigencies of globalized economic development, which are nevertheless indispensable for obtaining the necessary resources to face urgent problems relating to poverty, housing, public services, education, employment, etc.

In this context, only recently has urban form for a sustainable city been the subject of urban planning discourse (often promoted by international credit agencies). Today the basis of urban politics in Colombia is the promotion of "compact" cities, with efficient public transport and the prioritization of urban public space. It is still possible to build this model in Bogotá, because of the precarious state of roads in the periphery, security problems that led the wealthy classes to choose multifamily buildings in the city, and the rise in the price of rural property caused by the development of the flower agro-industry. Given these circumstances, Bogotá has experienced dense and compact development unlike the automobile-oriented suburbanization (sprawl) models of the 1960s–1980s typical of many other cities.

14.3 Recent Urban Development

14.3.1 The Urban Crisis of the 1980s

During the 1990s, a great urban crisis that had been incubating through the previous decades became evident in Colombia (Salazar and Del Castillo 2005; Martin 2006). It crystallized in a deep institutional crisis, growing insecurity, mobility and public transport problems, a housing shortage, and grave social divisions. Bogotá had accumulated the problems of any city with accelerated population growth, given its lack of the resources or the institutional and technical framework necessary to face them. The crisis in the public sphere and the low credibility of urban institutions in planning and, in general, in the city's future, revealed an "urban crisis" of huge proportions.

The crisis was characterized by the following eight features.

- *Increasing insecurity*. During the 1980s, Bogotá was among the most violent cities in the world; in 1994, it registered a rate of 82 homicides every 100,000 inhabitants, one of the highest in the continent. The violence in the country, enhanced by the power of drug-dealing, which contributed to the persistent guerrilla warfare of the 1960s, had resulted in a series of murders of political leaders and others, which placed the country among the most violent nations in the world. Between 1970 and 1994, Colombia had the highest rate of homicides in the Americas (Martin and Ceballos 2004: 102) In the same year, there were 1,089 traffic-related deaths in Bogotá. These figures explain the citizens' lack of trust in the institutions responsible for security in Bogotá.
- *Weakness of public finances*. The financial crisis occurred because while population and its demands increased, revenues stood still. Bogotá's resources remained unaltered for almost 30 years; tax collections were stagnant until 1983, and then recovered slightly through the 10 following years, mainly due to the country's decentralization laws, which transferred the nation's resources towards the regions. According to a study conducted by researchers from University College, London, in 2000, even though the city's income had increased by 300%, "taxpayers in the capital paid the same amount in 1991 as they had in 1963" (Gilbert and Dávila 2002: 29; translated by the author). In 1994 the city was practically bankrupt. "In 1992, the city was broke. It had collapsed. It could not be governed, nor administered. It had no future." (Martin and Ceballos 2004: 99; translated by the author). Bogotá offered no investment opportunities. In this situation, providing its inhabitants with the appropriate goods and services for urban development was unfeasible.
- *Governance problems and lack of transparency*. It was impossible to govern the city; politicians interfered constantly with the administrative sectors of the city. District administration and the growing bureaucracy were inefficient because of their loyalty to "clienteles." Councilors co-administered the city with the Mayor and his technical team, which made public administration and political control more difficult as well. These problems promoted a government efficiency crisis.
- *Urban segregation and housing shortages for the poorest groups*. A strongly segregated region emerged with the displacement of

the city's poorest groups to the periphery, which had low-quality services and inadequate transportation. The wealthier households, meanwhile, occupied the north-central zone, near the tertiary employment areas. In the last two decades of the twentieth century, approximately 180 ha per year of informal developments were constructed. Altogether, about 6,000 ha of the developed city, home to 26% of the population, were illegally built. So while in 1980 there were about 2,400 ha of informal developments, by 2,000 the area had grown to 6,000 ha.

- *Obsolete transportation system.* The outdated transportation system (more than 40 private companies owned buses traveling different routes) and the bad state of the city's road network meant that in 1998, a citizen of Bogotá spent an average of 4 h a day traveling, and journeyed an average of 10 km from home to work. Despite the city's low level of vehicle ownership (850,000 private vehicles for six million inhabitants), congestion and accessibilit*y problems were high, especially* in the south and eastern peripheral areas, home to the poorest groups.
- *The inability to construct and defend public space.* The occupation of sidewalks by automobiles and small shops, as well as the closing up of parks and other public areas, resulted in a loss of the structuring function of public space. For the citizens of Bogotá, public space came to represent badly built and dangerous places, which they had to navigate carefully to reach their destinations. At the same time, the city failed to reserve enough free public areas to satisfy the growing demands of the population. In 1996, there were 3 m^2 of green space per inhabitant, a very low figure, according to international standards.
- *Unplanned growth.* Tertiary industry, initially located downtown, was displaced to other areas in the city. Commerce and offices displaced old residential areas, and houses were replaced by buildings on a lot-by-lot basis. This unplanned "spontaneous renovation" diminished the city's environmental quality, due to the disappearance of free public and private spaces.
- *An ineffective planning regime.* During the second half of the twentieth century, Bogotá tried various planning schemes, which were abandoned as they proved inadequate to address the complex urban reality. At the end of the 1980s the weakness of public governance became evident in the city's inability to develop public property and the apparent subordination of all public affairs to the private sphere (Garay 1999; Gómez Buendía 1999). The planning

regime was incapable of providing answers to the grave problems that hindered the city's development. The administration's and citizens' lack of faith in planning was evident.

14.3.2 The City in the Last Fifteen Years

Bogotá is a dense and compact city with a rapidly growing population: it has, at present, 7.3 million inhabitants – two million more than in 1990 – spread over an area of 345.8 km^2, for a population density of 21.192 inhabitants per km^2.

Bogotá's annual demographic growth rate has decreased from 7.4% (1953–1964) to 2.6% (1993–2005). Every year, the city grows by about 150,000 new residents: 100,000 as a result of its natural growth, and the other 50,000 as a result of internal migration. Far more dynamic than the central city, the "urban region" – a 1,500-km^2 area divided into 12 municipalities – has 7.7 million people and adds a further 75,000 new inhabitants per year to the city-region.

The evolution of densities during the last decades (see Table 14-1) shows important changes in urban structure. The city's center loses more and more inhabitants; between 1973 and 1985, the population decreased by 30,634 inhabitants; between that year and 1993, there were 113,538 fewer inhabitants. In 2005, data indicates important changes; the central areas have stopped losing population, while the sectors of the neighboring zones of the city's centre have started to lose inhabitants, in spite of the replacement of old housing by high buildings. Meanwhile, the communes of the periphery are growing much more dynamically, especially the southern and western ones, forming two vast and very dense popular residential sectors: a very large one in the south, and a smaller one in the northwest.

Table 14-1. Bogotá's density 1910–2005

Year	Population	Area (km^2)	Density (population/km^2)
1910	145,000	5.70	25,439
1938	335,512	25.14	13,346
1951	715,362	27.00	26,495
1964	1,697,311	146.15	11,613
1973	2,861,913	222.99	12,834
1985	4,441,470	234.24	18,961
1993	5,484,244	266.56	20,574
2005	6,778,691	340.00	19,937

Source: DAPD (2000)

In general terms, the city has maintained an average density of more than 20,000 people per km^2, which is still high in relation to that of other Colombian and Latin-American cities. The densest sectors are located in the low-income zones, which can reach densities of up to 60,000 people per km^2, both in consolidated zones and in new settlements, generally those of informal origin. High-income zones, where there are also commercial activities, services and offices, have densities of between 13,000 and 30,000 people per km^2.

Between 1993 and 2005, the western municipalities of the Sabana experience considerable population growth. Figures 14-2–14-4 show that the 12 municipalities of the Sabana registered an increase of 416,000 inhabitants (1993–2005), most of them concentrated in Soacha, a municipality in the southwest.

14.3.3 Urban Development

Until the 1980s, Colombia's urban development polarized around four major cities (Bogotá, Medellín, Cali, and Barranquilla), a phenomenon locally known as *cuadricefalia urbana* ("urban quadricephalia"). Nevertheless, during the last two decades, Bogotá has exceeded the other three cities both in population growth rates and economic indicators. Today, Bogotá is the center of the national financial system. Its GDP accounts for as much as 27% of the national GDP. It is the location of many of the country's main companies and educational institutions, and the most advanced sectors in technology (communication, services). It is the country's main source of exports, totalling US$29 billion dollars and a 6.8% growth rate in 2006, and a level of US$4,238 GDP per capita.

Inside the city, two big axes can be identified, to the north and to the west of the centre, where most urban employment is found. In turn, these axes also show some poles of employment concentration.

- The central zone of the city (Historical Center – International Center) is still the city's main employment area. Inside this zone, up to 558,000 jobs have been identified, for an employment density of more than 200,000 jobs/km^2.
- This center has expanded more or less continuously towards the north since the 1970s, with the substitution of former high-income residential neighborhoods with financial, business, and commercial centers. Along this axis, high employment densities in commerce and services are also registered.
- Towards the west, the traditional industrial zone developed in the 1950s–1970s along what is now the avenue leading to the airport.

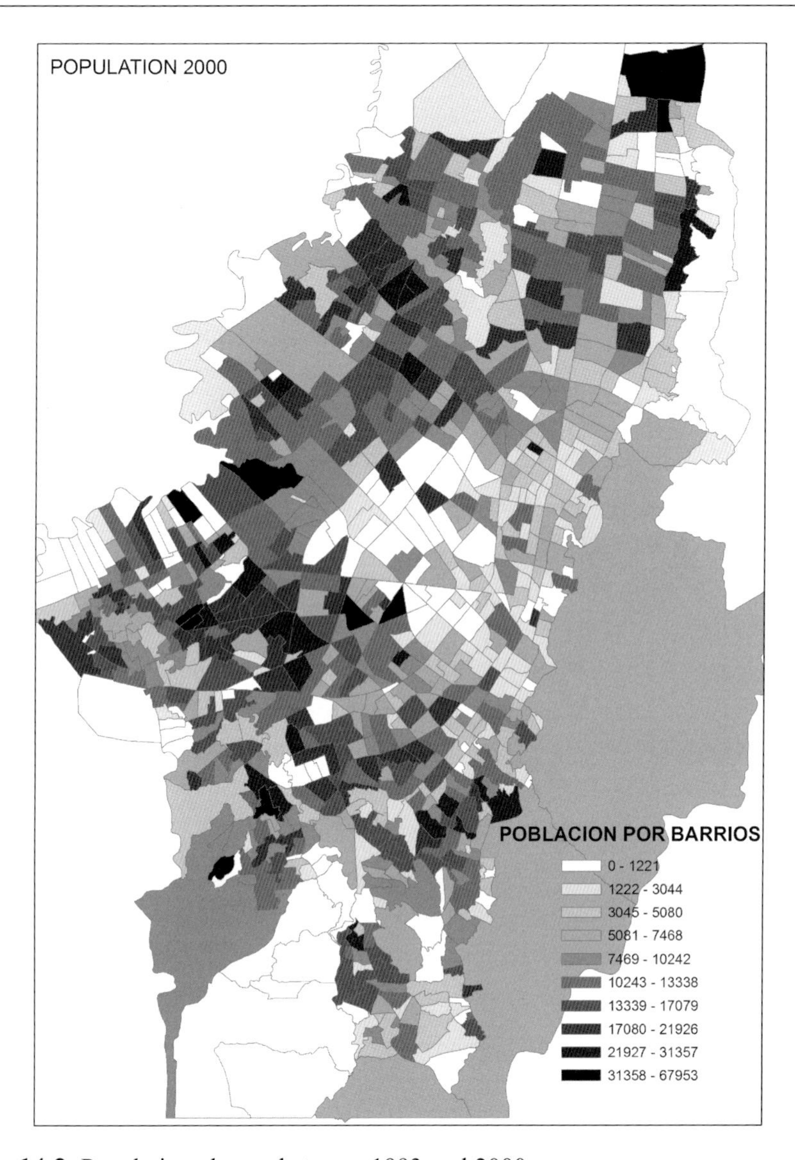

Fig. 14-2. Population change between 1993 and 2000

This axis was boosted by new expansions (Ciudad Salitre particularly), and today it is the most dynamic place for offices and services for enterprises, hotels, convention centers, etc.

- Employment decentralization towards other zones is visible in the Restrepo neighborhood to the south, Kennedy and Fontibón to the west, and some smaller nuclei to the northeast and to the south.

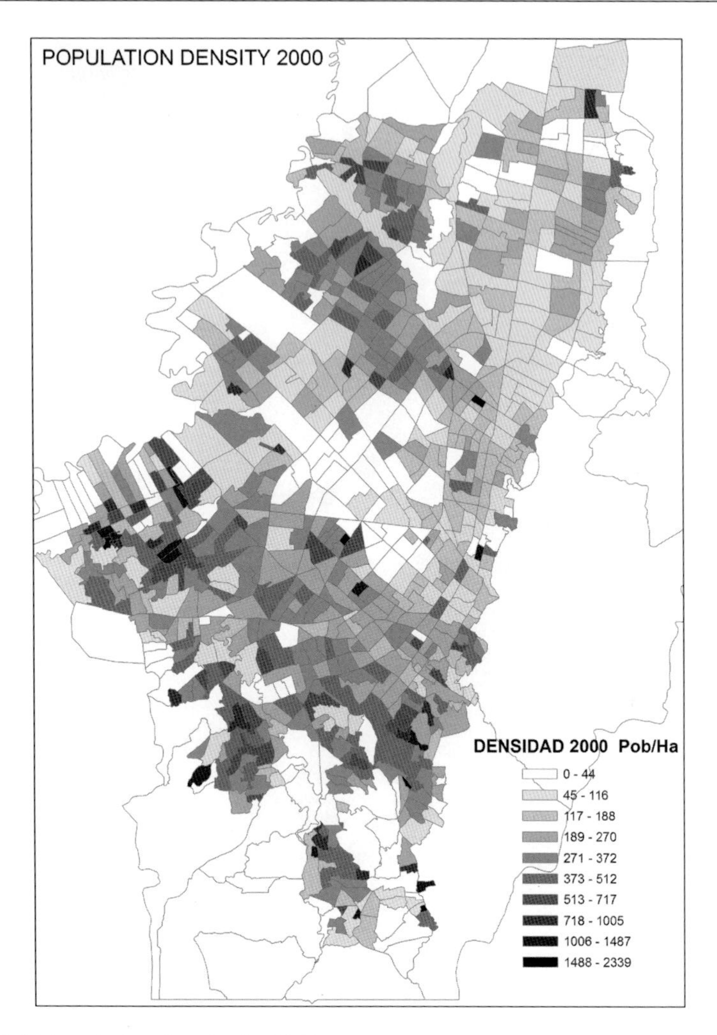

Fig. 14-3. Population density in 2000

14.3.4 Transport

The Bogotá Mobility Master Plan (Duarte Gutterman et al. 2006) showed that 67% of Bogotá's households do not own any type of motorized vehicle. Work and school were identified as the people's two main destinations (71% of the trips).

As shown in Fig. 14-5, public transport trips represent 57.2% of the total number of trips; 15.1% of the trips are made on foot, and only 14.7% are made on private vehicles. Walking and cycling combined reach 17.3% of the total number of trips.

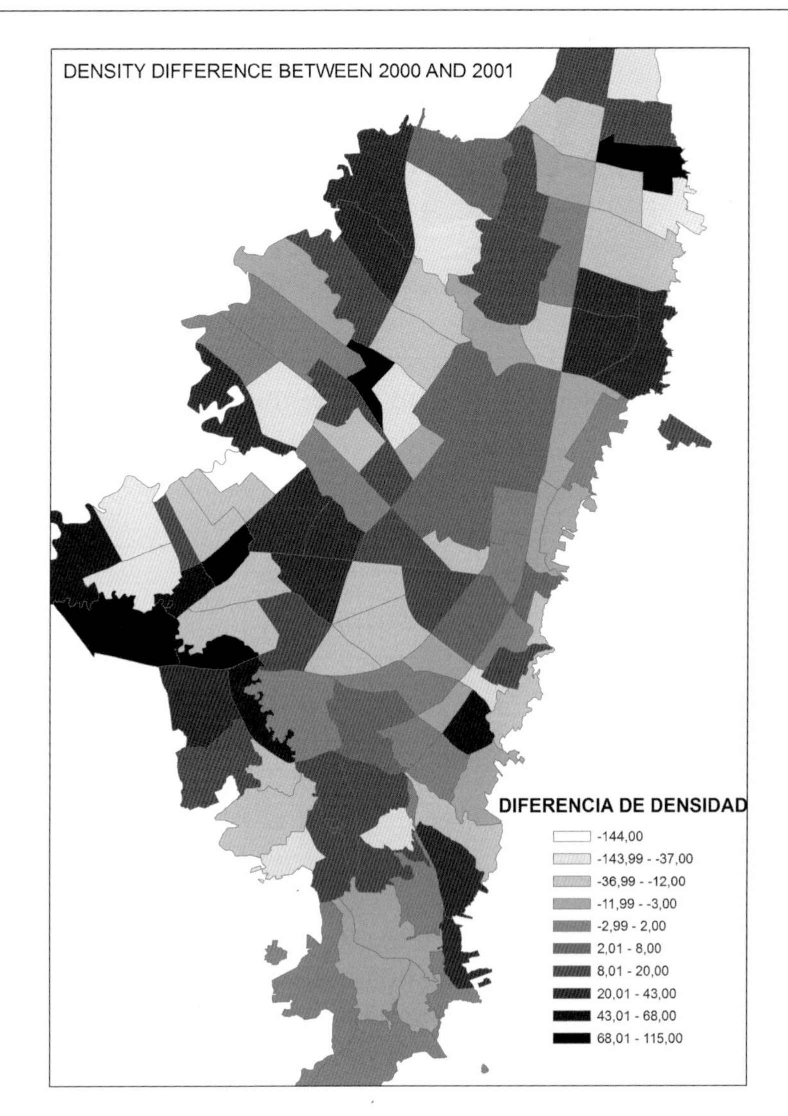

Fig. 14-4. Density difference between 1993 and 2000 (*). (*) *Figures 14.2, 14.3 and 14.4 were created by Luis Herney Rincón*

Considering travelers' socio-economic level, 55.3% of the trips of the richest population are made in private vehicles, and only 28.6% are made in public transport (8.6% in taxi). On the other hand, 68.6% of the poorest population uses public transportation, and only 4% private vehicles (see Fig. 14-6).

These figures show that, in spite of the important rise in the number of automobiles, public transport still represents the dominant mode for all trips, covering 75% of the motorized trips.

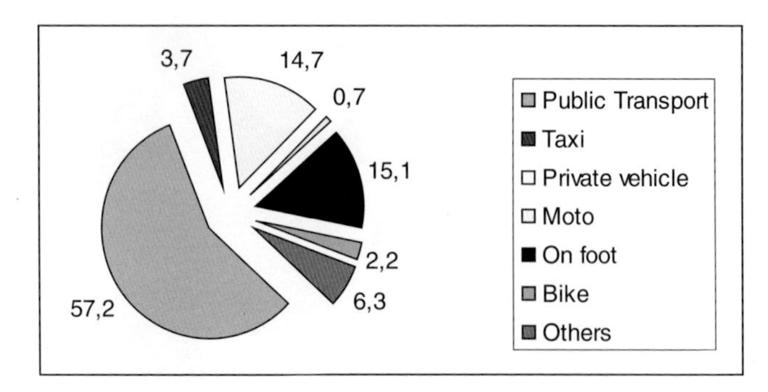

Fig. 14-5. Modal trip distribution in 2005 (Source "Formulación del plan maestro de movilidad para Bogotá D.C.", 2005)

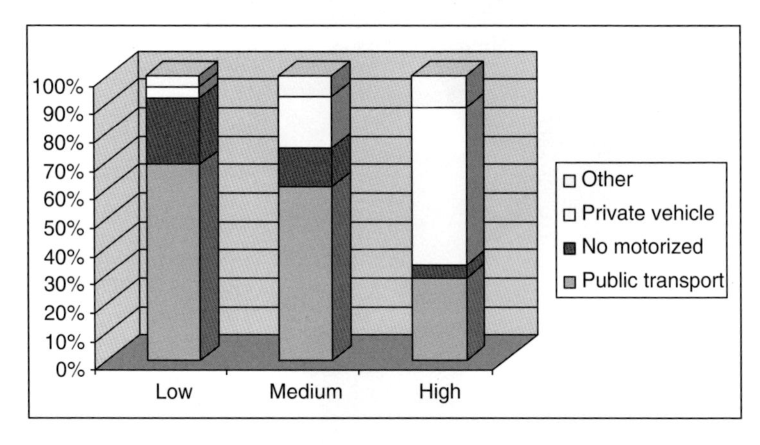

Fig. 14-6. Modal distribution by income level in Bogotá, 2005 (Source "Formulación del plan maestro de movilidad para Bogotá D.C.", 2005)

During the period 1993–2005, during which vehicle use increased significantly, public transport participation diminished only slightly. After only 5 years of operation, the new transport system, *Transmilenio*, already represents 25% of public transport trips (1.4 million trips per day).

Nevertheless, it is clear that private vehicles occupy 42% of the road space, while buses occupy only 26%. "On average, Bogotá households spend 14.22% of their family income on transport and communications … This percentage can be unfavorably compared with the 7.7% that prevailed during the 1980s, for it indicates that spending participation for these items practically doubled" (115; translated by the author).

14.4 The End of the Crisis

Bogotá's urban crisis is coming to an end. This fact is notable for three reasons:

- It has happened in a country that even today has not yet overcome its grave governance and development problems
- It represents the sum of many efforts, some of them coordinated with previous ones, others a response to particular programs, that ended up coming together in a collective project that was not thought through nor structured from the beginning
- The recovery of the public sphere is a central point of the process, which means developing the necessary arguments to support urban public goods and services

Within this process, the efforts of the city's mayors during the last 15 years in different areas should be cited. Jaime Castro (1992–1994) worked on governance and decentralization; Antanas Mockus (1994–1997 and 2001–2004), supported civic and democratic culture, efficient administration, and respect for life; Enrique Peñalosa (1998–2001) focused on mobility and public space improvement; and Luis E. Garzón (2004–2007) promoted social inclusion. Each of these mayors defended different ideas, each had his own programs, some wanted to be differentiated from the previous mayor, but all ended up supporting city projects that together, without a previously established plan, consolidated as a successful model of urban development.

Two of them (Mockus and Peñalosa) were supported by civic movements, different from traditional political parties. Their innovative government programs improved citizen behavior and public service management, built awareness of the collective ownership of public space and assets, and transformed citizens' apathy and mistrust towards the government, thus channeling generalized discontent concerning the country's overall situation.

Although citizens were initially skeptical about these efforts, their permanence and the real effects they have had on daily life (safer streets, improved mobility, better urban goods and services, among others) allowed them to have a multiplicative effect on the city's emergence out of crisis. Twelve years after its profound crisis, Bogotá's citizens once again believe that it is possible to live better through a collective effort, despite the critical conditions the country faces.

14.4.1 Strengthening Local Governance and Public Finances

The first point that should be emphasized in the process of ending the crisis is the adoption of a new institutional and financial framework for the city, contained in the "Bogotá Capital District's Organic Bylaw"[2] (Decree 1421 of 1993), issued by the President of the Republic as a development of what is stipulated in Colombia's 1991 Political Constitution.

This Bylaw was the result of a particular political situation: it was adopted as a part of the new Constitution, which had been conceived as a fundamental step for addressing the country's political and institutional crisis, resulting mainly from the expansion of drug traffic and the permanent presence of guerrillas. Within this scenario of public debate, the city's priorities were not the object of major controversies, which allowed the national government to propose a bylaw comprising innovative measures.

A special regime was adopted for Bogotá that implied a change in its form of government, consisting of separating the administration from the council, the city's body of political representation. This new regime increased the city's responsibilities, giving it more autonomy to organize its taxes and improve its finances. Civic participation was also promoted by implementing decentralization within the city itself: 20 *localidades* (districts) were created in Bogotá, which expanded the number of channels for the exercise of democracy.

Within the legal framework, and aside from the changes brought about by the 1991 Constitution, two actions should be emphasized. First, the 1994 Development Plan Law requires each mayor (elected since 1990) to introduce a Development Plan in his or her government program, describing all the investments to be made during his or her administration. Second, Law 388 of 1997 supports new methods of urban and regional planning based on urbanism as a public function. It requires the adoption of *Planes de Ordenamiento Territorial* or POTs (Territorial Management Plans or Land Management Plans), as a response to the need to transform urban planning and provide local administrations with contemporary urban development planning and management instruments to address the urban crisis.

14.4.2 Finances

There has been a spectacular recovery of the city's finances since 1994, an essential basis for future development. In 4 years, the city's revenues tripled (in constant pesos), as a result of new forms of tax calculation and tax collection. The highest rate of annual growth, 77%, happened between 1993 and 1994, after the promulgation of the District's Organic Bylaw.

[2] In the original Spanish the law is named the "Estátuto Organico de Bogotá". Such 'Organic' laws have a higher legal status in Columbian law.

That same year, the Industry and Trade Taxes (ICA) and the Land Property Tax grew at a rate of 90%. This increase was due to the implementation of "*autoavalúo*" (self-assessment), the direct collection of taxes by banks, and mandatory payments to the district's industrial and trade companies. In order to address the delay in updating the city's property register, the "*autoavalúo*" allowed citizens to fix the land value for which they would pay the Land Property Tax, which could not be less than 50% of the property's commercial value. This exercise in civic participation gave a boost to the city's finances.

Improving the city's income by 29% was the result of a "taxpayer culture" program, *110% with Bogotá*, designed to teach citizens about their responsibility towards the city and others: "all pay, all gain," was the slogan under which this "culture of contribution" was implemented. The "the culture of contribution" aimed to show citizens, through concrete examples, that paying taxes was a good way of redistributing the city's wealth. Citizens were asked to choose a project and pay more taxes – and 63,000 of them did. Before 1993, only 33% of all residents and businesses paid their taxes; today, 90% pay their taxes on time. The city manages its finances as a whole, therefore wealthier communities can subsidize poorer communities.

At the same time, costs were cut radically. For example, operation costs grew very slowly during the decade, decreasing from 45% of the total spending in 1993 to 25% or 30% in later years. During those same years, Bogotá's tax revenues grew at greater rates than the nation's, and internal indebtedness levels were lower than those established by law (Faimboim et al. 2001: 4), which helped to improve the city's BBB credit rating according to the Duff & Phelps Credit Rating Co., a financial advisory firm. (Today the rating is AAA.)

14.4.3 Increase in Welfare Investment

A very important part of the increase in revenues was directed to welfare investment. During the 1990s, welfare investment grew so rapidly that between 1992 and 1999, welfare spending multiplied by a factor of six. The last few years' budget shows that welfare investment has continued to rise significantly. Between 2001 and 2003 (without including transport and public space), it grew from 2.75 billion pesos (US$ 1.19 million in 2001) to 3.36 billion pesos ($US 1.17 million in 2003[3]).

[3]The exchange rate for one U.S. dollar was 2,300 pesos in 2001 and 2,877 pesos in 2003.

14.4.4 The New Planning Regime

The implementation of planning legislation in Colombia at the end of the 1990s produced a remarkable change in urban planning in Bogotá.

Bogotá's formulation and adoption of the POT (Territorial Management Plan) in 2000 led it to resume the physical planning efforts of the 1960s, and to tackle, at the same time, other subjects on the contemporary international agenda: environmentally sustainable development, competitiveness, and regional equity, as well as the "classical" urban problems (housing, public services and infrastructure) and those that characterize big urban agglomerations (mobility, suburban sprawl, urban center revitalization, asset conservation, etc.).

The response to this complex situation lay not in "choosing" one of the planning formulae of some developed country, but in adapting and consolidating planning instruments appropriate to the city's economic and institutional reality. It was necessary to distinguish the urban planning elements that had consolidated as a planning "culture" within the country from those that had to be modified, added to, or transformed.

14.4.5 The Recovery of Territorial Planning and Long-Term Vision: The Project Plan Articulated in a City Project

The POT was formulated at a time when the city had defined and begun to implement important projects that marked its future development: the new transport system, the recovery or creation of public spaces and parks, the setting of high architectural and urban design standards, the creation of social infrastructure, neighborhood improvement programs, and the building of social housing, among others.

Although these projects arose independently of the POT. The projects were incorporated and articulated in a "city project," based on a territorial model, conceived as a desirable vision of the city and its surroundings in the future, and its objective was to orient and concentrate government action, public inversion, and particular actions towards long-term goals: the sustainability of urban development, social equity, and improvements in the levels of urban competitiveness.

In this model, an urban structure is defined and the different parts of the region that require urban planning actions, projects and urban design standards are identified, as well as the general systems that support the city's development.

The POT identified and programmed public actions in the region, such as road and public service infrastructure, public facilities, transport, housing and neighborhood improvement programs. Coordinating and reaching agreements with the entities responsible for each of these actions makes it possible to define short-, medium-, and long-term scenarios, which propose reachable goals for each period, and constitute a base on which to define the Municipal Development Plans of the three mayors elected during their operation. This approach allowed the city to ensure that each urban planning action, each project, and each public program corresponded to priorities chosen by the citizens.

The POT also established management instruments that facilitate the development of public and private projects, among which the following should be mentioned: coordinated management for new developments, thanks to which lot-by-lot development can be overcome; the transfer of construction and development rights; and the city's participation in land value increases, which allows the city to share the benefits when the price of land increases because of an administrative decision.

Coordinated management distributes the financial burdens (land, infrastructure, and facilities, benefits (urban uses) among the different owners who contribute their land to the development of an urban project. At the same time, it allows for the zonal plan as a whole and the city to share profits, so that each urbanization process contributes to the development of the general infrastructure and facilities according to the benefits granted by the specific development standards.

Considerable debate has risen in Colombia concerning this aspect of the zonal plan: while some consider associate management the basis of a new form of urban management, through which total financing of infrastructure and facilities can be obtained, others consider it a complex procedure that hinders the execution of the partial plans. Its application has yet been tested in only a few cities, so it is still too soon to evaluate it objectively.

This advance in planning and urban management shows concrete and positive results. Key projects and decisions on the city's development have turned into shared and stable agreements between citizens and administrators, although citizens' degree of involvement with these objectives is still low.

14.4.6 The Different Planning Scales: Centers and Zonal Planning

The city planning exercise was conceived as the interrelation of efforts at different scales that define the structures of the region that should be articulated, seeking complementarities and eliminating problems that a decision at one level can cause at the other scales.

The POT defines a system of centers or nodes of activity in zones other than the urban center, at the urban, district, and neighbourhood scale. These centralities are intended to strengthen and complement the places of most intense employment and service activity (those of greater density). The objective is to bring urban services and benefits to citizens, in order to decrease the need for motorized trips to obtain goods and services.

Each of these centers is the object of a strategic urban planning exercise in which the general scale projects are redefined according to local objectives. Here, public investments have been reprogrammed to improve public space and accessibility, and to site district-level administrative activities and facilities, to promote the decentralization of shops, offices, post offices, insurance offices, banks, etc.

Within a defined radius in each center, mobility is facilitated through alternative transportation systems (bicycles, pedestrians), which are prioritized over large-scale transit systems (*Transmilenio*). This approach to mobility has led to a complete transformation of the approach to transportation, which was previously planned on a purely technical perspective, without considering its urban planning consequences.

At a smaller scale, the *Unidades de Planeación Zonal* or UPZs (Zonal Planning Units) were defined as planning divisions that allow the formulation and development of a district plan for each homogeneous sector of the city, defining at the same time standards that regulate private investment in the most developed (and richest) zones, and the infrastructure and public endowments required in populous neighborhoods.

14.4.7 Development Standards: An Instrument for Regulating Private Actions in the City and Making Them Sustainable

A statutory and management frame has been created, which specifies the standards of use and treatment for each urban district in order to regulate the use of private property.

The homogeneity of each zone, or district, was a basic condition for the application of a single development standard, so that its components would correspond to a specific period of development in the history of Bogotá, as described earlier in this chapter.

Regulation of land use is destined to protect residential zones from invasion and indiscriminate colonization, from uses that cause environmental deterioration and lower the quality of life of its inhabitants and, at the same time, to provide adequate space for the development of the economic activities required for the future development of the city. The objective is to rebalance the region through the decentralization of employment and productive activity, by strengthening or generating civic/commercial and service-type centers.

The standards specify the type of urban action that must be undertaken in a given area, public space, or construction. They define the interventions that can be made in each building, offering different answers for different areas of the city: conservation (of urban and architectural values), consolidation (of development), renovation (of structures and functions), improvement (of materials, infrastructure, and public space in lower-income neighborhoods), or development (of undeveloped lots).

The POT prioritized conservation zones, demanding that new developments respect the neighborhood's existing conditions, so that new construction would contribute to a sector's consolidation and improvement, and not to its abrupt transformation. Only in exceptional cases does the city allow a change of pattern or the complete renovation of a sector.

14.5 Actions and Policies Towards Sustainable Development

As the city emerged from crisis, it engaged in a series of actions to support sustainable urban development. These included actions to influence civic culture, as well as those oriented towards recovering public space and improving mobility.

Apart from the changes meant to strengthen governance and improve finances and social investment, described in the former chapter, the civic culture programs (cohabitation, secure city, and safe traffic) as well as the urban reconstruction of the city, are a part of a process of change that will allow the creation of a more competitive, sustainable, and fair city.

14.5.1 Civic Culture: Creating a Safer City

The objective of advancing and consolidating a "Civic Culture" took shape as part of Mayor Antanas Mockus's first administration. The Development Plan 1995–1998, known as "Forming a City," was intended to build civic culture and strengthen democratic institutions.

The purpose of focusing on civic culture is to modify the city and its inhabitants' behaviors. Behavior can be controlled through sanctions, but without gaining citizens' effective cooperation. Change was attained through civil auto-regulation, government employee training, and the creation of places where relations between functionaries and citizens are constructed (Londoño 2006: 131). Civic culture seeks also to build a shared image of the city and "a respect for the rules that confer civic identity ... to promote popular culture and generate a sense of belonging to the city [and] trigger the community's participation" (Londoño 2006: 134, translated by the author).

The civic culture program has evolved since its beginning, when the emphasis was on culture and security – in particular, the *Ley Zanahoria* (see below), the Civil Population Volunteer Disarming Program, measures to strengthen the Metropolitan Police, and the application of justice without delay by specialized and permanent units. The Peñalosa administration focused its efforts on the recovery and collective use of public space as a fundamental aspect of "the public sphere." During his second administration, Mockus's main objectives were creating awareness of the city's achievements (pedagogical balance), and defending life and democratic culture. The emphasis was on recognition of the institutions, instead of civic culture.

14.5.2 Security

The most significant achievement in the transformation of civic behavior is the systematic reduction of the homicide rate.

Homicides in Bogotá have decreased from 80 for every 100,000 inhabitants in 1994, to 18 for every 100,000 at present (see Fig. 14-7). "The city's crime observatory – called *Sistema Unificado de Informacion sobre Delincuencia y Violencia* (SUIVD) – constantly monitors and maps crime data as an input both for planning and for the evaluation of interventions" (Alcaldía de Bogotá 2004).

The following programs have helped consolidate this process of change.

- The *Ley Zanahoria*: Studies show that most homicides are perpetrated by men, occur after 1:00 a.m., involve alcohol and firearms, and take place between people who know each other. In order to face this problem, the *Ley Zanahoria* ("Carrot Law"[4]) was issued in 1995. The establishments that sold alcoholic beverages at night were allowed to do so only until 1:00 a.m. Once the homicide rates improved, permission to open was granted until 2:00 a.m., and later until 3:00 a.m.

[4] In Colombia, "*zanahoria*" designates a reserved and formal person.

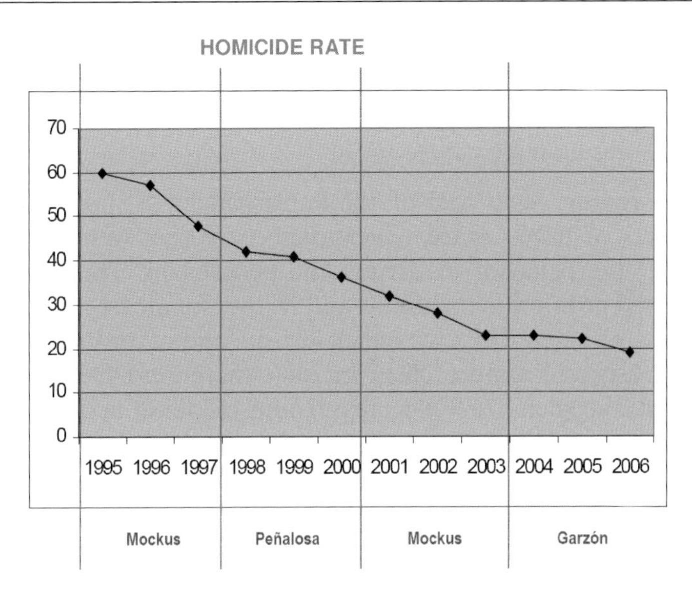

Fig. 14-7. Change in the homicide rate in Bogotá (Source Alcaldía Mayor de Bogotá)

- The Civil Population Volunteer Disarming Program resulted in the recuperation of thousands of arms that had been in the hands of the civil population. The program involved volunteer arms handovers and campaigns against violence.
- The creation of Justice Houses and Conciliation and Mediation Centers in marginalized areas allow citizens to gain access to a variety of national and municipal-level agencies that provide information, orientation, referrals and conflict resolution through formal and informal justice mechanisms.
- Civil Resistance against Terrorism: A series of terrorist acts perpetrated in Bogotá by illegally armed groups led the administration to unite all citizens in exercising civil resistance to confront violence. This included, for example, a symbolic defense of the Chingaza reservoir, which provides the city with nearly 70% of its water, from an attempted guerrilla attack. Guided by Mayor Mockus, the population painted three bright orange triangles around the reservoir, thus establishing that the property was protected by International Humanitarian Law.

Today, Bogotá's homicide rate is lower than that of Caracas, Mexico City, Rio de Janeiro, and Sao Paulo, among others. Citizens' perceptions of security have also significantly improved.

14.5.3 Complementary Safety and Security Programs

A series of parallel programs and events have also contributed to greater safety and security in the city.

- *Safer Traffic*. As a part of the improvement of mobility and the recovery of public space, educational campaigns were organized to change the behavior of drivers and pedestrians. These campaigns included promoting the use of and respect for crosswalks, as well as the use of safety belts by vehicle drivers and of protective helmets by cyclists and motorcyclists. In 2006, there were 497 fewer deaths in traffic accidents (a 9% decrease), and 183 fewer accidental deaths (a 15.9% decrease). Three innovative campaigns should be emphasized: (1) *Estrellas Negras* (Black Stars) is a symbolic campaign which consists of painting black stars in each place where a pedestrian has died as a result of a traffic accident; (2) *Caballeros de la Cebra* (Gentlemen of the Crosswalks), was an educational program for taxi drivers, designed to improve relationships between them, their clients, and pedestrians; (3) *Los Mimos* (Mimes) were used to caricaturize citizens' undesirable behaviors in public spaces and in areas of high vehicular traffic (See Fig. 14-8).
- *Appropriation and collective use of the city through bicycle paths and the night use of the city*. The *Ciclovía* (see Fig. 14-9) is a network

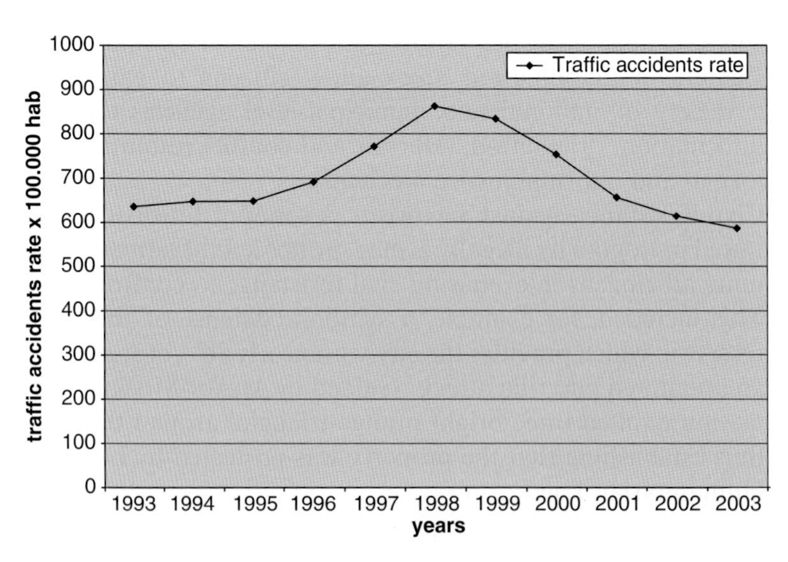

Fig. 14-8. Number of traffic accidents in Bogotá, 1993–2005 (Source "Formulación del plan maestro de movilidad para Bogotá D.C.", 2005)

Fig. 14-9. The Ciclovia

of 120 km of the largest roadways in the city, closed to regular traffic and reserved exclusively for bicyclists and runners between 7 a.m. and 2 p.m. on Sundays and holidays, and occasionally in the evening. An average of 700,000 bicycle riders, walkers, runners, and roller-skaters take advantage of this space every Sunday or holiday.

- *Collective events in public space.* A series of campaigns has been launched in conjunction with the public space program: music festivals (opera, jazz, zarzuela, rock, hip-hop, and Colombian music) are held in metropolitan parks; photography expositions on the city or other topics are organized in Bogotá's main plazas; while parades, gastronomic and kite-flying festivals, activities for pets, and dance competitions are held in the city's principal avenues. One event, the Ibero-American Theater Festival, has become the most important theater festival in Latin America.
- *Volunteer water saving.* A water shortage caused by the rupture of a main water conduit to Bogotá triggered the creation of a civic program to encourage water saving in everyday life. In a mere 3 months, the program diminished consumption 20% per inhabitant per day. Average consumption remains at that reduced level today, so investment in infrastructure has diminished.

- *Respect for diversity*. Respect for diversity and the visibility of social groups such as Afro-Colombians, natives, peasants, older people, and women, have been the goal of special policies in the city. An example of this is the LGBT (Lesbian, Gay, Transsexual and Bisexual) policy, implemented successfully by the local administration during the past few years.

14.5.4 Reconstructing City Spaces

The urban reconstruction of the city has played a determining role in the change the city has undergone during the past few years. Its most important contribution is probably related to public works in the city, complemented by the improvement of urban services. These improvements showed the citizens a new public management capacity associated with a new civic culture of respect for collective property, and the possibility of making progress even in periods during which the country faced serious development problems. It was a way of rendering the city's achievements visible in urban space.

14.5.5 The Recovery of Public Space

The public space recovery program is part of a larger initiative to build a more livable and friendly city that respects citizens and pedestrians, and provides the necessary spaces for their mobility, rest, or contact and recognition with other citizens. In short, the program consists of giving back to the city the dignity and significance of the spaces it uses as a collectivity, in which its inhabitants mix independently of their economic or social status. Based on respect for common patrimony, the purpose is to build a city that generates a sense of belonging, facilitates citizens' living together peaceably, and leads to the recognition of civic rights and duties.

In this sense, interventions were undertaken in spaces at different scales and in different places of the city.

Rather than public spaces – in terms of a non-private space, but not necessarily intended to generate social interchange – it is public domains this is all about: squares and parks animated by activities and cultural events, public libraries, sidewalks and boulevards that turn into catalysers of social life (Martin and Ceballos 2004: 101).

These public spaces were meant to trigger a new form of urban structure and improve its urban communities' quality of life. The following are some examples of the recovery of 764,000 m^2 of public spaces (sidewalks, squares) thanks to investments of close to \$273,196 million Colombian pesos (US\$ 119 million):

- The building of pedestrian spaces in areas of urban activity, recognized as urban centers, to allow the intense pedestrian use of commercial and service zones, in safe, comfortable and environmentally clean conditions. Most of these zones were built in peripheral residential neighborhoods which had had no appropriate spaces for these activities. The interventions in the Jimenez Avenue and Plaza San Victorino are two of the biggest recent public space restoration projects in Bogotá. Since the 1960s, San Victorino square, in the historic center of the city, became permanent informal market (see Fig. 14-10), that by 1998 had around 1,500 vendors.

Before

After

Fig. 14-10. San Victorino Square (Source Photograph by Cristina Salazar)

The recovery of the Plaza was made in 1999. The Colombian artist Edgar Negret made the sculpture that complements this plaza.

- The construction of an urban-scale pedestrian boulevard network as a set of corridors for pedestrian use, offering space for recreational use.
- The recovery, improvement, and maintenance of nearly 60% of the city's parks. The park network was conceived as an organizational element of the city's structure. The system of free metropolitan, urban, and district parks was built in relation to the strategic ecological systems (rivers, brooks, and hills), as a way to enhance them and support the preservation of natural spaces; at the same time, the park system is meant to complement the activities of the metropolitan center and the district and neighbourhood centers.
- Improving monumental public spaces to reinforce their status as representative places of the city, in which citizens recognize their role as citizens.
- The renovation of public facilities (public works, government offices, decentralized services), in order to recognize them as constitutive elements of the city, and ensure dignity in their forms and a welcoming attitude towards the city they belong to.

Since 1998, more than seven million m^2 of public space have been recovered.

14.5.6 The Restoration of Environmental Systems

Bogotá has a unique ecosystem. Its climate is tropical, but the city is at a very high altitude (2,600 m above sea level), with *páramos* (moorlands) and *humedales* (wetlands that consist of marshes and small lakes). Nearly 80% of these wetlands have been eliminated gradually in the accelerated urbanization process. The moorlands have also been affected by the extension of rural lands for agriculture and cattle-raising.

The city has engaged in restoration and conservation programs that included, where possible, the building of public spaces at the edges of sensitive areas, so as not to affect their environmental conditions.

Work has been carried out on almost all of the nine wetlands (667 ha) that remain in the city. For example, the largest survivor, Humedal Juan Amarillo (223 ha), was the object of a combined program of restoration and the construction of public spaces and a bicycle path.

The planning legislation integrated these elements in an ecological plan that supports the urban structure, articulated by environmental corridors between the hills and the river, following the course of rivers and brooks.

14.5.7 A New System of Transport and Mobility

The urban mobility program put into effect during the past few years has had a significant impact on the city. It includes five essential aspects:

- The recovery of sidewalks and the adaptation of road infrastructure. Providing the city with roads designed with adequate specifications for current traffic and, at the same time, providing roads with sidewalks appropriate for pedestrian circulation, with complementary street furniture, is a fundamental aspect of the mobility program.
- A new bus transport system through main avenues, the *Transmilenio*, started the total restructuring of the bus system. It is a high-capacity bus system (48,000 passengers per hour in one direction), that functions like a metro system. It is designed to respect citizens by providing a high-quality, efficient, consistent service at an accessible cost for users and for the district administration.

The system has four basic components:

1. An adequate infrastructure, composed of routes with exclusive central lanes in the most important avenues of the city (see Fig. 14-11). The routes have fixed stop points with covered stations that give access to the system, built and maintained by the public sector.

Fig. 14-11. The *Transmilenio* System

2. The operational system, in which articulated vehicles with a higher capacity (160 passengers) move through the exclusive bus routes. This network is complemented by *alimentadores* ("feeder" buses), which extend the system's area of influence. The feeder buses are operated by private enterprise.
3. The collection system consists of ticket production and sale, fabrication, installation and maintenance of reading equipment, information processing, and money handling, operated by private enterprise.
4. Planning, management, and control through an automatic control center is the responsibility of Transmilenio S.A., an industrial and commercial public enterprise created for this purpose.

In the first stage, completed in 2001, 38 km consisting of two routes were constructed (*Calle 80* and *Caracas*, *Autopista del Norte*), with 58 stations and 500 buses. In 2003–2004, the second phase was started with a new route, *Avenida de las Américas*, which connects the city center with the populous western districts.

In 2006, the second phase of the *Norte-Quito-Sur* and *Suba* routes, which serve the city's northwest and center-west, was finished, and the system consisted of 84 km of routes, 114 stations, 995 articulated buses and 403 feeder buses. About 1,470,000 passengers a day each pay the equivalent of about US$0.65 cents to use the system.

1. The bicycle path system was built as an alternative transport system in the city, cheap and non-polluting. It consists of a network of more than 250 km connecting different points in the city with residential and working zones. The bicycle paths are a project for Bogotá's future; the fact that they represent a non-contaminating, alternative mode of transport gives them a greater importance than that reflected by their current mobilization capacity (10% of all trips).
2. Private automobile restrictions. As a complement to the infrastructure and transport system programs, the city implemented the "*Pico y Placa*" ("Peak and Plate") program, which limits the circulation of private automobiles. Mindful of the effects that this type of standard has had in other cities (for example, it has led people to buy a second vehicle, and thus, pollute even more), the city limited the restriction to 40% of the daily vehicles during the peak hours (6:00 to 9:00 a.m. and 4:00 to 7:00 p.m.). This example of the administration's political will – which showed the citizens the urgency of controlling vehicle circulation – has had a positive effect on mobility indicators in the city but, above all, was well received by the inhabitants, who adapted their habits and schedules to the new measure.

3. No-car day. The city has decreed by referendum and popular vote the application of an annual no-car day. Probably the most interesting aspect of this measure, which has taken place for three consecutive years, is that bit by bit, it has become a normal day in the city, in which none of its activities are paralyzed. It is, like the bicycle paths, a project for Bogotá's future.

14.5.8 New and Better Facilities

To complement this urban transformation, the city has started various programs to provide itself with new and more modern facilities, constructed to the highest quality standards. Among these, attention should be drawn to the following:

- The public library network, which includes the construction of four big metropolitan libraries in strategic zones of the city (Virgilio Barco, El Tintal, El Tunal; the fourth, in Suba, is not yet complete at the time of publication), designed by renowned architects, which offer, in addition to basic library services, digital information, multimedia laboratories, and special areas for children's education. The District Library System (*Bibliored*) is composed of the four metropolitan libraries, six local district libraries, and eleven smaller neighborhood libraries, with educational as well as cultural programs, and interconnected services designed to reach all citizens equally. The program has had great success (Alcaldía de Bogotá 2000): the 6,500 m^2 of each of the big libraries are intensively used.
- An important increase in the number of schooling opportunities in the city's poorest areas (183,000 new student places in 4 years) has been made possible by the building of 50 new schools (some are still under construction) and the repair of 100 others, in an effort to adapt them to the needs of contemporary education. Schools have become central places in their respective areas, recognized and visited by the neighbors.

14.6 Challenges

As can be expected in complex and innovative set of programs, such as the ones developed in Bogotá, problems have arisen. Among others, the most evident for the citizens have become the following.

14.6.1 Mobility

The bus transport system, which uses exclusive lanes, has become a transport operation model for other cities throughout the world, but has presented the following problems, which must be overcome:

- Decrease in quality of service
- Decrease in the number of daily passengers: 1.4 instead of 1.5 million/day in July 2007, this has caused a profitability problem and an increase in the cost of tickets
- Considerable increase in the construction cost per kilometer; from US$5 million dollars during the first phase to over US$15 million dollars in the second

There have also been delays in the integration of the *Transmilenio* system with the other bus systems, a program which involves tariff integration and taking out of service nearly 50% of the present bus fleet. The transport industry has political power which it has used to delay urgent decisions. Technicians have not managed to build a viable integration scheme from the technical and political point of view.

14.6.2 Welfare Housing

During its first 3 years (2000–2003), Metrovivienda started four big projects that involved the construction of 34,000 units of welfare housing. After 4 years, 15,000 units had been built and occupied.

Unfortunately, these programs encountered obstacles that have held up the program during the past years – mainly objections from housing experts. They have criticized the size of the houses (an average of 35 m^2), arguing that they should be larger, and pointed out the relatively high cost of the solutions, which do not cover the lowest sector of the population nor, above all, the informally employed, who cannot acquire mortgage credit.

The administration of the last 4 years (2004–2008) put Metrovivienda into the hands of these dissident housing experts, who were not capable of managing it effectively, and created only about 8,000 units in 4 years, thus compromising the company's financial situation.

14.6.3 Planning in the City-Region

Perhaps the fundamental requirement for the future development of the region is the creation of a "metropolitan government," empowered to administer

Bogotá and the neighboring municipalities as part of an urban agglomeration. The annexation of six neighboring municipalities to Bogotá in 1954 postponed the creation of such a government and made it more difficult to develop a unified planning and administration system for public services and transportation. Today, Bogotá and every other municipality administers its jurisdiction independently, without any control or cohesion. The depletion of land available for urbanization in the city accelerates the urgency of this situation. Efforts made since 2002 to create a regional planning body and a regional economic development plan have not led to the desired results. It is a subject of absolute priority for the future development of the urban agglomeration.

14.7 Conclusion

Bogotá's experience during the last 15 years shows that the promotion of sustainable development in increasingly urbanized developing countries such as Colombia must be based on economic growth, social equality, cultural cohesion, and environmental protection. The construction of a strategy for the development of cities implies making the different approaches (globalization, local development, and sustainable development) compatible, in concrete terms, for each city's local needs. This requires a planning strategy, building consensus and solving conflicts, based on higher resource availability and better decision-making capacity by local authorities (Hassan and Zetter 2002: 14).

References

Alcaldía Mayor de Bogotá (2000) La Bogotá del Tercer Milenio. Historia de una Revolución Urbana, 1998–2000. Bogotá, Bogotá Viva

Alcaldía Mayor de Bogotá & Ministerio de Relaciones Exteriores de Colombia with the support of the University of Groningen, Netherlands, and Georgetown University, Washington DC (2004) Bogota, the proud revival of a city. Catalogue of the exhibition

Ardila G (ed) (2003) Territorio y Sociedad: El caso del Plan de Ordenamiento Territorial de Bogotá. Universidad Nacional de Colombia, Bogotá

Balbo M (2003) La nueva gestión urbana. In: Jordán R, Simioni D (eds) Gestión urbana para el desarrollo sostenible en América Latina y el Caribe. Cepal, Santiago de Chile

Borja J, Castells M (1997) Local y Global, la gestión de las ciudades en la era de la información. Taurus, UNCHS

Cortés M (2006) La anexión de los 6 municipios vecinos a Bogotá en 1954. Graduate thesis in Urbanismo dirigida por José Salazar Ferro, Universidad Nacional de Colombia, Bogotá

DAPD (2000) POT Bogotá: Documento Técnico de Soporte. Bogotá, capítulo 4

Duarte–Gutteman, Cal y Mayor y Asociados (2006) Formulación del plan maestro de movilidad para Bogotá DC, que incluye ordenamiento de estacionamientos. Bogotá

Faimboim I, Gaondour M, Uribe MC (eds) (2001) Misión de Reforma Institucional de Bogotá, Bases financieras para el desarrollo sostenible. Alcaldía Mayor de Bogotá, Bogotá

Garay LJ (1999) Construcción de una nueva sociedad. Cambio y Tercer Mundo Editores, Bogotá

Gómez Buendía H (1999) La hipótesis del Almendrón. In: Para dónde va Colombia? Tercer Mundo-Colciencias, Santafé de Bogotá

Gilbert A, Dávila J (2002) Bogotá: progress within a hostile environment. In: Dietz HA, Myers DJ (eds) Capital city politics in Latin America: democratization and empowerment. Lynne Rienner, Boulder, pp 29–63

Hassan A, Zetter R (2002) Sustainable development: between development and environmental agendas in the developing world. In: Zetter R, White R (eds) Planning in cities. ITDG Publishing, London

Londoño R (2006) De la Cortesía a la Cultura Ciudadana. In: Official catalogue of Colombia's exhibition at the Venice Biennale X international architecture exhibition. El Renacer de una Ciudad, Bogotá

Martin G (2006) La reinvención de lo público en Bogotá. In: Official catalogue of Colombia's exhibition in the Venice Biennale X international architecture exhibition. El Renacer de una Ciudad, Bogotá

Martin G, Ceballos M (2004) Bogotá, anatomía de una transformación - Políticas de seguridad ciudadana. Editorial Pontificia Universidad Javeriana, Bogotá

Salazar J, Del Castillo JC (2005) Estudio sobre el espacio público. CCB, Bogotá

15. Socially Sustainable Urban Development: The Case of São Paulo

Paulo Sandroni

The growth of Brazilian cities during the second half of the twentieth century has been intense. Large cities, including the former capital Rio de Janeiro (Brasília has been the capital since 1960) experienced rapid population growth, along with an expansion of the urban area and the concentration of poverty in peripheral regions.

The case of São Paulo is particularly significant. In 1850 the city, capital of the state of the same name, was not one of the ten largest in the country. But by the beginning of the twentieth century, São Paulo was the second-largest city in Brazil and in the 1950s, it surpassed Rio de Janeiro as the largest city in the country. São Paulo's population growth, population density, continuous constructed area, and GDP per capita for 1980 and 2007 are shown in Table 15-1.

This intense growth of population and area was initially determined by the expansion of the coffee plantations in the state's rural zones. As coffee was transported by railway to the Santos port (the largest port in Brazil), it necessarily passed through São Paulo. At the same time, immigrants from Europe and Japan who arrived in Santos and went inland to work in the coffee plantations passed also through São Paulo and many stayed there increasing the city population. After the crisis of the 1930s, import substitution resulted in intense industrial development in the city so that between 1930 and 1960, São Paulo became the largest industrial city in Latin America.

The city's growth at the beginning of the twentieth century was due mainly to international migration from European countries (Portugal, Spain, Italy, and Germany) and from Japan after 1908. But industrial growth from 1930 onwards attracted internal migrants, mainly from the northwest of the country and the rural areas of São Paulo state (Szmrecsany 2004).

A. Sorensen and J. Okata (eds.), *Megacities: Urban Form, Governance, and Sustainability*,

Table 15-1. Growth of São Paulo since 1980

	São Paulo municipality	**Metropolitan region of São Paulo**
Population in 1980	8,320,306	12,149,253
Population in 2007	9,967,061	18,584,893
Continuous constructed area in 2005	968.32 km²	1,957.00 km²
Population density in 2005*	7,119.99 persons/km²	2,376.16 persons/km²
Growth rate 1980–1991	1.15%	4.18%**
Growth rate 1991–2000	0.91%	3.68%**
Growth rate 2000–2007	0.55%	2.91%**
GDP per capita in 2005	R$ 24,082.86 (US$ 12,000.00)	R$ 21,771.63 (US$ 10,500.00

Source: de Miranda et al. (2005)
* This density refers to the population in the continuous constructed area. Part of the population is scattered along the rural area of the municipality of São Paulo and the Metropolitan Region of São Paulo
** Average population rate growth of the 49 municipalities belonging to the MRSP

The demand for urban land and infrastructure caused by this flow of migrants was considerable. Formerly, housing, water, sewage facilities, roads, and transportation had been provided privately by individual *fazendas* (farms). With migration into the city, the pressure on government to provide those services for newcomers who settled in the peripheral areas of the city increased sharply.

When new agricultural technologies were introduced in the 1960s, the substitution of crops (mainly coffee for soybeans) and the general mechanization of agriculture resulted in a sharp reduction of the labor force in the agricultural sector and a consequent increase in the urban population, especially in São Paulo. Workers who had lost their jobs had no other alternative than to migrate with their families to urban areas. In the cities, they settled into what was then considered the periphery, where land was cheap, and built shanties in areas where the reaction to this invasion was weaker – mainly in public areas at the edge of creeks or in conservation areas. The great majority of these new poor communities, or slums, had no infrastructure and the pressure for public investment increased considerably (Fig. 15-1).

During the 1970s, the devaluation of the dollar after the abandonment of the Bretton Woods Agreement and the economic crisis that followed the

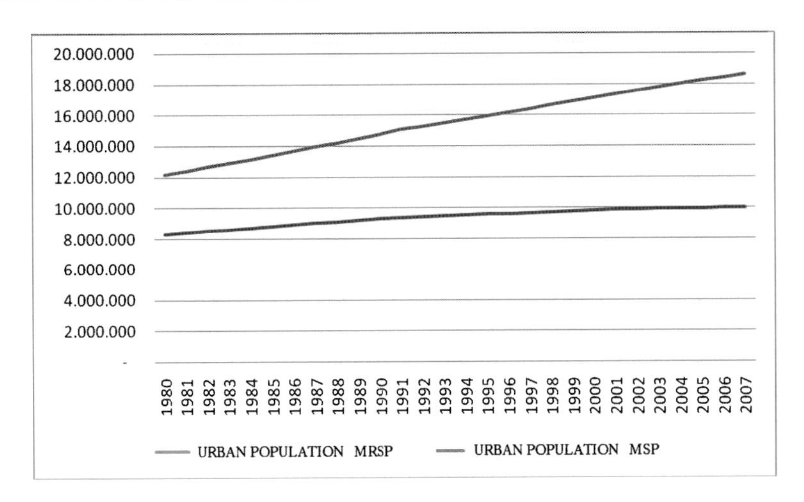

Fig. 15-1. Population growth of São Paulo

rise in commodity prices, especially oil, affected the Brazilian economy strongly. Both external and public debt increased sharply. Inflation soared as devaluation was used to stimulate exports in order to pay interest on the external debt. The government's investment capacity dwindled to almost nothing. São Paulo was one of the cities most affected by this process.

At this point, there was no capacity to maintain existing or build new infrastructure or provide services (such as transportation, water, sewage, or waste disposal). Nevertheless, the demands of the poor in the slums on the periphery of the city – and in some cases in the new areas where the middle and upper middle classes were living – could no longer be ignored. The end of Brazil's military dictatorship and the return to democratic institutions (such as free elections) meant that the new political parties had to try to attract votes.

No longer was it possible simply to demolish slums. The demands of the poor had to be considered, even if only in the pre-electoral period. New methods were needed to deal with the so-called "social question" and the city's management. The authorities not only had to address the presence of slums in the periphery, but also increasing traffic congestion in the central areas of the city where the upper classes lived.

Urban sprawl, resulting from high land prices in the central zones and the expansion of the city's peripheral areas, increased infrastructure costs (transportation, for instance) and led to negative and perverse consequences. The high costs of services such as transportation, lighting, sewage, waste disposal, or paving meant that poor families either received very low-quality services or no services at all.

This urban development process was not sustainable either from the economic, or from the social and environmental perspective. Economic sustainability required an investment capacity and expenditure on new services that the municipality could not afford. Social sustainability depended, among other factors, on the reversal of the segregation process (gentrification) caused by high prices for the best-located land, caused by the urban intensification process itself. And environmental sustainability was menaced by the occupation of conservation areas by lower- and middle-class housing, water contamination in the city's rivers by residential and industrial sewage disposal without treatment, and air pollution caused by industry and automobiles, particularly old buses and trucks.

The solution to or mitigation of these problems required new planning instruments, including new urban legislation, new institutions, new forms of city management, new ways to finance urban development, new relations between the private and the public sector, and a new approach to the problem of the slums. As we will see, not all of the needed instruments were created, and even where new planning instruments were put in place, in some cases the outcome was not what was intended.

15.1 New Urban Legislation: The Embú Letter

The need for a new approach to urban development emerged in the 1970s with the chaotic, unsustainable growth of cities, especially the two largest in Brazil: Rio de Janeiro and São Paulo. Architects, sociologists, jurists, urban specialists, and public servants began to propose and discuss new intervention instruments in urban development.

An important result of these discussions was the "Embú Letter" (Fundação Prefeito Faria Lima 1997), the product of a meeting in 1976 in Embú, in the state of São Paulo. One of the most important concepts of this document was the concept of *solo criado*, which means the opportunity to increase the floor area ratio (FAR) of a building plot or give owners or developers greater latitude in construction than they had had before. This was a consequence of the separation of the right of property and the right to build provided in the legislation. The opportunity to construct larger buildings could be granted if the public administration presented a proposal to the Council to change the zoning law.

Under the previously existing legislation, every landowner could construct a building for which the FAR could range from 1 to 4 times the plot area, and in some special cases 6 or even 12 times. But for the great majority of areas, the permitted FAR was 1 or 2. The new approach meant that plots that had a FAR of 1 or 2, if the builder met certain conditions (specially infrastructure limitations), could be increased to 3 or 4.

Another important contribution of the Embú Letter was the stipulation that the benefits of any increase in FAR (or a change in use) granted by the public sector to private owners should be shared. The principle on which this requirement was based was the sense that if the public sector grants more construction rights to the owner, it is in effect "creating" land value, and this new value created should be divided between them.

15.2 The Onerous Grant (*Outorga Onerosa*) Mechanism

Generally, all changes in zoning granting more rights to construct or changing the potential uses for plots increased the value of the land. This increased value had formerly benefited only the owner of the land. With the new approach under the Embú Letter, the question arose: how much of this added value should be appropriated by the public sector and how much by the private owner of the land? And, more important, in practical terms, how should this instrument operate? (De Ambrosis 1999).

With the end of the military dictatorship in the first half of 1980 and the reintroduction of elections, the old methods of slum demolition and expulsion of the families who formed slums on private land were not possible any more. So the first and concrete example of value increment appropriation by the public sector through the onerous grant mechanism (*outorga onerosa*) happened under the Operações Interligadas (Interlinked Operations) law, issued in the city of São Paulo in 1987 (Sandroni 2000).

The main goal of this new legislation (which was not inspired by the Embú Letter) was to solve the problem of well-located private land occupied by slums. A private landowner whose plots were occupied by slums could propose an increase in FAR or change the uses of the land and share the increased value with the public sector. The public sector received a minimum of 50% of this increased value. The benefits received by the public sector were destined exclusively to build social housing (at first, this was to be done by the landowner; later it was built by the government with money paid by the landowner) in other areas of the city for the families that would be displaced.

Many operations of this kind were approved, but with a very important change: the provision operated even in cases where the land was not occupied by slums. The majority of Interlinked Operations after 1988 were on land that did not contain slums. But part of the value appropriated by the public sector had to be used in the construction of houses for families removed from slums located in other places of the city, mainly areas subject to floods and landslides (Azevedo 1994).

These operations lasted until 1998, at which point they were declared unconstitutional because although there was a law permitting them, they contradicted the existent zoning law and regulations, and changes in these laws were attributes of the Legislative and not of the Executive. However, during almost 12 years (from 1987 until 1998), about 115 projects of this kind were approved and the value appropriated by the public sector (around $100 million U.S.) financed the construction of more than 11,000 houses for families that had formerly lived in slums.

For a city like São Paulo, this was not a large amount of money or significant number of social houses constructed. Nor did these operations represent better city planning; on the contrary, they were thought to interfere with the Master Plan (even if the existent Master Plan was obsolete and a new one had not yet been approved), because they were ad hoc, led to distortions in the zoning law, and created privileges for landowners and developers (even if they had to pay for the benefits received).

But this practice established the principle of appropriation by the public sector of part of the increased value of a property (because this increment was due to actions or new norms provided by the public sector) and negotiating this participation with the private sector. Until 1986 the private sector had appropriated (with few exceptions) *all* the increased value resulting from changes in urban legislation or zoning.

For landowners and developers, this new legislation, known as Interlinked Operations, meant that they did not have to wait for changes in the zoning laws that occurred only once in a year and sometimes were very complex and quite "expensive" (often they had to bribe legislators to approve specific changes for specific properties). Owners and developers learned to share these value increases with the public sector and were convinced that the arrangement was favorable to them. They agreed to pay for the additional construction rights they needed for their projects because it was faster and less expensive than it would have been if they had to buy additional land, which was not always available.

Another positive side effect of this practice was that public servants gained expertise in valuing land and negotiating the increment value with the private sector. Although in terms of planning, this practice did not contribute to the city's urban development, it provided extra financial resources to help solve part of the problem of slums located in risky areas, and thus contributed (on a very modest scale) to financial and social sustainability.

15.3 The New Constitution and Urban Development

In 1988 when Interlinked Operations began to be used in São Paulo, a new Constitution was approved in Brazil. Articles 182 and 183 concerning urban development established, among other things, the principle of the social function of land ownership (de Castro 2003) and enshrined the separation of the right of property from the right to construct. But the regulatory acts necessary for these two articles to become operational were approved only in 2001. In that year the regulatory law (Law 10.257, *Estatuto da Cidade*, or City Bill) was approved and only then did the new instrument begin to have practical effects in all Brazilian cities.

Nevertheless, many cities and states did not wait 13 years to approve the local regulatory acts necessary to use these two constitutional articles in their jurisdictions. They included these constitutional principles in their specific constitutions, approving the complementary legislation necessary to make them valid and operational (Furtado 1997).

The city of São Paulo was a pioneer in this matter and in 1990 adapted its Municipal Constitution (*Lei Organica do Municipio*) to the Federal Constitution, regulated Urban Operations, and sent both of them to the City Council for approval.

15.4 What is a Joint Urban Operation?

A joint urban operation, usually known as an urban operation (UO), can be understood as a structural transformation instrument for a part of the city, promoted through a partnership between public authorities and private developers. It involves the participation of landowners, investors, residents, and other stakeholders and has to be approved by the City Council.

For this partnership to take effect, UOs entail certain elements. The most important are urban incentives tied to contribution payments that attract private investment and induce developments to provide the transformations desired in urban policy. These incentives, originally defined by the specific laws of each urban operation, are now established in a general form by the *Estatuto da Cidade*. The incentives are changes in land characteristics (FAR, for instance), flexibility in land use and occupation requirements, and changes in building norms.

In certain cases, the city may issue and sell Cepacs (Certificates for Additional Construction Potential) in auctions to developers, which corresponds to additional rights to build. (This instrument will be explained in more detail latter).

The UOs affect certain areas of the city and are intended to promote urban interventions according to specific objectives defined in the Master Plan and in municipal urban policy. These interventions presuppose mid- and long-term management measures such as a new urban plan for the area, land readjustment mainly in areas occupied by slums, improvements to public spaces, the definition of real estate potential, and land use requirements (for a detailed description, see Montandon and De Sousa 2007).

In the city of São Paulo, UOs were mentioned in early Master Plans, but as a planning instrument they were incorporated only in the 2002 Master Plan. During the 1990s, the city administration sent individual proposals for Urban Operations to the Council. In other words, Urban Operations were used before 2002, but did not form an interlinked group of planning interventions for the city as a whole.

15.5 The Practice of Urban Operations

In practical terms, an urban operation is an intervention in a large area of the city that requires infrastructure and urban improvements such as avenues, drainage, housing for low-income families, public facilities, and other investments. The funds necessary to allow these investments should come from the incremental value realized by changes in zoning to permit increases in FAR and changes of use. Owners of properties inside the perimeter of the Urban Operation may propose projects that require changes in FAR, permitted uses, or building footprints (Sandroni 2004).

The administration examines the project and analyzes whether it is satisfactory from an architectural and urban point of view. If the project is approved, the next step is to estimate the value increment and determine how to share this value between the owner or developer and the public sector.[1] Each Urban Operation has specific instruments to determine the public-sector participation in the value created by the new zoning coefficients. In some UOs, participation is determined by a minimum percentage of the increment value created; in others, it is realized by selling Cepacs, as we will see later.

From 1990 on, 13 Urban Operations were proposed, but only five were approved before 2008: three during the 1990s and two in 2004. These operations were the Anhangabaú-Centro UO, the Água Branca UO, the Faria Lima UO, the Àgua Espraiada UO, and the Rio Verde-Jacu UO, which was included in the São Paulo Master Plan of 2002 (Law 13.872 of 2004). The total area occupied by these UOs represents about 20% of the total area of the municipality. Each one of these operations had particular characteristics and different motivations.

[1] After the approval of Cepacs in the Faria Lima and Água Espraiada UOs, the procedures changed, as seen in the description of these UOs, below.

The new Master Plan of 2002 consolidated four UOs created before its approval and created nine more: Diagonal Sul, Diagonal Norte, Carandiru-Vila Maria, Rio Verde-Jacu, Vila Leopoldina, Vila Sônia, Celso Garcia, Santo Amaro, and Tiquatira. But before April 2008, only the Rio Verde-Jacu UO was approved by City Council.

15.6 Urban Operations in Sao Paulo Since 1991

15.6.1 The Anhangabaú-Centro Urban Operation (Law 12.349/97)

Initially this UO affected an area of about 450 ha. Later the area was enlarged to 582 ha and the projects was renamed Urban Operation Centro, because it was located in the center of the city.

The main objectives were the renewal of the historical center of the city, the completion of some investments in infrastructure, the restoration of public spaces and buildings with historical and cultural interest, the doubling of the area covered by drainage system, and the regularization of the building occupied by the São Paulo Stock Exchange Market which had been enlarged beyond the area permitted, and was required to pay an economic compensation for this difference to be authorized to operate.

A few private projects were presented, most requiring regularization and/or change in uses and to a lesser degree an increase in FAR. The economic compensation of these operations was not very significant – about 12 million dollars (until 2007).

This UO did not produce the expected effects of attracting new private investments and population increment. Despite the incentives offered, many private firms and families moved out of the central area to other regions. Only departments of the state and municipality governments (and the City Hall itself) moved there and mitigated the outflow of investments and people from the Central area. Nevertheless, the consequence was a population decrease, income reduction, and a considerable number of empty buildings. But it is reasonable to point out that these negative tendencies could be much more intense if the incentives of the UO were not present.

The most deteriorated area inside the perimeter of this UO of the old center of São Paulo covered approximately 23 blocks known as "Cracolandia," where narcotics, crack, and other drugs were traded freely. The great majority of buildings were irregular, because they were constructed, maintained or operated not according to the building regulations and/or zoning norms.

Many commercial activities closed when the administration began to prepare the area for new investments after September 2005, when the city declared the area of public interest and created the possibility of urban and architectural revitalization. In October 2007 the administration began the expropriations of buildings and houses within these 23 blocks, but the revitalization process is very slow and up to May 2009 little significant change had occurred within that perimeter.

As this area was inside the perimeter of the Anhangabaú-Centro Urban Operation, the project could have used the mechanisms permitted by the UO to succeed. But the administration wanted to use a new instrument to finance the entire project: the Fundo de Investimento Imobiliário (FII), inspired by the REIT (Real Estate Investment Fund) used in the United States. The idea is to obtain and prepare land through expropriation, determine higher urban coefficients (FAR and others), and sell bonds to interested firms to attract new activities and spur the construction of new buildings in the renewed area.

This revitalization project is one of the largest in the city in the last decades but problems over expropriations and private partnerships have delayed the conclusion of the project and consequently the beginning of concrete interventions in the area.

15.6.2 The Àgua Branca Urban Operation (Law n. 11.774/95)

This UO covers about 500 ha and is located in a relatively downgraded area – the Barra Funda neighborhood. This area was formerly occupied by traditional industries, but is now home to commercial enterprises, service industries, and middle-class housing. As an industrial area, the land had a very low FAR (ranging from 0.5 to 1.0). The new activities required significant increases in FAR and, in some cases, changes in use.

Before 2005, only a few private projects were proposed, although one of them was a large one requiring more than 200,000 m^2 of additional construction area and an increase of FAR from 1 to 4. In this UO, the minimum compensation for the public sector from benefits granted to the developer was 60% of the increased value, which would have resulted in about 20 million dollars compensation to be used in infrastructure improvements and construction of social housing.[2] This proposal was to build 13 large

[2]This slum can be seen on Googlearth at 23 30′ 46.89″ S and 46 41′ 11.16″ W at an altitude of 570 m. Half of this slum is already urbanized. But after the approval of the UO, another slum was created inside its perimeter. This new one can be seen at 23 30′ 53.95″ S and 46 40′ 46.92″ W at an altitude of 490 m.

commercial and service industry buildings. But during the economic recession from 1999 to 2003, the developer suffered losses and could not continue the project. He finished only four of the 13 buildings scheduled. The compensation from the project ceased as well, and the entrepreneur delivered only 20% of the $20 million the city had expected.

After 2005, with the beginning of a new expansion cycle of real estate business, more than 15 new projects were proposed. Those already approved have so far yielded more than 13 million dollars in capture value to be used for infrastructure and social housing. Other projects for residential buildings that are currently being examined by the administration may yield up to 130 million dollars.

Among these new projects is a large one that is worth mentioning because it represents a break from the traditional developer's attitude towards the construction of houses for low-income families.

The Água Branca UO contains an area defined as a ZEIS (one of the *Zonas Especiais de Interesse Social* or Special Zones of Social Interest).[3] The ZEIS areas can be occupied only by social housing, or a specific percentage of the housing must be destined for low-income families. The main reason for establishing these zones is to avoid or minimize gentrification, and prevent the displacement of low-income families from areas where the price of land is rising as a result of public investments and the demand for land has shifted from low-income households to medium- or higher-income buyers.

One of the projects proposed was a large one in a ZEIS area. On a large plot of 63,000 m^2, the developer intended to build 27 buildings containing 2,714 apartments ranging from 45 to 100 m^2. This means that developers had found a way to profit from constructing houses for low-income families.

15.6.3 The Faria Lima Urban Operation (Law n. 11.732/95)

With an area of 450 ha, this UO is a quite different from the Centro or Água Branca UOs. While those UOs were located in derelict areas with considerable unused infrastructure capacity and a possibility for higher densities, this area was already dynamic, with rising land prices, intense real-estate development, and pressure to extend a road called Faria Lima Avenue. Although the existing densities were not high, developers demanded the maximum allowed in the legislation (FAR 4); this change could only be obtained properly by the approval of a UO.

[3]The 2002 Master Plan established 750 ZEISs (*Zonas Especiais de Interesse Social*), and 22 ZEPAMs (*Zonas Especiais de Proteção Ambiental*, or Special Zones for Environmental Protection) in the municipal area of São Paulo.

Therefore, the motivation for this UO was to increase FAR and permit changes in uses in the area affected by the construction of the avenue (which had no priority from a transportation point of view) to allow developers to construct high-quality residential, commercial, and service buildings (São Paulo 2000).

The decision to extend the avenue was taken *before* the UO proposal was presented to City Council and despite the protests of people who would be affected by expropriations. The easiest way to obtain an increase in FAR and the change in uses was to approve the UO. The alternative (in the absence of a UO) was to construct the avenue and then change the zoning in the UO area. This would be a much more complicated process demanding more negotiation between developers and City Council and the inclusion in the new zoning of individual properties. The public sector wanted a quick solution that would include all the area affected by the enlargement of the avenue. So the administration approved the UO, even though it meant that developers and owners had to share the value increased caused by the zoning changes.

The avenue extension began in 1994 and the UO was approved in 1995. The cost of expropriations and the construction of the avenue are difficult to estimate, because the administrations between 1993 and 2001 were not distinguished by transparency, but the investment was probably about 150 million dollars. This is a significant amount of money, and the expenditure was financed by the municipal budget, causing a deficit and consequently a public debt with an average interest rate of more than 15% a year.

By March 2009, the Faria Lima UO had produced about 400 million dollars in economic compensations and only now, 13 years later, we can say that the pay back of the initial investment of 150 million dollars (interests considered) has been completed.

Moreover, this UO contains more than 800 thousand m^2 to be sold over the next five or so years, so a considerable "profit" will be realized. The problem is that this "profit" cannot be used to pay down the debt incurred and inflated by the interest paid during these years by the expropriations and the construction of the avenue. The income obtained can only be used in new interventions *inside* the perimeter of the UO. It may even be that the income obtained in the future by selling Cepacs will be more than is the amount needed for work inside the perimeter of this UO. If that happens, how will the extra income be used?[4]

[4] One of the conditions of a UO is that all the income appropriated by the public sector must be used inside its perimeter. This restriction should be changed to allow the development of less developed areas of the city. It is reasonable to use a percentage of income, say 20%, produced in UOs in affluent areas for infrastructure improvements in low-income areas.

It is important to point out that the Faria Lima and Água Espraiada UOs, by the removal of slums[5] and the displacement of low- and middle-class families by high-income families provoked the highest level of gentrification among UOs. This topic will be discussed further below.

15.6.4 The Àgua Espraiada Urban Operation (Law 13.260/2001)

The Água Espraiada UO occupies about 1,425 ha and was approved in 2001 after Água Espraiada Avenue had been constructed. The construction of the avenue required the demolition of slums (Fix 2001) and was associated with a process of gentrification.

In the Água Espraiada UO, as in Faria Lima, the construction of the avenue and the necessary expropriations demanded a huge amount of money. This money was obtained through increasing public debt, although the figures for principal and interest paid are not available. Nevertheless, as the avenue was built many years before the onerous grant mechanism began to operate, it is likely that (as with Faria Lima Avenue) a considerable amount of money was dedicated to pay interest on the debt produced by the initial investment.

This UO was approved after the introduction of the *Estatuto da Cidade*, so it could use the Cepacs mechanism to capture value from the onerous grant.[6] The avenue is not yet finished and its extension required funding for a bridge over the Pinheiros River (already completed with funds from Cepac auctions) and for a link to a road (Imigrantes) that connects São Paulo and the Port of Santos. At least eight slums must be removed and it will be necessary to construct social housing for the affected families inside the perimeter of the UO, in addition to the high cost of constructing the avenue itself.

The Água Espraiada UO has 4.85 million m^2 of additional area to be sold through auctions of 3.75 million Cepacs (each Cepac may represent more than 1 m^2). As of November 2008, 1,180,000 Cepacs (or nearly 24%

[5]The last remaining slum in an area declared a ZEIS can been seen using Googlearth at 23 35′ 36.11″ S and 46 41′ 24.66″ W at an altitude of 390 m.

[6]There is some evidence that between 2004 and 2007 there was a kind of "cannibalism" between the Faria Lima and Água Espraiada UOs. The initial price of Cepacs in the former was R$1,100.00 and in the latter R$300.00 and some areas were very near each other. So the developers preferred to buy Cepacs in Água Espraiada and not in Faria Lima. All the auctions in Água Espraiada were successful, and the first two of Faria Lima were failures: the first one sold only 10% of the total offered, and the second 27%, but in this case only 10,000 Cepacs were offered.

of the total stock) had been sold, with an income of 320 million dollars. The extension of the avenue will demand the removal of many slums located in the edge of the Água Espraiada creek and the construction of new houses for these families inside the perimeter of the UO. The funds to finance the construction of these houses and finish the construction of the avenue are already in hands of the City Hall. It is interesting to say that the money obtained in the first Cepacs auctions in 2004 was to be used for the construction of 600 units of social housing for families from the Jardim Edith slum[7] and a bridge over the Pinheiros River. The bridge was constructed, but only now (June 2009) the decision to build the social housing was taken.

15.6.5 The Rio Verde-Jacu Urban Operation (Law 13.872/04)

This UO covers nearly 7,400 ha, making it the largest one studied here. It is located in the periphery of the city and one of its poorest areas, so the construction of the necessary infrastructure could not be financed with funds collected through the sale of additional potential construction rights, because developers were not interested in investing there immediately.

The main objective was to attract industrial, commercial, and services activities through incentives such as the reduction or temporarily elimination of taxes. The creation of employment is also an important objective. This UO is also intended to improve transportation and connections with the rest of the city while creating public and green areas for leisure and environmental preservation and protection. The UO established an additional potential construction area of 3,570,000 m^2.

This UO introduced an element of public participation, as its Executive Committee was composed not only of City Hall experts and administrators, but also included representatives of local businesses, workers, and people living inside the perimeter. However, since its creation in 2004, this Committee has met only once. As of 2008, very little had been done to implement its possibilities.

Another problem with this UO is that it includes many environmental protection areas, and for some projects it takes too long to secure the necessary permits. Moreover, the high costs for the necessary Environmental Impact Studies and the low returns expected by private developers offer

[7] Until April 2009 this slum could be seen using Googlearth at 23 36′ 48.62″ S and 46 41′ 39.01″ W at an altitude of 420 m.

little incentive for investment, except for projects with high state participation. This UO is not yet fully operating, although the municipal government through other mechanisms has attracted investments of about 20 million dollars of private firms with the creation of around 1,000 jobs.

15.7 Impact of Urban Operations

Even a superficial look at the Urban Operations created before the 2002 São Paulo Master Plan indicates that they do not constitute steps in a clearly articulated plan. They were introduced to solve particular problems, not linked with other regions of the city or not answering questions arising from the analysis of the city as a whole. But at least they created mechanisms to capture value and contributed to a sustainable process of financing infrastructure and social housing. Even if the construction of avenues in the Faria Lima and Água Espraiada UOs meant the expulsion of poor communities living in slums and facilitated gentrification, the instrument represented by the UO helped to mitigate these processes.

It is important to note that the process of gentrification had already begun *before* the approval of the Faria Lima and Água Espraiada UOs, and were intensified with the construction of the two avenues in these areas. The creation of ZEISs inside the Água Branca, Água Espraiada, and Faria Lima UOs helped mitigate the problem of slums and blocked (at least until 2008) the expulsion of the remaining slums, especially in Água Espraiada and Faria Lima (including the Coliseu and Jardim Edith slums). And, although developers' lobbies are exerting pressure to eliminate them, the UO and the Master Plan have determined that these slums must be urbanized where they are, or if families are removed, they have to remain inside the perimeter of each UO (and not expelled to the periphery), thereby mitigating the gentrification process.

But there are many menaces against ZEISs. During the revision of the Master Plan of 2002 in 2007 (every 5 years the Plan may be revised) there was a frustrated intent to eliminate ZEISs from the Água Espraiada UO. Currently additional UOs have been proposed and it is probable that the offensive against ZEISs will be relaunched.

UOs were the only instrument the administration had at its disposal to direct or control (or to try to control) urban development until the approval of the São Paulo Master Plan of 2002. Nevertheless, practices and instruments created and used in the UOs and in many cases their contradictory results can show the narrow limits they provide in attempting to plan the development of the city in a balanced and sustainable way.

We will now examine the Cepacs as a tool for capturing value from the onerous grant mechanism, or as an instrument to support the financial sustainability of urban development.

15.8 Cepacs: A New Instrument of Value Capture

The Faria Lima and Água Espraiada UOs included a new instrument, the Cepac, which means certificate (bond) for potential additional rights of construction. This instrument could be used by the city to capture value or receive economic compensation from projects proposed by developers. It was created and included in the Faria Lima UO in 1995, but only began to operate fully in 2004, after the approval of *Estatuto da Cidade* in 2001, when Cepacs could be used in all Brazilian cities.

The Cepacs are issued by the City Hall through EMURB (Empresa Municipal de Urbanização) and sold in electronic auctions in São Paulo stock market (Bovespa) and may only be used inside the perimeter of the UO in which they were issued. They give the bearer additional building rights as larger floor area ratio and footprints and change uses in his plot. Financially speaking the result of selling Cepacs means that developers give the public administration economic compensation for the new building rights received.

In São Paulo, only two (Faria Lima and Água Espraiada) of the five UO approved can use Cepacs. The others don't use it because when they were approved they did not include Cepacs as a tool to capture increment value. The total amount of Cepacs that can be issued depends on the total additional area each UO is able to support. This number depends on the previous analysis of the group of architects, engineers, economists and public servants that compare this upper limit with the existent infrastructure and all the additional works that will be financed with funds originated by selling Cepacs.

In each UO Cepacs have the same face value but correspond to a different amount of m^2 depending on the location of the plot where they are going to be used. For instance, in Faria Lima UO the initial price of Cepacs (determined by Faria Lima UO Law) is about 550 dollars but may correspond to a minimum of 0.8 m^2 to a maximum of 2.8 m^2 depending on the sector in which these Cepacs are going to be used. This difference is due to the different prices of plots depending on the sector inside the perimeter where they are located. If a developer uses his Cepacs in very expensive plots each Cepac will correspond to 0.8 m^2; if the use is in very cheap areas each Cepac will enable him to construct additional 2.8 m^2. The final price of Cepacs in auctions may be higher than this initial value all depending on the interest of the buyers. Between Dec. 2004 and March 2009 this price rose from 550 dollars to 850 dollars. In Agua Espraiada the initial value of Cepacs was 150 dollars and the correspondence in m^2 ranged from 1.0 to 3.0 m^2. Between July 2004 and Oct. 2008 prices rose from 150 dollars to 270 dollars.

One of the main advantages to the city of this form of value capture is to obtain compensation *before* the developer begins the construction of a project, so the public sector may finance the construction of infrastructure without incurring a deficit or public debt or using budget resources that could be employed in other activities, such as education or health.

For the developer, to buy Cepacs is to buy a right to construct. These rights may be used whenever the real estate business cycle recommends doing so, or when the entrepreneur decides is the best moment to launch a project. The City Hall may also use Cepacs, through private auctions, to pay contractors (if they accept) who have contracts to build infrastructure. In these private auctions there are no bids as in public auctions. The City Hall sends letters to creditors offering to pay the debts with Cepacs at a determined value, generally the price of the last auction. In Faria Lima UO between Dec. 2004 and Oct. 2008 these private auctions produced an income of about 80 million dollars.

In other words, Cepacs may be used directly as a non-budgetary fund to pay for necessary goods and services, renew infrastructure or construct social housing.

Between July 2004 and March 2009, the income produced by Cepacs in the Faria Lima and Água Espraiada UOs was, respectively, 260 million dollars and 320 million dollars or a total of 640 million dollars considering all public and private auctions.

The income from each square meter sold by Cepacs yields a bigger revenue for the public sector than was produced using the former mechanism of a percentage ranging from 50 to 60% of the land value increase. A sample of 12 important projects in Faria Lima UO shows that if Cepacs had been used, the income would have risen from 31 million dollars to 140 million dollars. Moreover, in the auctions held to date, prices have risen around 25% over inflation in the Faria Lima UO, and in average more than 50% in the Água Espraiada UO.

15.9 Price Increase of Land in Urban Operations

To exercise the additional construction rights provided by Cepacs it is necessary to have land in the physical sense of the word. In other words, the use of Cepacs depend on the ownership of land inside the perimeter of an UO. So the demand for land rises, along with prices. This is especially true of the Faria Lima UO. We have no consistent data to demonstrate this effect for all UOs, but indirectly we may estimate the rise in prices in the Faria Lima UO.

Some important differences can be noted by comparing the situation before 1996 with the later period, when the Faria Lima UO projects had begun. The average price per square meter of constructed area in the perimeter increased from R$1.681 in the 1991–1996 period, to R$1.916 in the 1996–2001 period, a 14% increase, while during the contraction of the business cycle in the metropolitan region of São Paulo (RMSP) in the same period, prices *decreased* from R$1.211 to R$1.064, or by 12%. Therefore the relative increase in prices per square meter in the Faria Lima UO relative to that of the São Paulo region, was around 26%. This considerable price increment contributed to the gentrification process. But this increase reflected not only the rise in land prices, but also the high quality of construction.

15.10 Real Estate Concentration and Tax Collection

To estimate the impact of UOs on land concentration and the increase in income from property taxes, we will also use data from the Faria Lima UO, where a considerable land concentration can be observed.

This concentration was due, on one hand, to the fact that since the 1950s the region has been occupied by single-family houses on small and medium-sized plots (between 200 and 400 m^2) and, on the other, to the fact that new commercial and, to a lesser extent, residential buildings need greater areas for new architectural projects, especially those incorporating luxury elements.

For instance, 115 selected projects approved between 1996 and 2003 required the use of 657 plots, for an average of 5.7 plots per project. Approximately 65 projects involved the construction of residential buildings and the remaining 50 were business buildings.

The changes caused by the replacement of single-family constructions by upper-middle-class residential and commercial buildings resulted in a substantial increase in the income of IPTU (the urban property tax or tax charged over land and buildings in urban areas) in the region. Many blocks previously occupied by single and two-story homes constructed in the 1950s and lasting for 25–30 years, enjoyed a tax (IPTU) discount for building obsolescence of up to 30%. They were replaced with new buildings of several floors and of a high construction standard for which the discount was zero. A higher tax is levied on higher quality buildings, and our estimates indicate that the tax per square meter constructed may have been between 2.7 times and 4.4 times the former tax.

As the number of square meters constructed increased in the region, the total amount of IPTU collected must have risen considerably. Therefore the mechanism of value capture (in this case made viable by the UO) also helped increase the amount of tax collected for the city. Nevertheless, this is also a manifestation of the gentrification process, because not only did the prices of land and construction rise, but also the property taxes. These increases restricted the access of lower-middle-class families to the region.

15.11 Impact on Construction Density, Population, and Gentrification

During the 1990s, some indicators show that the population was abandoning the Faria Lima OU area. The same phenomenon was happening in other traditional and central areas of the city. This process of population decrease had already been observed before the approval of the UOs, but it intensified after 1996.

In the case of Faria Lima, building density increased: a simple examination of aerial photographs between 1994 and 2001 shows this clearly. This apparent contradiction – less population, more buildings – is explained by the considerable presence of commercial and service buildings, which replaced the homes of lower-middle-class families. This finding is confirmed by the census data, since residential densities fell considerably between 1991 and 2000, from 27 to 22 persons per hectare.

The combined increase in building height for residential and business buildings and in income, with the reduction in household density, is another signal of the gentrification process in the Faria Lima OU area during the 1990s.

This gentrification process intensified when the extension of Avenue Faria Lima (and the construction of Avenue Água Espraiada) began in the mid of 1990 with the demolition of slums and displacement of middle-class residents through expropriation of the necessary areas for the construction of the avenue. This was the first stage of the gentrification process.

The second wave occurred when developers who needed large areas to construct high-quality buildings offered large sums to lower-middle-class owners of small plots or the owners of small business units. In this sense the replacement of lower-middle-class families and small business units by high-income groups and large international firms resulted also in a concentration of land ownership.[8]

Yet even if these lower-middle-class families suffered pressure to leave the area and social problems created by displacement, they were at least financially compensated, because the price of land rose considerably. The same did not happen with families living in slums: they were simply expelled with a very small amounts of compensation.[9]

15.12 A New Master Plan

A new Master Plan for São Paulo was approved in 2002. Between 1987 (when the first legislation for value capture was created) and 2002, the main instruments of urban intervention were the Urban Operations, since Interlinked Operations were forbidden in 1998. But this new Master Plan created at least three instruments to promote sustainability, one related to financial sustainability, one to social sustainability, and the third to environmental sustainability. The new Master Plan also consolidated the existing UOs and created nine more.

15.13 New Urban Operations and the General Reduction of Floor Area Ratio

The Master Plan of São Paulo approved in 2002 incorporated and adapted all the instruments permitted by the *Estatuto da Cidade* approved in 2001. The four UOs operating were consolidated and improved (with the creation of ZEISs inside their perimeters) and nine more were created.[10]

---

[8]A sample of eight projects with land areas ranging from 3,500 to 5,500 m^2 showed an average fusion of 17 independent lots per project.

[9]The last slum remaining in the Faria Lima perimeter is Coliseu, with no more than 100 houses. The area occupied by the slum was declared a ZEIS (Special Zone of Social Interest) and it will likely be urbanized. But considering the pressure exerted by developers, it is possible that the present administration (2009–2012) will try to change the law to eliminate the ZEIS status of the area, because it is one of the more valuable areas within the Faria Lima UO perimeter. This slum is interesting, because it is surrounded by very modern and expensive buildings. It can been seen in Googlearth at 23 35′ 36.11" S and 46 41′ 24.66" W at an altitude of 390 m.

[10]The present administration (2009–2012) sent to City Council a project (PL 0671/2007) proposing the creation of three more Urban Operations: Amador Bueno, Terminal de Cargas Logístico Fernão Dias, and Pólo de Desenvolvimento Sul. At the same time, the Carandiru-Vila Maria UO changed its name to Estrutural Norte.

Among other instruments connected to the increment value mechanism (*solo criado*) concept, the new Master Plan reduced the average FAR for all urban land not included in UOs. Now there is a basic FAR and in the largest part of São Paulo area it is equivalent to 1.0, but in some more distant areas this basic FAR can be a maximum of 2.0. Owners/developers who now intend to construct above this basic level (with exceptions for social houses, hospitals and other activities with public and social interest) to a maximum of 4.0 have to pay for the value increment produced by the difference between the basic and the maximum FAR permitted. It is interesting to note that many landowners whose land had formerly FARs of 2.0, 3.0, or 4.0 with the new Master Plan lost part of these rights and now if they want to construct more area they have to pay for it.[11]

The value capture in areas not within UOs began slowly after 2002, because developers, anticipating the approval of the new regulations, had obtained their construction licenses according to the former (and cheaper) conditions. During the next 3 or 4 years, they had licenses in accordance with the former zoning legislation and had to pay nothing to the administration if their lots exceeded 1 or 2 FAR.

But with the beginning of a new real estate market boom in 2005, a number of new licenses following the new rules were demanded and approved. According to the Master Plan, there was a stock maximum of 6.9 million m^2 of residential area to be used, of which 1.3 million m^2 (18.8%) was contracted up to February 2008, according to this new method. As for non-residential activities, the stock was 2.8 million m^2 and 0.155 million m^2 (5.5%) was contracted up to the same date.[12]

This means that the entire São Paulo municipality area now may be subject to increasing land building potential and the conversion of the benefits in onerous grants. Depending on how much developers want to build (to a maximum FAR of 4.0), a bigger or smaller share of this increment value may be appropriated by the public sector. These conditions are important to the financial sustainability of the city, because formerly the pressure exerted by growth on infrastructure was all financed by public funds. With these new procedures, part of the value created by city growth is used to finance the expansion of the infrastructure this growth has demanded.

[11] In Urban Operations the maximum FAR is 4.0, except in the Anhangabaú-Centro UO, where it is 6.0.

[12] In 2008 the total income by this concept was around 60 million dollars.

15.14 ZEISs and Social Sustainability

The new Master Plan created 750 ZEISs scattered around the urban area, representing a total of 32 km^2 (see Fig. 15-2). These areas are intended to provide land for the construction of social housing. The majority of these zones are already occupied by slums and are in peripheral areas of the city. But in some cases, these slums are in expensive areas near or even inside the most dynamic districts of the city.

By creating ZEISs, the land has lost its economic highest and best use, and where slums exist, they will likely be urbanized. This may be the most powerful instrument to avoid or to mitigate the gentrification process, although most of these ZEIS areas are already in the periphery of the city.

15.15 ZEPAMs: The Right of Preference and Environmental Sustainability

The new Master Plan also created 22 zones where there is the right of preemption or preference. This means that the government has the option to buy the land from the private landowners to build public parks and large reservoirs to mitigate floods.

Environmental protection is supposed to be ensured by the creation of ZEPAMs (zones of environmental protection), mainly in the south where the great city reservoirs and the sources of rivers are located, and in the north, where there are still some native forests and some water sources.

Although the Master Plan created this instrument of environmental protection, there is no guarantee that these areas will be respected. Invasions of poor, middle-class, and rich families are very common, for various reasons. And there is no punishment for those who flout the Master Plan. In other words, it is necessary but not sufficient to create official mechanisms of environmental protection. The forces that are impelling urban development are strong and chaotic and conspire against environmental sustainability. Other instruments are needed to tame these forces on behalf of a balanced urban development.

15.16 The Problem of Transportation

Since the beginning of the twentieth century, the intense growth of the city in area and population caused problems for public transportation. From 1900 until the 1930s, the main form of public transportation was tramways

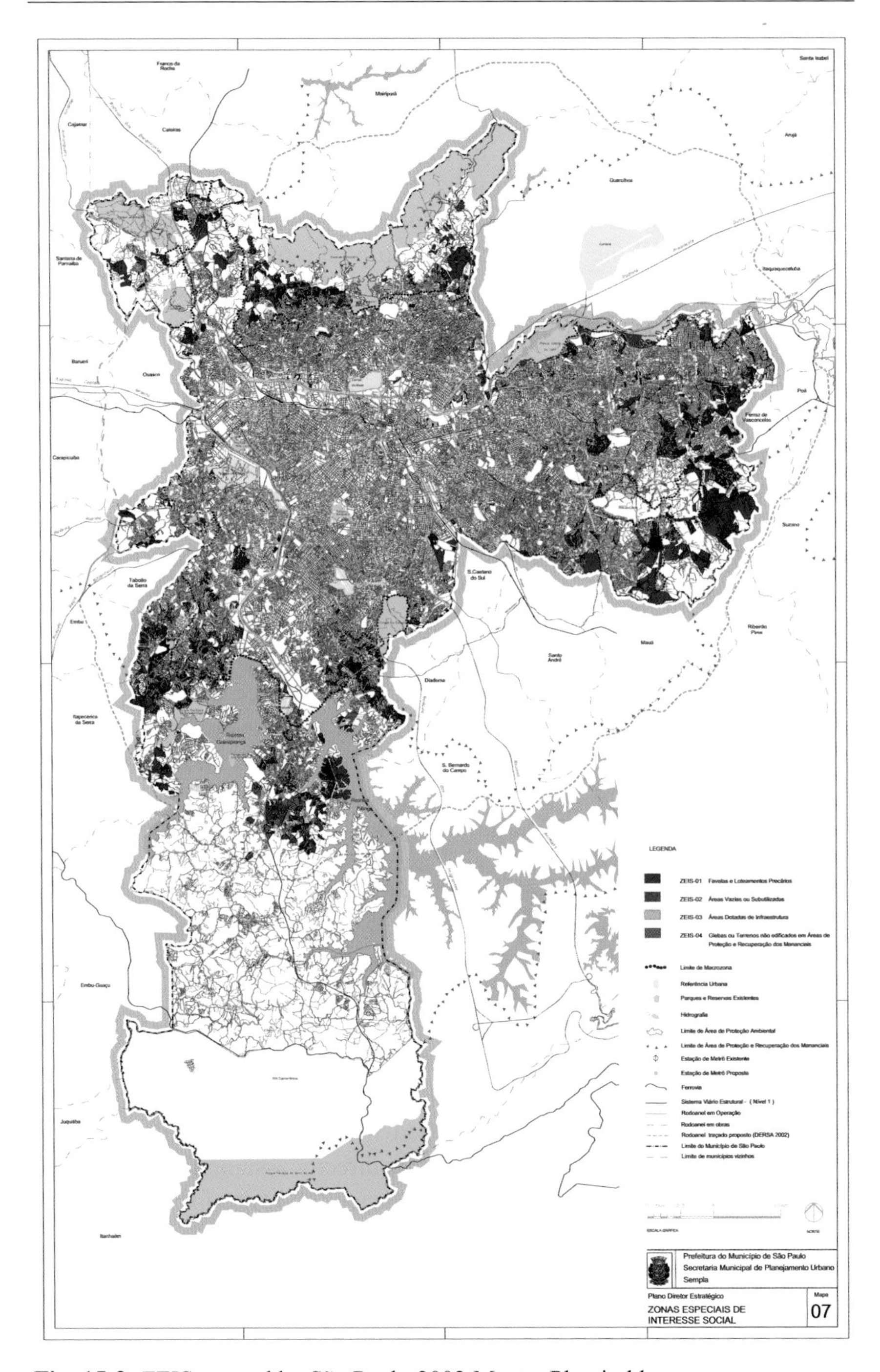

Fig. 15-2. ZEIS created by São Paulo 2002 Master Plan in blue

(streetcars) that used electric energy, although some motor buses came into use in the 1920s, along with private cars.

But in the 1940s, the Light and Power Co. responsible for streetcars was not interested in expanding its lines following the growth of the city because of the low level of the tariffs, which were controlled by the government. These tariffs did not pay for the considerable investment necessary to extend the rails and the electric cables. So public transportation by motor buses began to increase, first in the newer neighborhoods (where the Light & Power Co. was absent) and within a few years, buses replaced streetcars throughout the city.

Only in 1970 was the first line of rail-based transit built. But this decade was the decade of cars. Traffic congestion increased and the speed of buses diminished, making the transportation service even worse, particularly transportation to the most distant communities.

At the end of the 1980s and beginning of the 1990s, public transportation by buses was provided 30% by the public sector and 70% by the private sector. Both services were poor, although communities in periphery of the city were attended mainly by transportation provided directly by the public sector. Public transportation in São Paulo faced an important crisis in the 1990s, when the service was completely privatized. Since then, many efforts have been made to improve the service, with the construction of exclusive corridors and the extension of the subways, but public transportation remains one of the most important city bottlenecks.

In São Paulo, as in other large cities, there is a contradiction between public transportation and people who need it most: the high price of land in the central area forces poor families to the periphery, where they have to pay more for transportation to the city's central zone to get to jobs and other opportunities to make a living. So the highest fares are paid by those who have the lowest income and cannot afford an alternative. If the government sets low and affordable tariffs, private transportation entrepreneurs cannot make a profit and the service will be bad or non-existent.

The consequence of this contradiction is that public transportation in cities like São Paulo must be subsidized if social sustainability is to be preserved. The public administration must directly assume the function or contract with the private sector for the service (allowing for a reasonable profit without raising fares). This arrangement should guarantee the normal function of the transportation system.

But in doing so, the city must divert financial resources that could be destined to other activities as education and health or investment in other forms of infrastructure. To mitigate this problem the Master Plan aimed to create new employment centers in the periphery, such as the Verde-Jacu UO. The intent is to reduce the need to commute (and its cost), while revitalizing and increasing densities in central areas (particularly the Anhangabaú-Centro and Água Branca UOs), and avoiding the process of expelling poor families to the periphery.

15.17 Conclusions

The urban development of São Paulo was intense during the twentieth century, but it was not planned for sustainability, even if after 1960 Master Plans were approved and adopted by the municipal administration. Development was unbalanced, causing exclusion and a shortage of public services among the poor, who lived mainly in peripheral zones. The economic crisis of 1980–1990 reduced the capacity of public investments and maintenance and worsened the situation for these groups.

At the same time, democratization and a new Constitution brought new instruments of intervention and an increase in social participation in important political decisions concerning urban development. These new instruments allowed the public sector to recover legal and financial power to intervene and increase the capacity of planning in the urban areas. São Paulo city was a pioneer in approving and using these instruments and constituted a benchmark for urban development in Brazil.

With the 2005 recovery from the economic crisis, the legal instruments created by the *Estatuto da Cidade* in 2001 (regulation of articles 182 and 183 of 1988 Constitution) and the new Master Plan of 2002, the city was in a better position to face the chaotic tendencies of urban development.

From the perspective of sustainable development, it is reasonable to say that Urban Operations contributed to contradictory results. From a financial perspective, they helped the administration to capture value which in other circumstances would have be captured by owners or developers and to use this money to build infrastructure and social housing without using budget resources. But they accelerated the rise in land prices and so increased the pressure on poor families in slums and on lower-middle-class families in other areas to move. The introduction of the ZEIS helped to mitigate these tendencies, but even this instrument has had only limited results because up to now only in the Água Branca UO has a slum been partly urbanized. In the Faria Lima and Água Espraiada UOs, the slums have not yet been urbanized and there is pressure to suspend the ZEIS areas.

The first two UOs (Água Branca and Anhangabaú-Centro) did not demand previous investments from the public sector and the works in infrastructure are being made with the economic compensations provided by the private projects approved until now. In other words the pressure on budget was eliminated.

The last two (Faria Lima and Água Espraiada), by comparison, demanded considerable public investment for expropriations and the construction of avenues before economic compensations were received, increasing public indebtedness and precluding financial sustainability.

The extension of Faria Lima Avenue and Água Espraiada Avenue to a lesser degree resulted in gentrification, with the expulsion of poor families living in slums and lower-middle-class families, who were replaced by the upper-middle-class households. Small shops are being replaced by malls, shopping centers, and the modern and expensive offices of multinational corporations. The UOs created in these two areas with mechanisms of value capture and ZEISs as an instrument to mitigate the displacement of low-income households are still operating and the results are not yet clear.

The Água Espraiada UO has many slums located in areas that will be needed for the extension of the avenue. Other are located in ZEISs and are to be urbanized. Cepacs already sold and the available stock will provide the funds for these investments, but the offensive against ZEISs may continue.

The growth of the city in area and population and the absence of efficient forms of mass transportation such as subways, trains, and bus corridors have resulted in an extraordinary growth of individual transportation by automobiles (from lower-middle-class households to more affluent families) and a great expansion of commuting by foot by the poorer segments of the population. This process has caused traffic congestion and air pollution and increasing costs in services such as sewage disposal, garbage collection, security, and lighting, and does not contribute to a sustainable environment from an ecological and social perspective.

At least three out of four of São Paulo's UOs (Água Branca, Faria Lima, and Água Espraiada) included the construction of large avenues and created new areas for cars and buses. As public transportation services did not improve, the opening of these avenues, even if they at first relieved congestion somewhat, stimulated the increased use of automobiles. In a very short time, these new avenues were as congested as the others, as cars and buses competed for space, preventing higher speeds in public transportation services.

Before 1987 all changes in zoning and increment value due to public investments were generally captured by the owner of the land and/or developer of real estate projects. After 1987 the new legislation allowing Interlinked Operations, Urban Operations, and the reduction of FAR, separating the property right and the right of construction, together with the determination of the social function of land, brought new procedures and a form of participation by the public sector in all value created by urban development. But the way these instruments have been used by São Paulo's administrations since 1988 (with some exceptions) did not necessarily result in the mitigation of unsustainable situations produced by market-oriented urban development.

However the effects of Urban Operations and the 2002 Master Plan over the dimensions of sustainability in the economy, equity and ecology are currently being developed and there are promising results from ZEISs, Cepacs, and the reduction of FAR in all areas not belonging to UOs, but the results of creating special zones of environmental protection (ZEPAMs) are not yet available.

References

de Ambrosis C (1999) Recuperação da valorização imobiliária decorrente da urbanização. In: O município no século XXI: cenários e perspectivas. Fundação Prefeito Faria Lima, CEPAM, São Paulo

de Azevedo N, Domingos T (1994) O jogo das interligadas. Uma política pública em avaliação: a Lei 10.109/86 do Município de São Paulo. Dissertação de mestrado em Administração Pública apresentada à FGV/Escola de Administração de Empresas de São Paulo

de Castro, S Rabello (2003) Justor indenizações urbanas: Justiça social e o enriquecimento sem causea: Amatomia de um conceito. Mimeo

Fix M (2001) Parceiros da exclusão. Boitempo, São Paulo

Fundação Prefeito Faria Lima (CEPAM) (1997) O Solo Criado/Carta de Embu. São Paulo

Furtado F (1997) Instrumentos para a Recuperação de Mais-Valias na América Latina: debilidade na implementação, ambigüidade na interpretação. In: Cadernos IPPUR 11, (1 & 2). IPPUR, Rio de Janeiro, pp 163–206

de Miranda EE, Gomes EG, Guimarães M (2005) Mapeamento e estimativa da área urbanizada do Brasil com base em imagens orbitais e modelos estatísticos. Embrapa Monitoramento por Satélite, Campinas. Available at: http://www.urbanizacao.cnpm.embrapa.br

Montandon DT, De Sousa FF (2007) Land readjustment and joint urban operations. Romano Guerra Editores, São Paulo

Sandroni P (2000) La Operación Interligada West-Plaza: Un caso de apropiación de renta en la Ciudad de São Paulo. In: Iracheta Cenecorta AX, Smolka M (eds) Los Pobres de la Ciudad y la Tierra. El Colegio Mexiquense y Lincoln Institute of Land Policy, Mexico

Sandroni P (2004) Financiamiento de Grandes Proyectos Urbanos. In: Lungo M (ed) Grandes Proyectos Urbanos. Lincoln Institute of Land Policy & UCA Editores, El Salvador

São Paulo (Cidade), Secretaria Municipal do Planejamento (2000) Operação Urbana Faria Lima, São Paulo, 2000

Szmrecsany T (2004) Historia Econômica de São Paulo. Ed. Globo, São Paulo

16. Sustainability and Urban Form: The Metropolitan Region of Buenos Aires*

Eduardo Reese

16.1 Introduction

The Metropolitan Region of Buenos Aires (MRBA) has the largest concentration of political and economic power in Argentina and presents characteristics and specific modes of development that distinguish it from the other urban agglomerations in Argentina. The MRBA should be understood as part of a larger dense and complex region, referred to as the "Buenos Aires Industrial Axis," which constitutes a semi-continuous alignment of cities, ports, and industrial settlements extending from La Plata to Rosario (60 km south and 300 km northwest of Buenos Aires, respectively). The region is the most important urban agglomeration of the country, with close to 15,000 km^2 in surface area (2% of the country), of which 18% is urbanized. It includes the capital city (Buenos Aires) and 42 other municipalities, it has nearly 13.5 million habitants, 50% of the industrial workforce and 55% of the GNP, and it constitutes the main financial center of the country and the biggest production and consumption market, with a high degree of diversification.

The purpose of this book is to highlight the different debates about the relationship between sustainability and urban form in megacities around the world. Thus the first question that arises is: Is it possible to speak of a "sustainable urban form" for the MRBA? This article does not intend to present an "ideal model" of sustainable urban form, but it does pose some questions to take into consideration when attempting to achieve this objective in the context of the particularities and complexities of Buenos Aires.

*The English version of this text was prepared by Hayley Henderson.

A. Sorensen and J. Okata (eds.), *Megacities: Urban Form, Governance, and Sustainability*,

Therefore, and in function of the objectives of this publication, the area studied for this article represents a part of the MRBA and consists of a physically defined and agglomerated urbanized area that represents a spatial continuity of urban conditions (see Fig. 16-1). This area is composed of the City of Buenos Aires and 32 municipalities belonging to the surrounding Province of Buenos Aires, and it has 12.7 million inhabitants and 2,360 km^2 of continuous urban surface.

During the last 25 years, Buenos Aires has experienced a series of transformations in its growth processes (sprawl, segregation, fragmentation, etc.), which can be explained in the context of the neoliberal policies that prevailed until the crisis of 2001 in Argentina. At each stage, new problems have been superimposed upon unresolved situations inherited from the previous development model. This situation poses a number of questions with respect to urban sustainability, including (1) the relationship between the types of growth, occupation of land, and urban form; (2) access to land by low-income groups; (3) emerging conflicts over environmental issues and the urban quality debate; and (4) governance and model of urban planning and metropolitan management.

Fig. 16-1. Layout of the MRBA in 2006

16.2 Urban Configuration Processes in the MRBA

The layout of the MRBA, as an expression of complex socio-territorial processes, presents the following main characteristics:

- A central city (Buenos Aires) that hosts the highest and most important concentration of political, institutional, cultural, administrative, financial, and residential activities, supported by complete coverage of urban services. The central city articulates a wide spectrum of activities, which generates intense daily flows between places of residence and employment.
- A distinctly radial transportation system that has historically oriented the process of urbanization and defined the concentration of commercial and service activities. This system is becoming more complex and has begun to change, in part since the early 1990s, as a result of the expansion and extension of the region's concentric arterial routes.
- An expanded grid that supports residential uses and allows for the identification of local "centers" (areas of concentrated commercial, administrative and service activities – shown as "Metropolitan Centers" in Fig. 16-1) as the nodes of train and bus transportation. These local centers are relevant in terms of the general organization of the MRBA and they fulfill important functions in the provision of services within the region's connective fabric.

Since its origin, Buenos Aires (200 km^2) has occupied a central place in the economic and political processes of the country. Towards the end of the nineteenth century, the development model centered on the export of agricultural products turned the port of Buenos Aires into the heart of the national economy. Subsequent development of industrial activities, which were consolidated in the import-substitution stage during the 1930s, organized a new model of capital accumulation centered upon manufacturing that is reflected in the present metropolitan layout of Buenos Aires. During the first phase of import-substitution, industrial activity tended to localize in the central city and contiguous municipalities. During the second phase, the development of manufacturing promoted expansive urbanization forming a single agglomeration based on productive and residential uses. Simultaneously, and without the port losing its primacy in overseas commerce, Buenos Aires became a national node that concentrated specialized services and articulated a development model in which the secondary and tertiary sectors of the economy developed in the metropolitan area, mutually benefiting the city and the region.

In this way, the MRBA consolidated itself as an industrialized metropolis with a broad service sector that benefited from a development model whereby productive processes were concentrated in a small number of urban agglomerations that hosted a substantial part of the country's human, economic, and innovative resources. Simultaneously, the growth of the city was fundamentally marked by its function as the national capital and, therefore, as the headquarters of the most important political–institutional decisions. Thus, Buenos Aires can be best understood as a "port-city" and power center wherein the logics of "capital accumulation" and of "political accumulation" have historically been concentrated.

In relation to the radial character of the transportation system, the metropolitan territory is structured upon axes of expansion to the north, north-west, west, south and south-west, which organize the various areas of local centrality. Since 1857, the layout of the railways has left its mark on territorial organization as it directed urbanization processes and consolidated (and was the origin of) the formation of the region's centers.[1] Since the early twentieth century, bus transit has played a predominant role in connecting previously dispersed areas and facilitating urban expansion around new axes of expansion (Torres, 1978, 2001). Among the aforementioned axes of expansion, the "northern corridor" stands out with the highest concentration of investment levels in the country.

Lastly, regarding the third aspect, the growth of the metropolitan city as a grid has responded almost exclusively to market mechanisms and speculative interests. By 2006, the study area had grown to around 2,360 km^2 (Reese 2007) and continues to grow approximately 10% between each census period. The historical growth model was based on low-cost "popular subdivisions,"[2] with minimal levels of infrastructure coverage and the provision of subsidized transportation (based on policies of assistance to public-service companies). In this way, affordable subdivisions became the

[1]"The importance of railroads as a structuring agent in the system of regional centers manifests itself in the chaining of centers, which have a high level of connectivity with railway stations. The difference of levels that are observed between the chains made by the distinct railway lines is explained by the efficiency of their operation, the socioeconomic characteristics of the residential population and the presence of trip generators along their path." (Ternavasio et al. 1994).

[2]Popular subdivisions are created by the division, minimal urbanization and monthly sale of land parcels, promoted by private agents, for residential purposes in low-entry markets. Subdivision has been a central element in the socio-economic organization of land. The municipality of Moreno, located in the second ring of the MRBA, can be cited as an example. According to figures provided by the municipality, public authorities approved plans between 1950 and 1980 that generated close to 118,000 urban lots.

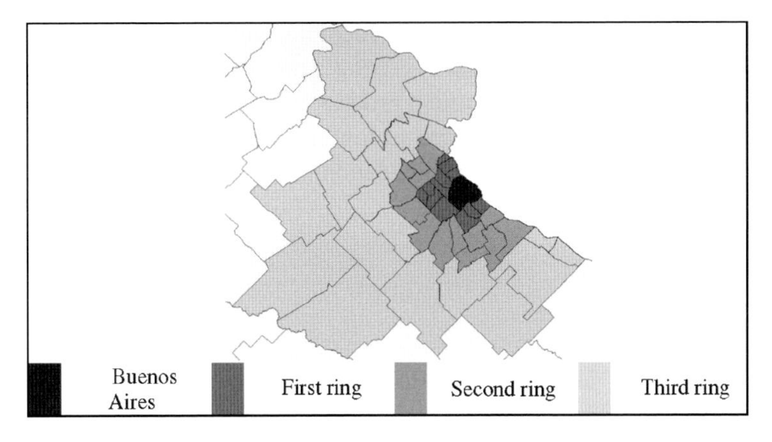

Fig. 16-2. Jurisdictional division of the MRBA and the municipalities of Buenos Aires Province in crowns or rings around the capital city

primary mechanism by which the urban form expanded. This expansion resulted in low gross densities of 10–30 inhabitants per hectare in vast sectors of the periphery, which substantially increased urbanization costs.

At the same time, as urban research has shown, the MRBA can be analyzed within three concentric territorial semi-rings or "crowns" around the city of Buenos Aires (see Fig. 16-2). The capital city and the first crown have the highest levels of infrastructure coverage, land values, land occupation, urban consolidation, and density of population and development.

Within the districts that make up the MRBA, growth has been severely unequal. Since the middle of the twentieth century, the resident population of Buenos Aires has not varied significantly, retaining close to three million inhabitants with only a slight drop in the last census period. In recent census periods, the population of the first ring of municipalities has stagnated, while the population of the third ring has substantially increased (between 30 and 45% in the decade 1991–2001). It must be noted that the municipalities of the third crown, which are farthest removed from the capital city, experience the highest levels of poverty and deficits in basic infrastructure.

The continuous growth of the city, with the consequent conversion of rural land into urban land, was carried out with scant and inconsistent municipal and provincial regulation, which has permitted the free play of the speculative real estate market. Starting in the mid 1970s, the traditional growth model faced a crisis for two main reasons: (1) the implementation of Decree 8912/77, which limited the subdivision of areas without infrastructure, and (2) structural adjustment policies that reduced the subsidies for economic activities as well as the incomes and livelihoods of the middle- and low-income sectors.

The sequence of the development process followed the urbanization logic in Argentina: growth by expansion at low densities in the peripheral areas (Fig. 16-3), the filling out and consolidation of the intermediate urban fabric

Fig. 16-3. Area of urban expansion. Growth has historically occurred with very low levels of services. Virrey del Pino (La Matanza) – 2006

Fig. 16-4. Suburbs in the finishing phase of basic social infrastructure and services provision. Burzaco (Almirante Brown) – 2006

Fig. 16-5. Metropolitan municipal centers play important roles in population densification and the concentration of new activities. Central area of San Fernando – 2006

Fig. 16-6. Buenos Aires (gross density of 15,000 people/km^2) has the highest level of service provision and a dynamic real estate industry. Buenos Aires – 2007

(Fig. 16-4), densification of metropolitan centers and along transport corridors (Fig. 16-5) and population stagnation with densification of service activities in the central city (Fig. 16-6).[3] Consequently, the urban form presents a vast internal variability of densities with coexisting spaces of highly concentrated urban activity and spaces of semi-rural character where acute problems of urban dispersion are manifest. Urban services coverage follows a decreasing gradient from the center to the periphery, typical of cities in developing countries.

16.3 Transformations in the MRBA's Layout in the Last 20 Years

There are two distinct stages within this period. The first stage spans between 1990 until the crisis of December 2001 and is characterized by the consolidation of neoliberal reforms. The second stage began in 2002 and extends to the present, and it is characterized by signs of rupture with the previous model, fundamentally through changes in the role of the state.

The most important features of the first period are the following:

- Significant state reform based on principles of neutrality and subsidiarity, with central political components of deregulation, privatization, focalization and decentralization
- Market liberalization, deregulation and liberal monetary policy promoted the concentration and deindustrialization of economic activity as well as the rupture of networks used by small to medium-sized businesses
- Informal-sector work, impoverishment and increasing social inequity
- Limited social assistance policies and the abandonment of universalism in social service coverage
- Important institutional changes, including constitutional reform at the national and provincial levels, as well as the modification of the legal status of the City of Buenos Aires to constitute an Autonomous Government, which culminated in the approval of its own Constitution in 1996

Market liberalization and the widespread privatization of government services restructured urban form in the metropolitan area. This process not only represents a change in property regime, but also a transfer of coordinating functions from the public to the private sector without an articulated system of planning and control.

[3]The analysis follows the scheme proposed by Hardoy (1972).

The improvement of road infrastructure, starting with the concessionary regime, exacerbated the incorporation of new border territories, which absorbed rural and agricultural areas that were unable to compete with new developments, such as gated communities, large commercial zones, or industrial parks. This led to the emergence of enclaves of varying scales within and along the edges of the expanding metropolitan fabric and promoted an increase in the value of urban land, widening the market to incorporate new land suitable for such developments that affect the MRBA in different ways.

Likewise, new forms of urbanization emerged in housing as well as production, consumption, and recreation. In parallel, a renewed real estate sector generated land market tensions, induced by an increased demand for new, high-quality products and the direction of capital into real estate investment whose profitability requires localization in "opportunity areas". These tensions were generated because the new developments were located in areas that were generally occupied by lower-income groups who were later unable to access the revalued land. This process therefore created a new kind of segregation.

The new gated communities in the periphery of the region highly value security (understood as restricted or controlled access), landscaping, contact with nature, and a lower cost of land than in central areas. The emergence of these communities correlates with increased accessibility provided by the private automobile and the extension of the highway system. This tendency has restructured the form of the metropolitan area so that new centers that locate along highways and other major arterial routes compete with the traditional nuclei of municipalities which were developed around train stations. This process has accentuated the fragmentation of urban space and the socioeconomic inequalities that are, in part, manifested by the isolation of lower-income groups and the self-segregation of higher-income sectors.

In general terms, it is possible to identify two urban trends relating to new forms of industrial production and localization in the MRBA. One of these trends tends toward concentration in large, high-tech establishments, known as "industrial parks" or planned industrial areas, located next to fast access routes. The other trend is very dispersed and tends to promote the articulation of small workshops.

This new logic of territorial organization generally manifests itself as competition between municipalities, caused by the subordination of urban policies to the logic of competition between locations to attract capital. The selective action of investment defines "opportunity areas" for expansion into certain locations or networks of locations. A common response is to create "modern" centers within metropolitan regions, directly connected by networks of high technology to the global system. The marketing of such modern centers symbolizes a dual urban reality, which is the product of exacerbated and planned technological, economic, and social segregation.

The patterns of locating new developments in the "legal" or "formal" city are generating a juxtaposition of two types of growth: one continuous and one discontinuous.[4] The continuous form of growth can be seen in Buenos Aires, which was essentially constructed following urbanization patterns similar to those of its central nucleus. Its urban grid layout responds to divisions of several decades that follow a fairly regular pattern that has become denser through increasing building heights (Fig. 16-7). Discontinuous growth refers to the selective choice of investment, which generates "opportunity areas" that are linked with the rest of the agglomeration by highway networks (see Fig. 16-8). New means of communication reinforce themselves and augment the use of private automobiles, resulting in reduced usage of public transit relative to the total number of trips taken, a phenomenon that was accentuated in the 1990s.

This juxtaposition of growth types is evidenced in the city by the densification of old "villas" (informal "slum" communities) (Fig. 16-9) as well as the informal occupation of peripheral land (Fig. 16-10).

Although structural changes did not alter the traditional role of the MRBA in general or of the capital city in particular, what has emerged as a result of these transformations is a tendency towards a polycentric morphology, based on the location of certain urban functions (production, commerce, higher education, entertainment) and the reinforcement of the centrality of

Fig. 16-7. Densification of the "formal" compact city by building up. Buenos Aires – 2008

[4]These challenges plant new dynamics in relation to urban growth that superimpose with existing problems of the previous model of development.

other functions (finance, business management), based on a series of productive processes that require proximity to each other.

With respect to the second stage, which began in 2002 after the profound crisis of 2001–2002, the national government has made changes in its own role and in the rules for some privatized public services. One of the most

Fig. 16-8. Expansion of the "formal" city into the periphery by means of "gated communities" for high-income earners. Cañuelas – 2006

Fig. 16-9. Compaction and densification of "informal" urban settlements. Buenos Aires – 2007

Fig. 16-10. Expansion of the "informal" city into the periphery through occupation by low-income sectors. Lomas de Zamora – 2007

important transformations the recovery of decision-making power regarding how and where investments are made and who is to carry out such investment projects, even though the integration of policies into a system of public service planning and regulation still has several problems. Both the national government and that of Buenos Aires Province have repealed the concession contracts of sanitation services providers so that now such services are provided by state-owned enterprises. Similarly, there has been a reactivation of social housing construction through increased public investment. Nevertheless, the traditional subordination of land policies to market logic has not been modified, as weakly regulated land markets persist, along with speculative activity. Thus, the new policies of social housing also contribute to the deepening of peripheral segregation.

16.4 Sustainability, Livability, and Planning in the MRBA

Over the last 20 years in Argentina, as in most of the world, there has been a broadening of the environmental debate, dealing with matters such as the protection of natural resources, the effects of new types of agricultural production, and urban problems. The processes that took place in the MRBA were not marginalized from this debate nor from associated conflicts. Nowadays, people are aware of the fact that sustainable urbanism in the MRBA is a decisive factor in the struggle against climate change, but also that the correct management of urbanization processes would help reduce transportation costs, stabilize land and housing prices, decrease the costs of construction and the provision of basic services, as well as mitigate socio-spatial segregation. Furthermore, recent conflicts about the management of the metropolitan hydrological basins brought to light the fact that environmental quality not only reduces environmental risks and health impacts on the population but also stimulates the economy, which is of fundamental importance in an increasingly demanding global order.

The principal issues associated with sustainability, livability, and planning in the MRBA are the following:

1. The type and form of metropolitan growth. Distinct political factors and real estate interests have impeded the possibility of reaching a consensus on public policies that pursue regional urban development.[5] The analyses that relate urban form to the city's modes of production (which recommend, for example, establishing growth limits in the MRBA and developing management tools) are generally found in technical documents (e.g., Garay 2007; Reese 2006, 2007) that so far have not had much resonance in political and social debates.
2. Management of the metropolitan transport system. The issue of mobility has, for some time, brought about numerous debates regarding the need to restructure and strengthen the public transport system, which currently accounts for about 46.6% of trips as opposed to 40% of trips using private cars and 13.6% by other means (taxi, motorbike, bicycle, etc.). The public policies that have been implemented so far are ambivalent and the public system suffers from structural problems in design, investment, and management.
3. The lack of an integrated approach to the management of the hydrological basins and a system of large open spaces. These matters have had greater diffusion in the public arena due to concerns raised by environmental and neighborhood organizations about elevated pollution levels in the two largest basins of the MRBA.[6]
4. The issue of access to urban land by low-income groups. The profound crisis of 2001–2002 and the persistence of informal urban development have led to a significant mobilization of territorial and technical NGOs in defense of squatters' rights. At the same time, this implied a significant change in the debate from housing rights to "the collective right to the city."

[5]The MRBA grows by approximately 1.3 million inhabitants every 10 years.

[6]The basins of the rivers Matanza–Riachuelo and Reconquista contain about 5,900km^2 of urban, suburban, and rural areas that affect over 7.1 million inhabitants.

5. The expansion of infrastructure networks and basic social services. In this area, the changes that have occurred since 2003 have resulted in the reformulation of policies and public investment grounded in the universal provision of services (particularly water and sewerage), while prioritizing those areas with the greatest deficits. This change is beginning to have a direct impact on densification in the intermediate neighborhoods in the second metropolitan crown.

In light of this summarized background, the remainder of this chapter focuses on three central axes of reflection about the relationship between sustainability and urban form in Buenos Aires[7].

16.4.1 Types of Growth, Land Occupation, and Urban Form

Even though the population growth of the MRBA shows a clear deceleration when compared to the high growth rates that the region experienced until the last third of the twentieth century, issues of growth and forms of urban occupation will continue to be of serious concern in the following years. In the last 6 years of economic expansion, the real estate market and land consumption have grown faster than the Gross Regional Product.

Accordingly, the challenge is to reinterpret the issue as not only a quantitative problem (as it has traditionally been viewed in urban plans: how many houses are needed, how much land is necessary, with which indicators, etc.), but also as a matter of quality and of modes of urban organization: what territorial structure to adopt, what type of urban designs are appropriate for specific localities, what planning model should be implemented for the periphery, what ought to be the relationship between new urban areas and open space and nature, and so on.

As previously stated, the growth model of the MRBA was traditionally based on popular subdivisions with limited infrastructure. However, the fragmented urbanization of rural and natural areas over the last 20 years responds to a different logic from that of traditional models of growth.

With respect to servicing and infrastructure costs, denser urban development models have always emerged in debates and in the expectations of our urban policies as a way to address the difficulties and demands of suburban

[7]Due to lack of space, several issues currently being debated in the MRBA cannot be discussed here, including solid waste disposal (which, like the hydrological basins, has also led to many conflicts and debates promoted by environmental NGOs), the control of polluting agents (especially industrial pollution), and the urgent need to create an efficient infrastructure system for economic development.

development. Nevertheless, the dense urban model has several limiting factors to be considered (for example, determining the appropriate balance of open space and built form), especially the verifiable transformation of consumer demand in favor of less dense residential development patterns.

It is also fundamental to incorporate into urban plans an integrated conception of the city's functions and activities that allows for a more "complex" urban development, one which does not segregate diverse urban spaces through zoning. The option of mixed-use development should be seen not only as overcoming the simplification of traditional urbanism, but also as promoting urban vitality and diversity, and minimizing social segregation.

From this point of view, the creation of an inclusive and sustainable metropolitan city requires the strong articulation of urban regulations and political decisions that have considerable impact on growth and densification (such as housing policies, decisions about extending infrastructure networks, access to land by lower-income groups, tax policies, the regulation of public transportation, and so forth). These policy actions and activities are usually influenced by public- and private-sector representatives whose decision-making power goes beyond that of the municipal sphere (Provincial Housing Institutes, construction companies, real estate agencies, politicians during campaign periods, etc.). In terms of the analysis of urban land production, this need for articulation may seem obvious, but it represents a critical issue that is usually absent from decision-making processes in the MRBA. Consequently, local urban management is often hampered when attempting to negotiate effectively and drive actions that result in a cohesive urban form.

16.4.2 The Right to the City and Access to Land by Low-Income Groups

While varying in degree according to different moments in history, access to land by low-income groups is a problem that has always been present in debates about the growth of the MRBA. The metropolitan layout is largely the product of the mechanisms of the speculative land market. Changes that have taken place since 2003 are having noticeable impacts on the socio-territorial layout of the region:

[8]According to a new UADE document, the construction sector grew at twice the rate of the economy as a whole, reaching 21.2% during the first half of 2006, compared to the same period in 2005.

- The reactivation of economic activity and the general expansion of demand operate as "cause and effect" factors of construction growth[8] and increase demand for land for new uses and activities.
- These combined processes have generated and transferred significant income to private landowners and have increased prices at rates higher than the growth of the economy as a whole.
- Argentine society (like most Latin American societies) has an established and widespread tradition of renting, which is explained by, amongst other things, economic instability and cycles of expansion and contraction. Consequently, since it is highly valued, land has historically provided a refuge and place of protection for company and family savings. These elements have created an extended culture that not only permits rent speculation and private appropriation of socially produced value, but also accepts such activities as a legitimate income source.
- Public policies have also contributed significantly to differential land valuation through land use regulations, public-sector construction, the promotion of certain projects, or actions that affect accessibility, generating larger socio-spatial inequalities in the city.
- The direct result of growth in land speculation is that growing sectors of the population find it impossible to access land through the formal market. This is verified by the growth in informal settlements, despite a drastic reduction in poverty and unemployment levels since 2003. As the 2005 Declaration of Buenos Aires notes:

> Urban land markets in Latin America tend to produce cities that are economically unequal, politically and socially exclusionary, spatially segregated and environmentally unsustainable. The high and often irrational prices for land aren't only attributable to structurally imperfect markets, but also to the absence of effective urban land management practices. Land markets are social relations and, therefore, can be influenced by policy (Smolka and Mullahy, 2007).

In this way, a central theme of urban sustainability in the MRBA is the search for equity in the distribution of the costs and benefits of the urbanization process. The challenge is to promote a more integrated city within the context of increasing pressure on land markets as a product of the increased

[9]In this point actions and discussion spaces opened by different provincial organizations stand out. See National Declaration for Urban Reform (2005).

demand for housing, construction equipment, economic activities, and civil and social services.[9]

At this point, another problematic issue becomes apparent within the debate on the MRBA – land market regulation mechanisms.

In order to have an effect on the functioning of urban land markets (formal and informal), to promote a sustainable and fair use of this resource, to reduce urban land prices, to produce serviced land for poor people, and to distribute costs and benefits in a more equitable manner, it is necessary to:

- Integrate policies of urban development and policies of land taxation
- Promote a new urban vision and legal framework that distinguish property rights from development rights and recognize that the total generated added value of development belongs not only to the landowner and should benefit the whole of society
- Create mechanisms for the recovery and distribution of added values that make it possible to produce serviced urban land for lower-income social sectors and to compensate for urban inequalities. (Declaración Nacional 2005)

So far, the experiences of the MRBA in this regard have been few, politically tentative, and constantly threatened by the pressures of developers and large real estate groups who are protected by a weak and obsolete legal framework.

16.4.3 Urban Quality and Environment Related Conflicts

The incorporation of environmental concerns into the city's management mechanisms implies the adoption of the concept of sustainable development as a framework for the design and implementation of urban policies. Sustainable development is one of the major challenges that all societies face, but the operational definition of this concept is still ambiguous in the case in of Argentina. The most widespread conceptions of relationships between environment, planning, and urban management are unable to go beyond simple resource analyses (of land, air, water, etc.) and have yet to produce integrated and concrete practices. Despite these limitations, urban plans are gradually introducing environmental management and urban landscaping principles in strategies of urban development.

Two complementary matters that emerge from the incorporation of environmental concerns in urban management deserve discussion herein. The first is the exponential growth in demands by the population for a "healthy" environment. The serious environmental conflicts of recent years (of which neighborhood struggles against contamination of the two most important hydraulic basins of the city stand out as the most significant) are the visible expression of many other environmental conflicts (of a less visible and more dispersed manner) that challenge the entrenched approach of land politics. In essence, these environmental conflicts represent a kind of emergent social questioning process that calls for a sustainable urban development model in the MRBA, where the unregulated actions of developers and the piecemeal and often negligent actions of policy-makers promote the indiscriminate and unsustainable use of land. The second complementary matter is that the incorporation of "the environment" in the urban problematic tends to constitute a reductionist exercise of adding natural landscapes to public space and incorporating more plazas, trees or green space in the city. This is not to question the necessity of more plazas, trees, or green space, but simply to highlight the confusion of "the environment" with "nature," which is one of the most common mistakes made by present perspectives. The urban environment is essentially a constructed environment and, as such, urban design and planning obviously has a central role to play in urban environmental management. The environment of public space should be understood from an integrated perspective that incorporates cultural components of each locality. The notion of place as a constructed symbolic representation (reinterpreted from the language of architecture) of the past (perhaps better understood as multiple pasts) is a fundamental component of the urban environment that gives meaning to metropolitan public space. This explains the importance of restoration initiatives, which can be observed in the City of Buenos Aires as well as in the other municipalities of the region.

16.5 Governance and Planning Approaches in Buenos Aires

Argentina is a federation with three levels of government; one global (national or federal), and two territorial (provincial and municipal). The territorial configuration of the MRBA does not coincide with political-administrative limits.

The MRBA consists of a "macro center" (City of Buenos Aires), which has nearly three million inhabitants who have access to services of the highest standards, and a periphery, which is characterized by acute deficits. This situation correlates to an institutional asymmetry. The political entities

[10]The Province of Buenos Aires has its own constitution and its government has its headquarters in the city of La Plata, making this the capital of the province.

that form the MRBA correspond to a state system in which different jurisdictions have different status levels. Since 1996, Buenos Aires has had an autonomous government with its own local constitution.[10] Beyond the limits of the capital city, the municipalities of Greater Buenos Aires form part of the Province of Buenos Aires.

As identified by Badía (1996), the management processes of the MRBA have always suffered from the lack of a public actor specifically dedicated to managing its unique needs. Accordingly, the government of the MRBA consists of a network of governmental bodies of different levels (federal, provincial, municipal, inter-jurisdictional) that exercise their responsibilities, not always in a coordinated manner, in the (total or partial) territory of the MRBA. The particular way in which each level of government organizes its institutional structure and assigns functions and responsibilities to their respective bodies are elements that explain the "institutional map" through which, at least from a formal point of view, decision-making should flow and metropolitan management of the region should be structured.

Four types of state entities have jurisdiction within the MRBA: the national government (which in recent years has again taken an active role in investments in basic services, housing and transport), Buenos Aires Province, the municipalities of Greater Buenos Aires, and the government of the City of Buenos Aires.

In matters of urban planning, the Province of Buenos Aires has an integrated law for urban development. Decree 8912/77, approved on October 24, 1977, structures the provincial territory and regulates the use, occupation, subdivision, and servicing of land. It was the first legal tool implemented in the country that was conceived as an organic body of principles and regulations that covered broad land use and planning issues. This decree also constitutes a base legislation that provides a legal framework for the entire provincial territory and for the vast diversity of urban nuclei within it.

Decree 8912/77 is not essentially and directly intended to regulate the conduct of individuals, but rather establishes standards that aim to regulate municipal actions. It has a technocratic and authoritarian conception of urbanism, which is characteristic of the period in which it was written. The law fundamentally instructs what "must be done," and it does not recognize the complexity and the practical problems of the real city. In this way, the law sets the standards for a middle- and upper-class city, ignoring the ways in which low-income sectors operate in the production of urban space. For example, the law contains a wide set of abstract urban indicators that regulate the shape of the "formal" city, but does not contain a single article concerning policies directed to the production of land or the improvement of conditions for poor people (in the "informal" city). Furthermore, there are no concrete specifications regarding the preservation of the natural environment, but only general principles. The law is out of date and strongly questioned by the municipalities for its centralized design, lack of flexibility and outdated management instruments. However, for 31 years, the metropolitan municipalities have defined their plans and urban policies within this framework. When it comes to carrying out policies, urban projects, and regulatory action, the political, institutional, and financial weaknesses of the municipalities make it difficult to act efficaciously.

The Constitution of the City of Buenos Aires, however, has a strong emphasis on land planning[11]:

- Article 19 creates a Strategic Planning Council, an advisory body that has the power to introduce legislative proposals, presided over by the mayor and made up of representatives of institutions and social organizations, which has the task of periodically proposing agreed upon strategic plans that provide the grounds for State policies.
- Article 29 requires that the City define an Urban Environmental Plan, prepared with cross-disciplinary participation of academic, professional, and community organizations, which will constitute the base law to which the rest of the urban planning and public works regulations must adjust.

Based on these and other important precepts in the City's Constitution, the new Urban Environment Plan (prepared between 1997 and 2000) was recently approved to replace the 1962 Master Plan. The 8 years that passed between the formulation of the plan and its approval is a clear indication of the difficulties that surrounded its preparation. Unfortunately, neither the original version nor the final approved text had a sound urban proposal, political agreement, and social consensus to legitimize it.

Traditionally, the urban and environmental politics of Buenos Aires had an important autonomy from the rest of the metropolitan region. Despite the change of legal status of the city in 1996, which increased its autonomy, it has remained difficult to reach a political consensus.

---

[11]The Constitution of the Autonomous City of Buenos Aires also incorporates the principle of citizen participation. The first Article mentions that the City "… organizes its institutions as a participative democracy…" This concept of participation is repeated throughout the text more than 20 times.

[12]The Urban Planning Code of 1977 was reformed several times and contains a text based on the Law 449 of the year 2000. However the different reforms did not substantially modify the planning described in the original text.

Likewise, it is important to emphasize the timing of the two urban planning regulation tools that remain valid and govern the MRBA: Decree 8912/77 of Land Use and Planning of the Province of Buenos Aires and the Urban Planning Code of the City of Buenos Aires. Both legal instruments were approved in 1977 and they were closely associated with more generally authoritative and conservative policies implemented by the last dictator.[12]

In this context, it is important to note that the municipalities have many weaknesses when it comes to the implementation of different policies and projects that affect the urban form and therefore metropolitan sustainability. Cutbacks in management capacity together with the absence of sufficient real income have generated a strong political, instrumental, economic, and financial dependency at the municipal level. Consequently, effective exercise of power at the local level to make decisions and define priorities is usually subject to the stipulations and actions of the provincial and national governments, sources of external financing and/or private agents with investment capacity. On the other hand,

> Land planning had, and unfortunately in many cases it still has, a technocratic and centralized way of functioning. Technicians of different levels make decisions on development with a "top-down" logic where only supply is considered and where resources are assigned following model-oriented procedures. In this way, actual planning has been divided into sectors with little integration and it suffers from a grand absence of effective operating capacities. (Catenazzi and Reese 2000).

A series of obstacles therefore persist in governmental organizations responsible for planning and urban projects, which complicate the preparation and implementation of new urban planning tools. These include:

- A strong tradition that reduces urban policy to a regulatory action that merely applies codes and zoning ordinances
- The disconnect between urban tools (plans and projects), fiscal and administrative tools (simplification of paperwork for certain activities), tax regulation tools (tax incentives and disincentives), and active economic policies (bank financing with differential subsidies in interest rates)

Nevertheless, in the area of management and public control of decision-making and project execution, there is an emerging debate about the merits of abandoning rigid regulation systems and replacing them with consensus-building processes oriented towards outcomes and concrete interventions. In short, the current debate emphasizes quality and relevance in management rather than rigid procedural formalities. In this manner, several management tools are being developed in order to pursue more active and less prohibitive urban policies, which are less rigid and more efficient, without neglecting the quality and sustainability of results.

The possibility of deepening this debate means an opportunity to consider a set of alternative approaches that, based on a reconsideration of the relationship between government, urban space, and communities, are more active, more participatory, and more sustainable, and, therefore, diametrically different from "traditional" planning in the Metropolitan Region of Buenos Aires.

References

Badía G (1996) Mapa Institucional del Area Metropolitana de Buenos Aires. Informe final para la CONANMBA, Buenos Aires

Catenazzi A, Reese E (2000) La construcción de estrategias de desarrollo local en las ciudades argentinas. En Revista Pobreza Urbana y Desarrollo, 20. IIED – AL (Instituto Internacional del Medio Ambiente y Desarrollo – América Latina), Buenos Aires

Declaración Nacional por la Reforma Urbana en Argentina (2005) Buenos Aires

Garay A (ed) (2007) Lineamientos Estratégicos para el Area Metropolitana de Buenos Aires. Subsecretaria de Urbanismo y Vivienda de la Provincia de Buenos Aires

Hardoy JE (1972) El paisaje urbano en América del Sur. En: Las ciudades en América Latina – Seis ensayos sobre la urbanización contemporánea. Paidós, Buenos Aires

Reese E (2006) La situación actual de la gestión urbana y la agenda de las ciudades en la Argentina. En: Medio Ambiente y Desarrollo, revista del Instituto de Medio Ambiente y Desarrollo de América Latina (IIED – AL) 65

Reese E (2007) Estudios y Propuestas para la Planificación del Ordenamiento del Uso del Suelo de la Cuenca Matanza – Riachuelo. ACUMAR (Autoridad de la Cuenca Matanza – Riachuelo), Secretaria de Ambiente y Desarrollo Sustentable. Buenos Aires

Smolka M, Mullahy L (2007) Editores. Declaración de Buenos Aires de la Red Latinoamericana del Instituto Lincoln de Políticas de Suelo. En Perspectivas Urbanas – Temas críticos en políticas de suelo en América Latina. Lincoln Institute of Land Policy, Cambridge, MA

Ternavasio A, Brennan P, Arcusín S (1994) Centros de conectividad Región Metropolitana de Buenos Aires. Jerarquización según nivel de conectividad en transporte público. Estudio relizado para la CONAMBA, Buenos Aires

Torres H (1978) Las transformaciones recientes de Buenos Aires a la luz del contexto global. En: La cuestión urbana en los noventa en la Región Metropolitana de Buenos Aires. Catenazzi, A. y Lombardo, J. (compiladores). Instituto del Conurbano, Universidad Nacional de General Sarmiento, Buenos Aires

Torres H (2001) Cambios socioterritoriales en Buenos Aires durante la década de 1990. Revista EURE 27(80). Santiago de Chile

Part IV
Conclusion

17. Megacity Sustainability: Urban Form, Development, and Governance

André Sorensen

The historical experience, governance systems, level of development, and geographical settings of each megacity are so different that it may be foolhardy to attempt to draw any conclusions based on this sample of cities. Clearly the most interesting aspects of each city's experience must be found in the individual chapters, yet there are some significant parallels in the experiences and issues faced by these very different cities, which are worth further exploration.

And, although we must keep in view the enormous differences between the conditions and policy approaches of megacities in the developing countries and those of developed countries, there are also profound differences among megacities in developed countries, and among those in developing countries. The issues faced by Calcutta are quite different from those of Buenos Aires, and Tokyo and Toronto are equally dissimilar. So a neat division into "developed" and "developing" is just as likely to obscure important issues as it is to reveal them. It is past time to move beyond a conception of cities in developed countries as "models" and those in developing country cities as "problems" (Roy 2005; Robinson 2006).

There are significant shared challenges in many of the megacities examined in this volume. Fundamental issues such as water supply and wastewater treatment, urban redevelopment and intensification, automobile proliferation, and governance fragmentation are basic drivers of policymaking in megacities everywhere, a consequence in part of the intersection of great size and inevitable demands for water, mobility, housing, and risk management. Similarities also result from the rapid dissemination of ideas, such as Bogotá's Transmilenio express bus system – itself borrowed from Curitiba in Brazil – which has inspired imitations around the world, including in rich cities. Also shared are

A. Sorensen and J. Okata (eds.), *Megacities: Urban Form, Governance, and Sustainability*,

larger forces such as global neoliberalization and competition for inward investment that put pressure on governments everywhere.

This chapter focuses on three major sets of issues faced by megacities today, informed by the findings and ideas of the case studies. The first is urban form, a primary focus of this project. Extensive growth is producing a number of shared challenges for the governance agendas of giant cities. A second set of issues relates to land development and land development control policies, respectively the generators of changes to urban form and a primary instrument of public policy in megacities. The third relates to the governance structures and challenges of these vast and dynamic megacities, and to attempts to influence changes occurring in the first two sets of issues.

17.1 Urban Form

Urban form is one of the fundamental concepts in urban studies, yet it is a surprisingly elusive one, lacking even an entry in the otherwise encyclopedic *Dictionary of Human Geography* (Johnston 2000). Urban form is a difficult concept in part because it includes so many urban phenomena. Probably the best definition is that of Kevin Lynch: "Settlement form is the spatial arrangement of persons doing things, the resulting spatial flows of persons, goods, and information, and the physical features which modify space in some way significant to those actions, including enclosures, surfaces, channels, ambiences, and objects. Further the description must include the cyclical and secular changes in those spatial distributions, the control of space, and the perception of it" (Lynch 1981: 48). Lynch's useful definition conceives urban form as not just the spatial arrangement of the city, but also the way this arrangement shapes everyday life – urban flows – as well as changes to these forms and flows and their meaning. Because urban form shapes urban flows and processes, it is a powerful determinant of urban quality of life, livability, efficiency, and health.

Urban form has in recent decades been the topic of vigorous political debate in many countries, primarily because of the rapid growth of cities and concerns over urban sprawl, or what are seen as problematic patterns of urban form. The big questions of urban form, sustainability and megacities are: What are the most significant contemporary changes in megacity form, and what are their impacts? How does urban form influence sustainability, livability, and social justice in the city? To what extent are planning and governance processes able to influence such changes? What is the potential role of urban form interventions to reinforce or reduce poverty and unsustainability in megacities?

The cities discussed here are so diverse that any prescription of a preferred urban form would be pointless, but a number of issues addressed in many of the chapters are worth highlighting. Here the focus is on:

1. Extensive patterns of growth, with a marked tendency in many cities towards ever lower densities of development
2. Growing polycentricity, both planned and unplanned
3. Marked increases in socio-spatial polarization: the sorting out of rich and poor into different locations, risk profiles, quality of life, health status, and relationships with state provided services, closely but not exclusively associated with the increasing prevalence of gated communities for the wealthy, fragmented and dispersed patterns of peri-urban growth, and the concentration of poor people in slums in the developed countries and vast informal settlements in developing countries

17.1.1 Sprawl

Perhaps the most significant change in patterns of urbanization during the last half century has been the spread of space-extensive urban development over ever-larger areas at ever-lower densities. Urban sprawl is not just an issue for rich countries with high levels of automobile ownership. For example, as Valenzuela shows, although the population growth of Mexico City is slowing, the land area continues to grow rapidly: between 1990 and 2000 an 18% increase in population was accompanied by a 31% increase in urban area. In Tehran over the last 50 years, the population has grown fivefold, while the municipal area grew sevenfold. Such growth patterns have long been common in the developed countries, especially the United States, where population grew by 17% between 1982 and 1997, and urbanized land area grew by 47% (Burchell 2005). But this is a more recent pattern in the poor cities of the global south, which had remained more compact.

Managing the urban forms of growth is extremely difficult in megacities everywhere. Extensive patterns of growth are in large part the product of the search for affordable housing by millions of newcomers, who settle in ever-more-distant urban fringe locations. In most megacity regions these newly urbanizing areas are almost always outside the planning jurisdiction of the central city, in municipalities that are suddenly confronted with huge development pressures and infrastructure demands. Such conditions mean that larger-scale patterns of regional growth are extremely difficult to plan and adequately service. As discussed below, this outcome is in part a function of fragmented governance in megacity regions, which often include hundreds of municipalities, each with its own planning functions.

In poor countries, in addition to jurisdictional fragmentation, the difficulty of planning is compounded by the fact that most areas in the suburbs are settled informally, in organized and unorganized invasions of available space. In such conditions, "planning" becomes a somewhat abstract exercise, urban form becomes more or less uncontrollable, and infrastructure deficits increase. As Valenzuela argues, urban form in places like Mexico City is often the product of extremes of wealth and poverty more than of planning and regulation. He asks: how can a city be subject to regulation when more than a third of the population lives in informal settlements with extra-legal land tenure and infrastructure arrangements (p. 293, this volume)? Informal settlements also emerge in places where settlement is formally prohibited, or in locations that are simply too dangerous or inaccessible to be of interest to formal land markets. These areas include seasonal floodplains and riverbeds, mountain slopes, and toxic waste dumps, where the risk of disaster or ill-health is high, and there are no services such as water supply or schools. As shown in the chapters on Calcutta, Buenos Aires, Mexico City, Bangkok, Jakarta, and others, major infrastructure is primarily provided to enclave developments for the wealthy, including transport routes to connect them, in a perverse skewing of public investment towards the needs of the rich rather than the poor.

Although the poor traditionally crowded into central city slums in order to be near their work, growing polycentricity with the spread of peripheral gated communities and large-scale planned developments for the wealthy in many developing countries is creating employment in the service sector for the poor residents of informal peri-urban settlements, allowing their increasing dispersal. As Winarso explains, in Jabotadebek, for example, the vast majority of migrants to the city make their own inexpensive housing in informal settlements called *kampung*, often relatively near where they find work. Similar patterns are found in the mountains surrounding Bogotá and Mexico City, where squatters invade public lands and build their own housing, or on the fringes of Buenos Aires, where unserviced subdivisions provide opportunities to create inexpensive self-built housing, or in the southern desert areas of Tehran, where private entrepreneurs subdivide and sell unserviced land to poor migrants.

Dispersal is compounded in megacities such as Mexico City, Seoul, and Tehran, where car ownership among middle-income sectors of the population is growing rapidly, encouraging the spread of formal residential developments outside the city. This is especially true in Mexico City and Seoul, where a dynamic car industry is a driver of the economy. As Valenzuela notes, in Mexico City the number of cars is growing at four times the rate of population growth, allowing rapid peripheral growth of both formal and informal settlements.

Attempting to shape patterns of urban form at the megacity scale is notoriously difficult, especially where significant amounts of development occur informally. As Sidhusingha argues, however, it may be at the micro scale of the urban neighborhood that the most important interventions can be made. He shows that Bangkok's master plans were all preoccupied with the larger regional scale of land-use and infrastructure networks, and that there has been little effective planning at the local scale. He suggests that the most pressing need is for innovative solutions to micro-scale urban form issues – and that the specific context of each city is integral to finding locally relevant solutions. Bangkok has seen a transformation from its traditional urban forms based on canals and water to a road-based city. Unfortunately, this conversion of urban form has not been very successful, as the city lost its former integrating logic without creating a new one. It moved "from fluid *khlongs* to clogged roads" (p. 146, this volume). He argues that in Bangkok today the urgent question is how to make better use of the superblocks that have developed informally in the interstices of major road systems and have little internal connectivity and few public spaces.

In most megacities, informal development represents an ever-increasing share of new urbanization. The traditional planning response to such informal development has been to borrow the models and standards of the developed countries, and make informal settlements illegal, attempting to prevent, contain, or bulldoze them, as has occurred recently in Zimbabwe. A growing movement, however, argues that such approaches are not merely unjust and ineffective, but profoundly counterproductive. Alternative approaches began with slum upgrading projects such as Jakarta's "Kampung Improvement Programs" of the 1970s, and "sites and services schemes" to supply low-cost land so the poor could build their own houses.

More recently, however, with the emergence of ever-vaster areas of informal, unserviced and unplanned development, it is increasingly recognized that despite the problems created by a lack of water supply and waste disposal in informal settlements, it is precisely the informality and extra-legality of such settlements that is essential to their economic vitality and affordability for the poor (Benjamin 2004; Roy 2005; Pieterse 2008). Informality is not disorganized, but is characterized by highly complex and diverse arrangements of tenure, economic and social arrangements. Attempts to "fix" such urban forms, while sometimes well meaning, are likely to lead to the displacement of existing residents and destruction of important social and economic networks (Benjamin 2004).

Worse, as Roy shows in her chapter on Calcutta, such interventions are just as likely to be self-serving moves by powerful political actors to create profitable opportunities for land development. She argues that in Calcutta the formal planning approach is used to promote inward investment by diasporic capital in enclave urbanism, with the ostensible goal of promoting Calcutta's world-city status. Planning thus permits "spaces of exception created by the sovereign power of the state, a territorialized flexibility that allows the state to create value" (p. 100, this volume). In Calcutta, "New Communism" uses the displacement of the poor to make space for frontiers of accumulation.

Processes of peripheral land development are diverse, but megacities everywhere are seeing a trend towards ever more dispersed development at lower densities. Peri-urban development is a profoundly contested process in most megacities because undeveloped land at the urban fringe presents an opportunity: for the poor the affordable opportunity to create some life space, or for landowners and developers the opportunity to generate a profit. The roles of the state in these processes are examined further in the discussion of land development below.

17.1.2 Polycentricity and Social Polarization

A second important trend in urban form is increasing polycentricity, closely associated with growing socio-spatial polarization. A polycentric form of development has long been seen as an ideal pattern for very large cities, as it can provide wide access to high-level services and employment opportunities without the need for long-distance travel to the metropolitan centre by residents of a city-region (Breheny and Rookwood 1993; McDonald and Prather 1994; Cervero and Wu 1997). In some rich megacities, polycentric development has been the product of strategic planning and long-range infrastructure investments, such as in Seoul and Toronto. In Seoul the state responded to population growth with massive new towns to augment housing supply, and one of history's most intensive bursts of planned new town development. Huge new planned developments outside the greenbelt provided housing for 1.2 million people in less than 7 years, helping to stabilize inflation in housing prices, and contributing to the 82% rate of homeownership in the Seoul Metropolitan Region. In Toronto, most peripheral growth was carefully planned, some as private large-scale comprehensive developments with commercial centers, and some as state-led attempts to form new subcenters. In London, a much earlier form of planned polycentricity was seen in the postwar New Towns; more recently the strategy has shifted to the Thames Corridor of development and redevelopment eastwards along the river towards the North Sea.

More common is the fragmented, unplanned, postmodern polycentricity of Los Angeles, and newly emerging large-scale private enclave developments such as Gurgaon outside Delhi, Santa Fe outside Mexico City, the north-west of Istanbul, and the dozens of shopping mall–centered developments around Jakarta. In these cases growing polycentricity is driven by private investment rather than planning, and is closely associated with one of the most profound and disturbing trends in megacities everywhere: the increasing spatial sorting of classes into different areas. This is in part a function of a largely unplanned dispersal of informal development by the poor into urban peripheries, and the growing scale of private-sector comprehensive developments for the wealthy associated with the securitization of real estate investment. Major private enclave projects now include hundreds of hectares, thousands of housing units, shopping malls, golf courses, hotels and schools, all with high-quality public services (Balbo 1993).

Many new "subcenters" are thus entirely private-sector driven, cater to a wealthy transnational elite that can afford them, and (apart from service workers) are effectively sealed off from the surrounding sea of informal development. Jakarta is a primary example of this dualism of formal–informal, planned–unplanned, rich–poor metropolitan growth. The continued growth of informal settlements without running water, electricity, or toilets is accompanied by a huge increase of high-end real-estate developments in the form of high-end "new towns" with high-security perimeter fences. Major public and private investments for the wealthy, with comparatively little for the poor contributes to a splintered city of growing socio-spatial polarization over time, not convergence, and a profound and growing distance between classes and urban settlements.

Madanipour describes a different type of socio-spatial polarization in Tehran's dualistic development pattern, with affluent development moving north, and the intensification of environmental problems in poorer areas towards the south. Here the divide between affluent, salubrious neighborhoods and poor, environmentally challenged neighborhoods follows the local geography, with the wealthy moving towards higher altitudes up the mountain slopes to the north, along tree-lined streets with larger houses, lower densities, and major municipal amenities and parks. At the same time, the informal settlements of the poor spread towards the south into the lowland desert areas. These settlements have much higher densities, lack adequate infrastructure, and are in areas prone to flooding, with a worse microclimate and higher levels of crime. Tehran provides a powerful illustration of the almost universal ability of elites to insulate themselves from major environmental problems and make a profit in the process. Not only do property values grow more reliably in affluent areas, elites are also able to ensure that municipal investment in infrastructure and facilities benefits themselves disproportionately, producing a self-reinforcing process of gated communities for the wealthy, isolated from the environmental and social problems of poorer areas.

Such skewed public investment priorities are also seen in Buenos Aires, where, Reese argues, the political system has responded most consistently to real estate interests rather than democratic political processes, which have been focused on other issues. Similar patterns are seen in Calcutta, Mexico City, Bangkok, Istanbul, and Los Angeles.

One of the most significant urban technology developments of the last 40 years has been the emergence of a range of technologies that allow small-scale deployment of high-quality water supply and wastewater management outside monopolistic municipal grids. This useful advance could have facilitated better provision of clean water to an ever-greater share of megacity populations. In practice, however, it appears to have permitted the wealthy to remove themselves from large-scale municipal networks and supply their own infrastructure within gated and privatized communities, abandoning any shared responsibility for public infrastructure. This stands in great contrast to earlier eras, when the fortunes of urban residents were inescapably bound together, and self-interest compelled the urban elite to push for infrastructure such as water supply and waste management systems that served all and were affordable to all.

Many of the case studies presented here provide a confirmation of Graham and Marvin's (2001) "splintering cities" hypothesis that the decline of the modern infrastructure ideal in the second half of the twentieth century has led to the abandonment of the goal of public provision of municipal services throughout the urbanized area; the increased differentiation between high-value locations served by such infrastructure and locations that are bypassed by it; and the promotion of a "secessionary" (2001: 268) approach by urban elites who increasingly self-segregate into enclaves and avoid contributing to larger networks.

At the same time, however, other forces are at work in some places, moving towards the use of land, land development, and municipal powers to create new forms of network infrastructure on a more equitable basis as discussed next.

17.2 Land, Land Valorization, and Infrastructure Building

Cities are extraordinary machines for the creation of wealth through the appreciation of property values, although usually characterized by inequality in the distribution of that wealth, and misery because of the lack of affordable housing that rising land values routinely produce. Urban policies, public investments, regulations, and plans also have enormous impacts on patterns of land value, quality of life and the distribution of the costs and benefits of urban life.

Among the most significant powers of municipal governments in cities around the world is the regulatory power over land use, building standards, densities, public space standards, and infrastructure provision. Changes in permitted development on particular parcels of urban land and the provision of public facilities can produce enormous increases (or decreases) in land values. And larger projects, planning frameworks, and investments can redistribute patterns of land value over whole districts. In principle, these powers can be used to benefit all urban residents. In most developed countries the provision of municipal services to all residents equally, including clean water, free public education, public transit, public libraries, public health services, and community centers has been a redistributive mechanism essential to urban livability, especially for the poor, who cannot afford to buy equivalent services on the market.

In many cities, however, municipal policy levers have routinely been deployed to the primary benefit of urban elites. As the "urban growth machine" literature (Logan and Molotch 1987; Jonas and Wilson 1999) convincingly argues, urban elites have huge incentives to influence local government decision-making, and are often successful in doing so. The huge profits available from land development has given rise to an almost limitless variety of creative ways – both legal and illegal – in which private interests draw on public resources to aid their schemes. These range from simple pro-growth policies such as facilitating large-scale new development on the fringe, to investments in infrastructure or policies favoring investment such as tax breaks, to major public land-assembly and redevelopment projects and public spectacles such as the Olympics.

In recent decades, such policies have commonly been justified on the basis that in the new global economy, cities are engines of the economy and must compete for the inward investment that produces economic growth and jobs. At the same time, this situation creates incentives for a "race to the bottom," as cities attempt to position themselves as attractive locations for investment by multinational firms that seek low tax regimes, lax environmental standards, and weak labor laws (Leitner and Sheppard 1998; Swyngedouw 2000; Brenner and Theodore 2002: 346; Peck and Tickell 2002; Brenner 2004).

All too often such inward investment involves the displacement of the poor, as in Haussmann's remodeling of Paris in the nineteenth century (Harvey 2008), the urban renewal projects of the 1950s and 1960s in the United States (Anderson 1964), and the current plans to redevelop Mumbai's

Dahravi area (Brugmann 2009). Harvey describes such urban investment as "accumulation through dispossession," as urban land redevelopment is predicated on the removal of existing land uses and residents and the transformation of low-cost land into high-cost land. As he recently put it, "urbanization… has played a crucial role in the absorption of capital surpluses, at ever increasing geographical scales, but at the price of burgeoning processes of creative destruction that have dispossessed the masses of any right to the city whatsoever" (Harvey 2008: 37).

The most egregious example of this process among the case studies here is that of Calcutta, where, as Roy explains, planning interventions such as Operation Sunshine cleared sidewalk vendors from public spaces, and the poor were displaced to create opportunities for investment by diasporic capital in upper-class enclaves, both in the pursuit of "world city" status. Most interesting is what Roy describes as an inversion of conventional concepts of planning in that the key power play of the new order in Calcutta is the "unmapping" (p. 100, this volume) of land, and the political leverage that supplies. In this case, some forms of informality are deployed by the state to permit illegal practices in the enclave development, while other modes of informality – the hawkers – are criminalized.

Roy suggests that while the common story in cities in developing countries is of a lack of planning capacity, her Calcutta story reminds us that it can also be an issue of how the available planning capacity is used. She argues that in this case, the central role of planning is to generate political capital for the ruling party, creating "spaces of exception" (p. 100, this volume) through the sovereign power of the state to promote inward investment by diasporic capital in enclave urbanism and new frontiers of accumulation. Calcutta's major sustainability issue is therefore not its inner-city slums, which are surprisingly resource-efficient, but the exurban enclave developments, which are able to skew public investment disproportionately towards their own needs.

Another, somewhat less one-sided case is that of Seoul, where the redevelopment of informal settlements in inner-city areas was initiated by the local state and carried out by the private sector. The Seoul municipal government has long had a policy of redeveloping areas of high-density informal settlements in inner-city areas, many of which were once squatter settlements on public land such as hillsides, railway yards, and floodplains. These have all been cleared since the 1970s, and the renewal agency has granted partial compensation to squatters by allowing the displaced to buy new housing units at less-than-market rates.

During the last decade most redevelopment has occurred in informal settlements where property owners had legal title to the land. The municipality has initiated redevelopment by rezoning these areas to permit very high-density redevelopments, and development companies provided capital to demolish existing settlements and put up new high-rise buildings for sale. In these areas about 40% of the population were owners who profited from the redevelopment by contributing their land and receiving housing units in return. The remaining 60% were tenants, of whom only about 35% were re-housed in public housing. The rest, including residents and shopkeepers, were simply displaced. Kim and Choe suggest that these projects can be considered a form of state-sponsored gentrification, while also noting that they contributed large amounts of inner-city housing during a housing crisis, and provided other benefits, such as better street networks, pedestrian amenities, bicycle paths, and green spaces.

Examples like this are well known, in large part because they are so common. These examples are, however, only one side of the story. Much less attention has been paid to the ways in which the regulation of urban land development and municipal investment can be a positive force, a powerfully redistributive mechanism that can promote social equity, livability, and sustainability. In the great urban crisis at the beginning of the twentieth century, many urbanists believed that municipal governments and planning held the key to a more just society, good housing for all, and a healthy environment. The essence of Ebenezer Howard's Garden Cities plan was not the physical development plan or the greenbelts, but social ownership of land that would allow the redistribution of land profits in the form of housing, public goods, and old-age pensions (Hall and Ward 1998). In practice, that ambitious goal was not achieved, but there have been many innovative approaches to the use of planning powers to improve the lot of the poor.

These include strategies that rely on direct municipal expenditure or resources and strategies to impose conditions on private developers. Examples of the former include providing municipally owned land for social or self-built housing and the creation of community gardens, markets, and centers in poor neighborhoods. More common are exactions on private development projects as a condition of development permission. Common strategies include requiring contributions of land from developers for roads, parks, public space, and schools in newly built areas; requiring financial or land contributions for affordable housing; or requiring contributions to other public goods such as schools, libraries, and community centers. The city of Vancouver in Canada has used such contributions to add public amenities and public spaces during the redevelopment and intensification of its downtown area (see Punter 2003).

There are many difficulties and shortcomings of such strategies, however. First, while legal structures vary, in most cases municipalities are in a weaker negotiating position than the developer, and generally receive only a small share of the increased value that the developer acquires through changes to planning regulations. Second, such strategies work only where there is strong market demand for space. Third, such contributions may persuade municipalities to approve developments that are undesirable in other ways. Fourth, without transparent management, such exactions create opportunities for corruption. Finally, municipalities can become dependent on the revenue raised in this way. Still, the benefits can be so great that careful examination of these strategies is important.

An excellent example of such exactions is Tehran, where strong market demand for intensification, a cash-strapped local government, and huge infrastructure deficits combined to produce a system in which the municipality is in the business of selling development permissions. This strategy, known as "density selling" has transformed the city, particularly in the affluent northern areas, from an urban landscape of large two-story villas to clusters of high-rise condominiums. It has also transformed the municipal budget, providing funds for a huge program of public works, including road expansions, parks, cultural centers, and municipal shopping centers. Madanipour reports that at its peak, such value capture represented about 80% of the city's revenue. This development has generated controversy, however, as large buildings have been built fronting on narrow roads and in places where other infrastructure was inadequate, promoted the destruction of the historical built fabric, and led to charges of corruption.

A more sophisticated approach to land value capture has emerged in São Paulo over the last 30 years, where rapid growth had produced widespread infrastructure deficits, and large areas of informal development. In 1976 a new law established the principle that wherever changes in planning regulations permitted more floor area on a given site, a share of the increased value should be returned to the public sector. This approach was widely used in slum clearance projects, where the public share of land value increase was used to build social housing for households displaced during redevelopment. This approach was criticized as gentrification and for distorting existing planning frameworks by permitting ad hoc intensification, but it established the principle that land value increases had to be shared with the public sector, whereas before this time, all such profits went to the private sector.

With the end of the military dictatorship, the passage of a new constitution in 1988 enshrined the concept of the social function of land ownership and separated property rights from the right to develop, making a more sophisticated approach to "Urban Operations" possible. As Sandroni explains, "In practical terms, an urban operation is an intervention in a large area of the city that requires infrastructure and urban improvements such as avenues, drainage, housing for low-income families, public facilities, and other investments. The funds necessary to allow these investments should come from the incremental value realized by changes in zoning to permit increases in FAR and changes of use. Owners of properties inside the perimeter of the Urban Operation may propose projects that require changes in FAR, permitted uses, or building footprints (p. 352, this volume). Five large-scale urban operations were approved by 2008, totaling over 10,000 ha in São Paulo, examined in detail by Sandroni (see also Montandon and De Sousa 2007). Such urban redevelopment projects are not perfect, as they still often tend to promote gentrification, but they have helped socialize a significant proportion of the increase in land value due to public investment, and contributed to a sustainable process of financing infrastructure and social housing.

A different approach and set of problems emerged in Toronto, where subdivision regulations were used to ensure that suburban developers provided or paid for all the infrastructure necessitated by their development. As Sorensen shows, this contributed to the evolution of a rational system of suburban development, with very high infrastructure standards and large amounts of land set aside for schools, parks, and green buffers along rivers. In this way far larger amounts of land could be allocated to these uses than would have been possible if the suburban municipalities had been forced to buy such land on the open market. It also meant that to a great extent, suburban home-buyers bore the full costs of the new development of suburban areas, instead of such costs being passed on to other taxpayers. Although this meant that the cost of new housing was higher, such costs were little subsidized from other revenues, which would have meant taxing renters to subsidize homeownership. At the same time, however, suburban municipalities became dependent on an unsustainable source of revenue and became locked into a cycle of growth and ever more development to balance budgets. The resulting delegation of most detailed planning and urban design to the development industry has also contributed to a proliferation of undifferentiated, conventional suburban development forms, and overall patterns of growth that many now criticize as suburban sprawl.

One way of solving the infrastructure and public facilities challenges of megacities is to ensure that the public receives a much larger share of the increases in land value created through public actions (termed "betterment" in the United Kingdom and "windfalls" in the United States), including regulation, investment, and infrastructure building. Most of the increase of land values in cities is due to factors other than the actions or investments of land-owners, yet in most cities they are able to keep 100% of that increase. Not only is this arrangement inequitable, but it also contributes to shortages of public goods that would help everyone, including property owners. In many countries around the world, measures to capture a share of such windfalls exist or new approaches are being attempted. This seems a promising avenue for future policy innovation, although it must be admitted that it is not easy to do well.

17.3 Governance Questions and Issues

All of the megacities studied here have serious challenges of unsustainability, worsening problems of social polarization, and disastrous living conditions for the poor. In several cases progress has been made in socializing a portion of the increases in land value resulting from development, but in most cases the larger problems created by market processes continue. The challenge for urban governance is to ensure that urban policies, public investments, regulations, and plans have positive impacts on quality of life for the majority, and produce a more equitable distribution of the costs and benefits of urban life.

An inescapable conclusion suggested by these case studies is that urbanization unavoidably requires guidance by the public sector. There is a fundamental role for careful planning and management to regulate and shape the development of land in the interests of long-term functioning, efficient infrastructure building, social equity, and environmental health. Leaving development patterns to private interests and self-help appears to lead inexorably to long-term dysfunctions, yet too often urban growth patterns are left entirely to private interests motivated primarily by profits and focused on short time-horizons.

The big question is what the nature of urban governance will be, and how to achieve governance institutions that are effective, democratic, and prioritize the welfare of the majority instead of that of a wealthy elite. Is investment of public resources made primarily to achieve benefits for investors in urban land development or for residents?

Of the many governance issues in megacities, we can touch on only three:

1. Governance fragmentation, exacerbated by the fact that many megacities are also capital cities and thus significantly affected by national government administrations
2. Colonial legacies of urban dualism, both in spatial patterns and infrastructure, and in governance approaches
3. A brief look at the case of Bogotá, a fascinating example of the transformation of urban governance

17.3.1 Fragmented Governance

In almost all the megacities studied here, rapid growth beyond the administrative boundaries of the central municipality has made governance much more complex, involving dozens or even hundreds of municipalities. In part this is simply a function of rapid growth, and municipal boundaries that are difficult to alter for one reason or another. Although such suburban growth transforms the larger urban structure, often placing increased burdens on the center and on regional capacity, it is usually not regulated by the central city at all. Most growth occurs in small peri-urban municipalities and rural townships surrounding the metropolis that have little governance or planning capacity and limited financial resources.

And while many urban functions are best planned at the local level, such as parks, schools, and local shopping areas, many functions must be planned at the scale of the whole region to be effective. These include large-scale transit and transport systems, water supply, waste management, and pollution control, among others. In many megacities social assistance and social housing should also be financed regionally or nationally, since poverty is often concentrated in particular areas, putting undue burdens on the municipalities that contain these areas. Fragmentation also commonly allows the wealthy to avoid their share of the costs of regional spending entirely, if they cluster into particular municipalities.

In the United States, this problem of regional fragmentation has led to the widespread practice of fiscal zoning: the exclusion of the poor by large-lot zoning and minimum housing cost regulations (see Orfield 1997). Metropolitan region fragmentation is thus also closely associated with urban sprawl, not only because of the inherent difficulties of coordinated planning, and the weakness of governments on the peri-urban fringe, but also because smaller municipalities on the fringe often compete for developments that are perceived to provide tax revenue, and are tempted to lower planning standards to win them. Peri-urban municipalities also routinely avoid providing regional public goods such as green space, public transit, or low-income housing (Fulton et al. 2001).

In Toronto in the early 1950s, small wealthy municipalities on the urban fringe had lower taxes and much better quality services than neighboring municipalities, even while they took advantage of the services provided by their neighbors. The analysis of this situation led to innovative governance arrangements in Toronto in 1953: a two-tier metropolitan government that included the suburban growth area and the central city under a single planning authority. Such interventions are seldom appreciated by the municipality being restructured, however, and take a great deal of political will by an upper-level government. If a government perceives that such reorganization would either threaten its political base or lead to increased financial burdens, such moves are unlikely to succeed. And even where the political will exists, it is difficult to achieve the necessary balance between strong region-wide planning powers at the upper-tier level of government, while the lower-tier government retains effective control over local issues. The Toronto case also shows that such arrangements need to be continually adjusted and reformed as conditions change and the city grows. When the urban area of Toronto outgrew Metro by 1970, but its boundaries were not expanded, it lost relevance as a regional planning agency and was abolished in 1998.

Creating region-wide metropolitan governments is not easy, and although often advocated, has seldom been successfully carried out. There are many reasons for this: senior level governments may be unwilling to cede significant power or tax capacity to another level of government; they may see it as politically unpopular to interfere with municipal government powers; or they may be afraid of establishing another large government that can challenge their policies (as did the Greater London Council in the 1980s just before the Thatcher government abolished it). Further, metropolitan governments often lack legitimacy, as they may not correspond with what urban citizens consider to be the place they live, tend to be top-down impositions of higher-level governments, and are usually too weak fiscally or jurisdictionally to carry out their assigned functions effectively. Their potential source of legitimacy – effectiveness in solving regional problems – is therefore compromised. Further, one of their fundamental roles is to redistribute tax revenues throughout their jurisdiction, from richer to poorer municipalities, a task that is not easily achieved.

Regional governance is hugely difficult, but the consequences of failure to govern effectively at that scale can be even worse. Cuff describes Los Angeles as a prototypically fragmented city, with no center, no unified vision of the future, and no planning apparatus for the whole city. She suggests that coherent planning has eluded Los Angeles since its founding, but recently there has been increasing pressure on civic leaders to solve some of the problems this pattern has created, especially traffic congestion. Part of the difficulty in planning arises from the fact that the urban space is difficult to comprehend, and an unintelligible urban space is hard to design and plan. Los Angeles was built almost entirely by profit-seeking real-estate interests, with no counterbalancing municipal agenda, and the result is fragmentation and polycentricity. Fragmentation further strengthens the hands of private developers, and weakens the negotiating power of municipalities. The six-county region has 187 municipal governments, each with its own planning agency, and the City of Los Angeles itself is notoriously fractured, with a weak mayor and 15 strong council districts. Cuff argues that planning fragmentation makes coherent plans for Los Angeles extremely difficult or impossible to carry out, but all the more necessary. In this situation, Cuff argues for "tactical incrementalism" (p. 280, this volume) or small-scale projects to repair small bits of the urban fabric and gives examples of such approaches.

Another huge challenge is the fact that many megacities – including London, Tokyo, Seoul, Bangkok, Tehran, Mexico City, Buenos Aires, Istanbul, Delhi, and Jakarta – are national capitals. There are some advantages here, as there is often a special relationship to central government, allowing some capital cities to draw in extra resources for showcase facilities and infrastructure projects. That largess seldom extends to the urbanized region outside the capital district, which usually is in even greater need of investment, as in the case of Mexico City.

But national governments can undermine urban governance with frequent interventions, and are especially likely to do so with capital cities. As Madanipour explains: "The history of modern municipalities in Iran, exemplified in Tehran, is a constant struggle between democratic aspirations for local autonomy and the central government's assertion of its powers. In the absence of the city council, mayors were appointed by the Ministry of the Interior. The relationship between the mayor and the city council on the one hand, and with the Ministry of the Interior on the other, can generate a tense power relationship" (p. 75, this volume).

London illustrates the challenges both of metropolitan governance, and of frequent interventions by a powerful central government. During the last 50 years, London government has undergone three major restructurings, from the creation of the Greater London Council in 1963, to its abolition in 1986, and finally the creation of a new directly elected Greater London Authority (GLA) and mayor in 2000. From 1986 to 2000 London had no citywide government at all, with the 33 boroughs taking full responsibility for planning within their areas, leading to a range of conflicting plans for the capital as a whole (Hebbert 1992). Even with the new citywide GLA, these problems are not easily overcome.

Rode highlights the contradictions between the need for large-scale planning of the whole urban structure (such as that by Transport for London and Design for London) with the need to maintain local discretion and powers at the borough scale. In London, however, the clear need for integrated strategic planning for transport and land use was the major factor that pushed the need for a unified government to the forefront. The new GLA is charged with developing and implementing a new strategic planning approach for London, and has had considerable success with a new congestion charge and rebuilding the deteriorating London Underground system. Even so, the national government has been careful about granting too much power to the new authority, which remains a small body without a large budget or autonomous powers. Significant planning power remains with the boroughs. Finally, the new GLA, while in charge of the old 33 boroughs within the greenbelt, does not cover the whole functional urban area, which has expanded to virtually the whole of the South-East of England as more and more commuters cross the greenbelt daily. Still, during its first 9 years, the GLA appears to have successfully created a new planning and governance approach, which will bear close scrutiny in the coming years.

17.3.2 Colonial Legacies of Dualistic Urbanism

One of the most problematic legacies of the colonial era in many megacities in the developing countries is the profound dualism between areas that are serviced with modern infrastructure such as water supply and sewers, and those that are not. In part this is a result of the high cost of such infrastructure, widespread patterns of informal development, and the lack of resources. To a very great extent, however, these patterns are a consequence of the institutional frameworks established under colonial rule. Colonial governments routinely established the latest European-style infrastructure in the European quarters and government districts of cities, while spending nothing at all for such services in the "native" areas. The "modern infrastructure ideal" that held sway in the metropolis usually did not survive the trip to the colonies. At the time of independence in many former colonies, large urban areas had no formal infrastructure at all. Perhaps more profoundly, in many cities a planning culture had become established for which differentiated service standards in different areas was seen as the norm, and universal clean water supply considered an unlikely and prohibitively expensive undertaking.

Hosagrahar examines these legacies of colonial attitudes and approaches to the supply of water in Delhi. She shows that whereas prior to colonization Delhi had a sophisticated water supply infrastructure that was deeply rooted in local history and culture, the colonial government imposed a new system designed to serve only part of the city. Today, much of the population has no supply of fresh water, or only intermittent supply, and Delhi faces serious water shortages. This is not, of course entirely the responsibility of the colonial government, as it has been more than 60 years since independence, and there has been rapid urban growth in that period. The fundamental problem of the colonial approach to water supply, she argues, is that the modern water system exacerbated the inequities in water supply and the exploitative extraction of water resources. As she puts it: "Having brought about the destruction of customary relationships with the environment and of community institutions of place-making, the forces of modernism have finally acknowledged the unsustainability of present modes of development everywhere. Urban development in Delhi has involved a four-part trajectory; first, the rejection of locally inherited knowledge about geography, terrain, and the built environment in the name of modernization; second, a history of exploitative policies and unsustainable urban development imposed in the colonial period; third, continuing unsustainable practices in the post-colonial period seen as necessary for modernization and competing in global markets; finally, having destroyed and lost local knowledges, Delhi, like other cities in Asia, is now compelled to find 'green' technologies for urban development" (p. 129–130, this volume). The huge question is whether such new approaches will be found, and if so whether they can be implemented in the face of existing institutions and cultures of water use and water abuse.

17.3.3 Bogotá

In this section on governance issues and strategies it seems unavoidable to make special mention of the case of Bogotá. We wish not to hold it up as some sort of utopia, which it is not, but as an example showing decisively that even in the face of huge obstacles, it is possible, especially in moments of crisis, to achieve profound changes in urban governance and civic culture, increase social cohesion and planning capacity, and create concrete gains in urban livability and sustainability.

Bogotá, like many other rapidly growing megacities, has spreading informal settlements, very poor segments of the population, a crisis of congestion, environmental pollution, and major infrastructure shortages. Informal development increased rapidly after the economic crisis of the early 1980s, and the neoliberal shift towards diminished government roles and taxation. Meanwhile, the ideology of subordinating public affairs to private sector demands fostered unplanned development.

As Salazar sees it, Bogotá's leadership was greatly influenced by the urban agenda established at the Rio Earth Summit, the UN Habitat 2 gathering, and the UN Millennium Development Goals. The solution involved several components. Perhaps best known is the Transmilenio, which transformed the bus network into a fast, high-capacity rapid transit system running in its own lanes. That was only a small part of the change, though. More important is that the municipality's financial autonomy was improved by the decentralization of powers from the central government, and an increase in the tax base provided by a share of capital gains generated by urban development. Before these changes, the city was almost bankrupt, services were declining, and infrastructure was deteriorating.

The close link between local democratic processes and spatial planning was one key to democratic renewal. The recovery and strengthening of the public sphere was another essential part of the success of the program, along with developing planning capacity, fiscal capacity, and civic pride in quality public services and spaces. As Salazar explains, "Bogotá's citizens once again believe that it is possible to live better through a collective effort, despite the critical conditions the country faces" (p. 325, this volume). One measure was a system of voluntarily higher taxes, in which 63,000 citizens gave more in tax than required, but even more important was that the rate of taxpayers who paid on time rose from 33 to 90%. Civic engagement and participation were considered important because behaviors needed to change too. Now urban safety is much improved, the homicide rate has dropped dramatically, and traffic accidents have decreased. The municipal administration also prioritized the creation of large areas of new and improved public spaces.

The Bogotá case supports Pieterse's (2008: 157) claim that for cities and citizens, the link between planning and democratic decision-making is crucial, because plans (master plans, strategic plans, regional development plans, etc.) express the ways in which broad normative principles are applied to specific territories. They create an opening for citizens and social movements to offer their perspectives on how to address problems in the city. This is not easy, but it offers opportunities to build an alternative way to imagine and talk about issues like integration, sustainability, or livelihoods, and link them to actual changes on the ground and everyday issues. The improvement of both governance processes as well as the fine-grained physical spaces of everyday life provide the links between micro-local issues and the bigger pictures of social and environmental sustainability for the future.

While it would be a mistake to see only the positive aspects of the Bogotá experience, or to pretend that here we may find a convenient set of solutions to the world's megacity sustainability problems, the Bogotá case does make one crucial point: positive change is possible, even though the challenges are great and the obstacles huge. If transformative change is possible in a city as beset by poverty, social, and political problems as Bogotá, then surely there is room for optimism that significant change for the better can be achieved in other cities as well.

The possibility of change that improves the sustainability and livability of cities seems somehow essential in providing the crucial social and psychological room to maneuver, and the freedom to imagine and work towards better and less unsustainable future trajectories for megacities. As David Harvey recently put it, “The freedom to make and remake our cities and ourselves is, I want to argue, one of the most precious yet most neglected of our human rights” (Harvey 2008). While the challenges facing megacities are clearly enormous as shown in all of the studies collected here, it is clear that transformative positive change is possible. That in itself is a major finding of this book. Perhaps the most surprising finding is that so many diverse megacities are experimenting with land value capture strategies, especially to help finance public infrastructure. This seems a highly promising approach, except that it goes against the prevailing orthodoxy of neoliberalism and the promotion of more competitive cities, so it remains to be seen whether such approaches will spread greatly or soon. Finally, the studies here all contribute to understanding the diversity and importance of the links between social and environmental sustainability, urban form and governance processes.

References

Anderson M (1964) The federal bulldozer: a critical analysis of urban renewal, 1949–1962. MIT Press, Cambridge, MA
Balbo M (1993) Urban Planning and the fragmented city of developing countries. Third World Plann Rev 15(1):23–35
Benjamin S (2004) Urban land transformation for pro-poor economies. Geoforum 35(2):177–187
Breheny MJ, Rookwood R (1993) Planning the sustainable city region. In: Blowers A (ed) Planning for a sustainable environment. Earthscan, London, pp 150–189
Brenner N (2004) New state spaces: urban governance and the rescaling of statehood. Oxford University Press, Oxford
Brenner N, Theodore N (2002) Preface: from the new localism to the spaces of neoliberalism. Antipode 34(3):341–347
Brugmann J (2009) Welcome to the urban revolution: how cities are changing the world. Viking Canada, Toronto
Burchell RW (2005) Sprawl costs: economic impacts of unchecked development. Island Press, Washington, DC
Cervero R, Wu K-L (1997) Polycentrism, commuting, and residential location in the San Francisco Bay area. Environ Plann A 29(5):865–886
Fulton WB, Pendall R, Nguyen MT, Harrison A (2001) Sprawl accelerates: exploring and explaining urban density changes in the US, 1982–1997. Brookings Institution, Washington, DC
Graham S, Marvin S (2001) Splintering urbanism: networked infrastructures, technological mobilities and the urban condition. Routledge, London; New York

Hall PG, Ward C (1998) Sociable cities: the legacy of Ebenezer Howard. Wiley, Chichester, NY

Harvey D (2008) The right to the city. New Left Review 53(Sept–Oct):23–40

Hebbert M (1992) Governing the capital. In: Thornley A (ed) The crisis of London. Routledge, London, pp 134–148

Johnston RJ (2000) The dictionary of human geography. Blackwell, Oxford

Jonas AEG, Wilson D (eds) (1999) The urban growth machine: critical perspectives, two decades later. State University of New York Press, Albany, NY

Leitner H, Sheppard E (1998) Economic uncertainty, interurban competition and the efficacy of entrepreneurialism. In: Hall T, Hubbard P (eds) The entrepreneurial city: geographies of politics, regime, and representation. Wiley, New York, pp 285–308

Logan JR, Molotch HL (1987) Urban fortunes: the political economy of place. University of California Press, Berkeley

Lynch K (1981) A theory of good city form. MIT Press, Cambridge, MA

McDonald JF, Prather P (1994) Suburban employment centers: the case of Chicago. Urban Stud 31(2):201–218

Montandon DT, De Sousa FF (2007) Land Readjustment and joint urban operations. Romano Guerra Editores, São Paulo

Orfield M (1997) Metropolitics: a regional agenda for community and stability. Brookings Institution Press, Washington, DC; Lincoln Institute of Land Policy, Cambridge MA

Peck J, Tickell A (2002) Neoliberalizing space. Antipode 34(3):380–404

Pieterse EA (2008) City futures: confronting the crisis of urban development. Zed Books, London, New York; UCT Press, Capetown South Africa

Punter J (2003) The Vancouver achievement: urban planning and design. UBC Press, Vancouver

Robinson J (2006) Ordinary cities: between modernity and development. Routledge, Abingdon, NY

Roy A (2005) Urban informality: toward an epistemology of planning. J Am Plann Assoc 71(2):147–158

Swyngedouw E (2000) Authoritarian governance, power, and the politics of rescaling. Environ Plann D Soc Space 18:63–76